Superconscienceholo-graphicexpialodocious
Modern Teachings of Life

Adam Cohan

AC Atlas Publishing

Published through AC Atlas Publishing

First Printing
Washington, D.C.

This book is not intended as a substitute for advice of physicians, or other professionals. These thoughts and ideas are personal opinions of the author. Readers are encouraged to consider, discuss, research, dispute and form their own opinions. Content and quotes are used to the best of the author's knowledge and may be subject to change as new information is discovered.

Superconsciencebook.com
Adam is anonymous

ISBN: 978-0-692-53468-7

Superconscienceholo-graphicexpialodocious

Modern Teachings of Life

Adam Cohan

AC Atlas Publishing

To all the Conscious Beings and
Enlightened Souls

Adam had'em

SUPERCONSCIENCE

Modern Teachings of Life

Table of Contents

PREFACE

In the beginning there was nothing. Then there was a sound, and that sound was a word... and that word was God. And from this one single word... from this one initial movement of vibration.... all of creation followed... and at that instant conscience began and by our act of measurement and observation the entire universe was created...and all that lies within it....

Once in a great while, throughout time, there have been intersecting moments that line up (harmoniously) with the cycles of the great cosmic clock, and we not only get a glimpse of all that is possible, but we actually have an opportunity to step beyond all that we have known as truth and participate in a grander truth that exists in a higher level of consciousness.

That shift in human conscience is happening now and you are already a part of the awakening. Any pure or fundamental change that will come... will come from the people — not governments. We are in essence the 'change,' the 'hope,' the 'messiah' that we all are waiting for...and it is already here...inside each one of us. Why has the 'universal truth' been hidden from the people on this Earth?

As one searches for the answer to this question, one will start to ask even more questions: Who made the universe? Who designed it? Who am I...and what is my purpose here on Earth? And with the search you will discover much more about yourself and the relationship you have to everything because you are immeasurably more beautiful and powerful than you have been told...

It is a challenge to know what I know. Our common bond is our perceived freedom and only that. To try to awaken people and instill this knowledge to them is not easy because people have protective walls built in front of them. Invisible walls made of false knowledge and understanding. 'They' are okay with being slaves, anything to the contrary, slaves to the modern agenda, but when you broadcast the truth, the real truth, you can 'unsettle' a lot of people. Many of these ideas and teachings are not solely my own. 'I' am purposed with this task to bring you this information, as others have, and let you make your own decision. Words, ideas and concepts such as self-empowerment, truth, knowledge, enlightenment and consciousness are what one should seek in this life... if you so desire. But enlightenment and consciousness are not easily attained. You are not 'enlightened' or 'consciously awake' just by reading a book or seeing a documentary...there is much more to it than that - but when the student is ready to commit...the teacher will appear and we are all led to the truth...but only...when we are ready to seek and accept it.

The 'one source energy' is both the designer and the creator. You are embodying a perfect replica of this 'one source energy.' Therefore you are the designer and creator of this universe. Our highest vibrational counterpart (ourselves) or future selves have created all this—there is no ability above you, in that, when you fully ascended you are the true light of the universe. You are everything and everyone.

All thoughts and emotions exist within you...today you are living in the third dimension which exists in linear/dharmatic time...so the anticipation of knowing the future seems like a 'power' or 'ability' above you – but you have chosen to come here to assist humanity – and within you is the encoded knowledge of that incredible ability. The more 'evolved' conscience has unconditional love for humanity and can assist humankind a great deal at this amazing time in our history — because the enlightened understand...'all' are one...and 'all' are equal.

Did we create ourselves? Yes – on the highest level of truth we created ourselves, but also created 'others' since we are all one related entity. Somehow out of this vibrant nothingness... came everything: matter, energy, space, time, and consciousness. When we say others it is because we, here on earth, can only think and relate to things in linear time and space. These others are just 'you' created from a higher density of existence (our future self). Realize, our ability is truly limitless. If you believe in limits then...you will have limits. When we lift the perception of 'limits' from our consciousness...then we are limitless! If you think 'it,' then in essence, you have also created it. We manifest what we think. Believe, understand and realize...there are no limits to our conscience.

The one common universal desire in every man, woman and child regardless of race, creed, religion or color...is freedom. Freedom may take on many different personal paths, but in general we seek freedom from any type of oppression from others. The freedom to be able to think freely without repercussions or fear is one of our greatest inner desires. We all want to create our own destiny, be who we want to be, do what we want to do and love who we want to love, without impedance or interference.

I use America as a perfect example of lost freedoms because America was originally founded on many of these same principals of freedom, but the real story for America and for most of the world's populations is that it has been enslaved over and over again for thousands of years. The world has been ruled by a 'hidden hand' of various global elite powers. The fact is...you're actually not free at all. There is only an illusion of freedom. And even today this very illusion of freedom is eroding away; the ones with 'power' choose to control the weaker through creating a paradigm of fear, debt and death. But as more and more people 'wake up' to what is really going on in the world a universal shift will take place and a new paradigm will evolve which allows for all people to become their own highest and best self through knowledge.

As we finally find our 'freedom,' it is essential that when we exercise this freedom we do not impede on others (to achieve the same). To be free (truly free), we need to allow others their own ability to express themselves freely too...by not enforcing our views upon them. And 'vice versa' - only as long as their freedom does not infringe on our freedom we should be able to achieve personal freedom for all following this universal moral code of life.

Things are speeding up. It took thousands of years to go through the agricultural revolution, it took hundreds of years to go through the industrial revolution and it took decades to go through the information revolution and now we are on the verge of an awareness revolution whereby humanity can use all this information to bring us to the pinnacle of our existence. This is truly the most dynamic time in all of history. And you have a front row seat to the greatest show on Earth. It is where the ancient spiritual world 'collides' with the modern technological world and from that union, a real utopian world can emerge based on love and knowledge.

How did we get where we are today? The answer is complicated and whether you believe what you read in these writings or not, it may help you arrive at your own truth. The Earth's astral planes were created as a free will zone. The free will zone invites any creative presence in the universe to come and contribute to the development of the earth. In the beginning, there were 12 'voids' similar in design and structure to the 'tree of life,' where 'celestial entities' could come participate in the creative design of the Earth and all of Earth's living inhabitants. Different creative energies filled these voids, but it was one of these voids that was taken over and occupied by a mischief-less benevolent entity; a 'fallen' angel called Lucifer. Understand that Lucifer was an angelic entity, bearer of light, and decided to go against the prime creator's vision and master plan and involve himself in the development of man here on earth. As Bible prophecies explain, man was made from clay and the 'breath of life' was breathed into him. Whether you believe we are created by God or evolved (here on earth) through natural selection and evolution the fact is that our design has been manipulated from its original concept. Not so much in the physical sense, but in man's composition of his memory, conscience and connectivity. Man's DNA is not 'fully' connected and it is this disconnection that prevents us from accessing our full potential. Lucifer was involved in this disconnection; by manipulating our DNA we are unable to fully remember our origins as well as many other limitations. We have been 'dumbed down' for the reasons that Lucifer did not want us to remember our origins and thus a 'disconnected man' could more easily be controlled. A less informed man was easier to manipulate and could be used as a worker here on earth for various tasks. Lucifer strove very hard to take over control of our mass conscience here on Earth. Lucifer flourishes off this control and negative energy. If we were fully connected (plugged in) our knowledge of the universe and our true natural powers would be much greater. Understand that evil may appear to be 'winning' the battle at this time – but good will always 'overcome' evil in the end.

How does one release themself from the shackles? Many think that by becoming financially independent that you will have attained personal freedom. This is not necessarily the case. In some ways the most financially well off people are the least 'free' and are 'mentally' miserable. Society predicts this and it seems we are programmed into thinking that the road to success and freedom is 'paved' with money...lots of money. This is not necessarily true freedom and one will never really achieve their highest and best 'self' by solely pursuing monetary freedom. Ironically, so many sacrifice so much to become financially free that they are the 'most' enslaved people; enslaved to money and debt. Many actually become depressed and destitute by putting so much financial self-pressure on themselves that they have lost the meaning of freedom.

There are different types of 'freedoms' that need to be considered in order for the individual to become fully free.

1) **Physical Freedom**- To live your life healthy and pain free.

2) **Financial Freedom**- To be debt free and do what you really want to do.

3) **Political Freedom**- A freedom from having to be tied to just one idea, group or party.

4) **Intellectual Freedom**- To question everything and guide ourselves accordingly.

5) **Emotional Freedom** – To be rid of toxic thoughts and unstable human interaction.

6) **Spiritual Freedom** – The ability to connect to a higher power and fulfill our destiny.

After achieving all of these types of freedoms to a certain level, then and only then, can we be truly free. We must first start with 'freeing' ourselves in order to free the world of the oppression and then be able to elevate those around us to be their highest and best selves. Each freedom interacts with the other freedoms and forms a symbiotic relationship feeding off each other. Much of the freedom that we seek comes from only one thing and that is thinking. Having time to think has become difficult. There is so much to do and so many distractions nowadays that it becomes mentally and physically impossible to take the time to sit for any extended period and just think. But this is where freedom really starts; in your mind. Take the time to free your mind from life's constant distracting and debilitating chatter. And from this 'silence' comes actions or more importantly non-actions. Man's ability to release his mind from constraints and think freely shall ultimately break the current system of enslavement that has been in place. With this freedom, man will be able to 'wake up' and become aware of what is happening around him in the world today. 'Wakening up' is the beginning part of the enlightenment process.

The following section outlines the five stages of awakening. I have gone through the awakening process and came across this list. I did not create the original outline, but believe that my 'embellished' version of this information most clearly represents the stages of awakening and parallels my journey. Your existence is mostly defined by what you do, how you look, what you wear and even what you drive. During and after the awakening process, many of these things won't matter as much. There is a 'shock' to your system and you must be eased into this awakening process. If you're thrown into it you won't see it as clearly and you may reject these teachings. Once you 'see it,' then it becomes easier to understand. I harken the awakening process to the feeling you would get by finding out your parents are not really your biological parents. You initially feel lost and abandoned, but understand this…you are still you and you will be free. Free to finally know your origins and realize the real point of life. These stages represent your old 'self' dying and a new 'self' being created in its place.

The Five Stages of Awakening:

1) **Denial** - anything counter to conventional wisdom is dismissed (protection of the ego). Whatever the authorities tell you is the truth and there is no need to question. Blissful ignorance and going along with the crowd. There are several types of specific denial which the illusion depends on

continuing. The three primary denials are based on your 'perceived' happy existence... i) You don't want to know...ii) Denial based on your welfare such as a job that makes good money...and iii) Your situation requires to conform with the 'status quo' to elevate your stature in society. In any case, the illusion is defended and those that think contrary are ostracized from society. The people that 'like' the false paradigm don't want to know - don't care to know - or don't want to make the effort to investigate the truth.

2) **Anger** - as you awake up to the new paradigm you get angry because you feel you have been taken as a fool, lied to and/or manipulated. In this stage you start to seek truths by the questions you ask. Finding the answers (truth) to the questions in this stage is what makes one angry because it is hard to face the 'real truth.' You must go through this difficult stage by not completely suppressing your anger to be able to continue through the rest of the stages. Harness this anger into positive energy. Finding out how the world really works (exists) is very eye opening. The reason being is because you 'question' the foundation of what makes you – *you* - and your very existence is vigorously challenged. Up till now you have been faithful to your core ideas and values yet now you feel you have been cheated out of something. You undergo a huge 'let down' since most everything you know and have been told has essentially been a 'big lie' and you are 'mad as hell.' Anger is the foremost reaction when you feel you have been taken advantage of and expends the most inner energy. Some channel this energy into intellectual research and seek knowledge as opposed to violent reactions. The push for acquiring knowledge in this stage is to not be 'taken advantage of' again in the future

and to base your own ideas and information on what you know – not what you have been told.

3) **Bargaining -** After you have calmed down a little from stage two you start to reach out to anyone and everyone who will listen to try to tell them what is really going on in the world. This is clearly the most annoying stage of the awakening process to the people around you. The reason for this is that most people you will reach out to are people still in stage one – denial. They will not see it the way you see it - or care to see it. They have not arrived yet as you have. In this stage you end up ruining many family gatherings. You ruin family parties, soccer games and social gatherings with friends because you are so focused on talking about the Federal Reserve, aliens, World Trade Center Building Seven or whatever other 'counter cultural' issues there are that day. You literally take all the joy out of everything and no one wants to be around you. If you have been vocal at work your position and standing at the 'firm' is compromised. You no longer are the 'model employee' and you may not 'fit in' anymore. Early on in this stage, you are really not awakening anyone. You are merely just trying to validate much of the 'heavy' information that has come to you over your recent history; you're seeking help. You know something is wrong and realize what you have been told doesn't add up. By reaching out - you are seeking guidance in your own search for truth. Much of the information you never noticed before because you didn't care to know or it seemed unimportant. If you choose to elevate your knowledge then you will go through this challenging stage which can last as long as it takes. It is up to you. You are seeking validation. It is not an overnight process. You won't go back to 'ignorance' because clarity has been presented to

you for the first time in your life...it feels right and you begin to understand...where you stand. It is empowering.

4) **Depression** - Now that you have reached out to everybody (and their mother — this really happens) an ominous sense of despair washes over you and depression sinks in. Those that already had some form of depression previously - this may be a very difficult stage on a personal level. You start to see that world problems seem too big (what can I do about it?) you are only one person no one wants to listen to you rant and nothing in your world seems to change quickly enough. At least nothing appears to change and certainly not on pace with how you're personally changing and growing. This can be one of the most painful stages and the toughest to work yourself out of because there are not many people you can turn to for help. Friends and family see that you have brought this on yourself and are not willing to care as much as a person that is dealing with depression from addictions or chemical imbalances. Though, there is no turning back at this point. You literally feel like you're 'drowning' and it can be debilitating and emotionally scary at times. Certain days you might not feel like going to work or doing the things you used to do and sometimes not even wanting to get out of bed. There is no way out of this stage except to go through it. But here is where you finally realize that you are growing and that inner strength can come from inner peace. Personal happiness comes from making progress in this stage and the more you progress the less depression will set in. It is all within you and soon the fear (self-inflicted or externally inflicted) that you had dissipates as you continue to grow out of the depression stage. On an even brighter note, as the shift in conscience continues to occur, more and more people will be 'shifting' with you...so

at some point, the fourth stage will not be as hard since you will be able to go through it together with many others. It is us who have gone before who have laid the pathway for you.

5) **Acceptance** - You finally enter the fifth stage when you can accept and become comfortable with the oncoming reality and you take active and positive steps to prepare. In this stage you will make significant changes to your life and begin to release much of the ties and burdens you have been carrying for so long. By 'accepting' to move forward, you may decide to change your job, sell your house and move or cut ties with old friends. In the end, you will see that this is a necessary process to go through to fully accept and move on with who you are and achieve real happiness. And you will achieve an enlightened happiness. This happiness is different than the 'blissful' happiness in stage one; it is a much deeper and introspective happiness. It is not a 'belly' type laugh of happiness, but a more subtle inner happiness of knowing. You will finally see the positive results from going through all of these stages and continue to guide your actions to align with the more positive aspects of your life. People will notice that you're happy again - confidence has returned and those around you will see the change within you, even those who thought you were 'crazy' not too long ago. Some may ask what happened to you and it is at this point - this verbal invitation that is the best time for you to share information and wisdom that you have acquired on your journey and now be able to do this on your terms.

Remember, no one really cares about you as much as you may care about yourself. You must do what you think is best for you to place '*you*' in the correct place to accept all this information.

You may ask, *"When is this awakening process going to start to happen?"* And my response, is, *"what it is going to take for you to <u>notice</u> that it is already happening!"* One cannot discuss human consciousness without also discussing the events occurring around us. It is important that a correlation be made to connect the dots between critical events and our ability to digest them on a philosophical level. So why go through this? It's life...and life is controlled by modern events and issues...so if you care to consider the full spectrum of effects on your life, continue to read on...

Politics, war, government and all the historical events that have occurred are not a series of isolated incidents, accidents or coincidences, but are rather conspiratorial in nature. Is a hidden unelected 'Cabal' group or organization with the 'end game goal' to takeover and control the entire world and its resources the cause of much of this evil? Is this the same 'Cabal' that has been pushing for a 'New World Order' over the past hundred years? Too much evidence points to the fact that there is a very small elite group of international people who are using the world as their 'chess board.' These people are brilliant. They are some of the smartest, wealthiest and well-connected people you have never heard of...or seen. They live in the shadows. They have no allegiance to any one country; they do not pay any personal taxes, they have more real wealth (gold-oil-diamonds) than the entire net worth of the rest of the world (est. 800 trillion) and are completely hidden from any public notoriety. Do they sit around a table each day and set the fate of the world on edge? I don't know because as of yet I have not been invited to a meeting, but if you look at this in a practical and rational manner with 'open eyes,' you will see that this is very possibly the case. Every market (stock, bond, commodity, energy, finance, real estate, gold, etc...) is controlled and manipulated. It all starts at the very top from where 'they' control nations, countries and governments with the laws they want passed and implemented. Presidents and leaders are literally 'pawns' of their system that have been groomed, paid and bought off through the corrupt political money system for their allegiance and service. To see it from their perspective, you must put yourself in their shoes…and when you do, it all really makes sense. They don't view the world as you and I do - they have a different set of moral values and vision. They believe they are privileged and above the 'fray.' They firmly believe their intentions are good. Skeptics will say that this is not possible; there is no way a small group could have that kind of control over everyone. This can occur and has occurred for centuries through the control of mass human consciousness. If you control 'conscience,' you can set everything else in motion including control of governments, laws, rights and freedoms.

People should ask questions…and more importantly…the right questions. God gave us our natural rights and government is here to protect those rights - nothing more, nothing less. The U.S. Constitution was created and founded as a Republic, not a democracy. History shows us that all 'democracies' eventually end up in tyranny. They don't teach this to our children in school because it would raise more questions. The schooling today does not look favorably on children asking those kind of questions. Democracy, or the pretense of 'democracy,' actually requires secrecy and divided social classes to survive and eventually always degenerates into some form of social upheaval with one group having control over the other. Secrecy serves only those who are in power. Our founding fathers understood this and attacked the idea of democracy yet it is spoken as our system of government and the reason and premise of why America has invaded so many foreign lands. The critical issue is that all this aggression costs money, resources and human lives.

We cannot continue to live with mounting debt till eternity. Debt is increasing at an alarming rate e.g., Federal, state, local, corporate, personal, student, mortgage, credit card, and automotive. We cannot keep printing money without destroying and devaluing the existing money supply. We cannot afford increasing costs of energy, healthcare, and food for the average family. Today we are a consumer-debt-based-economy where before (in the past) we actually produced and made things. Not only are we consumer based, but we are also 'instant gratification' consumer based; not waiting till we can really afford items, but sticking them on 'credit' so we can have them now. The American mentality to buy now and pay later, 'kicking the can further down the road,' is our modern day method of how we pay our debts.

All of these tactics keep people shackled in 'denial' for fear of losing their material way of life if they do not adhere to these suppressions. Trying to wake up the world to the reality of how our enslavement will impact what is coming is a daunting task. The simple fact is that the majority of humanity will be in denial well up until the next economic collapse or some other catastrophic world financial event occurs. Many of us are tired of dwelling on what, how, where, etc. I am not here to provide a 'play by play' or even say 'I told you so' when, in fact, something major really does happen. Most people have no idea how hopeless the situation is and how much we have all been played 'the fool.' Much anger and hostility will ensue when 'the collapse' does come. It will bring financial, social and political unrest to everyone and it will expose the corrupt system that has been a part of our society for years. Most people will be totally unprepared when the 'bill comes due' for having a life of trying to get something for nothing. There will be wars and riots in the streets during the collapse. The real damage though will be done quietly. The personal self-destruction occurs when everything you know and understand changes and shifts for the worse. This will not be easy for many to deal with and some who do 'wake up' during this time will be stuck in the 'hope and fear' loops which will lead to much depression and uncertainty. Some say ignorance is bliss, but it will be far worse to be 'sleeping' through or 'ill' prepared for what is coming. That is why it is so important for you to wake up now and maybe we all can prevent these future events. Many will worry about things completely outside of their control and yet a very small percentage of humanity will be close to waking up and will in the proper time start to question things and be able to do something productive to stop it from happening. So where do you stand at this time? Which side do you want to be on when everything changes…choose… but choose wisely…

Some people have an inner guide and don't need to follow others to make sound decisions. These people no longer need to hear what others say since they have clarity to take action in their own lives. They have freed themselves by identifying the poser within. This freedom provides inner strength to be able to release the love, passion and energy to others. Moreover, we then realize that there are no 'coincidences' in life and that the people, places and situations we encounter are supposed to cross our paths, there will be a feeling of ease. Understand, the more positive energy we give out the more we get back through inner freedom, inner peace, connectivity and synchronicity.

There will also be a time in our near future that it will be too late and certainly too dangerous to speak out. Since 2008 (and really beginning well before this time) the criminal elite have been trying to do everything to keep the 'system' going. They have tried to sustain the unsustainable. Today, with all the monitoring of the internet and CCTV cameras on every corner, it is far too dangerous to be right, when the government is determined to be right, when in actuality the government is so overtly wrong. But to know the truth sometimes you need to risk a lot…but it will be worth the journey. Understand that most everything is the opposite of what you have learned. As the insightful Yoda said, *"You must 'un-learn' what you have learned"* and *"re-learn"* it with an open and inquisitive intellect. 'Ah-ha' moments are those very special rare occasions that a thought or idea 'pops' into our head with a flash of clarity, insight and brilliance. It is as if the last remaining puzzle piece is found and placed to complete a puzzle or figuring out how to finally decode a tough problem. All of a sudden, 'it' just makes sense and you understand why, how and what. It can occur at any time and can be about any topic or subject, but is usually about life or life's meaning. Many times these insightful ideas bring answers to hard questions that we are asking. Much of the awakening process is a series of many 'aha moments'...one occurring after another. The clarity by which these thoughts come to you will be so 'profound' and so moving that it will immediately affect you and make you see the world with a different set of eyes. Sometimes it comes as intuition and sometimes it comes as inspiration, but it is all you. If you truly believe in what you have experienced...it will live with you for the rest of your life. These thoughts are there for a reason. They are there to help, assist and provide you with the direction of the path you should take. 'Ah-ha moments' are gifts to each of us and should not be ignored.

So, believe nothing. Not even what I am saying unless it syncs up with your 'inner compass' of truth. In order to do this, one must question and investigate. Question anything and everything that needs to be questioned. Question if it makes sense. Let your intuition guide you. Do not accept what anyone else says unless you can confirm it or it resonates within your soul as truth. Let go of the extraneous thoughts that will only lead to confusion and despair. It is at 'this place' that you will come to begin to be free. You're not committing to one side or the other, but 'melding' what is right, just and truthful from all sides. It is the middle road or what many call the 'middle way.' Listen to all, follow none and walk your own path as best you can.

"Don't let the behavior (or actions) of others destroy your inner peace."
-Dalai Lama

FOREWARD

This book is about life. It is written with love. Its intended purpose is to expand your vision of life and your relationship to the world and other people. It is a menagerie of information filled with many topics, concepts, facts, thoughts, philosophies, quotes, ideas, theories, poems and stories. You may not subscribe to everything that is being presented in these writings and some of the information may be hard to fathom, but if you encounter something that you disagree with that should not preclude you from digesting the rest of the information with an open mind and heart. Take that energy from your counter intelligence and use it towards a positive resolution. Do not harness that energy negatively with idle debate. This is merely a foundation from which you can work and strive to make things just and better. Each book (chapter) touches a separate important aspect of your life. Picture each book as a point or dot and as you uncover information you will see the relationship that is being made by connecting them. There is a distinct relationship between all the books and just like real life, you will start to see a larger picture evolve from connecting all of these seemingly unrelated dots. Ultimately, it is these dots that make up this matrix of a life we live here on earth. If you search the four corners of the Earth looking North, West, South and East...you may find Eden. It is all in the train of thought of how you perceive things.

Some books (chapters) have overlaying ideas and themes. This is not to be redundant, but to show how all of these topics interconnect with each other through commonalities. Some themes are pervasive and are mentioned several times in various books and it is these points that should garner most of your attention. It is these very points that are most crucial to address now in order to collectively assist in the awakening of common man to realize his true glory and to rise above the oppressive forces that have stifled man's creative spirit for so long.

The most important decision you will make will be your next one, because all of your other decisions are in the past. Make sure you're on good footing mentally, spiritually and intellectually to be able to accept these teachings and move forward. If any of the chapters (books), thoughts or ideas sync up with you then it is up to you to have the desire to investigate it further. These writings are meant to stir your appetite for knowledge and quench your thirst for information. It is the very foundation from which you can flourish to higher level of consciousness and forge a new pathway for new experiences along life's amazing journey.

Eve Kendall

INTRODUCTION

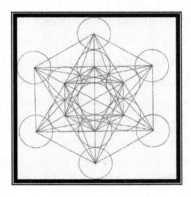

    This is a philosophical book about modern teachings of life. These writings came from journals written over many years. The reason these writings are being provided in this book is that many people are questioning what is going on and what their 'role' is in the world today...if any. These writings are here to assist and inform. To make you think and analyze what you know or what you may 'think' you know as truth and reality. Today, it is important as one learns the lessons of philosophy that they also be enlightened to the modern day events that are connected to human 'conscience.' One cannot know where they 'are' or where they 'stand' unless they become aware of everything going on around them. You are as much a part of the space around you as you are to yourself. So it is vital to understand how society is affecting and interplays with human conscience. Although many historical philosophical writings are in their own right brilliant, introspective teachings, I feel that much of their 'self-analysis' is antiquated. It is not providing an in-depth perspective for today's world with today's conscience. I do not ask that you believe (or follow) everything or even any of the information provided in this book... it is purely up to you.

The primary point of these writings is to provide you with the confidence to ask questions. To have you entertain alternative thinking and open your mind to all possibilities and do this only when you are ready. If you're ready and willing to handle truth, then take possession of the idea that you have the power and ability to simply question what you have been told. Go inside yourself and find the answers you have been seeking, because they are already there within you. If you have no questions, that is fine; you may be blissfully happy and life is good. You may be perfectly content in your existence and have no curiosity or desire to find out what is out there beyond your reach. You may also be in the first phase of enlightenment, which is denial. But if you want to know, and are questioning a lot of what you've been told about life's confusing journey...then step onto the path of enlightenment and continue reading.

The answers are there for you if you want them. Those that have already started on the path to awakening know tough times are ahead for many of us. If you sense and feel the changes of the elevation of awareness happening around you, then you can also sense and feel that our comfortable way of life is deteriorating fast. Those that are prepared will be able to navigate the (impending) coming collapse of our socio-economic system and align themselves spiritually and harmoniously with the awakening process. At some point in the future, there will be a total breakdown of our financial system and our infrastructure. One must understand that the current system is manipulated and is destined to fail. It is not sustainable. What many people may not know is that the failure of this system is by design. Who designed it? And why must it fail?

Writings in this book will provide information to assist you through these times and help answer these questions. This is not financial advice, but life advice. It is not doom and gloom if you don't want it to be. But it will be doom and gloom if you ignore the signs and don't pay attention to the happenings that are right in front of you. Many people's money and livelihood will be at risk because the forthcoming economic collapse will wipe out just about any type of paper money or asset. I'm referring to bank accounts, stocks, 401 Ks, IRAs and the 'quadrillion dollar' derivative market. Most people are not concerned to 'safe guard' themselves against a total collapse. They just don't want to acknowledge that there could be major problems or even small ones. They still have amnesia from the last economic collapse and are ill prepared financially, mentally, physically, emotionally or spiritually for another catastrophic event...one that will be even worse. It is not just about money, but elevating your awareness of what is going on so that you don't lose everything, especially your mental faculties. Most people believe what they want to believe and will either ignore these warnings or brush them off as someone else's concern. Unfortunately, this will affect every person on earth and especially in the western banking countries such as America.

There is an illusion so big, so large, and so vast that amazingly it will escape the people's perception. Those who see it will be thought of as crazy. Several fronts will be used as distractions to prevent the masses from seeing it. It will be hidden in plain sight. It will be accomplished slowly, methodically (literally one day at a time) to prevent people from seeing the changes as they occur. It will keep the lifespan short of its participants and the minds of individuals weak while pretending to do the opposite. Soft metals, aging accelerators and sedatives will be used (in secrecy) in food, water and in the air. They will be blanketed by poisons everywhere and they won't even suspect it.

George Orwell's <u>1984</u> demonstrates the direction the world is going at the present time. The 'New World' will be void of emotions except for fear, rage, triumph and self-abasement. There will be no loyalty except the loyalty to the state. There will only be the intoxication of power by the elite to regulate, control and monitor every man, women and child. If you want a picture of the future then imagine a boot stamping on the face of humanity...forever! The goal of the New World would be to transform "one nation under God," to a totally secular nation with the only power coming from the central state. The revolution that will take place is a battle for your soul. No guns needed or any violence for the revolution, but a need to wake up and start seeing the world with a set of eyes that is able to really see what is going on and move that vibration to others. As a collective force, we are stronger and bigger than any physical army that could be created.

"Until they become conscience, they will never rebel, and until after they have rebelled, they cannot become conscience."
-George Orwell

Why are we here? Why are you here? Have we been reincarnated? Is this heaven or is this a 'Prison Planet?' You are in the place you are by virtue of what you think, feel and believe. You are exactly where you are supposed to be right now at this time. You have created this. Don't question this. Accept this and grow from this point. Some extremely valuable lessons and teachings have come to me early in life and have been an important guide to help me understand the path of life. 1) "Everything is the opposite of what we know" and 2) "God cares not what you do, but why you do." The first one came to me when I was a little boy. I remember walking on the sidewalk out in front of my childhood home and a thought literally 'popped' into my head. It came as a voice of wisdom and confidence and that clear voice said to me that, "whatever I was told in life...that the real truth was the exact opposite." As a young boy this was the most outlandish idea I had ever heard and at that time it didn't mean much to me, but it obviously lived with me since. I believe that it was my 'inner voice' telling me this important information from experience. The experience was either from a previous incarnation (past, current (middle) or future self) or encoded information stored in my 'make-up' (DNA) that I needed to access at that early time in my life as a protective measure. As I have gone through life, it is amazing how true this statement really is and has helped me immensely with trying to make sense of things. The other came to me later in life in a similar voice which said, and I am paraphrasing, "that there is no right or wrong and that 'God' does not judge anyone by what they do, but more importantly...why they do it." This was my first real battle with my conscience. It is the motivation or the sponsoring thought of our actions that is important and that our time here on Earth is measured by the quality of our thoughts, emotions and actions. I never self-reflected or questioned 'why' I was doing something before. This was perplexing to me since up to this time in my life, I was taught and I believed, I needed to be aggressive and fight for what I wanted...not realizing that I was pushing only for material items, validation and success while compromising 'the bigger picture'...my conscience and integrity. These valuable teachings may help guide you through many difficult times and events as it did me and help show the correct pathway for your journey.

"You never know how strong you are 'till being strong is the only choice you have."
-Bob Marley

Some thoughts of inspiration......*I want to be like water... I want to slip through fingers, but also hold up ships. I want to be transparent, but also reflective. Do what you have to do to survive, but keep yourself balanced. Live simply and measure wealth by knowledge, not material items. And lastly, take care of your family and loved ones ...there really is no number two here...*

My desire is for us to stop being dishonest with each other. I want us to stop letting other people tell us how we should feel and act. There's so much goodness in the world between all humanity and you never hear about it. We let politicians and the media dictate to us how we're to form relationships and how to relate to one another instead of allowing humanness and spirituality to create our existence and follow our inner intuition of goodness.

This is difficult because educators want to take the real meaning of some words away from you under the pretense of being 'good' or 'bad.' This is called 'Double Speak or 'Newspeak.' If they take away the meaning then it can incapacitate your thought. If you can't think then you can't figure things out. If you can't figure things out, then you will never realize that you are a slave to the system. If you don't see you're a slave then you will never rebel and if you don't rebel you will never be free. You should want to be free to fill the higher purpose of why you were put here on this Earth. Most people are scared and feel disconnected from the rest of the world, but in truth we are all connected to everything that exists. Most of the answers to these questions lie in the opposite conscience. If you're in a mess and you got yourself into it, then don't use that same method of conscience thought to solve the problem to get yourself out of it. It is like saying...I got into debt for free! Maybe more debt can provide me more freedom?! Many warp reality to fit their own 'story.' Wherever you are now, use the opposite conscience to break free in order to move forward.

As tough as it is to 'sit down' and try to explain any of this to another person, it still needs to be told for those who want to listen. Entire generations have been brainwashed into thinking there is no 'God' and that we have evolved from simple life forms over millions of years. History has been rewritten, packaged and sold to the masses. Most of the population is sitting on the sidelines thinking all is well and just passively waiting to see if anything happens. When you push people to the brink of collapse, they will revolt against the oppression. If anything does happen, such as a financial collapse or World War III, their world will go from 'zero to sixty' miles an hour overnight. There will be no slow burn for them to digest the situation and some will run to pick up a gun (if they can) and run into the streets, because they will be panicked and looking for retribution.

You can make a difference even without any type of violence. An approach to social media needs to be done, but carefully. People are generally scared to put themselves out there, because they fear criticism from others. Perhaps you have been very careful not to open your mouth and say the wrong things in front of the wrong people or talk about controversial topics when not appropriate. Or perhaps you just don't want to instigate a controversy. That is understandable. But when you see where we are headed it should be obvious to get over these inhibitions. We need to 'rock the boat,' we need to be pushing people out of their comfort zones and waking people up, even if they don't want to be woken up, through conscience and by example. The crowd is sleep walking towards the edge of a cliff and they are carrying you and everybody else with them. We need to build a network of awareness for the benefit of our children's future. Those of you that are afraid of being on some watch list (NSA) understand that's exactly what they want you to be fearful of. They want you to stick your head in the sand and claim that there is "nothing going on here." If they can keep you silent, they can keep you controlled and keep your ideas and thoughts isolated. And if you're isolated, they can (will) have you powerless. But you're not really powerless, because you hold the cards. This is the critical mass of awakening; that moment when we the people realize that we already have the power to stop this tyranny and we come together and organize to tell them it is over.

"If you tell a lie big enough and keep repeating it, people will eventually come to believe it. The lie can be maintained only for such time as the state can shield the people from the political, economic, and/or military consequences of the lie. It thus becomes vitally important for the state to use all of its powers to repress dissent for the truth is the mortal enemy of the lie and thus by extension, the truth is the greatest enemy of the state."

-Joseph Goebbels

Disclaimer: Do not believe anything you read. This is a very ironic statement since you are reading it in a written book. The fact is that it is very hard to differentiate between what is right and what is wrong in our 3-D reality world we live in. It is so subjective. What may be right for someone may not be right for another. The purpose of these writings and teachings is to expand yourself, your knowledge and understanding of why things are why they are. To step back and observe as many have done so before you. The pathway has already been forged... and at the end of the path is the moment of ease and accomplishment. Here is where you will be able to reflect on the reason (answers) why you had to go down this path in the first place. All the information contained in this book is public. The information has come to me through many different avenues and sources including public websites, videos, articles and personal discussions with people. I am not here to tell you the way it is, but to offer alternative perspectives on some very serious topics that affect your life today. All the perspectives are just those...perspectives. This book is not meant to be a perfect historical reference guide with endless footnotes and documentation. The knowledge here is to make you aware of the 'massive propaganda machine' that has been misleading you with false information on every aspect of your life. It is not really necessary to know the truth inasmuch as to know the extent of the lies. Everything that has happened has been based on a lie.

Everyone in government, in the media, in the entertainment industry and even in the public domain who accepts the *big lie* as the 'official story' is a traitor, a coward or even a compliant accomplice to injustices that have been perpetrated on society. This is the litmus test to who you are and what you stand for. Think about what you know and what you defend that defines you. It relates to your courage, your strength, your relationship with truth and principles and ultimately, what you will pass on to the next generation and your own children. Your conscience will tell you whether you are a hypocrite or a fool or whether something greater inside of you still lives.

Over centuries, systems have been subtly modified, manipulated and even corrupted, often to serve the interests of the few. We have continually accepted these changes because man can adjust to living under virtually any conditions. The very trait that has enabled us to survive is the very trait that has enslaved and suppressed us. Most societies have an 'elite' and the way they stay in power is not only by controlling money and the governmental system, but also and more importantly, the way we think. So much is left un-debated and unsaid through a system of gatekeepers that our cognitive way we think and analyze information has been compromised. What has countered this suppression is the dawning of the information age with the advent of the internet. This has provided a universe of instantly accessible, freely available information. The Internet has provided millions of people knowledge — in knowledge is the understanding — and when you understand something is to be liberated from it.

Empires like America last about 250 years or about ten generations. Six 'ages' define these empires: Age of Pioneers; Age of Conquest; Age of Commerce; Age of Affluence; Age of Intellect; and the Age of Decadence. It is in the Age of Decadence that shows clear signs of the end of the empire with undisciplined and over extended military force, the ostentatious display of wealth, a massive discrepancy between the rich and poor, a celebration of celebrities and personalities, and an obsession with sex. The Age of Decadence is the' time' where you can never get enough of the stuff you don't need. So what does it mean if we are at the end of an empire? Does that mean an end to life or is it a new chapter with a new beginning? It will be a new beginning and when it comes, it will come with a fundamental change in consciousness. Yes, life will change as we know it, but it will be better and more harmonious with nature and humanity.

People don't realize how a person's life can be positively changed by just one book...

LIFE

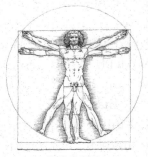

BOOK 1

"When I was 5 years old my mother always told me that happiness was the key to life. When I went to school, they asked me what I wanted to be when I grew up. I wrote down "Happy." They told me I didn't understand the assignment, and I told them they didn't understand life."

-John Lennon

What is the meaning of life? Most people have a difficult time answering this question because they don't know. It is a very tough, personal and deep question to try to answer. The meaning of one's life may be quite different from one person to another, but there is an underlying commonality that transcends everyone. The meaning of life — is the development of the consciousness, the development of the heart and the development of your character. Even with all the negative energy that is around — those that can circumvent this negativity and raise their awareness have the best chance of having a fulfilling meaningful life. We achieve meaning through our life experience and through our spiritual connection to others. This process is happening right now.

The spiritual connection can take on many forms here on Earth and there is no one right way and there is no wrong way either. But there are certain universal laws by which all must observe to achieve ascension and enlightenment. The universe is a living, expanding entity of eternal laws. We must observe our consequences of conduct. When we overindulge, we get ill. When we manage our desires, we are not ill. When we spend more than we earn, we are burdened with debt. When we are mindful of spending, we won't have debt. When we neglect children, they turn against us. When we are critical of others, we lose friends. Therefore, the answer to man's spiritual needs is self-discipline stemming from ideas that impel the believer to remake his own life; correct his faults, strengthen his character and deepen his awareness. Moreover — embrace nature in all her capacity, bringing truth to enlightened souls dedicated to passing these teachings of life on to future generations.

We are all enlightened beings, existing on many waves of vibration. Our soul desires to know and understand; the soul wants to remember everything. The ultimate goal of our soul is to "go back home." Home is the highest level of human consciousness and connects us to the prime source of our cosmic conscience. Some call this "God" or "God's hand," but it is not a person or one being, it is the energy from which everything exists. We have been given much misinformation from our governments and priests, and knowledge of the universe has been disconnected from humanity, compromising the freedom of our thoughts. Humanity is now plagued with the cancerous inability to grasp freedom — or at least true freedom. People have trouble governing themselves due to the assault on their psyche with misinformation immersed in terror, fear, and worry. The point here is that since we are all part of the same 'one' conscience, we cannot be any better or worse than the next person. The worst person you know is still one with us. And the holiest and the most righteous individual cannot be any better than the 'highest' and the 'holiest' that is inside each one of us. And thus, the strongest and the weakest may not rise taller nor fall lower than the highest or lowest which is in any of us.

Every human being has the ability to perform within them the most beautiful compassionate act or the most horrible sin.

The average person in the world considers their life uninspiring and that may be because they have given little or no intention to gaining information that will inspire them or develop their conscience. They are so hypnotized by their environment through pre-constructed concepts and ideas of what we should become through watching television and news – limiting ourselves, saying that we cannot be beautiful or expand ourselves and settling for a life of mediocrity all because we have been trained that way. People will live in denial even though their soul will have other aspirations and desires beyond what we see on the surface. But the questions do arise – such as, is there something more? Why am I here? What is the purpose of life? Where am I going? And what happens when I die? These questions are the ones asked of an individual on the journey of an awakening life.

To others observing an awakening soul, it almost looks like a nervous breakdown. This is so because the person brings into question the foundation of what they have been for so long. Old concepts start to fall apart. A new person arises from the old ashes. Regenerating unlike anything else that has happened in this life before. You are in a completely new territory within the new thought process. You're renewing and reconnecting the brain. You are 'hard wiring' it to think more decisively and clearly moving forward because you realize there is no going back. It will change you from the inside out.

If I change my mind – I change my direction. If I change my direction – I change my life. Are you strong enough to make this change? That is a question only you can answer and, at this time, you may not know. Many will ask what direction is right and what is wrong? If I choose this path am I going to get punished or if I go on the other path will I be rewarded? This poor self-analysis tries to map out our life for us to follow, but with deplorable results. There really is no such thing as good or bad—you are judging things way too superficially—you need to look at 'everything' on a deeper level to see how all of these decisions are being orchestrated, but have no guilt. You are here for the experience, and when you are on the correct path, your inner moral compass will chart your way. Good, bad or indifferent. This is the game of life and balancing all of life's aspects is challenging when you become enlightened in this 3-D world.

You are here to improve your existence, your soul and your conscience—but it is important to first understand that no one is judging you... except you. There is no ultimate right or wrong—but what matters is the motivation of your actions. God is the placeholder for the name of all people. We are here to share what we know with others – not to preach (just invite). We do not want to sow seeds of fear either with our invitation. We cannot do it for others—we are here to vibrate this energy (pass on) on to others for their self-evaluation and awareness. Put the things you have learned to work for the betterment of all. We are all ambassadors of light. A new frontier is on the horizon. The letting go of conventional wisdom becomes challenging, but will evolve as you grow and flourish. Bridge 'both' worlds to access your super consciousness. "Everything is energy and energy is everything."

"Come as you are...."
-Kurt Cobain

But it's all just an illusion. Once you realize how powerful you really are, you will never again act against your will. You know your instincts are correct when you break free from the confines of others' opinions and do what you know is right. All you have to do is remember who you are. You are the same soul 'born today' as the one born many years ago. So who do you want to be this time around? You are 'BORN FREE' and you will 'DIE FREE'...but will you 'LIVE FREE?' The choice is yours. Each one of us has infinite potential. Just start believing and you will create what you want. But you must believe!

Live in the here and now and create more time reflecting, thinking, meditating, breathing and living. Look to nature more. Be more tolerant of others, try to be at peace with yourself, have less inner turmoil and better appreciation for living in the moment. Accentuate the positive in everything. Have less guilt for the past and less fear of the future. Achieve a better understanding of the universe, time, conscious, subconscious thoughts, behavior and actions. Have less fear of dying and less concern to fit in (into old things) with others and less pressure or a need to fit in. Have less interest in 'trendy' social clubs and pointless organizations that steal your individuality. Aspire to show less outward hate, less evil thoughts, less anger towards people. Become more comfortable with who you are and what you are becoming. Know that the proper path is always the one right in front of you. Know who your true friends are...they are the ones that are supportive to you no matter what and are not destructive. Know that you may lose some relationships, but gain others. Understand that the hardest part during this process is your relationships with friends and loved ones. They will be confused and hurt by some of the ideas that you have acquired. And finally, if you are happy, then they should be happy for you too...if they really, genuinely care about you.

In life, we should be striving for love, happiness, friendship, kindness, peace and for a much better place for our children to thrive. Only in the happiness of others can our own happiness be measured. Live humbly and not compromise our integrity. Enter the path of wisdom. Guide your inner moral code and compass and use this when you are doing business with others. When you sell anything, you must be truthful and represent the product in good standing with integrity. If you cannot represent the product without pause/hesitation, then you shouldn't be selling it. When working with others on a project, try to be flexible. Merely complaining and not offering an idea or solution to the task at hand is worthless and offers nothing without posing a constructive alternative idea or solution. All collective work should be positive.

Heaven ends...where consciousness ends. This 'intersection' also is where the start of all creation begins and the farthest most moment of thought our conscience can comprehend. Is there anything beyond this point? I often wonder and believe it exists in a pure spiritual state of energy – the 12th dimension. All new creation is not really new in that everything that is being created has existed before. It has always been here – through consciousness. Does right and wrong exist? Yes and no. In our reality, there is right and wrong for we exist in duality here on Earth. We do have free will and choice and decisions to do right or wrong? In the truest reality – there is only what there is... neither right nor wrong. For in our true reality there is no duality – right is what we decide it is (nothing is wrong) just different levels of decisions. And from those decisions come different levels of experiences. Who is to say that those experiences are right or wrong? As long as no one 'gets hurt' how is anything wrong? We shouldn't judge. We just live the expression of experience we understand – and in all of this we can achieve love and goodness. A lot depends on the level of consciousness of the deciding entity. You need to abandon everything you have been taught. Abandon everything you have been disciplined to think, and trained to believe, since your first conscious memory.

All of this really starts making more sense when you abandon vanity. 'Vanity' is your external 'ego' persona that other people see. Abandoning vanity has little to do with what you wear, or how you wear your hair. Abandon all the 'bunk' that separates human beings from nature and what is natural. When I say abandon, I mean to let go only to the point where it doesn't consume you. We were born naked creations of the Earth to live, eat, drink and know of the Earth. We are here to live and die by the Earth within all her natural harmony. All in natural time and that time exists within us – not without us. Without us, conscious time does not exist because without us, there is no time on Earth – abandon all education and intellect — abandon all pomp and formality – abandon indoctrination and scholarship. Abandon all language, words and writing. Nature is pure and unadulterated, and is not cluttered with anything more than it can provide. Abandon ego. Everything is rather pointless destructions created by people that in reality cannot love. Some people desire to control others. They may not like themselves, so they press this on others because they can. Physically they are not happy with what was given to them so they surgically modify the outside appearance with plastic surgery, makeup, expensive clothing. These people force themselves through hours and hours of unnatural beauty; hours of hours of endless painful inorganic exercise doing more harm to the body than good. They are punishing their body for what? It is true that the things that we don't like about ourselves are the things that we are most critical about in others, physically and mentally.

To really live…let it all go…everything you have…your job, your possessions, your loved ones and all material items…everything. Then choose 5 things to bring back in the order of importance. So after you have done this in your mind… start to focus on that now… in real life!

The ascension process is happening right now. As 'ascension happens' we are met with changes in our life that are difficult to handle, but in the end there is a specific reason for going through this process. *A lot of what I used to believe in is dissolving, even relationships.* Life as I know it is essentially changing forever. There is something bigger, something more wonderful, something greater. Many of us question the traditional path we travel now and we sense there is a more poignant meaning to our existence. We seek to find what is good and just through a higher awareness. It is a greater power that is within and has always been there. We are not just physical beings. Some 'ascension symptoms' are as follows: My friends and family don't understand me anymore; I finally feel I care about life, but with no one to share it with; I am not interested in the same things I used to be; I feel energy changes; I feel I am more than just a body; I feel more spiritual in my connection to all things; my heart experiences waves of emotions I never felt before; my mind is awakening. When I dream – I have no real fear and feel connected to all past, present, and future events; no pain, no trauma, no discomfort, no confusion; no fear of separation between myself and everything else. Am I all I have? I realize now the cause of the pain I was going through was the fact that I wasn't here in the present. I have the opportunity to have a much fuller and richer experience of life.

Sometimes we are on or off this wave of universal feeling and we don't always have the 'flow' with us. But at least we understand and know where we want to go, and we want to take as many people with us as possible. Ascension is one of the greatest things that can happen to a human being. Ascension here on earth does have a certain dichotomy; on one hand you feel alive and connected, but on the other hand, you can also become more distant and alienated from your friends and loved ones. And yet because of this love, lies the reason why we so desperately try to help others. Many do not see that our intentions are trying to be helpful – to them we have become bothersome with our counter establishment-based ideas. We care so much in trying to help, that we have difficulty relating it to them on a daily basis. They think we have changed or gone 'nuts.'

When you become awakened on the ethereal plane, all things start to make sense...and your inclination is to share this with others. This is not for you to share with them unless they ask you to share it with them. The things many fear now are largely because they do not understand, (such as the fear of death), but if the experience of 'death' was something different and not as traumatic as many believe, then we may not fear it as much. The walls that are falling around us are the very walls that have kept us imprisoned. Financial walls, government walls and even some religious 'walls' are all falling to create a new, better world, free from control and fear. For a long time, the indigenous of this Earth have been saying this shift is coming, but the shift is really happening now. The world is changing – our bodies are changing – our DNA structure is changing – it is real and we will experience this shift. We are the ones that will be 'consciously' alive during this change. And it is up to us to change the way we think and live. The shift is occurring now and has been occurring slowly, but is speeding up. If we shifted 'too' quickly, we would not be able to handle the pace and many of us would perish. Mother Earth will go on and if we're not in harmony with the Earth, then we may not go on with her. But it is up to us to decide if we want to go with her.

There is a battle between light and dark forces. The Kabbala (Cabal of international elite) which is aligned with the dark is very strong and organized. They have been manipulating people of Earth over many centuries. They are building their empire while stripping us of our wealth, power, sovereignty, health, freedoms and our intelligence. This Cabal goes back thousands of years, prior to Egypt and has connections to ancient civilizations such as Limeira and Atlantis. Most people have heard of these places, but are unaware that they were real, advanced prosperous civilizations that also ended up destroying themselves. It is thought that Atlantis was either 'blown up' or succumbed to a great deluge or flood during a cleansing of the Earth, while Lemuria's destruction was brought on by human activity whereby humans began to 'mate' with the animal inhabitants which went against the moral codes established by the prime creator. When humans do not peaceably, amicably and fairly work out their differences among themselves, or go against morality, it can affect the survival of the human race. This is fate awaiting modern civilizations that do not listen and follow the practices of corruptness, hate and war. They chose to destroy themselves rather than pause to work out their sociological differences. Mature, wise beings can rise above the conflict. This devastation of their civilization was so great; it has continued to infiltrate our modern-day conscience. We still have problems, challenges and difficulties that we face today that stem from the past negative imprint and we must overcome them now since they were never corrected in the past. Call it Karma (dharmatic) residue. We are left 'holding the bag.' We are left to pick up the pieces and connect the past to rebuild the future from the ashes of these mistakes and come together as one human consciousness. But only if we have 'true' knowledge of the past that we can correct the present-moment ideology.

The New World Order (NWO) — is the modern version of the 'Cabal' and is the group who is pushing for a one-world global power...one in which the elite controls the total environment over the 'common people.' The fundamental difference is in what *"We the people"* seek is a world where all men, women and children are equally individual and yet connected as one. One world united, but not as one nation state. The goal for us is to build on unified kindness and create a society that is based on tolerance, understanding, love, cooperation, friendship and trust. Let's create amicable, peaceful agreements with each other despite any superficial differences that may exist. This is our purpose here on Earth. Our *calling*. Those who desire freedom, sovereignty, prosperity, health, safety, knowledge, love and trust will ascend — those who don't, will be removed. Those who do not want to participate (and that are married to this corrupt reality) will not be a part of the new enlightened dimension. Our challenge is to 'awaken' the corrupted beings, since these people want to create chaos. Chaos is a tool they use as their ally—it is their secret weapon even though it is being used out in the open. Confusion, fear, hate, separation, distrust are also tools in the 'chaos' arsenal that are used on us. They spread lies and disinformation—through propaganda outlets and social media. The newspapers and Internet are used to spread lies and deceit in an effort to keep all humanity blind from becoming properly informed; to keep us separate and divided—confused and in a perpetual state of fear, unbalance, suspicion and paranoia. It is up to us to 'see' and correct this as the manipulators attempt to guide us down the wrong path. We have to tear down these walls of deception that have kept us in slavery for thousands of years. The Cabal (and paid minions) do not spread positive energy. Be aware that some dark Kabbala pose as 'light workers' especially on the internet to misguide many that are looking for truth.

Everyone needs basic necessities such as food, water, shelter, warmth and security. We are all human beings trying to live in a society which is generally easier to do and more enjoyable with other people around. When you get into any type of hierarchy (kings or presidents) this is when it gets complicated with divided classes. But for now, we should keep it simple on a localized level where most people can achieve freedom and do what they want. Be mindful that as soon as you try to make a "one size fits all" solution to society, then some people, if not all, will be compromised.

Most people philosophize mid-stream about what is going on. You need to go back to the beginning. Back to the source (the mouth of the stream) and analyze it from there. You're only digesting one half of the story if you don't go all the way back to the 'origin' to fix a problem or cultivate a valid solution. For example: most criminals steal because they need something to survive.

Instead of 'legislating' more laws to put them behind bars, we should figure out why they are stealing in the first place. If they could flourish in society and have the proper means, then they could have everything to achieve happiness and not commit crimes. Many people only see their paradigm and don't bother to look any further to seek out the true cause behind the problem. It's hard to take yourself out of the comfort zone and question this. But the fact is, most people are invested in the wrong paradigm – mostly because this is what is told to them.

"If you are depressed, you are living in the past. If you are anxious you are living in the future. If you are at peace you are living in the present."

-Lao Tzu

When I was young I had all the freedom in the world to do pretty much what I wanted, yet I wanted <u>stuff</u> (cars, home, and merchandise). As I have gotten older and wiser in life, I realize that after having all that 'stuff' it is freedom that I really desire. True wealth is freedom. *'As an adult, I became overwhelmed with having to work to pay for all of that stuff.'* It is ironic because when you're a kid you just want stuff, but when you become an adult you have stuff yet all you want is to be a kid again to experience that freedom. Covet freedom until you don't feel you need anything. Life should be free no matter what age you are.

There is no corporate loyalty anymore. There are no raises or company benefits, or affordable healthcare to the faithful employee. If you could go back and do it again from when you graduated from school, would you say that you would work harder or would you want to be with your kids and family more? If you go to bed thinking and worrying about 'tomorrow' or money, then you're not living in the 'happy' vibration or enjoying the moment of 'now.' We have entered a time in history unlike any other time. Many people think that we are in the "middle of something big" and we are waiting for the proverbial "other shoe to drop." Something big is going to happen and whether consciously or subconsciously, we are preparing for it. We must look at who came before us and learn in the knowledge from the ancient text that has been left us. We are living at one of the most amazing and pivotal times here on Earth and many of these ancient writings tell us about this time that we are going through now. Thousands of years ago, they foretold of the 'now' times all pointing to this specific time in history, a unique time – a time of great change — prophecies — of what is happening. Many feel time is "speeding up." It is almost as if the heartbeat of the earth is accelerating. Our minds and bodies are tuned to this pull of the Earth so we are also moving along with this acceleration of Mother Earth's cycle and pulse. Along with this, it seems time is intersecting with a magnetic shift occurring from this third (3rd) dimension world into a higher, more complex 4th/5th dimension. A "great shift of the ages" is taking place. As the pulse increases, we are trying to keep up with the pace. Many historians point to this time that we are moving into now, the "Age of Aquarius," as significant. This 5th world paradigm shift will bring us closer to who we really are. We should look inside ourselves and become better people in order to fully align ourselves to accept this information. We are being tested. We must come to understand our relationship with each other, with nature and the planet Earth. We must prepare ourselves to accept this great knowledge, so we must elevate our understanding and love for others. Every emotion and feeling has certain chemistry. This chemistry (energy) needs to be with kindness, <u>not</u> hate because hate steals energy from the body. Compassion, tolerance, understanding infuses life into our bodies. It is of a higher vibration. We are going through many primary lessons and tests to prepare us for a much more important and relevant test. This test is being given by you. Encoded in these tests are teachings of life's meaning. We are all connected together through a field – an energy field that really provides the reflection around us from what we have become from within. So if we are in a society that is part of a corrupt and unjust existence…it is us who are actively creating this. The world around us is individually and collectively what we have become (inside). If we want to change this world, we must start with changing ourselves by becoming the very things we choose in life: love not hate; strength not fear; nurturing not destruction. We should not only choose, but demonstrate to live in the world as the very thing we want it to be – that we all should exist from within – the exact experience that becomes us. The young generation feels that this world doesn't make much sense to them. They feel alienated. The guidance they receive is from individuals just as confused as they are. The young are looking for something and may feel disenfranchised or separate from everything. They may not be looking to be a part of something yet they are searching for something greater and connected at this time– a collective movement of what's right, just, and a part of love. Not many are able to answer the questions they pose. But at least they are seeking; seeking and asking for a better way. Yet today it seems all the nations of the world are at war with one another. Do you think that this is the way? Can we stop <u>war</u> and <u>aggression</u> towards others? Each day we should take a moment for peace. Then the next day…take two moments. And then the following day take a whole minute and keep extending 'the moment' longer and longer each day until we achieve peace throughout the world. I know there was a past time we lived our life quite differently here on Earth; a simpler time. We lived much closer in harmony with the Earth and nature (not in a primitive sense) and we honored life. In a way we were much more advanced/civilized in our relationship with nature and the universe; today we have lost our way. We began to forget due to our disconnection. We have been disconnected from the divine, from our masculine/feminine origins and from the true purpose of why we came here in the first place. We long to understand the greater meaning of all this. We somehow embarked on a path for modern external invention and technology in an attempt to explain ourselves and our surrounding, but science is fragmented and it seems that almost everything we invent is, literally, something we can do from within our powerful selves. Our brain is no different than a super-computer. If our brain was fully operational (plugged in), we could outperform everything a super-computer can do and much, much more. Remember, if you can create it in your mind, it is created somewhere in the universe. Each cell in our body is a small microcomputer with 1.5 volts of electricity per cell. Times that number by 1 billion cells and that is a tantamount of electrical capacity within each one of us. We are over flowing with creative energy. Each cell contains information, stores knowledge, and works harmoniously with each and every other cell to make us who we are. We will continue to create a more technologically complex world out there not realizing that it is already created within us. We must find our balance. Modern technology is trying to recreate ourselves through artificial intelligence. The question is…is this a good idea?

10 Earth Shattering Truths:

1) Dinosaurs and dragons are the same.
2) We (*humans*) did not evolve from apes.
3) Cures for all disease and illness (including cancer) exist now.
4) The Great Pyramid of Giza was not built by the Egyptians.
5) All Mythology (*Greek & Roman*) is real.
6) Atlantis and Lemuria were real civilizations.
7) We exist in a holographic reality similar to the matrix.
8) Giants (*Nephilim*) have existed here on earth.
9) Technology exists to provide <u>free</u> clean energy (electricity) to everyone in the world.
10) Man never *landed* on the moon as shown on TV and what we saw was filmed in a movie studio.

Stop for a few minutes. Stop the hurried pace, and see what is really going on around us. More and more people are waking up each day and that is because they are all taking a 'pause.' By pausing, we go through a self-evaluation that leads us where we need to be and that place is 'home.' We need to keep our energy up during this time—not to get too drained. During this time of self-evaluation we come to realize that 'self' and 'other' are as similar as the north and south poles of a magnet, but it is still all one magnet. Yes, you are like one magnet and yes you have two ends (one that propels and one that attracts), but it is still all one. Not unlike many concepts of how we self-evaluate ourselves...people experience 'life,' but they don't know how to interpret it. We are one with the universe and at the proper moment of enlightenment, we will be able to see this irony through a set of 'wiser' eyes. An example of this irony is a 'king' is far more worried than the public about his security and must have guards on either side of him (wherever he is) fearing an attack. Yet the 'king' is really the same as you and me. They rule but how? Usually through tyranny so they have brought this situation upon themselves. The man who rules is usually the biggest criminal of them all and the only difference between him and the criminals in jail are the ones in jail are the ones who got caught. It helps to be able to make the rules, but at what cost?

We should strive to establish higher standards of just and unjust in our personal growth and through this process be able to pass on to the next generation a workable, livable philosophy of life. When you start to uncover the truth about one thing you will notice that other related events (and even some unrelated events) are then brought forward that require research and scrutiny. One truth uncovers more answers and even more questions. The overriding purpose of our existence in this universe is to experience free will, have a self-aware experience which advances our knowledge of who we are, learn personal growth and overcome evil forces. You did not come into this world, you came out of it.

If you think you exist only inside your skin, then you don't understand how we are *all* things. Billions of years ago, you thought you were a "Big Bang" — but you are not the end result of the Big Bang; you are the process – you are the primordial entity of the universe, not separate. There is no such thing as separate things or separate events and nothing intelligent or brilliant ever came from an explosion. The physical world is 'wiggly'. We try to create straight lines out of everything. The art of calculus is measuring the world and trying to make sense or 'straight lines' out of everything, yet this really can't be done. In the meantime, we worry that our world is going to end (the maternity ward to the crematorium) and we are what happens in between the ethereal plane. We must be aware that by you taking your point of view 'helps' me to be clear on what my point of view is. This whole idea of the universe being filled with unintelligent force playing around and not even enjoying it is a 'putdown' theory of the world. By putting the world down or saying anything is wrong with it is a game they (the elite) play to gain control of others. By putting the world down they are supposedly a superior kind of people. If you go along with this, you feel hostile and alienated. You may feel the world is a trap and you have to put up with a body and mind that falls apart over time — so why live on? For many reasons, but mostly for the experience of life and for the intelligence, love and beauty that are found in other people and in nature. There is a symptomatic scheme of all things. The earth is not 'infested' with people. We are all a part of it. To describe a person walking, you must describe the floor and to describe my behavior you must describe the environment. I am involved in 'one system' of behavior that is connected. We define each other. We are all patterns — and the external world is as much you as your body.

"I stopped explaining myself when I realized people only understand from their level of perception."

-Anonymous

Hide and seek is a game, yet this is how we pretend to lead our life for the most part. On the one hand, we spend our life hiding our true identity, while, on the other hand, pretending to seek for it. We know 'it' is there, yet we separate it from ourselves. It is like a bridge extending from one part to another part of the same shoreline. It is funny how Americans are the epitome of contradiction. We must understand that we are the eternal universe. Consider the world (life) as a drama (a play) that you know is not real—but the actors want to convince you it is real. If you cry during the play and you know it is not real, then you are buying into the drama of this play (life) that has been like a veil temporarily forced over your eyes. A newborn baby is pure. The one thing a baby, the most recent incarnation of God, knows is how to play hide and seek. Hide and seek is the basic game, and life is no different. So go out and play!

The eyes are useless *if* the mind is blind. Two things define you. *'Your patience when you have nothing and your attitude when you have everything.'* Remember you are the hero in this life...and you don't need to be saved. We think too much and feel too little. You are perfect exactly as you are. With all your flaws and problems, there's no need to change anything. All you need to change is the thought that you have to change.

Nothing in the world can bother you as much as your own mind. Others may seem to bother you, but it is not others, it is your own mind telling you that. Live your life devoid of fear and what others may think. Not fearing what the future brings. You are not ignorant and are going to jump off a building because you don't have fear—that is different. Having no fear of what reality brings and knowing that all that happens to me is just experience. What happens to me...is what needs to happen to me. What I need to learn will be relearned from within.

If you're not somewhat angry at this point in time, then you're not really paying attention to what is happening around you.

But in the end — only those things put forth: - *'How much you loved - How gently you lived - And how gracefully you let go of things not meant for you'* - will be the true measure of the person you become during this life. We need holy men and women to assist in the establishment of higher standards of right or wrong; to amend unjust laws on our statue books, to become the patrons of broader and nobler educational ideas, to foster the care of world peace, to aid in the achievement of economic justice, and most of all to provide the millions of this generation with a workable, livable philosophy of life.

Our greatest threat to our freedom today is not from a foreign enemy attacking us, but from our own government ignoring the 'constitution' (our rights) and the majority of the people letting them get away with it. As difficult and disturbing as it may seem, we must draw a conclusion that an elite group of people, and their corporations own, run and control, not just our energy, food supply, education and health care, but just about every aspect of our lives. A civilization built on ignorance will collapse under the weight of the very same ignorance. Those that have 'light' within themselves will pass triumphantly through the difficult years which lie ahead.

"All tyranny needs to gain a foothold is for people of good conscience to remain silent."

-Thomas Jefferson

Things have never been worse for people who want to speak the truth and highlight illegal practices in our own government. Laws and legislation are being implemented to keep us from accessing information on what the government is doing. People working for the government are making it virtually impossible (and illegal) for anyone in an intelligence agency to talk to the media and reporters. It is much more restrictive than in the past. Independent journalism is compromised. The smaller independent news outlets have very little clout. Some news groups have the illusion that they are independent, when, in fact, they are organized news source that are 'pawns' of the elite news media establishment spreading dis-information. Independent news blogs and outlets have been systematically taken over or infiltrated by our government intelligence. They have instituted rules, regulations and policies to close down legitimate press inquiries and replace this with its propaganda machine. At some point, it will become insurmountable to overcome the weight of the establishment mass media news machine and total access will be controlled.

'Listen to your own soul. If something doesn't feel right....it probably isn't.'

I'm at the point in life where I don't focus as much on losing friendships or relationships with family. People will come and go and I am not going to chase anyone or beg them for their friendship or loyalty and certainly I am not going to try to convince them to see it my way. They must do their own 'seeing' on their own. Sometimes the quietest people have the loudest minds. Only the most exceptional people become aware of the matrix without any convincing from others. Those who learn it exists must possess a rare degree of intuition, sensitivity and a questioning nature.

"We all know sometimes life hates and troubles...can make you wish you were born in another time and space, but you can bet your lifetimes that and twice its double... that God knew exactly where he wanted you to be placed...so make sure when you say you're in it but not of it...you're not helping to make this earth – a place sometimes called hell – change your words into truths and then change that truth into love...and maybe our children's grandchildren and their great-great grandchildren will tell...I'll be loving you..."

-Stevie Wonder 'As'

The mystical experience of life is a gift from God and to spread joy and happiness is our gift to other humans. But in order to spread joy and happiness one must already have it. Stephen Hawking said, *"Philosophy is dead. Philosophy has not kept up with modern developments in science particularly physics."* This is an arrogant, shortsighted statement that leads us to believe that there is nothing more to this life than what we can see. Can physics and science alone explain everything? Can it explain the grand design? Do we have to work the math to see the truth? The problem with science is that if the definition of 'life' does not fit into the equation – then it cannot be explained. Philosophy is the study of life and sometimes we need to go out of the confines of the pre-constructed box and entertain the idea that there is a higher power that is not quantifiable. Physics is <u>not</u> the study of everything! Consciousness is! Consciousness is truth – real truth – and can answer the questions beyond the study of physics. Physics is the science of the properties of matter and energy and the relationship between them. Questions such as..."what is the meaning of life"...is beyond science.

"Beware the barrenness of a busy life."

-Socrates

Consumerism is woven into the fabric of our life but it is a lie. It does not provide true happiness and security. Consumerism is a 'false prophet' to sell you the 'illusion' of happiness. We therefore spend a great portion of our lives in debt buying things we don't need. The point of life is to arrive here in the moment. Time is always now. You needn't be <u>guilty</u> because you feel <u>guilty</u>, but this is a hard concept to acquire in today's politically correct society. And always remember that truth has no agenda. The world is a phantasmagoria – a fluid flowing experience...so you can't hold onto it forever...

"You can ignore reality but you cannot ignore the consequences of ignoring reality."
-Ayn Rand

If you're interested in finding out information, please do your own research. The best part of doing research is that you feel informed. When you are informed you are better able to understand why this world is 'staged' to be so scary and confusing. You will grow from the place where you used to be. The unknown becomes known, and you may actually feel happier because you know where you stand. When you investigate past events on your own and you learn what really may have happened, it is different than when someone just tells you verbally. You have empowered yourself by taking the initiative – it has a much greater and profound affect. You also have a better understanding of why things happened the way they did and why things have been done to keep you from knowing the real truth. You can become less worried mostly due to the threats that have been shown to have been fabricated to instill fear in you. When you see past this fear ...you can more calmly assess the situation.

Conspiracy theorists are not bad people. They are just

inquisitive people. Challenging controversial ideas and questioning things needs to be done at this time in history by each one of us. The elite know that the masses are waking up and they want to prevent us from doing anything counter to their plan. If nothing is done now, there is little chance we will be able to do anything in the future. Growing does not mean excluding anything you have learned in the past, but adding unto as options that could be possibilities for now and in the future.

We have created a maelstrom of data, problems and information that encompass the earth by use of thought; Thinking of more solutions on how to fix the world's problems is not productive since it is our minds that have created them in the first place. Incorrect thinking has created the whole big mess which we are in right now. The paradox is that whatever you resist— persists. The more you resist something, the stronger it gets. The ego identity is always looking for answers and solutions. "Who am I? What is my purpose?" But the truth of who you are does not need an answer because all questions are created by your mind and you are not only just your mind. The truth lies in not asking more questions—but fewer questions and, more importantly, the correct questions. Quiet the soul. When seeking answers to the question of what life is...we need to understand that life itself is what we are seeking, the experience of being alive....being awake. A quiet mind can understand the nature of a stream...everything else falls into place when your mind is quiet—in that stillness—when your mind is quietest—inner energies wake up and work without effort on your behalf. By being quiet, you can hear all of creation speaking to you on the path of life. Our physical world is always filtered through our five senses. Be quiet...and listen.

My motive and I 'are' the same thing. Life begins with the present, not the past. The past is like the wake of a ship—it is behind you and will always be. The point of existence is now. There is only now. The future is an obstruction. It is a memory projected ahead of us and the prophecy is the contamination of the past. Live now. Be completely aware of now and what is — and if you can do that – then tomorrow will take care of itself.

My son asked me what I am doing. I told him that I am writing a book. He asked about what? I said about life. He abruptly turned around and started walking away. I asked him where are you going? He said that he did not need to know about life from my book and that he was already experiencing living life – so no need for me to tell him about it. Precious!!

The root of most people's sense of unhappiness is that our life has no meaning…at least no clearly defined meaning. Does life have a purpose? Why are we here? What is life's meaning? Setting you aside, what is the purpose of any of us… generally speaking? Does life have to have a purpose? Your purpose is conceived by you. The general purpose for all individuals to be here, is that we are a part of the singularity that is happening now. We feel that life ought to have significance. Many feel life has meaning when one belongs to a greater agenda; an enterprising endeavor that provides us a greater sense of satisfaction. Why is it though that we feel we need to be part of a fellowship or a group to have this experience? Fitting in and going along makes us happy. It is part of our nature to form into groups that provide solace and a certain sense of comfort and security. To be around others with the same mindset puts us into our comfort zone. It may also provide a sense of meaning on a collective level. Perhaps the meaning of life is God himself. It could be that our existence here is for us to find and build a relationship based on a bond of love and intellect with God. That could be the true meaning of the world. In certain moments, the significance of the world is right here in front of us right now. As each moment unfolds, so does the true reason and point of life itself and maybe nothing more. We get caught up in figuring out the purpose of life and that its purpose lies in some unattainable concept that is tied to something in the future when, in fact, it may be nothing more than what is going on right now. Very much like singing, dancing and meditating… there is no 'end point' to these actions. The point is the journey, the experience of just doing it and the feeling you get from doing things that are enjoyable. When you dance, you are not really going anywhere, but the act of dancing provides a higher vibrational energy that comes to us as joy and happiness. Could life really be that simple? Perhaps the true wisdom of life is 'play.' Life…at the core of everything – and if you don't take it all too seriously – is play. And the point is to play and see where it goes. It is, literally, what you make of it. There is no end goal but to enjoy and experience each moment as if it were a game of sorts; a serious game, but still a game. All of this is created for pleasure and the purpose of pleasure stems from creating new experiences. The purpose of life is not to just work and go through the motions. Break free from that mindset and behavior. You can live a full and happy life that provides the 'earthly trappings' that you need to survive, but also do it with a better balance and spirit. Perhaps certain moments of insight and illumination are when we understand the true meaning of life. Thus, the true meaning of life is… that there is no meaning. The purpose is that there is no purpose and although this sounds like nonsense, somehow it is a significant nonsense that has rhythm, complexity, and vibrational resonance – much like dance and music. Perhaps it is in this type of meaninglessness that we find the greatest meaning of all.

What is the meaning of life? Humanity is ever searching. Is it happiness? People have their own goals in the pursuit of happiness. Happiness, therefore, could be the meaning of life for some; however, it can't be a universal meaning of life for all. Some people say "faith in the Lord" is the point of life, but again each and every person can find their own way of finding the meaning of life with or without organized religion. One thing that is universal is conscious awareness. In the context of 'one lifetime' happiness could very well be the point, but if you step out of this lifetime and see all of your lives that came before and measured these 'lifetimes' solely on happiness – you may find that there is perhaps a greater point and meaning to life. What is this universal meaning then?

Consider, therefore, that the purpose of life is a journey of learning and experience – as you are a part of the oneness of all things, contributing your learning and experience to the great mass consciousness of everything. You are here to experience the ups and downs, the good and bad, the happiness and sadness of this lifetime. We are driven to experience happiness, but to truly know what happiness is, we must experience despair in one lifetime and then you will experience elation, learning the difference. All the while your spirit-self is learning and experiencing, and all importantly spiritually progressing. You are moving forward in your own personal evolution, while contributing to the evolution of the one infinite creation. There is not one big cosmic meaning for all. There is only the meaning we give to our life, an individual meaning, similar to a book of many books in a library.

'The important things in life are not things at all...'

Although there is likely an overriding cosmic/universal meaning for all, it is the individual experience of the collective consciousness that drives it. Our individual meaning (purpose) of life is the key contributor to the universal whole. If all personalities' perceptions were the same, then our experience would be redundant of others, universally learning nothing. We all have a higher personality and we all experience life differently. It must be this way. There is true equality in the 'spirit world.' The purpose of life is to experience it in your own unique way, not to fit in with a socially pre-determined purpose such as to make as much money as possible, consume material stuff, have a few vacations, obsess over social media, soak up entertainment and then die. The greater meaning is that it doesn't matter if you win or lose – you're experiencing it. Even if you spend your lifetime seeking your purpose, you have learned that experience whether you fully succeed or not. A soul may incarnate as human and experience a lifetime of suffering, but the learning and experience aims they set for that lifetime may have contained those objectives. Life's meaning is to experience whatever comes at us and go on a path of whatever you seek. There is no ultimate goal or horizon to search like crazy, because you are already there doing it – whatever your intuition tells you to do – and your soul knows the plan. Whether life is really good or really bad, from a spiritual perspective, it all has definite positive purpose — it is all contributing to your enlightenment, to your spiritual progression and to the universal mass conscious. Whatever you do, you are experiencing life just by doing it here on Earth. Karma tells us that we must experience "both sides" until we have (re) learned the lessons set down. If we fail to learn them, we may need to repeat incarnations until we do. It is preferable, however, to perform good works and be a loving, kind and selfless person in order to progress spiritually to positive higher realms of existence. The meaning of life is 'in' everything; because everything is a part of the 'oneness' of human creation, our souls, and everything on Earth. The universe (and beyond) are all one. The intelligent energy of the universal infinity is everything and everywhere; it is all one creation experiencing itself. The intensity in finding meaning gets stronger and stronger. We cannot escape these spiritual hungers. We are driven forward by a perpetual seeking and we cannot ever stop searching. It is possible that each of us possesses a subconscious remembering in varying degrees as to the nature of life.

Before our days were timeless ... now our days are scheduled ...

We keep searching because we know there is more to our existence than the tangible, 'physical' illusion that is presented to our senses. The meaning of life is known to us. We just can't remember. But the dim recollection 'bugs' us still. The meaning of life is the experience of being alive for the benefit of the oneness of creation of which you are a part.

"If you do what you need, you're surviving. If you do what you want, you're living."

-Anonymous

The vast populations of humans feel that they are winning the contest (game) versus life, but many are mistaken. They are part of the false paradigm – following profits and manipulation - thinking that this is good. Of course, life is not supposed to be an analysis of winning or losing, but rather the experience. We are here to achieve enlightenment in this lifetime, which is quite a remarkable feat by any measure in any lifetime. Here is an important thought: In order for us to think that there is a bigger, greater purpose to our life, the very first question we should ask is…does 'man' even have the ability (or capacity) to comprehend the full meaning of life. Are we even smart enough to see and understand this concept?

You were not born…to live in fear
You were not born…to bow your head or bend your knee
You were not born…to be a debt slave
You were not born…to be a corporate commodity
You were not born…to be a number on a report
You were not born…to pass your life in a cubicle
You were not born…to be a consumer statistic
You were not born…to live in fear

It doesn't have to be this way. It can be better. It can be right. It can be just. Who says that it has to be this way? Just because it has been this way for so long does not mean it has to continue. And to all of those who say life is good now…well, I will repeat it again in bold letters… **It can be better** (still)… if you want it to be.

"Simplicity is the ultimate sophistication."
-Anonymous

GEOMETRY

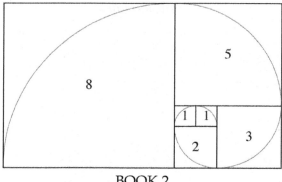

BOOK 2

Geometry, or more precisely "Sacred Geometry/Mathematics," is defined as the "architectural structure of the universe.... the fingerprint of God." Geometry is everywhere. Anywhere you look, the brilliance of geometry exists—from the largest thing imaginable such as our solar system, to the smallest particle of known existence, the atom. There are also certain repeating patterns in nature that follow sacred geometry called fractals. Fractals, on a microscopic level, make up everything solid and are constructed with reoccurring geometric patterns. Even if we cannot see all the beautiful, sacred geometric shapes with our 'naked eye,' it is right in front of us...and makes up this entire matrix which we live in.

Sacred mathematics is ubiquitous in nature. Set mathematical formulas exist in everything. Mathematics is just different vibrations of photons, but how or why it forms into what it does always follows the laws based on sacred geometry. Geometry is mathematics using shapes—so essentially we have a geometric construct that creates all matter and thus—all matter is based on geometry. There is a distinct purposefulness of everything that exists.   Nothing is random.   No matter how chaotic or random something in nature may seem—such as a cloud or a forest of trees – it is not random and there is always an underlying geometric pattern at its core. From a distance, a cloud looks very disorganized – structureless – no form, but when you move in closer (all the way down to the molecular level), there is a definitive structure. The makeup is repeating patterns all based on beautiful geometry, mathematics and the "Phi" ratio. The Phi ratio or Fibonacci number or the Golden Ratio is the number sequence by which everything in nature (and the universe) grows.

Question: If natural 'evolution' is a random, unrelated series of events occurring over time, then why is the evolution of nature not even 'more' random? Why do clouds always appear in the sky and why do trees usually grow straight up from the ground? Though there is a 'Random Factor' to everything natural, there are a definitive mathematical number of sequences and variations that make up all matter. These sequences, although random, still have a structure and follow a natural set of laws. The Random Factor, although peripherally and superficially may only show marginal intelligence in design, they are based on a universal geometric sequence of numbers which could only be derived from a supreme intelligence. Because this same sequence of numbers are found in everything natural (man, animals and plants), one must conclude there has to be an intelligent creator that made everything exactly like it is and for a reason. There is no chance 'evolution' happened by accident. So creation happened with a guiding creative hand of an overseer. Nature's construct was designed by an intellectual genius. But we are not geniuses. Did we have anything to do with creation? Yes, actually, we did and although we may doubt our supreme ability we should ascend to this conclusion. Reality itself, then, is a mathematical construct created by us. Max Plank – the father of quantum physics — demonstrated that all creation has quantum possibilities and that our existence is just one of those possibilities playing out. He showed that all matter is really a matrix of possibilities and that this reality is just one quantum possibility of our experience with and all of those possibilities being applicable to the laws of mathematics and sacred geometry.

Everything is sacred geometry. Geometry is math using shapes. No matter how chaotic 'matter' appears to be such as moss on a stone or a pile of leaves, there is on a molecular level a perfect geometric pattern and relationship to mathematics, phi ratio and the Fibonacci number sequence. And this is true in all 'reality' without exception. Sacred geometry tells us that we are all one. Each person is like a droplet of water in an ocean of consciousness.

Art and architecture is all based on Sacred Geometry. For centuries, stonemasons, which over time became Freemasons, have used these principals to construct some of the most incredible structures on Earth. The designs of revered 'holy' places from the prehistoric monuments at Stonehenge and the Great Pyramid of Giza, to the world's most wonderful cathedrals, mosques and temples, are all based on these same ancient principals of Sacred Geometry. The question is did the stonemasons of ancient times, who we know built the mosques and cathedrals, actually also build Stonehenge and the Pyramids of Giza? Perhaps assistance came from somewhere else...perhaps the hand of an intellectual architect. Although all of these magnificent structures follow Sacred Geometry, it is thought that the actual construction of these 'monolithic structures' may have been too advanced for that time or maybe anytime. If, in fact, assistance came from an advanced intelligent entity, or from extraterrestrial beings, (or even from just really smart men of the time), the Pyramids of Giza hold many mysteries in that no one may really know how or why they were physically built. This, among other amazing facts and oddities too numerous to cover in one book, let alone one chapter, make for many more questions than we have answers. The one conclusion we can make is that the Great Pyramids of Giza were not constructed as the tombs for Pharaohs. No hard evidence tells us of this and the anomalies of the Pyramids are so profound that any conclusion to the contrary is pure ignorance.

The Great Pyramid demonstrates the following brilliant characteristics: It is really eight sided not just four (two distinct planes per side); Its placement on earth is perfectly aligned with the North-South-East-West compass headings; It is perfectly in the center of all land mass in the world. Together with the other two pyramids, it is lined up perfectly with 'Orion's Belt' constellation in the sky; Every stone laid is of a different size and weight yet it all fits together perfectly like a 'jigsaw puzzle'; No mortar was used; You cannot even fit a piece of paper between the seams of any of the stones; The base is a 'perfect' square with less than a quarter inch of deviation; Its exterior was all laid with perfectly polished smooth white flat casting stones that made it shimmer like a jewel in the sun and could be seen from miles away; Its base to height measurement follows the Phi Ratio proportions exactly, and its design integrates sacred geometric patterns and mathematics. Lastly, it needs to be highlighted that the actual physical construction of just the Giza Pyramid would have required men to place a stone every four minutes for 'twenty' years nonstop (all day and all night), which is not only improbable, but virtually impossible. This does not even take into account the locating and moving of the stones to the work site or how they got each stone to the proper elevation to be placed. To put it in a better perspective...the 'measure of error' of the pyramid compared to the newest sky scraper construction, the pyramids exterior is to within 1/100th of an inch of perfection and the sky scraper with all of our modern technology and computers would be off by inches.

Stonehenge is equally amazing. Not so much for its actual physical construction, but for the fact that it aligns perfectly with the winter and summer solstice occurrence and by the precise location on the Earth which it was built. There are "energy lines" that are imaginary lines that 'crisscross' around the entire Earth's surface. These are called "Ley Lines" and these straight lines that circumvent the Earth connect energy 'nodes' or centers to one another. It was believed that if you built something on a Ley Line, then certain energies would be created. The incredible fact is, that if you take a straight Ley Line from Washington, D.C., through Columbia Maryland, through Philadelphia Pennsylvania, through New York City, New York, through Boston Massachusetts and continued the line over the Atlantic Ocean, you would end up intersecting with England, but not just with England proper but specifically with Stonehenge. That in itself is incredible, but even more telling is that one would had to have knowledge of the curvature of the earth in order for all of these cities and locations to line up exactly in a 'straight' line. Which either means that thousands of years before Christopher Columbus (which was not his real name) sailed to America — the builders of Stonehenge would had to have prior knowledge that the Earth was round or the Earth is indeed flat, but either way they had prior knowledge of the New World (America). This is not what our history books have told us, but of course it could just all be a coincidence. Perhaps the better theory is that The Giza Pyramids and Stonehenge, along with many other structures such as the amazing Gobeckli Tepe in Turkey, Easter Island, and the beautiful Nazca Lines in Peru (all very remote locations on the Earth) were all created by the same 'hand' much earlier in our historical timeline than we have been told and all constructed based on the same sacred geometric principles and laws.

The strands of our DNA, the cornea of the eye, snowflakes, pine cones, flower petals, diamond crystals, the branching of trees, a nautilus shell, the stars in the sky, the galaxy we spiral within, the air we breathe, and all life forms as we know them, emerge out of timeless geometric codes. Very sophisticated, geometric shapes exist in nature such Fractals, (a curve or geometric figure, each part of which has the same statistical character as the whole), perfect Isosceles Triangles, Platonic Solids, The Archimedean Solids, Metatron's Cube, and the Flower of life.

"The universe cannot be read until we have learnt the language and become familiar with the characters in which it is written. It is written in mathematical language, and the letters are triangles, circles and other geometrical figures, without which means it is humanly impossible to comprehend a single word."

-Galileo

As far back as 2,500 years ago Greek Mystery schools on Mount Olympus, which were religious schools based on secrecy and mystic teachings – it was taught that there are five perfect 3-demensional forms — the tetrahedron, the hexahedron, the octahedron, the dodecahedron, and the icosahedron...collectively known as the Platonic Solids; and that these form the foundation of everything in the physical world. The ancients knew these wonderful and beautiful pattern creations were symbolic of our own inner realm and that the 'experience' of Sacred Geometry was essential to the education of the soul. Viewing, analyzing and contemplating these forms allow us to gaze directly at the face of deep wisdom and see a glimpse of the inner workings of the creation of the universal mind.

In nature, we find patterns, designs and structures from the most minuscule particles, expressions of life not discernable by humans, to the greater cosmos. These inevitably follow geometrical archetypes, which reveal to us the nature of each form and its vibrational resonances. They are also symbolic of the underlying, metaphysical principle of the inseparable relationship of the part to the whole. It is this principle of oneness underlying all geometry, that permeates the architecture of all form in its myriad that diversity. This principle of interconnectedness, inseparability and union provides us with a continuous reminder of our relationship to the whole, a blueprint for the mind to the sacred foundation of all things created.

In order to better understand the mindset of the elite ruling cabal and their fascination and connection to what is going on in the world, you need to understand the importance of Sacred Geometry and Numerology. Both Sacred Geometry and Numerology, which is the relationship of events based on numbers, number cycles or number sequences are connected to ancient cultures that have possessed hidden knowledge and information passed down over centuries. Numerologists are very focused on the seven year agricultural cycle of the Hebrew "Sh'mitah" which some say foretells economic collapses and has occult symbolism. The end of the next Super-Sh'mitah was September 13, 2015. This 'cycle' holds many keys to not only the timing of our financial cycles, but also historical events such as world wars, depression and recessions. The Sh'mitah follows an agricultural cycle where every seven years food crops are halted and all monetary debts are forgiven which may directly relate to how in modern day financial cycles, debts are 'wiped' clean following economic crashes in the market.

Through geometry, you can visualize things three – dimensionally and this helps explain how conscience can exist on many multi-dimensional levels. There is more than just one 'plane of existence' and this holographic matrix has been kept hidden from us. This means that other worlds could exist right where you are now, but in a different dimension. It could even be a different time (past, present or future), but it exists in the exact same place and space.

Starting with what may be the simplest and most perfect of forms, the sphere is an ultimate expression of unity, completeness, and integrity. There is no point of view given greater or lesser importance, and all points on the surface are equally accessible and regarded by the center from which all originate. Atoms, cells, seeds, planets, and globular star systems all echo the spherical paradigm of total inclusion, acceptance, simultaneous potential and fruition, the macrocosm and microcosm.

The circle is a two-dimensional shadow of the sphere which is regarded throughout cultural history as an icon of the ineffable oneness; the indivisible fulfilment of the Universe. All other symbols and geometries reflect various aspects of the profound and consummate perfection of the circle, sphere and other higher dimensional forms of these we might imagine.

The ratio of the circumference of a circle to its diameter, Pi, is the original transcendental and irrational number. (Pi equals about 3.14159265358979323846264338327950288419769). It cannot be expressed in terms of the ratio of two whole numbers, or in the language of sacred symbolism; the essence of the circle exists in a dimension that transcends the linear rationality that it contains. Our holistic perspectives, feelings and intuitions encompass the finite elements of the ideas that are within them, yet have a greater wisdom than can be expressed by those ideas alone.

At the center of a circle or a sphere is always an infinitesimal point. The point needs no dimension, yet embraces all dimensions. Transcendence of the illusions of time and space result in the point of here and now, our most primal light of consciousness. The proverbial *"light at the end of the tunnel"* is being validated by the ever-increasing literature on so-called *"near-death experiences."* If our essence is truly spiritual omnipresence, then perhaps the 'point' of our being 'here' is to recognize the oneness we share, validating all individuals as equally precious and sacred aspects of that one.

Life itself as we know it, is inextricably interwoven with geometric forms, from the angles of atomic bonds in the molecules of the amino acids, to the helical spirals of DNA, to the spherical prototype of the cell, to the first few cells of an organism which assume vesical, tetrahedral, and star (double) tetrahedral forms prior to the diversification of tissues for different physiological functions. Our human bodies on this planet all developed with a common geometric progression from one, to two, to four, to eight primal cells and beyond.

Almost everywhere we look, the mineral intelligence embodied within crystalline structures follows geometry unfaltering in its exactitude. The lattice patterns of crystals all express the principles of mathematical perfection and repetition of a fundamental essence, each with a characteristic spectrum of resonances defined by the angles, lengths and relational orientations of its atomic components.

The square root of 2 embodies a profound principle of the whole being more than the sum of its parts. (The square root of two equals about 1.414213562...) The orthogonal dimensions (axes at right angles) form the conjugal union of the horizontal and vertical which gives birth to the greater offspring of the hypotenuse. The new generation possesses the capacity for synthesis, growth, integration and reconciliation of polarities by spanning both perspectives equally. The root of two originating from the square, leads to a greater unity, a higher expression of its essential truth, faithful to its lineage.

The fact that the root is irrational expresses the concept that our higher dimensional faculties can't always necessarily be expressed in lower order dimensional terms - e.g., "*And the light shineth in darkness; and the darkness comprehended it not.*" By the same token, we have the capacity to surpass the genetically programmed limitations of our ancestors, if we can shift into a new frame of reference (i.e., neutral with respect to prior axes, yet formed from that matrix-seed conjugation. Our dictionary refers to the word matrix both as a womb and an array (or grid lattice). Our language has some wonderful built-in metaphors if we look for them.

The Golden Ratio (a.k.a. Phi ratio a.k.a. sacred cut a.k.a. golden mean a.k.a. divine proportion) is another fundamental measure that seems to encompass everything. (The Golden Ratio is about 1.61803398874989484820458683436563811772O...) The Golden ratio is the unique ratio such that the ratio of the whole to the larger portion is the same as the ratio of the larger portion to the smaller portion. As such, it symbolically links each new generation to its ancestors, preserving the continuity of relationship as the means for retracing its lineage. The mathematician credited with the discovery of this series is Leonardo Pisano Fibonacci. Fibonacci ratios appear in the ratio of the number of spiral arms in daisies, in the chronology of rabbit populations, in the sequence of leaf patterns as they twist around a branch, and a myriad of places in nature where self-generating patterns are in effect. The sequence is the rational progression towards the irrational number embodied in the quintessential Golden Ratio.

This most aesthetically pleasing proportion, phi, has been utilized by numerous artists since (and probably before) the construction of the Great Pyramid. As scholars and artists of eras gone by discovered (e.g., Leonardo da Vinci, Plato, and Pythagoras), the intentional use of these natural proportions in art of various forms expands our sense of beauty, balance and harmony to optimal effect. It is thought that the most appealing faces to the human eye are ones that have the 'Phi' proportions and more closely adhere to the Golden Ratio. Leonardo da Vinci used the Golden Ratio in his painting of "The Last Supper" in both the overall composition (three vertical golden rectangles and a decagon), and also on the alignment of the central figure of Jesus. The outline of the Parthenon structure at the Acropolis near Athens, Greece also follows the Golden Rule of architecture which lends its beauty to the proportions set forth from the Golden Ratio.

The Vesica Piscis is the shape that is formed by the intersection of two circles or spheres whose centers exactly touch. This symbolic intersection represents the 'common ground,' shared vision or mutual understanding between equal individuals. The shape of the human eye is a Vesica Piscis. The spiritual significance of "seeing eye to eye" is the eye is the "mirror of the soul" and was a highly regarded shape used by numerous Renaissance artists. They utilized this form extensively in both art and architecture. The ratio of the axis of the form is the square root of three, which alludes to the deepest nature of the triune which cannot be adequately expressed by rational language alone.

This spiral generated by a recursive nest of Golden Triangles (triangles with relative side lengths of 1, phi and phi) is the classic shape of the Chambered Nautilus shell. The creature building this shell uses the same proportions for each expanded chamber that is added; growth follows a law which is everywhere the same. The outer triangle is the same as one of the five 'arms' of the pentagonal. Rotating a circle about a line tangent to it creates a torus, which is similar to a donut shape where the center exactly touches all the 'rotated circles.' The surface of the torus can be covered with seven distinct areas, all of which touch each other. In this 3-dimensional case, seven colors are needed, meaning that the torus has a high degree of 'communication' across its surface.

The progression from point (0-dimensional) to line (1-dimensional) to plane (2-dimensional) to space (3-dimensional) and beyond, leads us to the question: If mapping from higher order dimensions to lower ones loses vital information (as we can readily observe with optical illusions resulting from third to second dimensional mapping), does our 'fixation' with a 3-dimensional space introduce crucial distortions in our view of reality that a higher-dimensional perspective would not lead us to? Instead of paying attention to the messenger, we need to pay attention to the message. The message holds the construct of relevant information. This is important and shows the relationship of our heart to our brain.

Similarly, we need to pay attention to the individual components that 'make up' the whole. By analyzing the geometry of things, we can then be able to understand how and why things are like they are and their relationship of the parts to the whole and ourselves. We are all creators and implementers of this geometry — it is innate — and much of what we create is a part of the sacred geometrical universe.

LIGHT-BODY

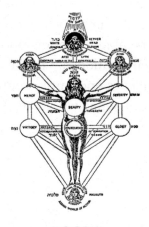

BOOK 3

The laws of 'free will' require us to ascend on our own with very little assistance. A "Light-Body" is the definition of a person that has been able to develop a mind-body relationship to ascend into a lighter, healthier and more spiritual existence here on Earth. A healthier mind-body will, in turn, come from inner peace and a true knowledge and understanding of the ascension process in your lifetime. Physically, the Light Body will ultimately feel lighter with less aches and pains, be healthier and look more youthful. Mentally, the Light Body will feel like it is connected to an energy source of knowledge that powers the universe. We currently perceive this ascension process experience as something out of this world, but it is not. It is real and can be attained by anyone who becomes a conscience and aware being. As we move from our carbon-based human form into the crystalline form, there will be more dexterity and balance within our body we will feel lighter and indeed shall actually be lighter and less heavy as our bodies will have less density to them. But these changes will be subtle and not necessarily happen overnight and will start 'mentally' rather than 'physically.' You will actually have better control over how you look; your health and your ability to regenerate will be much greater. Disease is not something (you) the ascended one will need to worry about. There will still be some inconsistencies in our 'physical balance' which can be easily remedied by healing practices or by your own inner healer guide. There will also be elements of surprise for the enlightened one which may be unique to each person, but this will be likened to something as desired gifts as if it's your 'birthday.'

There is a spring in your step and you don't feel the entire weight of the world being carried on your shoulders (e.g., Atlas). But the Light Body is more than just physical and actually has more to do with the mind and its connection (mental state) to the individual. "Light Workers" are people here in human form that have achieved a light-body existence to guide and assist us in our ascension process, but not show us too much as we must do it ourselves. Light Workers have been given different names here on earth e.g., Pleiadians, Indigo Children or Star Seeds. Light Workers started coming to earth 'again' through a new wave of natural births starting in the early 1960's and continue to come here to this very day to help in mass consciousness, awareness and ascension.

Light Workers came to the United States because here we could have the most impact. This is also a place where denial is pervasive. Those of us with many questions now are those for whom ascension is occurring right now. All the answers to our questions are not handed to us on a silver platter...that would be too easy. We must come to ask these 'questions' naturally according to the energy flow of our bodies to guide us on the pathway of ascension. All the answers to these questions are already encoded within us, within our DNA, and by asking, searching and striving for answers 'is' shifting us into the Light Body form.

This biology change in our mind/body is really the question at hand. So what happens to us when we fully ascend? Do we disappear or evaporate or do we stay physical in our bodies? We will always remain 'physical' as long as you inhabit the Earth and full ascension does not occur until the time of death when the spirit is free to leave our body.

Initially, the changes taking place within us are not centered on just the ascension from the cumulative perspective, but also a time-linear perspective. The 2012 winter solstice was the return to the core (home) for all humanity. Upon this date, we made the cumulative ascension to the '1/2' way point, thus achieving ascension for the human race. All we had to do was get past the 'mid-point', and in the 'Laws of Nature', we are accomplishing our goal. In other words, we did not blow ourselves up and the human race will survive and continue. This moment of 'singularity,' where humanity and artificial intelligence (created by us) are brought together in the information age, is the pinnacle of the ascension process and the top of our life pyramid. But it's an ongoing process and shall continue for many years during this active time. Earthlings are entering into a pattern of ascent or decent, the realization of the soul. Currently - if you're reading this, you are ascending. If you're asking questions about who you are and where you came from, you are ascending. There are changes taking place in the human body, even ones you can't see and they culminate at its highest point when you reach the core (home). DNA connections and a crystalline encoding are taking place as you ascend. Changes will continue to take place as you shift during the ascension process. This is what we understand as evolution of the soul and spirit. But evolution occurs in a way that many of us have not been made aware of in our Earthly, scholarly teachings, therefore the pattern of evolution must be understood. Evolution is not that which functions solely in a linear time. Rather it is a loop with events that happen at certain times and can be quantified with geometry.

Phi - the Golden Mean (1.62)-evolution is managed by a carefully constructed time clock dial/face. It is not at all random and it is very precise. Evolution generally occurs slowly, but during these specific, precise moments of our universal history, the rate at which evolution occurs shoots up like a rocket. We are then approaching the core (home) of our spiritual existence. Evolution and the returning to the core (going home) are inexplicably entwined. These changes occur within our bodies, during ascension and starts at the molecular level. The positions and electrons change their forms. Matter and antimatter shall meet. This will move and ascend humanity from carrying the carbon based molecule to the crystalline molecule. Therefore it is true to say we are moving into a 'Crystal form' – and this is all occurring at the quantum or molecular level. How does that affect us? It means much more life force will be assimilated and a greater assistance to the enlightened you. It allows a far greater percentage of universal energy to flow through you and it allows the brain electricity to 'turn on' and start functioning at full capacity for the fully ascended individual. Your body is like an antenna and in the crystalline form you are able to pick up the vibrational energy that you would not normally be able to access in the carbon-based form. In a pure crystalline form, there would be no aging as we know it on Earth and death would be our conscious choice. The key to starting the process is to initially unlock your 'chakras' and to activate your pineal gland. There are twelve total energy chakras, not just seven as believed by most people. There are seven that are within your body and five that are outside. Chakras are energy points or nodes along your spinal cord that are a part of the esoteric (subtle) body and not actually part of the physical body. The way to unlock your 'chakras' is that you must start at the base (spine) chakra and unlock this first in order to move into the next chakras. The order or sequence of unlocking chakras is important so that the body is 'unlocked' from the base moving up through the spine and up to the dome (head). The dome is where your third eye or pineal gland is and this is your gateway to the higher realms. Once you have unlocked your dome chakra, then you can start to access the five chakras that are located outside your body. The eighth chakra is located virtually just outside the skin of your body. Sometimes you sense that a person has an amazing aura about (around) them – and this is the energy you're picking up from the eighth chakra that 'comes off them' naturally. The remaining chakras extend out from the body to varying distances with the twelfth chakra extending out to the furthest most point we can think of or even comprehend (infinity).

Do we disappear or evaporate when we ascend? No! We stay physical. The physical is different, yet still similar to the one we had before coming to Earth, known as lateral ascension. There is no evaporation or disappearance; nothing physical like that will happen. The disappearance will happen from the perspective that the completely un-ascended will not be able to see the vibration of our body energy. Good feelings will instigate good chemical changes in our body; clues and metaphors will be provided to us to help us find these new and wonderful 'tools' for the enlightened soul. A certain synchronicity starts to occur as we ascend and this can show up as (running into) meeting people that have a 'connection' to us or even as reoccurring series of numbers (e.g., 11:11 on a clock) that keep showing up in different places in our lives.

Fear and confusion are emotions and feelings that we wish to be eased or eliminated during this time. Fear and confusion must be dealt with by the self - which we all have the (inner power) ability to do with our inner healer. Light Workers have the ability to remove fear and confusion from others through our heart, our conscious thought and from our healing hands. The heart actually sends a lot of information to the brain. The heart is an electromagnetic rhythm keeper. The state of immense stress causes the body much harm. The state of extreme stress can cause the immune system to falter and affect all parts of our mind/body energy. During stressful times, the heart sends an electrical circuit through all our cells in the body. The energy can actually go out of the body like an electrical impulse generated from this electrical energy system. Both positive and negative electricity impulse can be emitted – people have different electrical voltages depending on makeup/environment. You've heard the expression that a person has either 'positive' or 'negative' energy and it is this energy that we feel when we are around them. The frequency of our inner body energy level is similar to a radio transmitter in that you carry either a strong or weak signal. The body helps with electrical conductivity. We are like an antenna trying to pick up signals. Stone masons understood vibrational energy and knew how stones and crystals could hold information similar to a modern compact disk (CD) which has a harmonic existence. This is similar to how a 'soul mate' can complete your energy like no other person. Different people can be connected to your unique vibrational energy. A thought can travel to another person within a second and even though no two humans are the same, we can identify people by this energy. Shamanism was part of the cornerstone of all early civilization and understood the mind/body energy connection. They used medicines from the Earth to heal, but also had an understanding of astrology, stars and dates that correlate to humans. Ancient civilization also used many creative aspects such as art, music and dance. Certain rhythms have benefits to humans and the Earth. Native American Indians were 'one' with the Earth and performed dances to heal the Earth. In a way, the ascended are reconnecting with this same type of energy that was prevalent in our past history.

When you ascend here on Earth you will go through many changes. Mentally you will worry less about things and physically you will worry less about how you look, yet your body will start to rejuvenate and look younger and feel lighter, but other changes will occur too. You do become less motivated, less hungry, less tired, less bored, and feel more purposeful. You also become less materialistic and less consumed with money. Less motivated but more creative. Sleeping patterns change. You have the ability to see right and wrong more clearly. You become more emotional. You identify love and hate in others, you become less manipulative. Intuition strengthens. Abstract ideas are not as foreign. Compassion for others increases. In language, you use less swear words. You watch what you eat. You will consume less red meat. You will eat more raw fruit and vegetables. Your body will change form. You can 'mold' and 'sculpt' how you want to appear. Hair stops falling out. You have less aches and physical pains. Your body feels lighter. You become stronger. You are happier with less to worry or care about. You are less motivated to watch television or sports and have more thirst for knowledge. Corruption becomes more apparent in day-to-day life, news, money and government. Your pineal gland starts to become more active and a more active pineal gland leads to intuition, telepathy, and elevated intelligence and insight. Finally, you start to question who, what, where and when. '24/7 fear' is the world we live in today so the hormone of fight and flight is continuously 'on' and thus drains the body of essential energy to combat normal sickness and illness. Most of our energy is used on protection. We have become deluded on working so hard to put up an image that we became physically and mentally tired wearing ourselves down to a point where we drain the body of vitality. A person (or humanity) cannot grow under these circumstances and if there is no growth, then we die metaphorically and physically.

The brain only has a limited capacity to hold onto certain amounts of stress or fear and then it must disseminate the excess into the body, or be 'discharged.' Brain stress will go into one place; back, chest, ulcers, neck, and head thereby channeling negative into energy into certain parts of the body making them ache, ill or sick. Stress reduces the performance output of body, correlating there is definitely a mind/body interaction. Many people channel stress into their heart and this causes negative adrenaline into the body. This is extremely detrimental to the heart and can cause problems leading to various diseases and medical conditions such as arrhythmia, clogging, high blood pressure and a host of many other heart-related conditions. Lastly, if you're sad or confused, looking for a solution is like admitting you have a problem. You have in effect created that problem by giving attention to it. Remember you create your reality. Admitting you have a problem and looking for a solution to that problem is the problem. When you think about something in a negative tone, you are just causing more damage to it. Don't think! Sometimes no thoughts are really good thoughts:

- Remember not to think (negatively).
- When you reach for the stars you are put onto your back.
- Admitting you have a problem is not the solution... it is the problem!
- All things are simple to simple minds.

"Ignorance is bliss..."

– Thomas Gray

The great American 'dis-ease' of nerves and chronic dispositional tendencies result in chronic physical ailments. The peculiarities of disposition as we nurse them through the years set in upon us as bodily ailments affecting our later years, with innumerable misfortunes, which destroy our happiness and peace of mind. Fear is only in your head. We don't pay much attention to our parts of the body until they are in pain. Then we notice how important each body part is to us, which we have taken for granted until we experience pain in that area.

Another important gland that interplays with our mind/body relationship is the Pineal gland. The pineal gland produces – DMT (N,N-Dimethyltryptomine) and serotonin which helps us sleep, dream and connect us to our spiritual world. Inner peace begins the moment you choose not to allow another person or event to control your emotions. Happiness comes from liking yourself, something completely unrelated to material items and money. When you're on your death bed...will you be thinking about money? Think about what really makes you happy. Then go out and make enough money to take part in those activities. Making more than you really need is a waste of the only non-renewable resource you have and that is your time on this planet. If you spend all of your time chasing money, you will never take the time to enjoy it...healthy balance...healthy mind...healthy body.

You finally have 'Arrived' and so it dawns on you, with a certain sense, that you have been cheated – because life feels the same as it has always felt. Nothing internally has really changed... you are 'conditioned' by society to be in desperate need of a future. So the final goal that this life prepares us for is retirement – when you will be a senior citizen and you will have the wealth, wisdom and the leisure to do what you have always wanted, but you will at the same time also have impotence, poor health (perhaps) and low energy. So the entire process is really ironic from cradle to grave. We are involved in a really dire situation whereby we divide our day into work and play; we work (job) to make money in order to play (leisure). The object is work to make money and the object of making money is to go home and enjoy the money and play. The illusion is that money alone can buy true pleasure. Unfortunately, we generally do not get paid to play, but this is something we might all try to aspire to.

The game of 'hide and seek' is one of the first things we play as a child. It is instinctual. Life is also very much like a game of 'hide and seek' since we search for who we really are for most of our life.

Those that 'wake up' during this lifetime are the ones playing the game of life correctly...while some give up playing the game because they feel they may never really find who they are. And yet others feel they won't wake up until they have paid a price for the search. Many try to find assistance in counseling or therapy because they feel a void or need help in this search. The running joke is that – "anyone who goes to a psychiatrist needs to get their head examined." But what you have really created is, that you have defined yourself as a person who needs to go to a doctor by going to a psychiatrist. Ironically, all the answers to these questions of "who I am" are already inside you. Once you know who you are, all the questions and problems that confront you that originally made you seek outside help from a doctor become superfluous. Having personally experienced 'talking' to a psychiatrist when my mother passed, I can say that it was helpful to a degree. Unfortunately, much of the therapy consisted of medications that not only affected my mind, but also my body in an unnatural way. In addition, I was remiss by the forced visits that personally made me feel controlled and somehow 'inferior' at the time. Maybe I was playing the victim, but I realize now, that I am stronger than that even though it was difficult to know it at the time. Are you also playing a victim of the world? Don't be a victim of the world. Being aware of being aware of playing a victim is the first positive step to understanding 'who' you are.

If things don't work the way you're doing it, then change the rhythm or tempo of which you're doing them. Especially physical movement for example: getting up or down out of a chair or bed; navigating stairs; getting in or out of a car. Changing the quickness or slowness or angle (hand placement) you do these movements can bring less pain. Have your physical body work with the mental body to become one, more fluid-moving energy- filled individual.

"As long as you're fighting something (anything) – you're creating it!"

-Anonymous

Spiritual people generally have concerns with money. Religious people have concerns with sex. Money and sex are energy. Spirituality is energy too. So what is the problem? Money, sex spirituality and power are the things most people seek more than anything else in this 'matrix' of our world. These items are the four 'set' programs of our society. You can only really embrace, in any combination, two of these programs at a time. It has been theorized that many people with money and power don't have much spirituality and they feel lost inside. We are infinite beings with infinite internal energy, but even here on Earth you <u>can't</u> have it all without conflict. Society and the matrix keep us from finding it all and disconnected from who we truly are. We are more than what meets the eye, but we are constantly fighting and resisting ourselves without realizing we are incredibly powerful beings.

We have the ability to heal ourselves by truly believing in it. This is not wishful thinking. This is a documented fact (i.e., placebo effect). We are so amazing that our system of energy can create anything — we can even create disease if we want. Most all disease is man-made. We have poisoned ourselves with man-made toxins and poisoned our thoughts with fear and worry. As soon as someone says they have cancer and they say they want to 'fight it' you give cancer the power over you. As soon as you're fighting Diabetes, Leukemia, any type of pain, depression, high blood pressure or any disease (it doesn't matter what it is) as long as you're fighting it or resisting it, you can never be well because you believe in it and you have empowered it. You have given it the upper hand. Disease is dis-ease in the body. Question: Then how are you going to break out of the endless 'sickness' routine? In order to break out of a disease or illness, you have to change your life pattern—you cannot believe in it. Awareness exists here on Earth, but only as an observation unless you truly commit to it, which then it will manifest itself.

Warning: If you really 'go for' the holistic 'Light Body' mindset and you live in a fairly 'normal' environment your friends, family and co-workers will probably try to commit you to a sanitarium. You will show signs of withdrawal from common practices, but remember you have lost nothing. You are the same person you have always been, but you have grown from 'here to there.' Institutional psychiatry is the enforcement and guardianship of standard reality. If you're in an alternative state of consciousness you will not fit very well into the standard vibrations of what the average person would call sane. But what is 'sane' anyway? What is self-improving? It's all relative. Joggers run for what reason – for health, to improve fitness? The punishment you put on your body may in fact be worse in the long run. If you like to run and want exercise, you can do this in conjunction with either a sport or activity such as soccer or tennis. At least you're playing a 'game' with others while you are exercising. Merely shaking bones, rattling brains and punishing knees are what you get on the pretense that it is healthy for you. The same can be said for your mental fitness too. Sanity can only be judged subjectively and all that matters is that you conduct yourself with confidence and balance. Letting others question your methodology is really their problem, not yours.

All of this enlightenment starts making sense when you abandon vanity and materialism. Abandon all the 'stuff' that separates human beings from nature and what is natural. Abandon everything you have been taught, or have been trained to think. We were born naked creatures of the Earth to live, eat, drink and know of the Earth. We are here to live and die by the Earth in natural harmony with her, all in natural time. That time exists within us - not without us. Without us consciously here, time does not exist.

Because without us, there is no time on Earth - abandon all educational intellect...abandon all pomp and formality. Abandon etiquette and courtesies...abandon all language, words and writing.

No, time is pure, unadulterated and only cluttered with anything more than it doesn't provide. Abandon ego. Everything is basically pointless distraction created by people that in actuality do not love themselves and desire to press on and control others through lies and manipulation. They physically are not happy with themselves and do not want (or like) what was given to them so they artificially modify the outside appearance with plastic surgery, makeup and clothing and hours and hours of unnatural beauty, hours and hours of pointless experience (of) inorganic exercise which constitutes painful exercise doing more harm to the body than good. Hours in the gym punishing the body for what reason: to look better; to be healthier? They are reflections of what was given to us and replacing it with false representation of themselves disguised even further with titles, badges, money, family names, wealth, class and anything directed away from nature and closer to a false existence.

"Whose property is my body? Probably mine. I so – regard it. If I experiment with it, who must be answerable? I, not the state."
-Mark Twain

Some people will tell you they are accident prone. This means they are not working together 'in harmony' with their energy body and their physical body. We tend to do things without even thinking about whatever we are doing; that our mind is 'off' thinking about something else. The physical action is simple enough like cutting a piece of bread, but if we do not concentrate on the task – something can go wrong and then we slip and cut ourselves. When the physical and mental (energy) body work as one, then we will accomplish the task with success.

Intuition is important and plays into the equation in that our intuition tells us what to do next. But is your heart, mind and body working as one? With so many distractions in today's world, even driving a car without touching your cellphone, or drinking coffee, is quite an accomplishment. We literally do 100 things a day without even concentrating on them and, again, there is the potential for things to go differently than we intend.

Vaccines are being used today for a multitudinous of reasons, but mostly as a preventative measure. When a vaccine is injected, it is literally placing foreign material into the body. This is not natural. Vaccines are blatant last-ditch efforts to control populations by injecting harmful chemical additives such as Aluminum, Formaldehyde and Thimerosal (mercury) along with a small portion of the actual disease you're trying to prevent. Question: Can we be assured that vaccines are not being used by certain controlling governmental or international entities to implement latent disease and illness that may show up in later life such as Autism and Alzheimer's? If ever someone, even of authority, orders you to take a vaccine without your consent, respectfully decline because it is your (or your child's) body so you choose what you put in it. Period.

The key to the matrix is this: We all created this matrix that we are living in. We created it so that we wouldn't have to really think about it when we choose to come here — we could just run on automatic pilot. This 'framework of life' is constructed from limitations of duality; rightness and wrongness and goodness and badness so it's all about resistance and reaction or more clearly about acceptance and agreement. So we are either agreeing or disagreeing with everything. The problem with that is every time you agree or disagree, you resist or react, you are in conflict because then you have to prove or verify your point of view. As long as you're trying to prove a point of view, you will never experience true ease, inner peace, happiness or true success. We can never reach the greatness individually or collectively, while consumed with 'making points' to others in that we will not be able to make positive improvements to the world collectively if we can't achieve this individually. Our heart tells us this. There will always be something that we are fighting, and as long as you're fighting something (anything) you're creating it.

"The only difference...between real heaven and heaven here on earth...is that in the real heaven you do not need to 'fluff' your pillows to be comfortable."

-Anonymous

Nirvana—means to blow out...to release. Breathing (breath) is life (spirit). But if you hold your breath, you will eventually lose it...so breathe out and let it go. It will come back to you. But if you don't let it go—you will suffocate. Don't cling, and you will be in the state of Nirvana. No need to say anything—just 'be' without words and without conflict. When you release your breath, you replenish life and relax. There is no need to be tense. There is no hurry either...go at your own comfortable pace, because everything will be there when you finally arrive.

A private message to the true Light-Worker(s): Everything you seek is already done for you. You have accomplished your work and humanity is applauding you for this now. It is at this time you need to travel to the place of creativity which many call 'home.' They call it many names such as the vortex, or the source, but it is really home for you and it is here you will feel the full celebration of the work that you have, and are continuing to do, for humanity. There has never been a time in all of history like the intensity of the time that is upon us now. Your patience here on Earth is greatly appreciated. Sometimes it is very difficult to balance yourself in this world. For this you have much appreciation from others and much love is coming to you now. So we wish to express to you the brilliance of who you are. You are 'physically' focused beings who are source energy instead of 'physically' focused beings. You are the leading edge of the universe...the creators of this universe and in your physical bodies, you are beacons who will lead millions of others who want what you have, but don't know what you know. You have no assignment to teach them, but it is through the clarity of your example that it will. And because of your participation, you have gathered around you in a rather consistence and intense fashion a cadre of non-physical energies...you can call them 'angels' of the universe or whatever you want to call them, who have always known you, but whom you have not always known. But you're feeling for them and your finding of them will be more vivid to you as you grow. And that feeling of standing out there on the leading edge is sort of lonely because others don't get you...is fast fading. Your new association with who you really are has powerfully taken its place. It will no longer be necessary for others 'to get you' in order for you to stand and know who you are. In fact, you will find it a very common thing that flows forth from you when others say..."*I don't understand what you mean*"... for you to say..."*it doesn't matter.*" You are going to find yourself teaching without anyone asking for a classroom. You're going to find yourself understanding without anyone really verbalizing a problem. You're going to find yourself 'vibrationally' speaking, knowing from inside your vortex on how it feels to be tuned in to infinite intelligence. Solutions are going to flow forth to you more emphatically than you ever experienced before, and you're going to find yourself often standing as a very clear minded-being amidst others who are standing in a place of confusion. And you're not going to feel uncomfortable in your leadership. As you hear people complaining, you won't take their complaints to heart at all, but you're going to feel a solution forming within you and words to back up the solution and you're going to find yourself telling people what you know on a more consistent basis without offending them, because you're not going to be considering their point of view and your point of view at the same time, but rather you will be speaking profoundly from your point of view with insight, clarity and love. One who is connected to this energy source, one who is flowing with the stream, is more powerful and more influential than millions who are not. In giving this all to you, it is our powerful desire for you to understand that this is not an assignment that is being given to you, but it is the fulfilling of your intention that you set forth yourself, for yourself, when you decided to come to Earth. This is the acknowledgment that you have accomplished what you set forth to accomplish. You are creators who have come here as a God-force to align with the untapped energies to assist in the ascension and awakening process of human kind.

It is your knowing that as you move forward from this day that, never again, will you feel negative emotions without blessing the importance of them. Because in the negative emotion is the indication that you are setting forth for the growth and expansion of the universe and instead of feeling a continuation of negative feelings, you're going to 'flip' and feel the bounce that takes the solution to the problems that arise. You're going to feel 'plugged in' more often as you explore the contrast of your experience of time space reality. Over the days that follow, you will start to increase the feeling of profound connectedness and although you may not feel it like some, your desire to have it will bring it to you. Because you have managed to activate your inner vibration energy with enough consistency and frequency, you have been able to receive coded information, which your point of attraction has shifted dramatically. And the lives around you that you call physical manifestations will begin to start to show this shift in human consciousness too. So flow with the new-found freedom and the release of the resistance that was set before you in the past.

There could not be more love focused on you right now. There could not be more recognition of the worthiness that which is you, that which is felt here and now. You have done the work and the energy around you has received the benefit which is exactly the way you so lovingly set it all up when you decided to come forth. We want you to physically feel the appreciation of that which you call 'God' (the prime creator) and that which we call 'all that is' for the expansion of the universe that is a result of the being-ness that is you.

VIBRATION

BOOK 4

Vibration is energy in motion. Life is a battle of sorts between light and dark in the universe. We seek to bring ourselves to the light vibration while many evil forces are trying hard to keep us in the dark and stuck in a low frequency vibration. Dark forces thrive on negative, or low-frequency vibrations such as, hate, evil, manipulation, etc. and are full of trickery; to the extent that the 'dark' may come to us disguised as a 'light force' pushing as human spirit, to aid us when, in fact, it is not here to help. Here again is a situation where mis- or disinformation can be spread, making it difficult for some to ascend. We as a people have evolved here on Earth for over 12,000 years, and during most of this time we have not known what true freedom is. Our spirituality and consciousness have been stifled with inadequate information, and a manipulated history that makes little or no sense, and evades the entire essence of love and goodness to humanity. It has highlighted violence, war, terror, fear, aggression and superstitions and yet many of us are able to circumvent all the negativity and 'put forth' good vibrations. Understand, a positive vibration will always create positive energy. The controlling elite have created sophisticated societal systems of control such as false governments and religions so that they can control and manipulate us. They are the ones creating the terror themselves so that they can <u>legally</u> give more power to the police state and military industrial complex, and set new laws and regulations that extract wealth, land, money, guns, gold and anything else of value out of our possession to de-power us and every other citizen from achieving a higher vibration of existence. They want to amplify the negative energy. Do you want to live in such a world? They know that you will not completely believe in all of this so investigate this yourself. Ask the question: Why? The evidence and answers are there...but you must make the effort to find them. Try to erase the negativity in your mind and concentrate on positive energy. That is our power against evil dark forces. They are essentially powerless against a strong, positive energy and 'they' do not want us to learn and tap into this amazing power.

'They' use radio, music, television, newspapers, religion, politicians, mimicking and electromagnetic waves to keep us contained. Keeping us out of the 'know.' Those that nervously laugh at this information must travel further on the path to enlightenment than others since they are starting from a further point from the truth. They are the ones with the actual fear. Their whole 'world' is brought into question once they start asking questions. Fear of the truth is ominous – especially – the happier and more blissful the person is in their 'fake world reality.' An intelligent human must investigate – ask questions, and not just dismiss or criticize. One must first do their own investigation or have firsthand experience, in order to have a sound opinion of anything and not just depend on heresy. For example: The universe is inhabited by many beings and our governments have kept many secrets about them. It would be shortsighted on our part not to entertain the possibility that other 'human-like' life forms have come to Earth in the past 100 years or so. Any person laughing, joking or making fun of other people that may believe in this shows the conditioning and manipulation to which we have been submitted. We are living on this planet for a reason, and part of the growing process is to learn to think positively and accomplish this task even in such a negative world.

If you seek real knowledge, then a path will be set before you. But you and only you must make the decision to set forward and go down this less travelled path. But it is this path that holds the understanding of higher knowledge and demonstrates the mass control that has been put on us. Most people on Earth have forgotten to listen to their soul. We still have much to (re)learn in this life. Compared with most intelligent life within the Solar System, we are very much like a young, immature, adolescent teenager. We need to evolve by focusing our concentration on positive vibrational emotions and our consciousness. Create a positive journey to gain knowledge about our past. Don't let others disturb your journey. Be aware that others are stealing your inner energy to keep you 'primitive' just like they are.

Shift changes in our evolution have been occurring and are still coming. There is a feeling of uneasiness when you know it's coming. These sudden shifts will 'rock the boat,' in order to assist you in waking up, but we must keep an even keel to navigate the choppy waters ahead. Many sense this vibrational change and are preparing for this, therefore we feel we have many tasks at hand to prepare and resolve before the forthcoming deadline associated with the shift. Even regular tasks have a sense of greater purpose with others assisting mainly behind the scenes. This could be us wanting to clear up past issues (from this life or others), relationships, or past family dynamics. Our spiritual past identities are attempting to drop the 'density' of this reality, so that we store within ourselves the current vibrational energy. Several unaddressed issues creating an imbalance in ourselves need to be resolved since they have reached a breaking point. Our operating system should disengage from this system that technically 'pushes our buttons' – that makes us do things against our intuition. Many times, when we don't resolve things, we are 'placed' in situations to observe and learn from. Having the wisdom is to be engaged on a 'neutral basis' (to observe) be present (in the moment) and know what is happening right in front of us. We will know when the path opens for us and if we are required to take action. This is important and will show us how we are to use and integrate our life experiences for the good of all. We need to know when to censure or when to direct energy into something. This is the time for spiritual initiation and greater wisdom in our actions and lifestyle. At the proper time, we will apply the pressure ourselves in order to accomplish these changes and to 'sync' our vibrations in harmony with not only one another, but also as a method to elevate our awareness. The 2012 awakening cycle continued the informational shift and is causing us to 'NOT' procrastinate. This vibrational shift will intensify and become even more important over the coming years.

"There is a force in the universe, which, if we permit it, will flow through us and produce miraculous results."

-Mahatma Gandhi

Dimensions are 'vibrationally' shifting, causing a massive movement of information within the consciousness. If we can discipline ourselves by quieting the mind, we can see these new revelations being presented to us. Through this great period of consciousness, we are slowly awakening. We are entering a period of 'live review.' Live review will enable us to project our life as a streaming video that can be reviewed and evaluated – in between incarnation cycles – and participating in this 'live review' in this cycle, while still in our '3D' body, will be a massive, positive step in the direction of forwarding and accelerating consciousness in our world. Facing memories and reaching conclusions will slide your consciousness into a supportive form of unity field with other ascending beings – and into the unity platform of this '3D' architecture as a part of this transition along with other events lifting our inner vibration. We need to continually quiet the noise and focus on our inner signal which, in turn, shows us the correct way for life's direction. We have a vibrant and lively inner life that is our true navigator of the path that we take on the world. Your inner self is how we show up in the world. It makes perfect 'sense' that if you have 'anything' to do with where you are going, you need to have a distinct relationship with that driver. We need to 'co-exist' with ourselves and not suppress the true driver of love and kindness. Why do you think you will experience anything different when you're gone from here?

'And out of the great void of space, a small sound took shape and thus creation began.'

Everything in existence is the result of a frequency and vibration. The 'ancients' understood this about life. The universe, astrology, mathematics, magnetism, healing, and the unseen forces all correspond to a frequency of encoded knowledge. Encoded knowledge is information that is conveyed in sign and symbols – we have just failed to understand this for ourselves; sacred knowledge is only known to a handful of people and is kept hidden from the public. We perceive this reality with our five senses though it's not real; Quantum physics has shown us that space and time are just an illusion. Quantum physics has revealed that matter does not exist and that the substance of the universe is consciousness. Instead of a fear-greed-based existence, and the quiet desperation to accumulate material items, we should be collecting knowledge and truth to enlighten our behavior.

REAL EYES ... REALIZE ... REAL LIES

"The world is like a ride at an amusement park and when you choose to go on it you think it is real, because that is how powerful your mind is. The ride goes up and down and round and round. It has thrills & chills very brightly colored very loud and it is fun — for a while. Some people have been on the ride for a long time and they begin to question — is this real? Or is it just a ride? And other people remember and come back to us and say hey don't worry, don't be afraid this is just a ride and we kill those people."

-Bill Hicks

Quantum physics also tells us that we create our reality. The majority of humans use all their vast energy chasing after the little, relatively insignificant things in life. New beliefs generate new actions and that, in turn, creates a new reality. People ask for change and then when life does change they ask why. They still use the old 'baggage formula' for life and then wonder what happened. As changes begin, there is an evolution of energy (cleaning house) to make way for the new energy. It is like you place your food order with the 'cosmos' and it is being custom prepared. Don't believe that you don't deserve it. You need to keep up that vibration to receive it when it comes to you. All energy is there to serve you.

The laws that have been put before us are limiting, inasmuch and ultimately do more harm than good. The 'enlightened' truth seeker does not fit into society in the traditional sense and can see through the manipulation that has been put in front of us. The enlightened do not want to conform — they want to grow. Conformity is the stagnation of an individual and stagnation is extinction. The inability to grow beyond what we see is essential for ascension here on Earth. We must at least try to ascend here on Earth while we are alive. The height to which we ascend here on Earth is the ascended height we will be when we die. *'As above so below.'* We need to create heaven on Earth. We need to become better people to others.

We are all connected – so when you hate or show aggression

toward others, you are actually manifesting these ideas into yourself. We must not focus or prejudge people by what we see externally and concentrate more on their internal vibration. You may dislike a person's outward appearance or characteristics – but that person has the same 'heart' and 'soul' as you. They have the same concerns, wants, desires and lie down at night to go to sleep and dream just as you do. What makes them any better or less of a person? Even a prisoner in a locked jail cell has the ability to freely think and dream as he/she wish. It does not matter who, where, or what you are. We are connected to all living things. We are living brothers and sisters and when all humanity realizes this, then the corruption and killing will stop. We are connected to the Earth so the raping of the resources of the Earth must stop. We should seek only sustainable power sources and use our food and energy for the betterment of all, instead of manipulation of the few.

Once you start thinking on your own, and truly believe in these ideas and thoughts, then you will start to change your views and desires to a more positive outcome. We virtually reset our thoughts away from old and realign them to a new more just pattern of thinking. Be cognizant that these are not secret powers of our 'collective mind.' Everyone has the same abilities. Also, be cognizant that the collapse of a wave function on the quantum level will occur if a person is involved, watching or observing the event. This demonstrates that power of consciousness even affects us on the quantum level. Powers of human consciousness are like a life 'bond'– subatomic particles are invisible – but contribute to life's vibrational energy. The body works similarly. It is not a whole bunch of parts operating alone – they are all one connected system.

Every negative situation you experience in life is a test to see if you can be moved from who you think you really are. If your sense of self-worth can so easily be changed according to every difficulty, disappointment and failure that comes your way, then your identity isn't so true after all. True identity is unchanging and becomes even stronger with each opposing circumstance that seeks to destroy it. Your true identity is light. Your true reality is spirit. The more you may encounter negative circumstances the more you should realize that this is a test of your inner strength and self-worth.

As things become difficult, it may seem harsh, but try to get over it and stop playing the martyr. Don't wallow in your own self-pity. You have set up an imaginary enemy and by pretending to be a martyr, you blame other people for the way you feel. You blame them for stealing your life source (heart and energy) and your conscience has trapped you by letting it happen. Try to be whole, sovereign, strong and independent and stop taking from others and they will stop taking from you. It is that simple. You are an Angelic being. You are an expression of God, so begin to realize this and begin to act the part.

Vibration helps awaken people. There is a field at the root level of conscience. The 'Akashic Field' is where all records—all information—all experience past, present and future exists now and has always existed. It is this field from which subatomic particles arise to create galaxies, stars, planets and all life. Layers of vibration make our existence and are constantly changing and exchanging information. When the 'thinking mind' is still, you can see reality as it really is. All aspects of everything work together - nothing is separate. Life and death—self and other—are not separate. Everything has a spiritual vibration. Everything is connected to the one vibratory source consciousness evolving in one field, one force that moves through all. This field does not occur around you, but through you and is happening as you. You are the 'U' in universe. You are the eyes in which creation sees itself. You create your dreams the same way you create your reality. Our reality 'matrix' is no different. Everyone and everything is you, the 'one' conscience. Perhaps consciousness occurs in the same place outside the body which is how we can share the same thoughts collectively together.

"YHWH" the name of God, is a 'vibration' not a spoken word. We all share in this one unity vibration of 'YHWH.' Today our crises in humanity are not political or economic or even social - it is a crises in conscience...an inability to experience our true nature and the inability to recognize the connection in all people and all things.

"Praná" or (CHI) is your inner energy-less resistance. For example: In a metal wire there is more energy that can be transmitted, but there is also resistance...and it is the same within your body. Meditation is a state of nonresistance. More energy to the chakras allows more energy to flow and a stronger physical connection. Physical patterns and connections are enhanced by repetition; blossoming the power within and increasing our physical connections. By placing attention to what's within and not on the physical, you lower resistance to the experience and you increase your energy capacity. So how do we capitalize on these vibrations? Neurons wire together most when a person is in a state of sustained attention. This means it is possible to direct your own subjective experience of reality. Literally if your thoughts are ones of fear, worry, anxiety and negatively, then you 'grow' the hard wiring for more of these thoughts to flourish. If you direct your thoughts vibrationally to the ones of love, compassion, gratitude, and joy, you create the wiring for repeating these experiences. How do we sync up with positive vibrations if we are surrounded by all this negatively, violence and suffering? This is slightly different than when you 'create your reality' because you experience it at the root level (the base vibration level) of sensation without the prejudice of thought involved. This wiring that goes on is interpreted as different from normal reality wiring. It is a more 'desirable' reality because we consciously are focused on it. We have our thought process backwards most of the time. We let ideas of the eternal world shape our network wiring, when we must start thinking and originating our thoughts (rewiring) more positively.

"All matter is merely energy condensed to a slow vibration, that we are all one consciousness experiencing itself subjectively, there is no such thing as death, life is only a dream, and we are the imagination of ourselves..."
                                                                -Bill Hicks

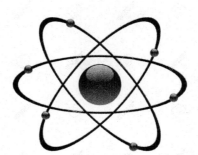

SPIRITUALITY

BOOK 5

It seems that every person you encounter will tell you that they are 'spiritual.' What does that really mean? There are some truths to this in that spirituality can take on many forms and that each person does have a spiritual component to their 'makeup.' You may have heard the expression that, *"we are not human beings having a spiritual experience, but rather a spiritual being having a human experience."* This shows us that our true nature is firstly spiritual and secondarily physical. As we quiet the noise around us ...each one of us can access a higher 'spiritual calling'...this is the voice of wise direction...that will guide us on life's amazing journey.

Inside every person, there's another person just like him or her, this inner person looks exactly the same as the physical person, but it is subtle and invisible (to the physical eye). Its name is spirit, and it's the real and the actual person.

Modern civilization is missing the point. The problems of life cannot be solved by material means alone. We must then look to the spiritual world and God for guidance. The human life experience is coming to understanding human values. Real knowledge is...'knowing yourself,' who we are, who God is and understanding our relationship and duty to God and spirituality. Through spirituality, we can know and love God and solve our problems as earthlings. When men are not governed by God...they will be ruled by 'tyrants.' The material world is just like a prison (the spirit soul is imprisoned into a material body, which is imprisoned into a material world). We do not really belong in this material world. It is not natural. We are spirit souls that belong to the spirit world. Modern civilization is geared wrongly to the immediate gratification of a material life. It is a demonic belief that materialism is the ultimate goal of life. It is not possible to become truly peaceful and happy in the attempt to gratify our senses on a temporary basis. The result is usually the opposite. The existence of material things agitates our senses and unless you can control your mind, senses may not be able to attain any spiritual advancement. Spirit is permanence, while matter is temporary. Our present culture entangles us more and moves with the materialistic world so that the path to the spirit world is blocked. The demonic goal of a few is to block what our planets (and citizens of it) are here for, what we are intended for. The material world is here for us to actually rid ourselves of the allure of the material world...for the aim of life is to go back 'home.' A demonic person cannot go back home until they rid themselves of the demonic mentality. This makes it tough for many to return home. This becomes a type of psychological warfare—to tie man down so that he is not able to return home. Home, back to the Supreme Lord – the prime creator – the true self.

When we observe all that is going on around us, it seems easy to fall out of love with life. It is easy to get pessimistic and desperate, but to me, the spirituality crisis has matured to the threshold point of mass awakening of all humanity. There is a feeling inside of me that no matter how small or insignificant I may see myself, that what I am doing will have an impact on the greater good. From these thoughts I can conclude that:

1) *There is no ascension after death... that is beyond what you do here on Earth. Where and what you achieve here on Earth is where you will be when you die. ("As Above so below").*
2) *Our destiny has been decided by us since we elected this upon ourselves to come here and figure this out and in doing so elevating all consciousness of humanity.*

We can reach the levels of the 'avatars' – no hate, no judgment, no testing, and no rules. We are who we are and can be who you want to be without any confines. We are gentle, powerful giants of energy that share a common bond of light. We are all connected and you're not alone. Spirituality is this – to make something of this life – evolve yourself on a personnel level. It has nothing to do with giving anything materialistic, charity or money.

- *Salvation is not a person place or prize; it is a state of mind. Face challenges with grace and gratitude and know that it is within you.*
- *Does conflict breed consciousness? Some believe there needs to be a major outer shift in this reality to adjust our inner thinking process to come to a higher level of conscience.*

The universe is a living, expanding entity of eternal laws. We must observe our consequences of conduct. When we overindulge, we get ill. When we manage our desires, we are not ill. When we spend more than we earn, we are burdened with debt. When we neglect children, they turn against us. When we are critical, we lose friends. Therefore, the answer to man's spiritual needs is self-discipline stemming from ideas that impel the believer to remake his own life; correct his faults, strengthen his character, and deepen his knowledge. Moreover – nature in all her capacity will bring truth to those spiritual souls dedicated to passing this secret of 'life' on to future generations.

We need holy and spiritual men and women to assist in the establishment of higher standards of right and wrong; to amend unjust laws on our statue books, to become the patrons of broader and nobler educational ideas, to foster the care of world peace, to aid in the achievement of economic justice, and most of all, to provide the millions of this generation with a workable livable philosophy of life. From all this information around us, there is a nagging sense that the sacred history of the world is being supplemented by a new religion of science, engineering and void of human spirit. We are told that everything before 1900 was considered fallacy, superstition and myth. Everything after 1900 was profound, glorious and true (which it is not). Truth does not belong to one century – it belongs to all time…eternity. Live by your heart, not your mind. Our physical bodies are gifts from existence. They hold our spirit. We forget that our human bodies here on Earth are not what we are, or who we are, but rather of 'how we are.' Our bodies are not our identity – not ultimate reality – not a permanent expression of who we are. They are temporary. They are on loan to us only as long as we really need them to have the experiences we need to have in order to wake up here on Earth. Your body is here to serve you. Use positive reinforcement.

Star seeds are spiritual human Light-Bearers of this world who come here to assist in the awakening and ascension of the human species and yes, they can also get homesickness – we feel this when we come back to this reality. There is a wanting to be connected to the home light energy, but in many ways this reality becomes boring/mundane, almost redundant and very tedious. All people everywhere need to be challenged by a noble cause. We need to live in harmony with all-including celestial entities. We have to become spiritual beings and practice what every religion trumpets - the <u>Golden Rule of life</u>! Every single 'system' in place that is controlling and enslaving us will be defeated without any confrontation or violence. Not one shot needs to be fired from a gun. All we need to do is act within the conscience of God. It is neither a religion nor a religious-based idea. It is a creative and spiritual idea common to all people. It possesses the true spirit of the understanding that you are free (and always have been free) to use the conscience power of thought.

The legal system may try telling you differently, but there are no laws that can control one's spirit or soul. You are already free...and will always be free. Once we all realize this — no physical revolution will be needed; we can align with each other collectively and overcome any type of tyranny or evil, by peacefully turning to documented facts and raising our conscious. Your self-conscious creates the right conditions for your energy to grow. If you are trying to make something happen, then you're creating resistance to what is the higher spiritual evolution. In removing all the resistance that you have created, allows the evolution of energy to unfold. If resistance is diminished, then a level of happiness is achieved which quite possibly could be the initial reason that you were trying to make something happen in the first place. We pursue happiness like it is a product or a commodity; consequently we can't find it out there at the shopping mall or at some store. Happiness cannot be purchased. Spirituality and happiness is not in fact out there somewhere...it is in here...in you. Now go find it...

Playing the 'victim' is a very common practice among people of the 21st century. Most people let others into their mind pattern and allow them to intrude into their energy space to abuse or traumatize them. Much of this is done 'willingly' because it is the attention (good or bad) from others that the victims really seek and the wanting to place blame on others for their own short comings. Unfortunately, most of humanity today is conditioned to play the victim. As soon as you believe that you are in a cruel world and cannot do anything about it, which is exactly when you become a victim. Mind control patterns have been constructed to think a certain way and we as individuals attract the 'drama' of being the victim and all the attention and chatter that it comes with. If you're tired of being the victim and want to release yourself from this mindset, you must first recognize the victimization mind pattern and then learn how to undo it.

Deprogram the connection with the 'over soul' and be present in this moment to empower yourself. Understand that what you seek from others is already inside yourself and their attention to your situation should have no bearing on how you feel. When you 'let go' of the expectations or the perceived benefits of playing the victim, you will harness that energy towards a more constructive goal of overcoming the initial reason why you needed to play the victim in the first place. Playing the victim, when you are not, is a selfish behavior that benefits no one and ultimately depowers you from your natural energy source. Victimization feeds off negative energy. As one elevates to this conclusion and is able to move forward without the attention of others, this will, in turn, help others to deprogram and overcome this evil cycle that has covered our consciousness. Some people fear this information. It is because they fear their own inability to overcome. They feel comfortable being a victim, but when they step outside their comfort zone, they will realize that they can do this. At some point, playing the victim is somewhat of a game – and part of the 'human experience, but at some point you see it is this low-level conscious thought that imperils the overall state of consciousness. Enabling this behavior only makes it significantly worse.

With this understanding, you are able to know the secret meaning underlying all events and release yourself from traditional confines of thinking. With this achievement, you have essentially 'rewired' your thought process, but be wary...critics loom. Many 'practical' people will observe that you have lost your way or that you're falling down on the job. They may believe that you have 'escaped from normal life' because they firmly believe that this existence is the only one real world reality. They believe the world is filled with many unrelated events. They don't see the spiritual connection among us. Those who don't seek the greater meaning of life take hold of the materialism of life because it is the only thing they can see in front of them. They make a success of things and may appear happy, but it is only temporary. You believe you're an important person – and that you're contributing to humanity – but all of this is void of the creative spiritual vibration that actually connects all of us to the one unity. Understand, success is relative and that chasing success and material items only lasts for a little while. But in time, ultimately, it will also dissolve as everything does. Where does your earthly success go when you're dead? In a book of footnotes perhaps, but even this is not permanent. What happens to all the money and material items that you accumulated? At least maybe your surviving relatives are getting to enjoy them, but where are you?

Don't 'guild' the living - adding useless improvements that actually don't help at all (i.e., legs on a snake). Institutional activities are really superfluous. Eventually, many so called 'spiritual' practices such as religions and obedience to the 'state' will be eliminated – because traditional governments (the state) will no longer be applicable. All will become unnecessary, since every individual will be able to be self-governing and self-reliant. As more individuals embrace spiritually and have a connection between all 'brothers and sisters' of the planet, the manipulative practices of these institutions will vanish. Even to some extent, the church. Humanity shift is in consciousness.

Gold and silver are important symbols of spirituality throughout history; both metals reflecting a different light energy and can provide a bounty 1) of emotional warmth and wealth and

2) of spiritual purity and enlightenment. Gold and silver, which can take on many different forms and uses, is representative of the enlightened spiritual being and its natural beauty, transcends all eternity and will take a very vital role in our next incarnation here on Earth. The right and left hands also are meaningful spiritual symbols. The right hand represents the material world and the left hand represents the unconscious or unknown world. 'Sinister' means left (in Latin) and describes how many believe that the minority left-handed people have a clearer understanding of the unknown. Left-handed people are naturally connected to the 'sinister', or evil because they possess this unknown knowledge. It may be interesting to highlight the fact that many of our recent American presidents have been left handed (Reagan, Clinton, Bush, and Obama). Our 'hands' can open spiritual doors (left) and material doors (right); both exemplify strong messages of our existence and of our duality here on Earth.

Everything has been recycled — everything is related — everything is one. There is really nothing to be afraid of, because it is all 'you.' Everything is an extension of you. The difficulty is that we have the illusion of separation and by being born, given an individual identity and a name, we have created this separation from the Oneness. We are also continuously told through certain religions and institutions, that we are not part of a greater oneness. People yearn to be a part of 'one' and it is our spiritual calling. You can achieve this without 'religion' per se. Question: Who also knows what you are thinking when you are thinking thoughts? Most people will say God — only God knows what you are thinking. No other person would have the ability to precisely know your thoughts, unless they are 'inside your head.' If you know what you're thinking, and God knows what you're thinking, how does God also have the ability to know what everyone is thinking? Perhaps by collapsing all of this into 'one' you will have a better understanding of how God and you are related. One can only deduce from this exercise of thought, that the spirit of God is, literally, inside each one of us regardless of any social group, affiliation or religion we may belong to...and this is true for all people. Therefore by seeking answers and listening to what's within our conscience is our spiritual connection to God.

"Be Careful what you think...your thoughts run your life...Creativity is intelligence having fun..."

-Albert Einstein

Tao (pronounced 'Dow') is an ancient Chinese concept signifying the 'way,' 'path' or 'flow.' Tao is the intuitive knowing of life that of which cannot be grasped fully as just a concept, but known as the present living experience of one's being. Tao is considered to have ineffable qualities that prevent it from being defined or expressed in words.

"If you dig deep you see that the 'multiplicity of things' are not all separated and are all related – you have become 'aware' and the perception of separation dissolve into one unity."

-Anonymous

SEXUALITY

BOOK 6

Sexual suppression supports the power of the establishment (church and state) and has sunk very deep roots into the exploited masses by means of sexual anxiety and guilt. Sexuality has many attributes and is important on many levels to us being able to thrive here on Earth. Sexuality is a form of freedom and expression. We are sexual beings, having been created by a sexual experience, so I ask this next question with a little sarcasm. Since we are all born with sex organs, why not use them responsibly? Several resolutions come from this sexuality suppression. First, it results in a certain submission to church/state exploitation and authority that tells us it is unacceptable to have any sexual encounter other than to procreate. Secondly, it 'stagnates' the intellectual powers of the oppressed masses by harnessing the greater natural part of our biological energy. And finally, it paralyzes the resolute development of creative forces and renders the architect helpless of all aspirations for human freedom. It is ironic though, that we live in a world where we have to hide to make love, while violence is practiced in broad daylight.

The one thing that differentiates us as humans from other species here on earth is that both the male and female can experience an orgasm. The orgasm is one of the only human events by which a person can naturally experience the purest moment of ecstasy; a multi-dimensional, out-of-body experience that is connecting us to our true reality of energy, spirituality, light and love. The orgasm is one of the best emotional feelings that pours through us and spreads electromagnetically to others. But the orgasm is also personal, very personal. Some feel guilty because it feels so good. It is self-indulgent by some standards, but it is also self-healing. It revitalizes us. Religion seems to be the biggest obstacle in society that predicts how we should act and even conduct our personal life. Simple guilt and fear are thrust upon the congregation in teachings and preaching that tell us that self or even mutual gratification is unholy—when in fact, it is the single most important thing one can partake in to reach higher realms and have true spirituality—one with nature— to everything that is just and correct. The moment of orgasm is timeless. We are suspended in space at that moment. We have gone to another world, another dimension that has no worries or fears. The physicality of the orgasm is really not physical at all. It is mental. The orgasm is taking place in your brain. And every time you ejaculate, many beautiful things happen to your body. Aside from complete satisfaction for lack of worry or fear and the obvious state of relaxation, there is a multiple, complex, chemical reaction going on inside your body. Endorphins such as serotonin, melatonin and possibly DMT all are registered in the body. And specifically, the brain is what gives us our orgasm. Electromagnetic pulses send off vibrations to relate all the chemicals in your body to make you feel good. In the middle center of your brain is the smallest organ called the Pineal Gland that is our doorway to reaching the mental place of the orgasm. The orgasm is a mental process. It all takes place in your brain. The physical stimulation upon your genitals and the physical activity that you're doing to stimulate you to orgasm is just the function by which an orgasm can happen. Many times in order to achieve an orgasm, the person may need (besides physical interaction) visual, or even smell or sound, stimulation to reach orgasm. Visual, sound and smell all interplay with one another to create a very complex cocktail of external stimulation in order to bring us to orgasm. One must be very comfortable with their partner in order to reach the highest and purest level of orgasm.

We have been taught by our 'sex education classes' that the orgasm is generally a local event of the genital area. It is not. It is a cosmic event that has been interpreted as a local event so that we would miss the greater point. It is a timeless ongoing point of Goodness (and Godhood) of pleasure connecting to the life pulse of existence. It can occur anywhere. It can occur at any time. Eating delicious food may cause an orgasmic experience...if we were indeed that free. It is the height of appreciating - the divinity of anything in all things. By definition, many denote an 'orgasm' for both men and women as 'cuming', but I believe that they are not actually one in the same thing. Cuming or the act of cuming is brought on by physical stimulation, but in some aspect may lack the true connection to the higher realms.

Why is the orgasm so powerful? What is its true purpose excluding the obvious procreative aspect? Why do we have the capability of an orgasm and why does it feel so good? Why is it the obsession of all young men and any sexually active adult? Is there any harm done to the body when you orgasm? Quite to the contrary, orgasms are healthy and provide much balance to one's state of mind. Anytime you can place yourself in a higher state of joyful vibration, then it can only be a positive effect on the whole. Orgasm is the ultimate state of all human emotions coming together for the benefit of the person having it. We associate orgasm with guilt when [in fact] it should be celebrated, since it is one of the easiest ways we can achieve a higher state of consciousness in this heavily 3-D laden world. The moment of orgasm is the extreme state of consciousness. It is one of the purest "now" moments we can experience. We are connected to all that is within us and all that is around us. All that we experience during orgasm is true reality which is our connection to who we really are.

What is an orgasm? An orgasm, for either a man or women, is to achieve an extreme state of excitement and ultimately ejaculation (cuming). This feels great (really great). The moments leading up to ejaculation are blissful levels of arousal. The moment just before, during and immediately after ejaculation is a timeless series of moments that are truly one of the best feelings a person can experience. The actual moment of orgasm is cosmic. During orgasm, our body and mind becomes one and the vibrational energy that the body experiences are truly a magnificent release and acceptance of power. The body undergoes a transformation from a normal state – to heightened state – in a brief moment that is difficult to put into words. Like the word "love," it transcends explanation. It is the precise time that our bodies reach such a heightened level of satisfaction that we are literally swept to another dimension. In this dimension, it is the pinnacle of self-gratification and the body reacts with the release of 'cum,' but more than cum it is unconditional vibration that reverberates through our entire body. It is the best feeling a human can experience...mentally, physically, spiritually and emotionally. At the moment of orgasm, we are not worried or concerned about anything. That moment is timeless; you are not thinking about the past or the future. It is the exact moment that we are consciously aware of the precise present moment of 'now.' The moment of bliss takes us to our elated happy place or what some may refer to as "home." At that moment, we are home and at one with ourselves. This is the moment of unconditional love.

The precise moment of orgasm is us experiencing our true reality and is the zenith of now moments. True reality is a unique place that many have not experienced. To experience true reality, we must ascend here on Earth. The orgasm tells us that there is proof of a more connected blissful existence for us here on Earth. Orgasm is the key to the door that connects us with our spiritual soul and brings us to the forefront of creation. The orgasm is the most pleasurable thing a person can do in their waking life. Eating, sleeping, swimming, etc. can have moments of pure joy, but if you ask any person, the pleasure that orgasm gives would be considered the highest of all actions. I've heard people refer to ice cream as orgasmic, but I have never heard anyone describe an orgasm as a 'Chocolate Sunday.'

"Everything in the world is about sex... except sex. Sex is about power."
                                        -Oscar Wilde

Each person you have sex with leaves an imprint on you. Sex is a 'God Force' and needs to be shared only with those whom you want to share your force with. This event should be joyous. You inherit each person's energy you have sex with, so essentially you have acquired their 'Karmatic Imprint' onto your imprint. When your body comes together with another in intercourse, your seven chakras are stirred and your Kundalini is moved. Kundalini, is a spiritual energy, the energy of the consciousness, which resides within the sleeping body and is aroused through awakening, enlightening and spiritual discipline. It is said that Kundalini, in Sanskrit specifically means coiled up or coiled like a snake. As the 'snake' unravels it lets go of your chakras (from base to dome) to allow the individual to achieve a higher state of conscious and release the body into a more healthy and aware state. If your Kundalini is moved even only a little bit, you have moved in the correct direction. The lower two chakras' infusion can have 'hooks' into the other person's energy field, and 'vis-a-versa,' they can have hooks into yours. This is why it is important to be very selective to whom you share this with. If the person you have selected to sleep with is an 'evil' or 'bad' person, that imprint attaches to you. This imprint stays with you and becomes a part of you. People sometimes wonder why life's journey is so difficult and things don't always go the right way for them. They may not need to look any further than who they are having intercourse with. A 'troublesome' mistress may actually be much more trouble than a person realizes. If you're going to have sex with someone new, it is important that you have a certain bond and commitment (good foundation) and that you can be there for them mentally, physically, emotionally and spiritually. In today's fast-paced society, this is usually not the case. Sex is wonderful. It is the most glorious gift you can share with another human being here on Earth and it is a pathway to discover your true identity. However, you must learn how to use it with the correct intentions. Very little real education is taught to us about having sex and the ramifications in doing so...except the physical manifestations and implications such as contracting a disease or getting pregnant.

We all think it is ok to work hard and talk about our jobs with others yet when it comes to sex, we don't necessarily think it is appropriate to openly discuss our sexual fantasies. We don't have the same set of values for each. There are no awards or accolades for the regular person having sex (porn industry excluded). Society believes you're a better citizen if you're working hard at a job rather than working hard having intercourse. In that sense, our sexuality is quite governed by religion, politics and the narrow-minded establishments. But when we are more sexual, it connects us to the higher realms. If we could just enjoy our human sexuality more freely we could all enhance our lives and achieve better relief from the pressure of really working hard and daily stress. Sexual experimentation with a loving partner is saying "yes" to life. The orgasm is transcendent and you can experience pure 'every-thingness' and 'nothingness' all at the same time.

The human genitals are the doorway to our living library and we should recognize this and learn how to use it correctly; it serves as an opening into 'who' we really are. Sexuality has healing powers and opens us up to the heavens and the stars. Sexuality is a bonded, loving relationship that can be profound and take you into other worlds, revitalize your body and remind your body of its most idealized patterns using sexual expression to rejuvenate yourself. Sexuality involves hormones and can affect us positively with a healthy 'glow' and better body chemistry. Sex excites the very core of yourself and all your 'light encoded filaments' become alive and 'tuned' in with one another. Touching and feeling another person's body is joyous and can form a strong bond and connection between two people. Picture a magnet. Your body energizes itself when you become sexual and at this time your hormones (like a current) pulse through your entire body. When you come in contact with your partner, it is like two magnets attracting each other and the currents of your hormones are creating a beautiful wave of energy together. There is a heightened electromagnetic force between each other. This electromagnetic current can occur without ever touching one another. And if the wave is strong enough, it can help us reach higher dimensional worlds. Sexuality is one of the most exciting gifts we have. This should be enjoyed here on Earth. And that means every part of your body. Talk about sex. Help each other explore those parts.

Men can practice holding their ejaculation and integrate certain techniques that can help do this to achieve a heightened and more fulfilling level of orgasm. The perineum pouch (scrotum and anus area) can be held during pre-ejaculation and can change your orgasm for the better.

Humans have been led to believe that only the genitals experience the orgasm which is localized, but there are full-body orgasm experiences too. There are different levels of pleasure and with awareness you can experience different types of orgasm – not just the 'local' genital orgasm. When you're with someone you really love, you can literally 'look into their eyes' and exchange coded messages and DNA. This is a heart connection which relates to the eyes of our soul. Opening the 'eyes' figuratively provides a different sexual experience. Practice slow sexual pleasure not reaching climax too soon (we are always in such a rush to reach orgasm). The best orgasms are reached slowly and with great patience. Have fun and build momentum to just before climax and try to hold that frequency – subside to a point – and then build it again... and again. Take your time with it. Enjoy sharing time and exploring. The experience will be more pleasurable and on a deeper spiritual level with the other person.

Masturbation is another way to achieve self-satisfaction and there is nothing wrong with this activity. It is a fine practice to honor your body and to stimulate certain feelings within yourself. Masturbate without shame and without guilt. The point of masturbation is to have an orgasm which is placing our mind/body connection in the highest vibration. It is a fine art form. You should masturbate for pleasure not solely to eliminate stress or release tension. It's 'OK' to love and honor yourself and it is essential before you can provide love to others. You should know and understand what excites you. Masturbation is considered by many a 'taboo' topic of discussion. It is shunned in public conversations and is avoided in just about any social circles. It is a private matter, but it is something real, true and when comfortable – can be shared openly with others without shame. The irony is that when you banish and ostracize a topic like masturbation you actually make it more mysterious and intriguing. Self-gratification is fine. If you enjoy it fine, and if you don't – that is fine too.

There is no right or wrong here…there is just the experience. To the individual, there may be several reasons for masturbating, but the primary one is to have an orgasm. It is taught that self-gratification is an 'unholy' thing. Masturbation is deterred by most religions and educational teachings. Even in sex education, it is taught as something that should not be done and can prevent you from a normal upbringing. We are admonished against the habit of masturbating largely due to the stigma attached to it, yet each day more and more people are arriving at their own conclusion, that it is a normal, healthy and natural practice not to be ashamed of.

Semen (sperm) can carry a tremendous amount of information, data and DNA coding of the human species. Blood is also a human substance that has coded DNA and information similar to semen. It is believed in some occult circles that the mixture of these two substances (i.e., virgin blood and semen) when consumed together creates a healthy source cocktail called the "elixir of life." This 'drink' offers revitalization and rejuvenation individually and sharing these substances in a relationship is the ultimate in sharing your power. (Perhaps this is part of the lore of why vampires live so long.) This elixir's secret ability, whether believable or not, has been hidden from us since pagan times.

Sexual expression happens continuously throughout your life. Sexuality is our birthright and our heritage as humans while we are here on Earth. The 'ever' expanding 'now' moment is an accumulation of the past and also the future. Each moment forward holds more events than in the past moment. The 'time concept' of things, although seemingly linear, has sped up the pace, and velocity we create and this also applies to sexuality. If you haven't noticed, sexuality is prevalent everywhere and sexual deviant behavior is not so much hidden in the shadows anymore. This could be due to many factors, but I believe mostly because the 'now conscience' has more sexuality 'running' through our thoughts with our exposure to the media and, specifically to the Internet.

One of the most natural things for a man is to look at a woman's breasts. In Western cultures, we are fascinated with women's breasts. Ironically this appreciation and practice is very healthy. This may be the primary reason men watch TV for hours on end to see some 'skin' or a 'boob'. But seriously, looking at women's breasts makes a man's heart healthier because it opens up the capillaries and exercises the heart muscles. This may harken back to our subconscious when we were a baby. To a baby, the breast represents a comfort zone for warmth, food and love. A good 'ogle' can equal up to a 30-minute workout and can prolong life by as much as 5 years and make a male healthier and happier, but definitely happier.

If we are not living a full healthy and open sexual life in our normal existence, it could lead to creating a "fetish" of sexual deviant behavior. A fixation of pornographic material on an all-consuming level is also detrimental to a normal existence. These behaviors can also compromise and make for an unhealthy relationship with another person, spouse or partner – especially if it is hidden. All images and pictures that contain sexual imagination – in-turn is not bad – erotic imagery can be a part of life as a consenting adult as long as it is tasteful (of course who determines if it is tasteful or not). Imagination is very important to sexuality. Sexual fantasies can become addictions if they are not exercised with balance or with a real partner in a natural, safe, caring environment. Sexual deviancy can also interfere with our daily functions of life when the preoccupation with it interferes with work (Internet porn) or when the desire is so strong it negatively affects others that are near us. When this type of behavior is expressed publically (in a social environment) one can fear punishment and ostracism from society. But that is also a part of society's problem (hang up) because personal pleasure or public sexuality is 'fine' as long as it is natural and doesn't harm anyone.

The pornography industry thrives on us. They have basically taken what is pure and vital to our well-being and have made it into a depraved culture of salacious and pervasive business conglomerates that are essentially evil to the core. If some people want to enjoy pornography, then that should be their decision alone. Society predicts that it is wrong even though it allows its distribution through numerous media outlets including even The Walt Disney Corporation – the makers of many of our children's movies. That is because porn makes a lot of money for some elites and companies at the corporate level. So, this brings us full circle, back to our own minds and actions being suppressed and manipulated in a way that redirects a natural process of life into something 'corporate' and tied to profits. Sex sells...but are you buying?

"My girlfriend always laughs during sex...no matter what she's reading."
-Steve Jobs

As far as homosexuality and same-sex marriages go, I am not necessarily against it, but I don't understand it because it seems unnatural to me (personally). I don't promote it – but being the freedom-based thinker that I am – I really don't care what you do as long as you don't hurt anyone or infringe on the rights of others while doing it.

I do believe that this 'push' in the exposure of the homosexual agenda in the media is actually hurting the cause. It is compromising the majority of people, while protecting only the minority few and sacrificing the traditional family values of our nation as a whole. The entire "politically correct" society we are creating is actually damaging the fabric of the country and, in turn, stifles creativity because everyone must conform to a prescripted and pre-approved way. We should not be in the difficult position to have to choose one or the other.

Some religious people's views disagree with the 'agenda,' so let us not forget that these people have rights too. We must be cognizant of the majority and protect their values as well as the minority. Let people be who they want to be without forcing the 'agenda' on the majority. The fact is, that same-sex marriage has never been illegal and you can get married to anyone you want. It just may not be recognized by the government. Any two people can be married or write up a contract of marriage without limitations. What modern sexuality really comes down to is not about love, marriage or who you have sex with, but more about marriage subsidies, tax credits and government benefits handed out to married couples. The cash and prizes dished out is really a small enticement if it means having to compromise our free will to be married to who we want, where we want and when we want.

ENLIGHTENMENT

BOOK 7

"Expose yourself to your deepest fear: afterwards that fear has no power. And the fear of freedom shrinks and vanishes. You are free."

–Jim Morrison

The word enlightenment contains the word 'light.' Those that are enlightened are able to see in the dark (what's hidden) when others cannot. By being able to see in the dark one can obtain valuable knowledge. The owl is very wise. The owl's wisdom and knowledge comes from the owl's ability to see at night (in the dark). Like the owl, if you are able to see what others cannot, then you have a great advantage. When you have knowledge that others cannot access, then you can use this knowledge to empower yourself. Over history, smaller, elite groups have acquired important sacred knowledge, and have hidden this information. By hiding knowledge those 'in the know' would have the power to control over others not in the know by means of manipulation.

Those who have been able to become enlightened during their lifetime become a threat to the enlightened elite since if you know what 'they' know then it will weaken their advantage and ultimately their control over you. Information is enlightenment and enlightenment is power.

For the first time in history, most of the Earth is 'politically' awake and at our doorstep. We have the spiritual age of the past colliding with the technology age of the future. Never before have we lived in such a dynamic time. We literally have a front row seat to the real "greatest show on Earth." Humanity is facing challenging times, but it is not only the amount of information or events, but the velocity of all this information (news) that is coming at us that is unprecedented. How are we going to navigate through this time? Are we going to subscribe to the fear-based reality created by the corrupt few or are we going to choose freedom and reconnect with our true selves as part of the unity of conciseness? It is crucial at this time to free ourselves from the establishment shackles that have been handicapping mankind for hundreds if not thousands of years. It is important though that we handle this in a productive, peaceful non-violent way through non-compliance. Not anger. The powers that be, want violence and revolution because this contributes to the mounting polarizing energy which divides us. They want you to use all of your energy fighting your neighbor (through racism, religion and social class warfare) just as long as the energy is not directed toward them. They understand the power of the masses and know if the people ever do 'wake up' and direct the energy toward them, their control is over. They personally may be finished too. The world then could reset to a better more harmonious existence here on Earth. People need to embrace the one law of love and its connection to the heart and stand up to do the right thing. The more people that wake up, the more energy will be charged into the field with positive frequency (grow exponentially) and, in turn, the more souls will wake up.

At some time, there will be a 'tipping point' of awakening souls whereby we will be able to break free from the negative energy and its hold on our conscience.

The Earth is reaching the end of a cycle and is moving into an awakened state of information and conscience. The new cycle, which some may call the 'Age of Aquarius' is coming into creation now. The shift started back in about 1986 and will continue well into the 21st century. Evolution does really happen, but not in the same way that is portrayed in the 'Darwinian' model of evolution. Species don't just turn into other species as Darwin theorized. True evolution is the evolution of consciousness, which provides enlightenment. This evolutionary process occurs over large periods of time as it has for thousands of years. But that process is dramatically speeding up and can now change in an instant. That is the power of the 'now conscious' occurring and we are fast approaching that pivotal time right now in history. The Earth is a conscience living being with the human race evolving right in step with it. This evolution is not just localized to Earth and its inhabitants, but this transformation is occurring universally with all creation everywhere. Conscience is on the verge of creating a new reality and the medium is human kind. This is the gateway between the above and the below. So choose love over fear and align yourself with the natural evolution of what the universe is telling us at this time. Listen.

"The quietest people have the loudest minds!"

-Anonymous

Sometimes the 'enlightened' seem to be a little distant, lazy, impartial, passive, apathetic, cold-hearted, or even uncaring or mean to others. Many do not understand why the enlightened are like this, but the reason is simple. The truly enlightened look at things differently and have assessed what is important. Many things that people care or are passionate about are not things that need much attention in the higher realms (such as watching a professional sporting event or watching reality TV) and so the enlightened view much of this as just (relatively) not important in the 'big picture' of life...that is 'not' to say that sports and TV are not enjoyable, they are, but should be enjoyed in moderation. One may assume that if a person is 'enlightened' that they would have immense tolerance for others and be 'all' about peace and love. This is true to an extent, but as we enter the dynamic time of awakening, it will become harder for the enlightened to be patient with the unenlightened. To bring awareness to important issues becomes the focus of the enlightened spirits. Protesting in the streets or staging a revolution is not the answer. Placing ribbons everywhere for improvement or a cause is not the answer either. A more passive (collective) revolution is our spiritual connection and the correct pathway to solving many of the world's problems is through our conscious awakening.

We cannot lose sight now. We must keep focus. We must set our compass heading in the correct direction; some people have lost this heading and are drifting off course. That direction should be towards the light - to love - to truth - to understand - to tolerance - to kindness - to friendship - to cooperation - do not lose track of your compass heading; keep moving forward – to head home. There is a place many of us want to go and dwell. That place is home. Home is not the place you live here on earth, but rather a place we go with our 'mental' thought. It is the place between mind and matter and is the place we finally feel at ease with life. Home is our comfort place – home is where we go after we finally 'get it'...the point of life. Some equate being 'enlightened' to becoming 'awake' and this is a very good analogy.

Deep down inside – these feelings and emotions will take

you to the correct place, home. Use your creative powers of 'manifestation' and 'choice.' Choose your thoughts carefully. These thoughts will get manifested. Your words, your actions and your emotions are a compass charting a course on a map and holding true to this pathway is very challenging at times. You may not fully understand where you have to go to finally get to your destination, but you must be firm in your convictions to hold to this path and move ahead. The conscious choice to move forward ultimately comes from within you. Many have questions about what this path is about. Keep vigilant and be cognizant of the headings that you are navigating. Think about your current attitude — demeanors — words and actions toward others – will all of this take you 'home' to the higher realms? The rewards are not gifted or accomplished just by want. In a sense, the right to exist in the higher realms in the universe must be earned. You will not achieve this just by pure desire. It is learned and earned through our experience gaining wisdom and knowledge. You are not given this right (e.g., keys to the door) until you reach a certain plateau of your being – and some have demonstrated beautifully that they have reached this plateau. It must be earned through love and light and this is the way it is. Kindness and generosity for others is the key and an individual must understand and teach this to others to pass into the higher realms. That no one government or religion has all the answers and we must rise above the domestic distractions to pass into the higher realms and if not...then the soul will continue to be 'schooled.' This lower dimension houses us until such a date and time that we master this for ourselves.

'Good words can never cover ugly actions...love yourself – then you can love everybody else.'

At first you may believe the Bible writings as the infallible word of God... and all that is associated with religious teachings as 100% true. But at some point it dawns on you that most of the religious propaganda is used to control people, and it becomes clear there is no real 'enlightenment' going on in the world. The entire 'enlightenment journey' occurs when you 'personally' become aware of what is going on around you. At that point, you begin to realize that you are a lot more connected than you have been told and that you have a distinct personal relationship with 'God' aside from traditional religions and through enlightenment you're no longer beholden to certain labels or classifications… I am not Christian, Jewish, Muslim or Atheist. I do not assume that I am anything but a child, a parent, a human being and nothing more…..

These labels I have given up, they are limiting and imprisoning. I am not any religion; I am not any political affiliation; I am not a citizen of any one place; I belong to no group with no agenda; I have moved away from all those divisions that have limited my beliefs and understanding that are only bound to that group. Inevitably, one group always disagrees and fights with another group with opposing beliefs. We need to release ourselves and be freed of all labels for true enlightenment. Labels are used to enslave and pit us against each other and that ultimately divides and controls us. We are born, indoctrinated and reared to believe whatever we are told by our elders. We initially don't find much reason to question our parents, teachers, or our religious leaders-yet it is at the point now we see things are not going well. We are 'off course' and the real truth is not being told. Television and media supports the same basic conditioning (claim), but their 'truths' (lies) are served mainstream breakfast, lunch and dinner. Bon appetite!

The 'Illuminati' consider themselves to be enlightened. This brilliant, well connected elite group makes up an extremely small percentage of the total population, yet they have tremendous influence on our daily lives. Many of these 'Illuminati families' claim to be related to the 13 bloodlines that have descended from 'Jesus' through time and into the modern day families of the elite.

Obviously this goes against the religious beliefs and understanding that Jesus was never married and never procreated.

When a musician or actor indicates that they are part of the Illuminati through messaging, they are really not a part of the bloodline but rather have been 'tapped' as personalities who 'work' for the Illuminati conveying the messages through music and entertainment. They have been recruited to promote the 'agenda' and help indoctrinate the next generation. They are rewarded very generously and provided with any and all material comforts fame and fortune that a person could imagine, but it is at a very high cost...their soul. A 'deal' is made with the 'devil.' This has been very well documented by many artists in interviews. Ultimately, the elite (Illuminati) want to reset the system, but this time without the American Constitution. They want to align America with the other NATO nations under U.N. guidelines following Agenda 21 which is the bylaws of the New World Order. It will get to a point in the not too distant future, that no state will be able to threaten the power and control of the U.N. backed U.S. government. If you don't have a plan for your life, then someone else will plan it for you. Just remember that freedom will never go out of style, no matter what.

The current socioeconomic system that is in place today is corrupt and run by psychopathic people that don't care about the average person. The way to real substantive change in the world is ultimately through 'non-compliancy' of the current system, but it must be done in a non-violent and constructive manner. That doesn't mean quit your job, give away all your money and run for the mountains either. Noncompliance is about doing the right thing, disconnecting from the 'forced fed' mainstream illusion and being truly responsible for yourself and your actions and intentions. Do what is right. Be compassionate to others by following your heart. Be mindful of the type of energy you are 'putting out' and know you will harness the energy that is flowing back to you. Much of what we have been told through education systems and religion institutions are extremely compartmentalized. We need to become aware that everything is connected on a higher level of consciousness and any limitations that you have been told simply do not apply. Feelings and emotions are the 'language' that communicates us to the creator of this universe. The creator is the single consciousness of mankind. During the past 100 years mankind has 'shifted' so far away from its true essence that we almost have come close to losing our humanity. We have been trained to be dependent on the 'system' and robbed of our individuality, self-esteem and independence. We believe anything the television commercials tell us and that the accumulation of 'stuff' is the purpose of life. Through the slow poisoning of our mind and bodies by television, fluoridation, toxic chemicals, vaccines and substandard food, we have been robbed of basic nutrients – and our ability to access our spiritual connection to the higher realms of critical thinking.

Much of the structure of things today is by design. Our enlightenment is at odds with an evil counter-presence. The bigger 'picture' suggests that the evil hand of the elite that control and has been in the driver's seat has guided our reality. The original sect was a sun cult, very pagan in origins, and has evolved over time under many different guises, but still uses many of the ritualistic techniques to carry out certain events. There are also many arms to the octopus that use secret organizations with covert methods and agendas to control the general population and do this in plain view of the unsuspecting public. A lot of the control comes from channeling the energy (whether it be positive or negative) over the masses to reach everyone. This group controls the flow of the world resources, its manipulation of the global money supply, and most importantly the control of information pushing us to what is a one world government. Much of the knowledge and information is hidden from us, the general citizens of the world, and is kept secret by the ruling bloodlines. Unfortunately, a lot of (real) history has been hidden and many of the great inventions through time, including 'real hardware' to benefit man, have been lost or suppressed. They know if you control the beliefs and emotions of the population, you can control the entire species. And by doing this they can also create whatever reality they want which in our case is a fear-based, debt-ridden existence. The key is to inform and educate yourself so that you do not have to be consumed by this false paradigm.

Everyone is here as conscience. The creator is conscience and everyone is an expression of that conscience. Christ Consciousness is when we realize this for ourselves and achieve this enlightenment. Many religions either don't understand or claim ignorance, but ultimately hold you back from achieving Christ Consciousness. We are told in traditional religious teachings, that what we are 'looking' for is external, in a book or in a church or temple when in fact it is already within us. Your inner thoughts affect the outer world around you. Your feelings (and the connection to the world) are not something you can turn on or off. Every conscience moment of your life, you are communicating with energy around you shaping the reality with thoughts and emotions. This information may be discomforting too many because when you realize this it comes with a great responsibility.

You're the one in charge of what is happening and all of this comes from you. What are you going to create? The energy you give out is literally drawn upon, and absorbed by others, and is shaping the physical world in front of you. You've heard the expression, "That person has great energy." There is great truth to that. Jesus was an enlightened Christ conscious being in a projection that came here to assist in the ascension process of mankind. You, also, are a Christ Conscious-trying being in a projection. What purpose are you here for? The difference is that Jesus knew who he was…most people do not. He came here to give us this vital message and for over 2,000 years that message has been compromised and manipulated. The fact is, that most people do not realize that they are like Jesus. They live under the illusion that this reality is, all there is and what you do here on Earth today has little or no impact on the higher realms.

The "good versus evil" conflict that many people allude to in the Bible is being waged right now. The battle is over your mind and soul and it is up to you on how you want to encounter this. The outcome of this 'war' is either mankind will have awakened his DNA to realize his or her true potential and become one with love (good) or he will succumb and lose the last bit of innocence of his existence to hate (evil). Right now, we are on the precipice of this moment in time and the key is within you. Look inside yourself. The power and direction is there — embrace your true potential — the truth will set you free. Stop complying. Wake up.

Your body is like a big solar system made up of millions of smaller solar systems called atoms. Each atom is ninety-nine point ninety nine percent (99.99%) empty space and is also a mini-solar system. Somehow all this empty space makes up your physical body and this physical world. Based on this fact all that can exist in creation is consciousness; there's no true substance to the physical world. Consciousness is energy and the physical world is an illusion. Humanity has suffered a great forgetting. Man has been here on earth much longer than we have been told. Man has lived quite well on this planet in the past and for long periods of time. This truth has been suppressed. Most everything that is taught to us, especially in our history books and much of religion is not true. We are told that we are separate, insignificant entities when in fact this is far from the truth. You're it! You're the creator of all this that is in front of you. What are you going to do with it? Each one of us holds the key to the universe in our hands. We are not just merely spectators of all of this and we are in the main event that is going on now. Human kind is the vector and the link between the above and the below.

Each one of us is here now participating in creation at this particular time and for a specific purpose and that purpose is to create this reality, to perceive the experience and to gain insight and knowledge. The tools given to us to interpret this information are our thoughts, emotions and feelings. Ultimately it is our free will that is the basis of everything. Free to think, free to feel and free to love what we want and have free choice. The freedom of choice allows us to choose what energy we want to align and center ourselves in. It is from this center that we perceive our individual reality. And that, in turn, is a part of the total collective consciousness which is what many believe to be God.

It is beginning to be accepted that consciousness occurs outside of our bodies. This is actually very significant. This would mean when you look in the mirror, the individual that you see is not actually you. It is merely the vessel that you use to move around here in the 3rd dimension to be able to experience this world. The world you live in is purely illusionary. It is a construct of your beliefs and everyone else's beliefs that manifests this into reality. So the person in the mirror is not who or what you really are, it is just a container and everything around us, the solidity of everything again is just an illusion that you're experiencing. Matter is just the concept of divisions in space. Space is what is real and matter is just a creation of consciousness. The conscious field around you has been called many names, such as the Matrix. It is the field that combines all things into what we perceive as real. This is how you can shape your reality by your perceptions (and interactions) of your thoughts, feelings and emotions which all occur within you. It is like a language that runs through you and communicates with the world that is external to your physical vessel. Electromagnetism allows us to be able to communicate with the external world or space around us. The greatest harness of electromagnetic energy is the heart. The heart is the center. The heart is where we start to think, not our brain.

Certain powers have gone to painstaking lengths to keep much sacred knowledge hidden from us. These forces have succeeded in trapping the collective consciousness of humankind and this has been achieved by the manipulation of the mind. Methods have been implemented to keep us separate from who we are and the connection of power that is among all of us. This has been going on for a long time and has made use of suppression of knowledge, manipulation of religion, patriotism, race, wealth, class and every other form of separatism to the population in order to keep us separate and fighting among ourselves. 'They' will use anything they can to make human kind feel separate from one another and even from the planet you live upon. The main tool to use this separate society is fear. This is done on purpose and by design. Unfortunately, most people do not see this or want to see this since they don't want to accept that this is the way the world is run. Since most of the information that we obtain comes from newspaper, TV or the Internet and that most all of these media companies are consolidated into just a few, that we are very hard pressed to get anything close to the truth in our news information. This is what our news media does, and this is by design. Mainstream media's purpose today is not to keep you informed, but rather is focused on the control of information that has been whittled down to shape the thoughts of its listeners. Mainstream media uses theories and propaganda as facts in reporting the news and promotes ridicule of any who question it. It is very cleverly constructed through the haze of propaganda and many people cannot or do not have the ability to see through much of this. Some people do not want to care since they will say that it doesn't affect them, so they do not care.

The way to see past all the lies is to free ourselves from this control. Each individual has to stand up and reclaim their birthright. Each government, military man and police officer needs to ask themselves the question: Am I going to 'unquestionably' do what I have been told (my job) and follow some corrupt legislation which compromises the liberty of my fellow citizens rather than going after the real criminals who created the unjust laws? They must realize that this 'assault' on us also affects them and their families too, since their rights as a citizen are also being compromised. Much of what is 'going on' is going on because we let it go on. Somehow, we choose to let it go on because that is what we have been told to think through social programming. If we came together (collectively) things could change. Public awareness is a big part of the key to success. Spread the word and stand up and say NO! We need to assert ourselves and choose freedom of choice. The easiest way to start this is first turn off the TV. Avoid any public programming. We are treated as chattel, so as consumers refuse to be treated like that moving forward. Remember the government is here to serve the people, not the other way around.

How did we end up letting the world get like this? Everything has been corrupted to an extent with wars created by design and corporate interest set above people's needs. Our food is poisoned from toxins; our water has been compromised with toxic waste under the guise that fluoride is good for teeth. Just about all aspects of our daily life have been corrupted without most people knowing or doing anything about it or even knowing there is a problem at hand. Most people are consumed with the 'meaningless' collection of material items that they never consider to think about what is going on and why. More people are consumed with the physical improvement of the external body with no focus on improving the mind-body relationship. More focus on what separates us as opposed to focusing on the similarities of all of us. Too many of us are waiting for a savior to make this all right, when we are not taking the responsibility ourselves.

"The further a society drifts from truth, the more it will hate those that speak it."
-George Orwell

The elite have worked very hard to get this to this point and don't want to relinquish the control and power that they have built up for centuries. They are the ones that have implemented the fear and the negative energy that sustains the fear. They know all about the occult, numerology, group- think and how to create the most fear they can. They know that all of humanity works as a single conscience. They also know that if they create enough fear in the world, then that is the reality we will experience. Rise above this. Don't buy into the doomsday end of the world prophecies they tell you through the media and Hollywood. If we choose, there will be a shift to the higher conscience. The only way we even could entertain an end of the world scenario is if we let them take it that far, but it is in our control when enough people wake up.

'Culturally' you're not allowed to believe there is a small, elite group of people ruling the world...because if you do you will be ridiculed and labeled as a "conspiracy-theorist." But your government is lying, your media is lying and your leaders are lying. It is an empty feeling of disbelief. Ironically, it is the same entities saying they don't lie, that are lying. Whenever a person of authority tells you they are not 'lying,' they are probably lying too. Everything is the opposite of what you are being told.'

These people are brilliant. Not everyone who champions world government is a knowing part of the Master Plan. They are there for self-serving reasons — personal advancement and 'sign on' since this is the easiest and quickest way to financial rewards and power. Those who don't support are shunned from advancement. Moral people cannot be bought with money or advancement. Moral people won't allow themselves to be suckered into the 'agenda' — they see through that illusion and understand the 'agenda' is ultimately unfair to the masses. Top conspirators seek out these people that will comply and reward them with money, power and access. The people that ask, *"What's in it for me?"* are the ones that help the enemy achieve those goals and milestones of deception.

Here is a story:

A middle-aged man with slightly graying temples, crystal blue eyes and some old worn boat sneakers is fishing with a net and wooden pole in some shallow ocean waters in a small European town on a beautiful beach one day. He is having very good success catching several fish within a few minutes and he is being observed by another man that is relaxing in a beach chair close by. This other man is from New York City, a well-to-do businessman who is vacationing in the nearby town. The businessman gets up from his chair and approaches the fisherman as he is walking back in from the water's break. He greets the man and tells him that he marvels at his ability to catch so many fish in such a short period of time. When asked how he does so well, the fisherman humbly tells him that there is no secret to his success, but that he knows these waters and they have provided well for his family through the years. And that some of the extra fish he catches, he gives to his friends and relatives in exchange for some bread, olives and cheese. The businessman goes on to explain that if the Fisherman could catch that many fish in an hour or so, he could be able to create a very successful fishing business. The businessman asks the fisherman what his normal day consists of doing. The fisherman goes onto explain that he wakes up in the morning and has a light breakfast before heading out to fish, and that when he either gets tired or has caught plenty of fish that he heads back to his humble home for lunch. Upon getting back home, he is greeted by his lovely wife of twenty-five years to share a quiet lunch on the veranda before taking a long nap in the porch hammock. He goes on to explain that after the nap he gets up to either read a book or play his guitar with anticipation of the evening festivities. At night, he and his wife get together with friends to eat the fresh catch of the day, drink wine, and talk about the day's events and reminisce about the past. Sometimes there is music and dancing. He goes on to explain that it is a simple life and there is not much fanfare. The businessman looks at him with astonishment that the fisherman is not more ambitious. He goes on to explain that the fisherman could set up a fishing business with boats and crews of men. That he could take over the fishing industry in this and other nearby towns and villages and sell the fish to stores, markets and restaurants. He could make lots and lots of money selling his fish and grow the business into one of the biggest fishing businesses around. In a short period of time, he could be making so much money that he could buy some of the finest fishing gear, and a bigger more luxurious home and be able to do whatever the man could imagine. The businessman goes on to ask the fisherman what if you had all the money in the world what would you do? The fisherman looks down at his old, battered sneakers and thinks and pauses for a second before he gently looks up at the businessman with his crystal blue eyes and says that he would probably wake up - have a little breakfast before heading out to fish and after that he would have a wonderful lunch with his wife, take a nap and......I think you get the picture. Happiness is a state of mind. Neither a place nor a bank account with a ton of zeroes... and the simple fisherman already had exactly what he wanted.

'We are all magicians...' The concept of magic (Maji) comes to us from antiquity and is Biblical (and is referred to in the Bible), but much of it is hidden. We create our reality and in effect this is truly a kind of magic. We create this 'third dimension' without realizing it by allowing miracles and synchronicities to occur in our path. The secret is that thoughts create your reality. The first step is what is up for grabs—your mind. Imagination: You see it in your mind before you create it 'here.' All creativity is imagined before it is made into reality. The important point here is that all magic has a reverse side (Black Magic) — Disney's '*When you wish upon a star*' is black magic. The star represents an inverted symbol, which is basically a pentagram.

'They' use existing symbols, but just invert them. Everything can be inverted or made opposite.

What *if* everything that you thought you knew about the last 100 years was actually a lie?

What if ...an elite, international banking cartel infiltrated the American Government in 1913?

What if... in 1914, this elite banking cartel funded both sides of the First World War?

What if... in 1929, this elite banking cartel intentionally caused the Great Depression?

What if ...the goal was to bankrupt America, in order to enforce a new "tax" on all wages?

What if ...the "Social Security" tax was levied as collateral to pay the debt to these bankers?

What if ...in 1933, your birth certificate became legal evidence of your share of this debt?

What if ...this banking cartel pulled the same 'scam' in nearly every country on this planet?

What if ...this banking cartel funded all sides of the Second World War including Hitler?

What if ...the goal of World War II was to create the United Nations and the State of Israel?

What if ...the United Nations was signed as the framework for a future world government?

What if ...9/11 was used by the bankers to justify invading any country not under their control?

What if ...9/11 was also a pretext to destroy the American Constitution and set up a police state?

What if ...a global police state has been set up to enforce this future world government?

Some have looked on with anger at the Prime Creator because of the harm and suffering brought forth onto man, that each one of us must remember that in accordance with the universal law of 'karma' we always get what we deserve as determined by the joy and pain we wilfully impose on others. When they see that the only reason there is so much suffering in the world is because humanity has rebelled against the creator's will—all should live in peace... and instead man lives by the false law known as 'survival of the fittest' and in so doing, man in his willingness to fight does so at the cost and suffering of others. Man does this in an effort to attain success and survival, yet man does not realize that the same suffering will always come back on him. Thus, one who is willing to 'humble oneself' and see it is man's willingness to continually struggle to fight his way through each successive challenge against each 'new' opponent - makes he himself responsible for perpetuating the pain and suffering on Earth. The illusory law condoning the 'dog-eat-dog' nature of our existence would have many amongst humanity believe that one has the right to maim, condemn or even kill another person.

Somehow this aggressive behavior is falsely justified because it serves as a means to achieve a certain resolve for the betterment of society. In doing so, however, what few people understand is that we are 'provided the power' and 'free will' to do such things not because we should do them, but rather that we have the ability to demonstrate the quality of our souls through the choice of our actions. One who has the power to overcome and take what he desires for himself from the world and not harm others in doing so – demonstrates the quality of his soul by choosing to use this power not to hurt anyone else, but rather to help them.

"When the people fear their government, there is tyranny; when the government fears the people, there is liberty."

-Thomas Jefferson

Elitism is very dark since it excludes others. Everyone wants to be special—or more correctly they believe that they need to 'feel' special, but true deliverance and salvation come from being ordinary and simple. There is no need to be special—so drop being special and you are already headed in the correct direction. There are certain experiences we must go through here on Earth before we can ascend into the higher dimensions. Even bad or unsettling experiences are essential to the human growth experience. These inner lessons and growth go 'hand in hand.'

'Someone asked me if I believe in conspiracies. Well sure. Here's one. It is called the Political System. It is nothing if not a giant conspiracy to rob, trick and subjugate the population."

-Jeffrey Tucker

Words of advice for the newly enlightened souls: Many of us must try to live a 'normal' life as we wake up during the enlightenment period. We must still try to be a normal person as all this information comes to us and we grow beyond our old self. Initially, we must still go to happy hour with our co-workers and have dinners and share holidays with friends and family, but at the same time attempt to compartmentalize our life. You really don't want to be the one ruining all festive social events with gloom and doom (the sky is falling scenario). When I say compartmentalize - you end up wearing different hats to socialize with different groups of people in order to just exist. In order to get along and not have yourself 'stand out,' you must go with the flow and pick your battles and, more importantly, to pick your audience carefully when you do talk esoterically or philosophically. The main reason is that many of us are raising kids and you can easily alienate yourself from your children, especially if 'mom or dad' is too far 'out there.'

Your children will learn and grow just as you did and all you need to do is lay the seed for them. Do not 'hit' them over the head with all the 'stuff' you have been enlightened to. But you must believe that they will find their own way and they will end up on the correct path...so set an example and let them go naturally. You also need to be careful when interacting with friends, family and relatives. All the people you know are at different points of knowledge and awakening and it is not for you to move them along with their education unless they want you to help. If they ask questions, this is an invitation and a wonderful opportunity to answer their questions honestly and with compassion. You can lay 'seeds' with them too, but it needs to be from a level-headed perspective and not from the 'Chicken Little' the sky is falling crazy guy. It is a balancing 'act'...and you are the actor. Yes, I understand how serious all this information is - that you have spent countless hours gathering and digesting it and you want to tell everyone about what you know. You literally want to yell it from the 'highest roof top' in your neighborhood, but trust me, this is not a good way to enlightened people. It will only get you noticed and not in a good way. The quieter you are, the better they will listen when you do have something to say. Understand that most of your friends and family are not equipped to discuss a lot of the topics that the awakened person deals with. Everything from the 'language' (lingo) of the topics to the details of the current events – they may not be able to articulate, so they are not interested or ill-equipped to partake in conversations on these matters. A lot of information the awakened person grapples with is scary stuff. Most people would rather not deal with talking about corruption, assassinations and manipulation. They have enough to deal with in their regular everyday life. The last thing they want to deal with is talking to you about how the government is trying to control you. Unfortunately, at some point it will be time for them to wake up and 'smell the coffee.' It may take an event (war, financial collapse, alien invasion) to get them to wake up. For some, it may be too late, but if you remain friends with these people, they may turn to you for answers at some point (perhaps in the future) and this is the time to not say, 'I told you so,' but to reach out and help them as best you can.

Many of us have tried to explain, warn or convince others (family, friends and neighbors) of the 'xtreme world takeover' by the global elite bankers, but you need to be patient and an opportunist to pick the appropriate time and place for your discussion. If you can select an appropriate 'lead in' that connects and identifies with whom you're talking to, that would be highly recommended. You need to tailor the discussion to them. If you pick a topic they are interested in, then they are more likely to investigate it on their own. Hot buttons that would 'push' us to 'wake up' quickly could be immediate harm to family members. This will get many to sit up and pay attention because it affects them on a personal level. For example: The fact that your money in your wallet is being devalued by the international bankers is not quite as pressing as the vaccine shots that were just given to your child to enter a new grade in a public school that gave them brain damage. As more people are hurt or affected by the New World Order agenda, they will go on their own journey of enlightenment. People can only take so much until they will revolt. But they must take that journey themselves and not be forced. When something is forced, it does not really become a part of you since you may still not believe and still have doubts. It is like taking the 'red pill' in "The Matrix" movie. You can't force anyone; they must want to take the 'red pill' on their own...

LOVE

BOOK 8

The Beatles sang, *"All you need is love."* Is this true? Is 'love' the only thing you really need to survive and thrive in the world today? From my perspective, life can be the most beautiful experience as long as the basis of this existence begins with a foundation of love. Love can and will solve every problem, every situation and every conflict in the world. By 'loving' more, you start an energy that goes forth and can provide for you in this lifetime. Love is universal. It is a common language with all cultures and the feeling you get from love is the same vibrational energy for every person everywhere. Love is that 'unexplainable' feeling of pure emotional bliss (joy and happiness) that emanates from the 'cockles' of your heart. Love is all vibrational energy. Love is the purest emotion we experience and hate is love's exact opposite. If you judge or hate, then you will create 'karma' imprints that will embody themselves within you. This adverse imprint makes it very hard to love others unconditionally and makes it especially hard to love and respect yourself. 'Omni Love' - is the purest state of unconditional love for all humanity. It is the point at which love and joy flows equally and harmoniously between you and others. Unconditional love: You must love yourself first in order to love anybody else. Have you ever heard this expression? As ridiculous as it sounds, it is the truth. It is important that you are able to decipher and differentiate the meaning and 'concept' of loving yourself. I use the term in the capacity that in order to love others, there needs to be a portion of your conscience that has respect and love for yourself. I do not mean that you are consumed with treating yourself to all your whims and desires nor that your day is consumed with self-gratification, but rather there needs to be a 'happy medium' – a balance within yourself. An appreciation of 'who' you are that empowers your self-esteem will ultimately resonate from you to other people. If you are unhappy, despondent or uncaring with the person you see in the mirror, then you are unlikely to care and love not only yourself, but others. It is very difficult to carry that love vibration over to other people if you don't have a love vibration already within. Remember, you are positive vibrational energy and that energy starts within you and you are the one that controls this, so it is essential for that positive energy to begin with a foundation of love. Love is the highest vibrational energy and can influence everything and everyone around you and by loving others, the love will ultimately flow back to you...

"When the power of love overcomes the love of power, the world will know peace."
-Jimi Hendrix

When you understand your identity, it will not end at the boundary of where your skin touches air. You begin to look into the faces of others and see yourself. You begin to notice that there is a commonality between you and everyone else. And for that reason, why would you want to harm others when ultimately you are only doing yourself harm – to serve/love others is to help yourself. I seek my own enlightenment for the sake of all beings. We extend an energy field that can effect and change other people's thinking and feeling. Each person has a soul and that soul has a spiritual agenda to be filled. No matter how hard things get or how many things are thrown at us, we must keep focus on our real purpose here on Earth and that is love. And with love, we can go 'home.' If you don't get 'it' right this lifetime – you can keep coming back over and over again until you do. It seems that once we have done this enough times we will get the point about loving others that we can finally 'graduate.' This is what modern day prophecies are all about – either we will come to love and save the world or alternatively – blow our planet up. The planet goes through energy transformations so if you're ready to go 'with it' and graduate you don't need to reincarnate ever again into this human body experience unless you want to. It will be your choice. But at some point humanity needs to 'wake up.' Everyone's soul energy must learn to balance itself within the physical body; the energies of the physical body have their own biases creating an egoist mind. That mind is based on your experiences, traumas and expectations of what you have built during your lifetime – and if enlightenment is your goal – love can do this for you.

The fool's equation is this: If I get _____, then I will be happy. This tells us that if it takes something in the future to make you happy...then you're not happy in the <u>now</u>. So we need to turn this statement around to this: If I am whole, peaceful and happy then I will attract _____. Or whatever I want. Create 'loving space' within ourselves then in turn love will fill this void. How do we approach our higher self? We have to listen for direction. We all have a wound. The 'wound' is the cause of much of our self-inflicted problems such as hate, violence and addiction. The wound is that our Prime Creator has abandoned us – in that we are alone and completely unprotected. That is why many seek religion or look to some form of higher spirituality for answers. That wound is manifested from childhood since we see our parents as a certain type of 'god' or archetype. Invariably at some point our parents too will disappoint us through either painful experiences and memories or the perception of what they did or did not do for us during our childhood. When our parents die, we feel abandoned, left alone and our soul feels empty. Something is missing. People (friends and family) will try to make us feel better, but to no avail we must go through this time in our own grieving way. Unfortunately, at these and other similar painful times, many feel that nobody really cares about them, or doesn't understand what they are going through. Even if this is not true... it still feels that way. We feel disappointed and the feeling envelopes us. We project that same disappointment onto the 'creator' and this in turn extends onto the wheel of karma where we will repeat the same painful experiences over and over again until we learn and grow from this experience. Sometimes people will come into our life and appear to fill the role of parent on an archetypal level. We may not become totally aware at the time that this person is filling a void, but at some point, we realize this is what is happening. These 'archetypal' mentors or role models are very important to our development and can help fill the void of a missing parent or parents during our lifetime. Sometimes, even with some guidance, we end up in the same place that we started, continuing to make the same mistakes as before, but we must realize that we need to love and forgive in order to move on, grow and ultimately go home.

In forgiveness lies the stoppage of the rotating 'wheel of karma.' The wheel of karma is the rotating experiences which we keep going through that are met with the same result from doing the same action over and over again. But it is only once we need to learn forgiveness that this wheel will stop and collapse. Our lives will become blessed and magical. And the experience of forgiveness that seemed so overwhelming at first has virtually taken us to the place where hate has little effect on us anymore. This is the higher self. Pure love is distorted by the third dimension. Pure love is not conditional. Unconditional love is what we should strive for. When you ask, "What do I get in return from giving love?" – It is entrenched in conditions and it is this type of question that prevents one from understanding what the essence of love is.

'There is no separation between you and anyone else. Love others unconditionally and thus you bring more love to yourself unconditionally. Serve without thought, intention or pretension. Be simple.'

The 3rd dimension operates with a specific set of rules and has certain characteristics, aspects, boundaries, edges and structures. Three main structures create this 3rd dimension:

1) Duality
2) Linear Time
3) Rational Mind

Love does not have a role in any of these structures...

"People were created to be loved. Things were created to be used. The reason the world is in chaos is because things are being loved and people are being used."

-Anonymous

Thought is an illusionary thing. Thought is responsible for all the suffering we experience. Who else is really aware of what I am thinking? Imagine yourself free from thought. Free from your problems. You are bigger than your body and bigger than your mind; you are not a fragment of the universe, you are the universe...and underneath all of our accomplishments should be playfulness and love. You can't unplug things in your life if you are still consumed by them. Look at all the wonder that has been achieved in the world... it is amazing to think that you participated in creating it...the good...and also the bad.

This also extends to 'truth' and how concerned you are about what others think of you. In a higher realm, you do not need approval or to seek confirmation from anyone. I understand that it is difficult to subscribe to this thought process in our superficial world of today. But when we do succumb to 'fitting in' or 'manipulation,' it prevents us from living in the highest truth. Living in truth means that all is consistent with what we think, say and do. It is a feeling of knowingness. Socially, we sometimes have to compromise or align ourselves with others and therefore we become more easily influenced or controlled. This is counter to seeking truth. Our truth can only be known to us. To follow the truth means stepping outside the norm. Truth seekers are not followers but leaders. Likely you now realize that judging others is just a distraction from truth. Always remember in real truth…there is true love.

How you feel is how things 'are'… the ideal place to love is the ideal place to live and it is all within you. It doesn't matter if you are projecting it on the outside as long as it is a part of you from the inside. When you're in love you feel good. It is like medicine for the mind. The question that you need to ask yourself is: "How do you feel about yourself?" We are conditioned to think physically about ourselves, but it is emotions and our mental state that does what your body feels it needs to do. Separation from 'the love source' leaves us isolated. The proper conscience is the "I Am" *conscience*. This may sound a little selfish or self-serving, but the 'I am' conscience is actually about taking care of 'you' by discovering yourself. This also just may be the greatest gift to humanity, in that by taking care of yourself, achieving happiness and love – will have a profound effect on the external world. Your perception of the world is helping you create the world. It sounds self-aggrandizing, but try it. Try loving yourself. Treat yourself, have compassion for yourself and stop beating yourself up over small trifle life events.

Imagine if everyone was able to achieve a positive confident perception of themselves, then we could literally help all humanity instantaneously. This, more than anything, will help heal mass consciousness. Instead of worrying or being afraid of everything that is going on in the world, try focusing more on your world (family and friends). When you stop involving yourself in everybody else's business and start to concentrate on your own happiness, then this will extend to everyone around you. Start with your own world, and by doing this it will extend outward to others and the love vibration will spread to those seeking the same. It all starts with you.

When I loved myself enough, I began separating myself from whatever wasn't healthy. This meant people, jobs, certain food, my own beliefs and habits. Anything that kept me small I gave up. My 'judgment' called it disloyal, but now I see it as self-empowering. By separating, you're letting go. By letting go, you release yourself from the constraints, but this still does not release you from your actions. Just because you "do what you're told" does not release you from your conscience. Are you a responsible human being or just a pawn of the establishment? If we spent 'half the time' loving people instead of spending all the time hating them – imagine the amount of love in the world there would be. We use so much of our time hating other people, or thinking about the hate for other people, that it consumes much of our idle thoughts and uses so much of our energy. We could be much better off as the human race as a whole if we move to the side of love. Don't hate…love.

"In the end, only three things matter…how much you loved, how gently you lived and how gracefully you let go of things not meant for you."
–Buddha

The vision of a fourth dimension is beautiful and anybody who has 'peered' into it from the third dimension has seen the love energy fields that surround us. But whether through practicing yoga, meditation, a religious revelation, a drug-induced event or even a 'near death' experience that ushers in the 'altered state' conscience of the higher dimension – it is forever life changing. But there is a real danger — because people that have experienced 'true reality' of the 4th dimension are looked at as 'way out there'. Trying to explain this experience to others is met with great skepticism unless the other party has experienced a similar vision. The danger also lies in that those that go through this experience don't recognize the beauty and can become a serious menace to society. They are unable to conform. Society categorizes people as 'sane' or 'insane' based on sound mental faculties and when the perception is that you have crossed that line, you can easily be misunderstood. Many acquaintances become worried about you because you are not taking the world seriously anymore (at least not like they are). You see through the fog and you know the world is an illusion. The concerns you had previously may not be important anymore, and you reevaluate your standing in society and your relationship to the illusionary existence. With the new found 'attitude' and vision of the world, people don't know what you're going to say or how you are going to react. They don't know if you are going to abide by the rules, conform to societal ways because you don't see the rules as applying to you anymore. You see through it all and the limitations that have been put in front of you are no longer limitations and you have the ability to look beyond in a more holistic way of thinking and doing things. For some, it may be difficult to navigate through this, and a few may lose the concept of reality. The important thing is to try to stay grounded during this time of ascension and maintain love. Some practices of Zen Buddhism may be helpful and can also maintain a discipline that is clear, clean and self-powering — the combination of all of this is 'balance.' Experiencing the 4th dimension is like traveling to outer-space. And when you get back, you will never 'see' things the same way you did before.

'The heart knows... the mind lies...'

Theoretically, wherever you ascend to, here on Earth is where you will be after you die. Our real 'home' for us is the 4th and 5th dimensions. Unconditional love increases ascension. Your love and appreciation for nature and animals increases ascension. Something tells you that everything is connected. Ideas, memories and dreams all flow through you. You feel you have a purpose for existence. You feel connected — less disconnected. You seek love, truth, knowledge and a simpler way of life. You desire a less complicated, more basic and harmonious existence. You start taking things off your plate and be less worried of what others think – become more comfortable in your own skin. There is less need to "keep up with the Joneses." Achieve less stress, less anxiety, less depression, less self-destructive thoughts, less concern with daily events and less dependency on political trends. Have more appreciation for music, dance, art and creativity. Have less involvement with money, stocks, banks, bankers, lawyers, doctors, military and government officials. Have less dependence and need for prescription medicine, less need for alcohol, harmful drugs, and more focus on your spirituality. What is a man worth when he has lost all his worldly goods? Exactly what he was worth before he lost everything! Learn to be servants of human needs for yourself and others. Truth is Love! There's divine protection when you speak the truth because love is at the center of it all. The long, quiet journey back home equals the spiritual growth back to who we really are. We are love...

"It matters not who you love, where you love, why you love, when you love, or how you love, it matters only that you love."

-John Lennon

When you love someone…truly love them, friend or lover, you lay your 'heart' open to them. You hand over a part of yourself that you would normally not give to anyone else. You expose yourself to let them inside a part of you that only you can touch. You also literally hand them a 'razor with a road map' to find where to cut the most painful and deepest part of your heart. If they ever do strike, it is crippling. It leaves you naked and exposed, wondering what you did to make them want to hurt you so badly…when all you did was love them.

"I am a conscious spiritual explorer experiencing an in and out-of-body 'astral projection' and when you get rid of all the fear — love is the only thing left."

-Anonymous

WAR

BOOK 9

War, what is it good for? Absolutely nothing! You can say that again.

"Of course the people don't want war. But after all, it's the leaders of the country who determine the policy, and it's always a simple matter to drag the people along whether it's a democracy, a fascist dictatorship, or a parliament, or a communist dictatorship. Voice or no voice, the people can always be brought to the bidding of the leaders. That is easy. All you have to do is tell them they are being attacked, and denounce the pacifists for lack of patriotism, and exposing the country to greater danger."

— Hermann Goering

Should the United States police the world? There is nothing new about government misleading their own people to start a war. Any government that desires to initiate a war (invasion) usually lies to its people to create the illusion that support for the war is just; that there is no other option to handle the situation except to go to war; or a staged event (false flag) that provokes a validated military response. The philosophy of war is then backed up and pushed on us by the 'media complex' (radio, newsprint, Internet and TV) to show everyone who the 'bad guy' really is. This means that our government not only lies to the public and its citizens, but they also knowingly are doing this aggression illegally, most likely without approval from Congress. America is in a 'Warm War' now. Things have been heating up ever since September 11, 2001 in the Middle East (by design), and now conflicts are spreading further east towards China and Russia and south into Northern Africa. The complicating factor is there is also a huge 'Currency War' going on internationally with the 'Petro-dollar' which has brought on sanctions and other economic tactics to fight our foes on the 'financial battlefield.' It seems we are heading toward World War III if everything keeps deteriorating the way they are going. But "we the people" have the power to overturn any government actions and have the ability to stop any and all military aggression overseas... and this can be done with not one more shot fired. It can happen through conscious awakening.

Racism within our military industrial complex has long been an important tool to justify the destruction and occupation of another country (especially people of dark skin color). The subversion and torture of another people based on racism or color is a method employed by this government and is a more dangerous weapon than a rifle, a tank, a bomber or a battleship – and is more destructive than our artillery shell or bunker buster or a Tomahawk missile. Though, if there are weapons of destruction 'owned' by our government, there are malicious people willing to push the button and use them on others. Those who send us to war, though, do not have to pull a trigger or lob a mortar round, they just order infantry men to do it for them. They don't have to fight the war; they merely have to sell the war. They need a public that is willing to send our soldiers into harm's way and they need these soldiers to kill and be killed, without question, for unjust causes. They've spent billions on sophisticated bombs, but those bombs only become weapons when those in the military are willing to follow orders to use them. IF you asked any military soldier if they were aware that they are fighting a war on behalf of a ruling class of international billionaires that profit from human suffering, who care only about expanding their wealth and controlling the world economy, would they in good conscience continue to do so?

All wars, assassinations and international corruption track back to the private central bankers. They have initiated it all by implementing a covert stratagem. They may not have perpetuated all of it after its initiation, but they have instigated it for a reason which usually has to do with money, power, control or oil. I realize many people will have difficulty comprehending the fact that every modern war fought had little to do with helping the citizens or some humanitarian reason – and everything to do with forcing the private central banking system onto that invaded sovereign nation and imposing massive debt that can never be repaid all the while stealing their natural resources and infrastructure. Have you ever wondered why America is mired in so many military conflicts around the world? Are we really that benevolent a country when, in fact, we can't even take care of our own citizens who are unemployed and starving on food stamps? If we are to really 'wake up,' waking up to the egregious atrocity of human sacrifice based on the pretense of artificial war is a good place to start.

When it comes to war, few will remember how massive fortunes are made by the elite bankers. They convince soldiers to go to war for the sake of "democracy" leaving their wife, kids, and family behind. Is this serving the greater good? No, it is surrendering to everything evil. Governments say it is a noble thing to 'give up your life' for your country. There is no nobility to die on the false proposition of goodness while 'filling' already wealthy people's pockets with more money. While their wars and aggression are created by this government, they (the elite) are held harmless. Those who send our young children to fight the war don't have to pull a trigger or face the barrel of an enemy's loaded gun ...ever!

"War is when your government tells you who the enemy is. Revolution is when you figure it out for yourself..."

-Anonymous

There is a new 'litmus test' that is being asked of all our military forces in America. That test asks, *"Would you 'fire' on your own people if you were ordered to?"* Could you find yourself carrying out the order to shoot an American citizen if the citizen were not obeying or laying down their arms? In addition, how would you feel if the premise of these aggressive actions were being 'ordered' of the military and all based on a lie or a 'false flag' event?

They lied about foreknowledge of Pearl Harbor
They lied about the Bay of Pigs
They lied about the Kennedy assassination
They lied about the Gulf of Tonkin incident
They lied about the Iran-Contra affair
They lied about the Gulf War
They lied about Waco
They lied about the Oklahoma City bombings
They lied about 9/11
They lied about the war in Iraq
They lied about Fast and Furious
They lied about Afghanistan
They lied about Libya
They lied about Syria
They lied about Iran
They lied about gun running in Benghazi
They lied about Sandy Hook
They lied about Ukraine

What else are 'they' going to lie about...?

We were told at one time that there was a bad 'bogeyman' in Iraq by the name of Saddam Hussein and that he had a regime and weapons that threatened our way of life here in America. We were told he was technologically, politically and economically powerful. However, from the onset, both sides of the Iraq war were 'orchestrated' in a war room from Washington, D.C. It was ultimately set up and controlled by the group of elite global central bankers that carefully and methodically created an illusion of a man with reckless power at the head of "a million man strong army" on the verge of "going nuclear" on us. We were told that this criminal had gained control of 'one fifth' of the world's oil supply virtually overnight. So which real criminal bank financed him? In reality, Saddam Hussein was just another pawn of many pawns of the N.W.O. and assumed undercover CIA operative; a 'puppet' pretending to be a 'bad guy' playing his part in the grand master plan and who at one point thought he had real power. But when he started going against his elite buddies...they ended up killing him.

The war on terrorism has been created. They don't hate us (America) because of our freedoms. They hate us because every day we are funding and committing crimes against humanity in sovereign nations. The so-called "war on terror" is a cover for our military aggression to gain control of the resources and set up western central banking and insert elite corporations in the Middle East, Western Asia and parts of Northern Africa. This is sending the poor of this country to kill the poor of many Muslim countries. This is trading blood for oil and creating genocide on most of the free world. 'We' (America and its central bankers) are in fact the real terrorist, and to observe this and remain complacent and silent on the 'sidelines' is also a crime...a crime of your conscience. It is our responsibility, to us and the rest of the world, to stand up together and put an end to the deceit and manipulation on innocent populations of the world. It is time to put an end to the oppressive behavior upon humanity and break free of the illusion that has been pulled over our eyes. The bankers are not there to establish democracy. It's the opposite. They are there to establish the basis for 'economic occupation' to be continued after the 'military occupation' has ended.

The capacity of a nation to make war is the greatest social power it can exercise: war making, active or contemplated, is a matter of life and death. The misconceptions of war are:

1) To defend a nation from military attack by another or to deter such attack.
2) To defend the national interest, economic and political ideology.
3) To maintain or increase a nation's military power to secure its borders.

We are conditioned to believe that war is the glue that holds society together. 'War' equals 'Nations' and 'Peace' equals 'Non-Nations.' So, theoretically, if you eliminate war it could break down all nations' sovereignty and economies. This is not true. We do need an economy in order to be independent and survive, but using war as an economy is insanity. Therefore, a substitute for the 'war system' must be found in order to provide stability for the people and legitimate control (peace) of the nation. Know and understand that nations use an invented threat (or propaganda) to control people (i.e., America must come together to fight "Global Terrorism" - it is, for the most part, all invented and contradictory).

"All tyranny needs to gain a foothold is for people of good conscience to remain silent."

-Edmund Burke

We are always eternal. We have been taught that reality follows certain rules. We have been taught to fear this reality. We are told to fear the world around us; to fear the people around us. To fear the very act of being alive and this storied lie has been told to us from birth to install this fear. We are actually part of the same conscience of everything that is evil on this planet. We are the ones that are 'evil' – because we are the only ones on this planet with the concept of evil. Hate and evil are a complex system of emotions and we humans are the only intelligent species with this creative ability. We create hate. So we are essentially the source cause of every man-made problem that exists today. Through reverse symbolism and secret codes, the 'powers that be' will have you believe that you are following and supporting military aggression for a 'just' reason. Unfortunately, when you hear the word "peace" used by the aggressors, they actually mean war. It is the opposite and when you learn the code, you can decipher the language of the corporate, corrupt, elite, military industrial complex.

As a side note, it was in 2000 that the stars on the Republican National Committee logo (elephant) were inverted upside down. Who did this? Why did they do it? And what is the meaning?

Yes, there will always be 'crazy psychotic' people that take pleasure in hurting and even killing other people. But these people tend to be 'sociopaths' when measured against sane people. These aggressive war loving people are out of touch so much that I don't see them being able to have the capability of creating a huge following of subservient people without either a lot of help or a lot of money. Meaning, many 'appointed' ones have been supported and financed by a 'hidden hand' with an agenda. Those who end up following a person with a psychopathic personality will quickly realize that nothing this person is creating will end up being good, and all that are involved will eventually be compromised one way or another — or even killed.

"War is a game that's gone too far."

- John Lennon

The answer is "No!" We should not support our troops if it means that they are invading sovereign nations and killing innocent people. We should no longer support the false dialogue that is regurgitated at halftime at every football game and sporting event. We should not support anything that fights aggression with more aggression. It is time to support peace and spread this across the Earth before we completely lose our way or lose everything. Send our boys and girls back home to be with their families and build communities here instead of destroying communities there…because the 'front line' could just as easily be on our soil next time.

If our fundamental goal is to create a heaven here on Earth and everywhere you look across the world there are military conflicts…and if the expression "war is hell" is true, then may we conclude that what we are all creating here on Earth right now…is hell? It is time to put down the guns and take our foot off the accelerator of self-destruction. We have mastered the act of killing so now let's master the joy of living. I always thought (how) if we just took one second to put down all our weapons of aggression that we could experience 'peace' for just a moment. And through this one moment, we could extend that to one minute and then two minutes, and so on and so forth, and eventually create an entire hour of peace and meditation each day for everyone. After the world could experience this and see how beautiful it could be, people would be hungry for more 'peace time.' This would be the best hour of each day for every person, and from this we could build and create a complete day of peace and eventually, exist in this moment forever…

FOOD

BOOK 10

If you are what you eat, then many of us are in trouble, especially in America. Food is very important. Food covers so many different aspects of our life, but most importantly you can't survive without it. It is also the source of great fun and joy at events such as birthdays, weddings and most holidays are planned around the celebration of food. Yet with the importance of food in our life, we really know very little about the food we eat. Back in the day before refrigeration you knew what you were eating. Most likely, it came from the farm and everything had to be fresh. Today most food is processed and can be purchased in a supermarket or grocery store. As of late, there has been a great movement towards 'organic' and healthier choices, but unfortunately much of our food has been compromised. Food today has been used as a weapon against populations and billions of people have been unknowingly affected– including you and your family. Internationally, there are scores of deaths due to either lack of food or malnutrition. The areas of the world that battle hunger are specifically targeted by the corporate food monopolies and the sad truth is that if everybody on earth were committed to feeding the hungry, then there would be no starvation anywhere. But this is not the case, and each day more and more children and families go without the necessary food and nutrition to survive. Question: Even with today's technology why are so many people still starving? And why is it that the food we do have access to so manipulated and manufactured that it is detrimental to our health? These questions can be answered by looking no further than the companies that bring us our food and the unbelievable story of manipulation that is being done by them. There is an evil presence (entity) that has manipulated all aspects of food from its seeds, to the planting, to the growing, to the production and to the end product. Food has become big business and if you're on the wrong side of the food equation...you just may starve.

Your food has been 'hijacked' by corporate greed. Cargill and more specifically Monsanto, the very same corporate-controlled agricultural companies that have been selling pesticides (Roundup®), fertilizers and chemicals are now controlling pretty much all food production in western civilization. They are spending billions of dollars to tell us that food production will be done their way or no way at all. The farmer who, in the past, knew how to feed us healthful quality food that was "all natural" is the one getting 'squeezed' in the middle of all of this manipulation. The farmers are faced with getting on board with the Genetically Modified Organism (GMO) program or get out of the business, leaving them virtually no options. They are forced into buying only GMO seeds each year for growing crops and stopping certain practices that keep the soil healthy for future crops. Farmers are forced into buying expensive "inputs" and infrastructure from these corporations to keep up with competition therefore mortgaging their futures and having to survive by complying with the food monopolies. A vicious cycle starts when you introduce chemicals into the production of food since each subsequent year it will take more and more chemicals to achieve the same results due to crop resistance to these chemicals and the depleted viability of the soil. This entire system is a mess, yet most people just accept it. Entire food chains are being destroyed, resources are being stripped and populations decreased (all by design).

The concept of "genetic modification" of food is not necessarily a new one nor is it necessarily bad. Genetic modification is essentially a form of natural selection of hybridization. Although, to a certain extent this occurs naturally in nature, man historically has taken successful seeds and crops and 'spliced' them with other successful seeds and crops to yield the best and most resilient future crop production for a more abundant and plentiful harvest. Man has also mated certain animals with other animals to produce a bigger stronger breed of offspring. What these food companies have done is taken it to the next level by combining plants and animals (genes/DNA) together in a laboratory to make food more scientific. By making food more scientific they can produce stronger and larger crops and even 'beefier' livestock, but the question is, what long term effects will this have on humans that consume this food. Polyploid is what it is called when cells and organisms contain more than two pairs of chromosomes. This can aid in the food hybridization since they already innately have versatility and natural 'built in' resiliency. Unfortunately, the corporate food monopolies understand farmers can 'hybridize' food themselves so they have introduced a "Kill Gene" that is spliced into crops so that seeds are unable to be used from one growing season to another. Food is ultimately a simple supply and demand cycle which is governed by a free market, but as more and more food is being processed in a laboratory, the more we should be concerned that the average food grower and consumer is losing control of their own fate and possibly health.

The most active form of anarchy is growing your own food. To be off the grid, and not dependent on any form of a food support system, is complete freedom. Governments don't want you to grow your own food because they can't regulate, modify or tax it. You are a threat to the system. It seems we are at a point in our society where we tell people what they need – we don't ask them. That is why we have so much processed food on supermarket shelves which is possibly making millions and millions of susceptible to illness and cancers. Because of the GMOs and pesticides in our food there has been a huge push towards organically grown foods. The label "organic" may be misleading though. Some food may be called organic because the farm it comes from may have an organic designation, but the actual food product in hand may not be grown any differently than the food from the competition down the road that is not organic. The concern here is that organically produced food is more expensive (ironic, isn't it?) and the consumer will be paying more for possibly an inferior product.

The foods that contain GMOs are known by many names: genetically modified; genetically engineered (GE); transgenic; recombinant; gene-altered; biotech; and even "Frankenfoods." Why should you care whether you are eating these so-called Frankenfoods? The many reasons include concerns over environmental stewardship, international relations and trade, biodiversity, chemical-based versus sustainable agriculture, the patenting and ownership of life forms, and a number of personal health maladies. It is not natural to take genes from one species and 'force' it into the DNA of other species, but by doing this, food manufacturers can mix and match between different species of food types and essentially clone new 'Frankenfoods.' It all starts with the 'Frankenstein' seeds that must be bought annually from corporations (like Cargill and Monsanto). These seeds have terminator genes which insure that the seeds can only be used for one planting. If a farmer is caught using repurposed seeds, they are sued by the manufacturer.

The CODEX Alimentarius Commission mandates use of recombinant bovine growth hormone (BGH) as well as bovine colostrum nutrients in food and milk. Every animal must be treated with antibiotics and artificial growth hormones which mean that practically anything you eat is causing you to ingest unnatural chemicals into your body. This, coupled with the deterioration and deplorable handling and care of the animals that are being raised for food in these facilities (not to mention the livestock that become sicker from all the unnatural chemicals and in turn must use even more drugs and chemicals to keep them healthy) makes for a very unappetizing meal. Vitamin and mineral guidelines have been suppressed for these foods too, so providers of 'clean food' and nutrients are being pushed out of business.

Over the past quarter century or so, there has been one very dramatic change to our daily existence and that is the food we eat. The food we consume today is far different than the food thirty even twenty years ago. We have gone from food in its natural 'whole food' form to food undergoing a 'scientific experiment' and the ginny pig in this case is the human species. The process of introducing a gene from one organism into an unrelated organism has made its way onto our grocery store shelves via items as diverse as cheese, veggie burgers, cereal and cookies. Most of the corn, cotton and soybeans grown in the United States come from genetically modified plants, and almost all processed and packaged foods contain corn or soybeans in one form or another. Other examples of GMOs include strawberries and tomatoes injected with fish genes to protect the fruit from freezing: goats injected with spider genes to produce milk with proteins stronger than kevlar for use in industrial products; salmon that are genetically engineered with a growth hormone that allow them to keep growing larger; rice injected with human genes to produce pharmaceuticals; and as mentioned before dairy cows injected with the genetically engineered hormone rBGH (also known as rBST) to increase milk production.

Controversy obviously surrounds these food crops. While they have undoubtedly benefited humans in some ways— worldwide life spans have lengthened during the era of GMOs, partially due to improved nutrition made possible through GMO technology. The profitability of the GMO industry has led large-scale agriculture companies to rush products to market without the level of testing many would consider adequate to ensure human and environmental safety. Despite this, GMO ingredients are ubiquitous. The Environmental Working Group conservatively estimates that each American consumes about 190 pounds of GMO foods every year. Unless your diet has been composed almost entirely of organically grown, unprocessed ingredients, you for many years (without your knowledge) have been a participant in a scientific experiment of grand proportion.

Organic regulations define the GMO process as "a variety of methods used to genetically modify organisms or influence their growth and development by means that are not possible under natural conditions or processes." In essence, genes for desirable traits are extracted from a plant, animal, fungus, bacterium or virus and inserted into a life-form that would typically not be able to assimilate that gene into its DNA. A specific example includes engineering corn with the pesticide Bt (*Bacillus thuringiensis*) to kill the corn borers that might attack the plant; inserting a gene that produces growth hormones into hogs to make them grow faster or into cows to make them produce more milk; or transferring a trait for herbicide resistance into plants so that they may then be sprayed with that herbicide without dying. According to organic regulations, genetic modification does not include the use of "traditional breeding, conjugation, fermentation, hybridization, in vitro fertilization or tissue culture."

When it comes to our food, there are a few different types of pesticide-resistant crops that are grown: 1) The 'herbicide-tolerant' crop which can be spread with herbicide, and 2) The insecticide producing crop that can produce their own toxic insecticide that if an insect eats that plant, then it breaks open their stomach and kills the insect, and 3) The fungicide-resistant crop which is immune to various types of fungus growing on the plant itself. Man has been exposed to subpar genetically altered food for what reason? Like most things it boils down to money and greed. We are sacrificing our health and welfare for profits and the profits, are not even ours. The sad truth of the matter is, that most people are unaware of what is going on with our food. They recognize the GMO labeling, but they don't necessarily have a bad association with the term because they have been told (or 'sold') that it is a good thing.

Vitamins have been 'suppressed' as a means for the average person to keep healthy and not partake in the healthcare system. Pharmaceutical companies actually encourage people not to take vitamins and suppress any benefits of natural supplements including Vitamin C. They have even been able to conjure up scientific studies to show that taking (any kind of) vitamins or supplements are bad for you. If you are healthy and take daily vitamins and or supplements, then you are not participating in the healthcare and pharmaceutical racket. It seems that any type of preventative measures to keep yourself happy and healthy is discouraged by 'big Food' and 'big Pharma.'

Soda pop is another interesting food-related discussion. We all have been told that carbonated soda is "bad" for us mostly because we perceive it to be somewhat fattening and full of sugar. Diet soda has become immensely popular because of this, but the soda you drink (diet or not) contains other chemicals that are detrimental to your health. Aside from the fact that there is no nutritional value and heavy consumption can lead to obesity, high blood pressure and diabetes, soda contains high fructose corn syrup, phosphoric acid, caffeine and tons of sugar. Diet soda is actually worse for you than the regular brand in that diet soda contains artificial sweeteners such as Aspartame which has been specifically linked to Leukemia, Heart Disease and Cancer. Why our society continues to advertise, push upon and consent to the consumption of sodas on to our children so that they will become lifelong drinkers of 'poison' is of profound disillusion and amazement.

Another food related topic is the use of Universal Product Bar Codes on store and grocery packaging. Everything you buy in a store in the western world contains a barcode. The barcode was originally conceived by N. Joseph Woodland in an attempt to help keep track of sales and manage inventory of products for stores and the companies that manufactured them. This tracking code is a series of coded bars (lines and numerals) that are usually scanned by an electronic sensor system (electronic eye) upon products coming into the store and also upon check out at the store by the consumer. Either it is ironic or a huge coincidence (please remember there are no coincidences) that every barcode has the number "666" encrypted in the code.

The Bible has told us that the mark of the beast is 666. *"Let the one who has understanding calculate the number of the beast, for it is the number of a man, and his number is '666.'* It has been prophesized that in 'End Times' that not only will all products carry the 'mark of the beast,' but that all humans will also receive the mark in order to keep track of us. The devil is literally in the details. The 'mark' may not be a barcode per se, but perhaps comes in a more subtle way via a small devise or 'chip' that would be inserted into everyone's arm or wrist. A RFID (Radio-Frequency Identification) makes use of electromagnetic technology and has been used in a small chip form in animals and even your credit cards and passports. The next stage of implementation and agenda of the New World Order is to place this tracking chip in humans to contain all information – medical records, bank accounts and citizenship coded on the chip. So in the future, if you have either done something wrong or if the 'state' just doesn't like you anymore they can 'turn off' your chip so that you would not be able to access money, healthcare or any other societal benefits – possibly even food. It would be the simplest and the easiest way to control large populations in the future.

WATER

BOOK 11

"To have faith is to trust yourself to the water. When you swim, you don't grab hold of the water, because if you do, you will sink and drown. Instead you relax and float."
-Alan Watts

We are about 80% water. The Earth is 80% water. We also share about the same percentage of salt in our bodies as does the oceans and seas of the Earth. The Earth has many similarities with the human anatomy. This is no coincidence. There is no more important substance to us than water. Water holds many unique secrets to our human experience. Water holds encoded information and can even hold thoughts and memories. It contains knowledge of our past, our current thoughts and has a conscience. Water is beautiful. It has uncommon characteristics in that it can take on so many different forms such as solid (ice), gas (vapor) and liquid and it is in this natural, viscous state that water is most amazing. From the effortless ability to reflect images, to its tensile strength, to its profound ability to transmit sound and light, it is the most versatile substance on earth and these properties and characteristics strongly point to water as the result of intelligent design. One of the most unique characteristics of water is its ability to be self-leveling. No matter how rough or unleveled a surface is (i.e., Earth) when water moves over, it is 'self-leveling'; It literally 'goes with the flow' of the terrain. When water comes in contact with an object, it will perfectly surround the object with no hesitation. When water comes in contact with an obstruction such as a dam, it will pool at the base then continue to rise. It will keep continuing to rise until it finds a place to move around the sides of the obstacle.

As a metaphor...we should use the flow of water as a method for movement of our own lives. Too many times we are confronted with obstacles in our life whereby we feel the best way to 'get to the other side' is to force a path straight ahead. If the obstacle is big enough then we must continue to push and push until either we painfully work our way through with some type of 'brain damage' or find ourselves hopelessly defeated by an unrelentingly worthy opponent. The better way to get to the other side is to flow like water. There is always another way, another path, another direction we may not see right away, yet it is there and, like water, we will always find it. When you go with the flow, you will see how uncomplicated things can be. When forced, you cause friction and frustration to the situation. Be like water and flow.

It is easy to alter the composition of public water as many communities have done. Chemicals such as sodium fluoride and curiously some heavy metal elements (Aluminum, Barium and Strontium) have shown up in public water systems. These elements are not detectable by normal sensory means (taste, sight or smell). 75% of our 'water' today is fluoridated in the United States – mostly in urban and populated areas. The authorities have decided that by adding fluoride to our water that it will help strengthen our teeth and prevent tooth decay. The irrational thinking behind this is if naturally occurring fluoride was good for us, then adding a whole lot more would make it even better for us? It is disturbing that these chemicals are found in our drinking water and at such high levels that can do irreparable damage to our bodies. Even though some of the added chemicals are found 'naturally' within our body and in our food, it is at these unhealthy heightened levels that should alarm any conscious person. It is thought that many illnesses and diseases are caused by the additives and chemicals that are in water today. Bone cancer, Autism, Alzheimer's, lower estrogen levels in women and the many tooth related issues such as yellowing and pitting of tooth enamel are problems that stem from excess and a buildup over time of sodium fluoride. So the big question is: Why do companies and authorities go to all the effort by spending money to fluoridate our water when it already comes packaged in toothpaste? We don't ingest toothpaste...we can't or shouldn't because the labels on toothpaste say it contains a toxic ingredient – "Do Not Consume." So they continue to treat our water to ensure that you're getting your daily dosage of fluoridated water through drinking, bathing cooking, eating, swimming, showering and also brushing.

Authorities say that drinking fluoridated water can protect your teeth against cavities. Municipalities all across the world today dump toxic Sodium Fluoride, which is a byproduct of aluminum production, into the water supply hoping to indiscriminately 'medicate' the population through their tap water faucets. The official story on fluoride sounds wonderfully nice, that drinking fluoridated water will prevent cavities. But there's another side to this story, (a side you probably never heard) and it starts with the astonishing but verifiable fact that nearly all the chemicals found in municipal water supplies aren't naturally or unnaturally occurring fluoride at all but are, in fact, a combination of 'similar' chemicals

Hexafluoride Solicit Acid and Sodium Silica Fluoride. These two dangerous chemicals are what really is being substituted in our water for the less harmful fluoride they tell us is natural. These two chemicals are considered highly toxic and are poison in larger quantities as classified by the Environmental Protection Agency (EPA). They're labeled as hazardous waste when packaged for transportation. Workers must wear industrial safety gear including goggles and gloves when handling these chemicals. So why are they being dumped into our water supply, and where did they come from originally? They come from phosphate mining companies. Phosphate is an important mineral used in fertilizers and is mined from natural rock deposits scattered across the world. Phosphate rock is then refined to produce phosphoric acid. If that name sounds familiar, that's because one of the main ingredients in carbonated sodas such as Coke-Cola and Pepsi-Cola is phosphoric acid.

Phosphoric acid is often compared with battery acid and it's a highly acidic liquid believed to be the primary reason of why drinking sodas can result in kidney stones and a loss of bone mineral density. Phosphate rock is also used to create fertilizers. One problem is phosphate is often contaminated with high levels of fluoride too. The Fluoride Sulfuric Acid is added to a 'wet slurry' of phosphate and water. This causes the fluoride to vaporize, releasing highly toxic gaseous compounds such as hydrogen fluoride and silicon tetra fluoride. These toxic fluoride chemicals used to be released directly into the air from the smokestacks of phosphate mining operations, but the nearby farms suffered such devastating losses of cattle and food crops that environmental guidelines changed and prohibited this. The phosphate mining industry put in to place a way to capture toxic fluoride so that it wouldn't be released into the air and kill the surrounding livestock and vegetation. This was accomplished by installing wet scrubbers that captured the toxic fluoride chemicals preventing them from being released into the environment. It is from these wet scrubbers that toxic fluoride chemicals are now harvested. The chemicals are collected, repackaged, then shipped to your local city and then dumped into the municipal water supply. This is called water fluoridation and when dentists and doctors say they support fluoride in the water supply, what they're really saying is that they support the mass poisoning of the population with a highly toxic and hazardous waste product. If the chemical was not put into the water supply they would have to dispose of the highly toxic hazardous waste under strict EPA regulations which would cost a lot of money to the company.

Curiously, it is a violation of federal law to dump these chemicals, Hexafluorosilicic Acid and Sodium Silicofluoride into the public water supply. Such an act is in fact considered an act of terrorism and yet it is mysteriously allowed today as long as it is companied by a loosely justified claim that we're doing this to stop cavities. Setting aside for the moment the inconvenient truth that water fluoridation involves the illegal act of dumping hazardous waste into the water supply, there's another important question in all this: Do these toxic fluoride chemicals actually prevent cavities? Roughly 99% of the municipal water pumped through any given city never ends up in the mouths of the people using it. Most water is used for showering, washing dishes, washing clothes, watering yards and filling pools and almost none of the fluoride in the water supply comes into contact with human teeth or what it was intended for. It does, however, end up downstream where it contaminates rivers, streams and ultimately our oceans and seas. In this way, water fluoridation policies have become a convenient loophole through which the phosphate mining industry can dump its toxic waste byproducts into the environment without adhering to any EPA regulations whatsoever. Phosphate mining companies even turn a profit by selling their hazardous waste to cities labeling it fluoride even though this name is scientifically inaccurate and all this raises an obvious question: If fluoride kills cows, crops and fish and is considered a hazardous waste chemical by the EPA then how could it be healthy for us to ingest? And why don't doctors and dentists, even though they openly recommend fluoride, sometimes with irrational exuberance, know where fluoride really comes from? If dentists knew fluoride was derived from the chemical waste the phosphate mining industry, would they still be recommending that we consume it? In reality, our bodies have become the toxic waste dump site for the phosphate mining industry.

Over the last several decades, an astonishing 24 studies have established a statistical link between fluoride exposure and low IQs in children. One study conducted by the Center for Endemic Disease Control in China found that each additional milligram of fluoride detected in every liter in a child's urine was associated with a 0.59 point decrease in their IQ score. Another study found that fluoride exposure slashed the number of children achieving high IQs by more than seventy percent. It shouldn't be surprising to learn that consuming a hazardous chemical might impair brain function. Water fluoridation could be the root cause of the alarming drop in academic aptitude among children in first world nations. Historically, comparing the mathematics they taught to eighth-graders in the 1950's are now college-level courses. *Maybe the reason why Jonny can't read or spell very well is because Jonny's been drinking too much fluoridated water.*

Here are three bits of advice for you: 1) Seek out a holistic dentist who understands the seriousness of the toxicity of fluoride and mercury. He or She should advise that your children not to drink toxic fluoride chemicals from your tap water. 2) Don't drink unfiltered tap water. In addition to the toxic Fluoride chemicals that tap water has, it is usually also contaminated with Chlorine and other dangerous elements from old water pipes. Purchase a good countertop water filter or get a whole house filter to remove chlorine and fluoride from the water entering your home. 3) Help bring water fluoridation awareness to your local city or town. Your city's, if like in most cities,' water fluoridation policies have been pushed by government programs that are technically ignorant to the origins and composition of fluoride. Local water supply companies are essentially compliant by mass medicating the entire population with what can only be called a drug or poison. The biologically active chemical they claim can prevent a health condition is essentially a drug that has never received U.S. Food and Drug Association (FDA) approval. Such a drug or medication should have recommended doses and outlined drug interactions considered for anyone being written a prescription. Fluoride is an unapproved drug being used in a highly illegal mass-medication scheme that provides an excuse for the disposing of a highly toxic hazardous waste chemical. It's time to stop fluoride demand and end fluoridation in your local cities and towns. Call for those who purchase and handle fluoride to stop what they're doing. Question the safety of these toxic chemicals being dumped into the water supply as these are actions that endanger the public and could be called and act of terrorism. The doctors and dentists, whom we have trusted, should be ashamed of taking part (actively or inactively) in the mass chemical poisoning of the people and causing untold harm to populations.

There is nothing more natural for a baby's consumption than a mother's milk. Breast milk from mothers contains practically no fluoride at all. Fluoride is not a nutrient; no natural biochemical process in the human body needs fluoride. Nothing is beyond debate and the science is not closed on fluoride. Would companies spend a lot of money to fluoridate water just to help us? No, I don't think so. During WWII the Germans suspected that by adding fluoride to drinking water, it would make people "passive" so they used the concentration camps to test sodium fluoride and its effects on people. They found that sodium fluoride was a good way to 'sedate' the people in the concentration camps. A sedated prisoner was an obedient and non-violent prisoner. If a prisoner was more at ease, they were easier to control and less likely to be aggressive or violent. Sodium Fluoride has a calming effect on the human body. The result was profound since the Sodium Fluoride made it easier to handle the prisoners because they were calmer. This enabled the Germans to reduce the number of guards required to watch over the prisoners. The real sinister purpose of adding fluoride to water is to calm down and sedate the American population as to pacify them into dumbness. It is no coincidence either that the main ingredient in rat poison is Sodium Fluoride. Never has there been any conclusive study or evidence to prove the benefit of Sodium Fluoride on children's teeth.

Once fluoride is added to the water supply, there is no way of controlling the dose; it goes to everyone regardless of age, weight, health, need or nutrient status. The addition of fluoride to the public water supply violates the individual's right to informed consent to medical or human treatment. Fluoridated countries are being overexposed to fluoride as demonstrated by high levels of Dental Fluorosis in children but also high concentration levels found in the Pineal Gland.

The Pineal Gland, so named because of its likeness to a pine cone, is no bigger than a grain of rice and science has barely discovered the fullness of all its functions within the body and its connection to the mind/body relationship. The Pineal Gland (third eye) is the interface between conscience and matter. Almost the entire body is symmetrical (even the brain) yet the Pineal Gland is not symmetrical and has two distinct sides. The Pineal Gland is vital for converting signals from the parasympathetic to the endocrine system. The Pineal Gland – believed in many spiritual cultures to be the third eye of the body is responsible for intuition. It is the 'seat' of the soul where spirituality and your body meet. The gland releases vital antigens and hormones essential to our emotional and intellectual health. The Pineal Gland also regulates waking and sleeping patterns.

The Pineal Gland is our single natural source and produces substances such as serotonin and melatonin. These two important hormones can provide a pleasant night sleep, a happy and joyful blissful state of being and will provide spiritual devotion. The Pineal Gland is also important in sexual development, hunger, wakefulness, sleepiness, insomnia and your mental state. Even more compelling is the esoteric connection it may provide. It may be our gateway to the spiritual world and linked to our abilities such as intuition, discernment, psychic awareness and expanding the minds capacity as ancient cultures have alluded to. The gland's location and its resemblance to a 'third eye' make it appear to be, quite literally, the mind's eye. Natural light can most definitely affect the gland positively and increase the activity of the gland. More activity brings more insight, intuition, happiness and a stronger spiritual connection. This gland does receive blood flow and therefore is dependent on the body for nourishment and survival. As a result any 'death' in the blood (toxicity) can easily accumulate in the Pineal Gland. The primary danger is the accumulation of fluoride and other toxins in the blood, causing damage to the gland through calcification. The Pineal Gland has the highest levels of fluoride in the body and is the main 'target' for fluoride accumulation in humans. A calcified gland will not function properly and can have immense adverse effects on the body. Artificial foods and ingredients can also contribute to the toxicity level, but Fluoride (Sodium Fluoride) is largely blamed for Pineal Gland calcification. Other side effects of the gland not functioning properly are possible weight gain, thyroid and kidney trouble, confusion, and lowered IQ. A healthy gland can contribute to our overall happiness, a healthy nervous system, better sleep, better dreams, better imagination and better cognitive functioning. Drinking clean, unadulterated water is the key to an uncalcified Pineal Gland.

"Empty your mind...be formless...shapeless...like water. You put water into a cup...it becomes the cup...you put water into a bottle...it becomes the bottle...put it into a teapot...it becomes the teapot. Now water can flow or it can crash. Be water my friend."

-Bruce Lee

'N,N-Dimethyltryptomine' (DMT) is a naturally occurring substance made in your Pineal Gland and is released in very small amounts at times during sleeping. The 'full' release of DMT occurs usually at two times during your life...once, at birth and the other at the moment of death. It is believed to facilitate the traveling of the human soul in and out of the body. It acts as a bridge between these two worlds (life and death), but adventurous people have been able to access DMT and produce it through deep meditation or at times where a cosmic conscience event happens. The DMT experience is said to be similar to some aspects of a 'psychedelic' experience, yet DMT is natural and does not have any ill or adverse effect on the human body.

You can eliminate Fluoride and these neurotoxins from your routine and diet so you are not stuck with a "calcified" Pineal Gland forever. The calcification of something is like a "hardening" – turning into bone or crystal (inflexible). When the gland works properly it should be physically soft and malleable as would be found in an 'enlightened' spiritual person. If the gland is not malleable and no antigens or DMT can be released from a calcified (crystalized) gland since it has become hardened. To decalcify your Pineal Gland you need to eliminate all fluoridated water (even cooking), all neurotoxins in what we eat or drink especially items like soda containing Aspartame and also incorporate daily meditation to work this gland free. Like a stuck door it may need to be 'pried open.' It may take time, but when it 'opens' it will burst open very quickly.

At that point, you should be able to connect better to the dream/meditative, visionary state. You will have the ability to see colors in dreams more vividly, enjoy meditation on a higher level and even connect to the higher state of consciousness and intuition. So, over time, the process is really twofold: 1) Physiological—watch what we eat/drink, and 2) Exercise our mind with meditation and creativity. We are discouraged from being creative by our structured, academic systems and the result is that it strips us of our natural, inborn creativity. So the Pineal Gland becomes calcified not only when we take in the wrong kind of substances, but also when we take in the wrong kind of thought processes. Thus, we can help decalcify ourselves by dropping the false patterns of society.

When the Pineal Gland is fully functioning, you'll be able to attain a state of pure inner peace by more easily letting things go to reach a "thoughtless-state." In a thoughtless state is where we can be most creative. When you close your eyes, you can visualize anything—that is your Pineal Gland working. You are able to construct elaborate imagery right there on your mind's blank canvas. You *literally* can build castles, write symphonies or paint the most beautiful sunset with your third eye. Creativity breeds here and the more creative and happy a person is, the more active Pineal Gland (third eye) the person has. Your center of vision comes from this central, third eye and is very powerful, very creative and very vital.

By unlocking your Pineal Gland you will be able to speed up your learning and memory abilities, increase creativity, sharpen your insight, increase wisdom (enhance intuition), connect to telepathy, sharpen your awareness (psychic abilities) and experience bliss. People will turn around and notice you in a room or hallway because you will have a glow about you. As your presence becomes more vibrational, you will be able to see right from wrong more easily. You will be able to see through the lies and propaganda; you no longer wish to view news television, read newsprint or listen to news radio. Television commercials will disgust you and you will notice how they talk down to you (and entertain) you on a 'kindergarten' level. The radio will seem like idle chatter; you will feel like you just woke up from a dream and none of this is real or important (anymore).

There are more crucial problems in the world today than water fluoridation, but it is still important since, ironically, it prevents us from doing what we are doing right now and that is critical thinking. Toxic water is the prime cause of depression. So it is essential that we try to put the purest water into our, 'water-based body computer systems' for a multitude of reasons.

AIR

BOOK 12

Is the air here on Earth fit to breathe? It sounds like either a ridiculous question, or a trick question. The Earth's atmosphere allows us to breathe air which is vital for our survival. But what if the air has been modified? What if the air you breathe has been altered to make you ill over time, dumb your intelligence, and negatively affect all natural animals, plants and water? Although this sounds unbelievable, this is the case in many countries (mostly NATO countries) where there are increased levels of heavy metals in tested samples of the water and soil. This is a sign that something unusual is going on and the toxins may not be originating from the soil, but from the sky! This topic stands above others as one of the most controversial and guarded topics and is shrouded in secrecy. Have you looked up in the sky lately? What do you see? Are you noticing what many others have noticed over the past few decades – that there is an all-out assault on our skies? What are these long, white lines being 'sprayed' in plumes behind airplanes? Most people would think these are "contrails" or condensation trails being left behind by passing 'hot' airplane engines in the sky. This phenomenon is what is referred to as "Chemtrails" and it is linked to the massive and illusive Geo-Engineering and also the High Frequency Active Aurora Research Program (HAARP) technology. Geo-Engineering is a complex undertaking that may sound like a benefit to us, but rather may have many dire implications. HAARP is the technology that was created by Nikola Tesla over a century ago, and the quick explanation is that this technology is being used against humanity now by sinister forces.

So what are "Chemtrails?" And why are they being sprayed? You might get a slightly different answer depending on whom you ask, but the conclusive answer is that military-type aircraft are being used to spray very long lines of chemical salts into the atmosphere. These "heavy, metal, chemical cocktails" include, but are not limited to aluminum, barium and strontium. Over a period of hours, after being sprayed, these trails spread out in an expanding pattern and form a thin blanket of 'film' in the sky. When the sky takes on a 'silvery' color as opposed to a natural blue color, this is evidence of manipulation and spraying in the sky. The sky tends to look overcast when it is 'completely treated.' Those that have watched the sky for many years know the difference between real clouds and the fake clouds, made by airplanes. When the sky is fully covered with fake clouds the use of electromagnetic pulse or some other form of frequency technology is used to make it rain and bring down the 'chaff' in the sky. It then falls (as weather) to Earth and accumulates in our soils and waterways. This is part of a secret global engineering program that is used primarily over North America, Europe, Russia and most NATO nations, although it has been reported elsewhere as well. Stratospheric Aerosol Geo-engineering has multiple purposes, but some of them are related to the use of a newer generation of high-tech plasma weaponry - technology such as HAARP.

HAARP shoots energy waves into the upper ionosphere atmosphere and the metals in the sky act as a conductor. Because these weapons of technology are supposed to be top secret, the U.S. Government will not confirm or deny that chemtrails are being used. The Government's answer is that people who see chemical trails are just imagining things and are seeing regular jet contrails. This government response shouldn't come as a surprise though; it's necessary to keep certain weapons technology secret. The government has a long history of denying things that people have witnessed to be true such as the once-mysterious "stealth bomber." Some go as far to say that they are spraying the sky to help mankind from the supposedly depleting ozone layer or as a defense mechanism from other countries such as Russia, but there's a problem with chemtrail and HAARP technologies that makes it a different and even more complex matter. The problem is that the chemicals sprayed in the sky eventually settled down on the Earth below contaminating water and ground surfaces from which we grow food and obtain our water to get our nourishment. This compromised food and water, in turn, can cause health problems and illness.

All this debate has led to the creation of organizations led by experts and scientists that are trying to get the word out to the public about the dangers of these chemtrails while the government wishes to keep the geo-engineering spraying secret, and is waging a propaganda campaign against the existence of chemtrails. It can take a while to go through the massive insults and mockery which is the primary disinformation weapon used by the government toward inquisitive people, but if you ignore the ridicule just long enough to research the facts behind chemtrails you'll find it is very convincing. There is too much information and pictures on the Internet of these long crisscrossing streaks from so-called commercial planes and the official story has been debunked a hundred different ways including testimonies from commercial airline pilots and confessions from whistleblowers in the military who have helped to load the chemicals onto the planes.

Another potentially catastrophic danger presented by the HAARP weaponry is the ability to create weather and change weather patterns. The electro-magnetic frequency capabilities that HAARP possesses have the ability to affect weather and create storms. Some people's conservative views prevent them from accepting the idea that the government is developing, using and hiding such technology from public view. What is difficult to comprehend is how some people ignore the overwhelming mountain of scientific evidence that supports the existence of chemtrails and HAARP technology. People, especially in the media, use insults and mockery as a method of debating sensitive topics such as chemtrails.

Thousands of photographs and videos exist of the skies above towns going from a beautiful blue cloudless sky transformed by planes into a sky covered with 'checkerboard' patterns of 'chemical trails.' This took place over a relatively short period of time performed by a half dozen or so military type (KC – 10's and KC – 135's Strato-tankers from Evergreen Airfield) jets streaking back and forth overhead. The photographic evidence is incontrovertible. The natural contrails dissipate in seconds as the planes pass by while chemtrails, on the other hand, hang in the sky and spread out creating a white blanket. It has been told to us that the necessary circumstances that a 'trail' of exhaust can persist is when the atmosphere the plane is flying in is cold enough and has high humidity. Yet we see these 'contrails' day and night even on the hottest day of summer and even when the atmosphere is not fit to hold persistent trails. It just does not add up. If it doesn't add up, then there is an alternative reason why things are the way they are.

The HAARP technology can also control your mood and behavior. The HAARP frequency can spread a 'spider web' effect over general populations and can, literally, send a 'fear frequency' to any place on the Earth. It can harness your energy for sinister purposes as well as controlling the weather. In fact, scientists predict that by the year 2030 the weather could be modified and controlled (man-made). But, the fact is the weather is being controlled right now. Regardless of why the government is using Geo-Engineering, conclusive evidence proves that the elevated quantities of metals are impacting our soil, water and food. For that reason alone - should be sufficient enough to wake people up now to investigate more thoroughly on behalf of our future generations.

When you're exposed to these chemicals long enough, it suppresses the ability of your white blood cells to defend you from airborne infections coming into your lungs. It also suppresses your immune system. Once these nanoparticles (that contain 'heavy elements' such as aluminum, barium and strontium) get into your internal system they can go through the membrane barriers of the cells and can suppress the ability of the mitochondria to help gobble up bad toxins in the body. This can affect the reproductive ability for cells to regenerate and heal and will bring on disease and illness to what otherwise would be a healthy individual. Simply breathing in this adulterated air your body places your immune system is under stress.

As far back as 1961, The United Nations (elite Globalists) started the "Geo-Engineering" program on paper and in 1968 the "Club of Rome" pushed to implement this onto the public for a plethora of reasons. It has been a full-on assault from 1997 to present day. The accumulation of barium salts and aluminum nanoparticles is turning everything alkaline and killing all plant and living matter. Today, plant(s) leaves show illness and stress. They are less bright, with more brown spots than in the past—leaves are falling off the trees earlier and the fall colors are less vibrant! The Monsanto Corporation (the same company that brought you Agent Orange) connection is very important to the 'alkaline soil' issue. These heavy metals and nanoparticles work their way into the soil and change the pH balance to be more alkaline. Plants require a certain amount of acidity in the soil to grow properly. More importantly seeds will not grow if the soil is not conducive to the proper 'pH' balance. Monsanto has genetically engineered seeds so that they are able to grow in a higher alkaline soil. Not only have they patented these seeds, but they have a monopoly over farmers, requiring them to exclusively use their formulated seeds, which the seeds only have one growing season so the farmers must purchase new genetic seeds every year. The farmers' situation is only one aspect of this sinister plan. The bigger concern is that these seeds are also growing genetically modified food that we are putting into our bodies. This is not natural and the devastating effects of this shortsightedness may not be too far off in the future since we are already seeing the mal-effects of this today. The powers that be keep denying everything, but we are at a tipping point. The question is: Are we really stupid to ask about this? The answer is "No!" We need to ask. We never saw airplanes in the sky at that elevation spraying like this before 1997 with streams of cloud dust from one end of the sky to the other. This Geo-Engineering and HAARP interrelationship is quite sophisticated. All of this is Tesla Radar Technology and is being used against us (not help or assist us) as Tesla intended. We will have no other option than to continue Geo-Engineering (GMO) the seeds to grow things because these seeds will be the only thing that will be able to grow in the damaged soil – and that includes those who want to grow their own food too. They have created the problem and packaged a solution with aluminum-resistant crops. As part of the urbanization agenda (moving all people to central living areas) one of the results is the lack of ability to grow food in your own backyard. It will be easy to move everyone because nothing will grow anywhere. People will be forced to go into a "living zone" to get their food. If we stop being able to provide our own food then we will have to go where they tell us to live. Supplies will be rationed. They have already targeted Europe, America and any U.N. country that has valuable, sufficient resources where they may be able to amount to something in the future; or any country able to mount an opposition to this is Draconian world plan. There is nothing more important than our Earth and without it functioning properly we won't function properly. This is the most important time of our lives and quite possibly in all of history. We need to wake up and unify, come together and bring awareness; put unity back into our community.

Perhaps "chemtrails" are the most ignored government crime because it represents government and private corporations joining as one playing 'god' with our weather system with no oversight or regulations. The universal global warming and the subsequent climate change 'religion' are intertwined together with the weather manipulation by the globalists who need to continue to push and usher in their all-invasive global carbon tax. Through taxation they can ultimately achieve control of all human activity on Earth in the name of the environment. By means of Agenda 21 they will implement the final stages of control over everything we do. While the admitted spraying of chemicals into the sky is intended to be a solution to countering "Global Warming" which in reality is a major lie and is the primary cause of the problem. Our government has over 150 patents for Geo-Engineering weather modifications of the sky. They admit to spraying, and many pilots have come forward and provided evidence on their spraying and manipulation of the sky. The end goal is to use Agenda 21 (2030) as a method of land confiscation and moving people into cities (urban areas), and shrinking their carbon footprint and taxing them while doing this. The tax is the way to help fund the impending one-world government which, in turn, is helping to fund your own enslavement.

The Weather Channel is another example of an elite–controlled media complex. The people that bring you The Weather Channel, Weather Central and all the weather reporting, are owned by Blackrock (Swartzman's company), Bain Capital (Romney's company) and Lynn Forester de Rothschild (wife of Evelyn de Rothschild). Raytheon does all the forecasts and tracks weather conditions for the National Weather Service and NOAA. In addition, Lockheed Martin does the weather modeling for the F.A.A. and airplane traffic. This tightly-knit elite group of characters is providing you with all the daily weather forecasting and there is no oversight or monitoring of the process. Perhaps there is a reason for this, and that reason is that our weather as a whole has been manipulated. Who better to manipulate it than the entities that are also reporting it? It would not be a stretch to assume that there is some kind of high powered collusion between these groups. At some time in the future, this fact will be made more public and people will know the truth.

Stratospheric Aerosol Geo-engineering is "Chemtrails." The word "Chemtrail" has no real scientific basis or relevance of meaning yet it is the common phrase that most often describes what people see in the sky that is being created by military type tanker airplanes spraying aerosol particulates in these long 'white' cloud formations. This subject of Chemtrails is not only one of the most serious topics in this book, but also one of the more complex ones. One cannot approach the Geo-Engineering, (chemtrails), climate change subject as a one dimensional matter, which is because the subject has so many (multi) layers that are interwoven with many facets of our life. Like many serious topics that have come to light, how does one go about the normal business of life when you know you are breathing toxic air that is directly related to Geo-engineering programs? You don't. And because this topic is so important to the welfare of all humans, it should be brought to the forefront and openly discussed with everyone. Immediately. Once you know what is really going on anyone with good conscience cannot pretend or ignore this anymore.

Disbelievers will tell you that what you see are 'contrails' left behind by airplanes, or if they admit that spraying is going on—that it is being done to counteract any type of "Global Warming" or "Climate Change" that is occurring naturally by blocking the sun's rays. Either way you approach this subject, the fact is that our air, water and soil (along with ourselves) are being contaminated with toxic levels of heavy metal particulates that are detrimental to all living things. First, don't be naïve enough to think that your government is going to ask you if they can spray stuff in the sky. Second, so much happens without our knowledge and this is one of the most guarded secrets going on in our government. They will continue to do it because they simply can. So much of what is going on with the Geo-engineering programs is hidden. Disbelievers will tell you that perhaps they are spraying the skies "for our benefit." This is partially true, because over the past century there have been changes to our environment, but this is a natural cycle of our weather. Man has complicated the situation by all the unnatural 'pollution' through CO_2 gases, automobiles, factories, aerosol cans and the burning of fossil fuels that are contributing to the natural deterioration of our atmosphere and ozone layer. But the most important point is this. Anything that is being done now to counteract the 'Climate Change' situation (caused by man or not) is making it far worse. The intentional 'grid and blanket' spraying in the sky is making the original problem (which is a natural climate shift that it was trying to help alleviate) much, much worse. The story gets even uglier from here.

The elite Central Bankers, who are financing the spraying and pushing for Climate Change awareness, are the ones who are escalating the problem by going to just about every country on the planet (and through the United Nations Agenda 21, Agenda 2030, and other globalist organizations) and are imposing a "Climate Tax." This huge tax is basically a huge fee (debt based) that must be paid over time back to the Globalists to fight climate change.

It is the biggest farce and to tax us on top of all the other horrible injustices is purely adding insult to injury. The Globalists are *literally* taking advantage of the situation they created in the first place. But this is how they do things. The real problem is they are playing with nature. They are changing the natural flow and balance of the environment. It's kind of like they are <u>playing</u> 'Mother Nature' and not just playing 'with' her, but against her. Either way, it could end very badly because they have managed to 'ruin' the balance of just about every natural and harmonious aspect of our life. They have changed the weather, manipulated our water, poisoned our food, modified the air, taxed us and lied to us about it all. These crimes are far worse than the money crimes the bankers usually perform on us through the banks. This is much more serious in that the damage being done could be irreparable to our planet. The people behind this are monsters. Complete and utter psychopaths who have no care for others (or themselves) and are unaware of their psychopathic behavior. They are breathing and eating the same 'crap' that everyone else is. A normal person could never image that anyone would act so inhumanely and do this to their fellow man by implement methods to depopulate the Earth on purpose. Many of these ideas are traced back to the "Club of Rome" whose foundation is set on taking away the autonomy of the individual and placing them into a group for easier control, and eventual easier extermination, through what is perceived to be natural occurring events. There is also speculation that the elite have methods of detoxifying their bodies through blood transfusions to eradicate the heavy metals which have worked their way into their bodies. More speculation and debate shows that there is a correlation between the increase in diseases like Alzheimer's and Autism due to the heavy metals in our food, water and air. It is unfortunate that very few people have come forward to expose this connection. Some have done so, but at an expense. These people have been threatened or their lifestyle will be severely compromised if they do "speak out." It would be a very bad career decision for a meteorologist or an airplane pilot to step out of line since they may not be able to work at another career. They are told not to touch or discuss the topic of Geo-Engineering. There is no First Amendment protection for these people either, yet when the information does finally come out, it will open a floodgate of people coming forward to disclose what they know since they will feel more comfortable when everyone else is coming forward. The problem is so big and complex that most people don't even know where to start.

The droughts in California are directly related to the weather modification created by Geo-engineering. California is a weather sacrifice zone. By changing the weather you change the natural weather patterns and California is dramatically affected by this. The Midwest states are also being 'droughted-out' from weather modification, affecting food production. Weather warfare on our enemies has been well documented over time. The "Global Diming" that is going on is causing a lower percentage of the sun rays to reach the Earth and it is affecting plant and wildlife growth. It is also decreasing the ability to harness solar power. You may think that by blocking the sun you would mitigate 'Global Warming' (Climate Change), but in fact you make Global Warming much worse not better—since you create a hot box effect between the earth's surface and the upper atmosphere and this in turn causes nature to dry out by producing more thermal energy. This 'drying out' is affecting the amount of water that gets to the plants, wildlife and crops. The species extinction rate is alarming. Over the past 30 years or so we have lost approximately a third of the animal and insect species variations on Earth due to manipulation and Geo-Engineering. If the planet cannot support life it is essentially "game over." The headlines are hiding the real problem that is going on. Do not look to your mainstream media to highlight or cover this story. It is way too sensitive or 'hot.'

It is extremely difficult to be aware of all of this and to sit idle. It is not only difficult, it is sad; mostly because no one wants to spend the time to investigate this for themselves. They just think it is so farfetched that it is all made-up. This contributes to the difficulty in educating others. If you are new to all of this, you will go through a whole bag of emotions: grief, devastation, and anger including 'disbelief,' because it so difficult to believe it is really going on. Life is busy with kids, work, paying bills and looking to advance ourselves in stature with the next promotion, but we 'must' look up at the skies and pay attention at this time. The only way we can stop this is by all people of the world coming together setting their differences aside and see beyond the political and social obstacles that have separated us. Together, we can overcome and solve any problem with collective thought for a more balanced, harmonious existence. We have to protect the air we breathe and do this now, not only for ourselves, but for future generations.

SLEEP

BOOK 13

Sleep is vital to our existence, mentally, physically and spiritually. Sleep is our natural state and is our true connection to who we are. We should spend about one-third of our lives sleeping, but ironically most people don't get enough sleep. Many of us feel that when we "sleep too much" we are being lazy and not getting things done. We are preoccupied with achieving mindless amounts of early morning work and late night chores that in the end steal our energy and depower our spirituality. Some people joke and say that sleep is something they will "do after [they] die" so they stay awake with caffeine, energy drinks and any type of stimulant pills to conquer their bucket list. "Grab the gusto" of life and "burn that midnight oil" to go out and make as much money as you can to keep up with the "Joneses" of the world. The world has become open "24/7" and international cities and global markets rarely, if ever, sleep. News programs and Mini-marts are open 24 hours a day and the media never stops pushing news updates at us from all sides and at all hours. If you want to try to keep up – you will very quickly burn yourself out. Your body and mind need to reset each day, so it is essential to rest your body (when it tells you) even if you're not feeling too tired.

Once upon a while ago, there was a story circulating about a Japanese businessman who worked 13 days straight and only slept an 'hour or so' on a cot in his office each night. On the 14th day he was dead. He was 35. There was another story about a young video gamer who decided to play a video game for 48 hours straight. He was also met with the same unfortunate demise. You can go weeks without food, and even days without water, yet the body and mind cannot function well without sleep and resting each and every day.

Some people have trouble sleeping; most of the time it is because they have too much on their minds. Maybe they do not have a clear conscience. Those that say they "sleep like a baby" are people with either a clear conscience or perhaps no conscience at all. Go figure. A healthy balance of proper food, exercise, quality bedding and pillows and a clear mental state are all ingredients for the recipe for a good nights sleep. We should not be influenced by others when we need to rest or sleep.

Neither should we be influenced or bullied when we want to relax or meditate. Meditation is not sleep, yet it provides some of the same healing mechanisms that sleep gives' us. It recharges the mind and relaxes the body. Meditation is a practice in which an individual induces a 'mode of consciousness' either to realize some benefit to the mind-body connection or his or her relationship to the universe. When you tell people that you meditate they may laugh a little, but that should not change you or how you see yourself. For a healthy balance it is essential, each day, to slow your mind and minimize the chattering of your "ego." Empty your mind of the thoughts that normally preoccupy it. You want your thoughts to come about from the cosmic consciousness that is encoded inside of you. In this lucid state you are able to clarify reality, see and solve problems better, self-evaluate and not worry as much about things.

I find that the simple tasks of 'forgiveness' and 'letting go' are a very important aspect of resting the mind and is the trunk from which everything stems from. Forgiveness is the acceptance of others as they are and by, accepting others, you have established forgiveness and acceptance for yourself. Ultimately, your mind is the cosmic mind... and the cosmic mind is your identity... and that identity is truth. So, in truth, one can gain cosmic energy which is provided to us through sleep and meditation. Sleep is conscious meditation.

Some simple sleeping suggestions: Since many of us spend many hours sleeping each night it is important to have proper and comfortable bedding. A firm mattress is recommended with a comfortable head pillow (not too soft or thick) and a smaller pillow for between the knees. This will limit back and neck pain. Some use a "body pillow" to hold onto while sleeping on the side. You may rotate between your back and sides and any one restful position is suitable. Achieve a position that is free from pain or pressure. You must be able to relax, let go and be comfortable. It is important to have a dark, cool room and all electronics should be off since artificial light flickers and will stimulate your conscience and keep you awake. Music can be used as a medium to fall asleep, but should be soft and relaxing. Never go to bed hungry (if you can help it) and drinking clean, pure water before and after sleeping is recommended.

When you journey onto the path of enlightenment and start to become aware of who you are, your sleeping patterns will change. We are so caught up with the regiment of the 9 to 5 work day schedule that we fill our evenings and weekends with the millions of things that we feel we need to accomplish that sleep is constantly being compromised. The enlightened will rest when they are tired—even if it means taking naps during the day. The enlightened are less concerned with the routine sleeping patterns and find sleep to be not only a healthy reset of the body and mind, but as a subtle escape from this reality. As one awakens in this life, it becomes harder and harder to navigate the mundane and trivial trappings of everyday existence. Sleep is our escape from this routine. During sleep, our pure conscious can move freely as it does in the higher realms. Our 'burdensome' body becomes less solid, and with less solidity we are able to perform life's events with less physical effort. Sleep is our time to dream. Dreams are very much a part of our natural state and have a far more significant relationship to our waking life than people may realize.

Dreams are reflections of only your world – your own psyche self. If you see the world change, it is only your world not the entire world. If you see yourself die in a dream, this could mean not a physical death of 'you,' but rather what you're experiencing is the unavoidable prophecy of death of part of your ego (a part of the self). It is the part of your mind that has been 'clinging' to this reduction of scientific belief that you're all alone in the universe and once you die there is nothing more to who you are or your existence. Don't forget your conscience is eternal and you are the co-creator of this world and your reality. You will always be 'here' and always have been here. Once the soul comes to grasp with this 'concept' then you can experience a true 'awaking' and you will be able to let go of what you have feared the most, death (death in reality and death in your dreams). Your dreams can let go of these limitations. When you let go of the part of you that doesn't want to forgive, that criticizes others and that feels a need to protect the corporeal body (in its own interest) above all else. In that accord, you recognize that by helping others you are helping yourself. Dreaming is quite different from meditation. Meditation is stilling your mind where your thoughts are in touch with your higher self (lucid dreaming). Though you are still 'pulling' from the same sub-conscious 'pool of thoughts' that come from your higher mind during both experiences, during dreaming, your thoughts are being absconded. In dreaming you are pulled into the past with guilt and pushed into the future with fear.

If you can get past this 'mental blockage' and create a 'be here now' mentality, then what begins to happen is you awaken the part that is present in this moment (the now moment). In this state of higher self-awareness you are connected to all things and you realize that you don't need to be so preoccupied with what others think or think about you. You have let go. At this point of awakening you will be able to customize your dreams so that you are not always lost in a past or future moment.

Dreams – our higher self uses dreams to convey symbolic information that gives us clues to the concerns that are affecting us in our lives right now. The big secret of dreams is that the entire environment is a reflection of our self. That means every character and every object and every event represents something'

Dream interpretation: There are two different categories: 1) the over soul dream, and 2) the programming dream. The 'over soul' dream is typically one where you are still you, yet you have abilities that are beyond your human form, e.g., you are able to fly. Some of our dreams are of the latter kind – the programming type dreams – which are conditioning you to conform to the way society has manipulated you and does this through your fear-based subconscious. These are the type of dreams where you are sitting in a classroom and all of a sudden you're naked. You will always have over soul dreams because a release of pent up energy is required as a natural body condition (call it a mind flush). An automatic release valve in your mind controls the energy and is like a self-regulating check and balance system. You are actually reporting your 'life progress' at that point in time. Look at the symbolism within the dream to help determine if it is an over soul or programing type dream. Many programing dreams are re-occurring and usually are trying to tell you something about yourself. These dreams can be unnerving. To 'undo' the programmed dream sequence one must un-do the program functions and alter the compartments of the matrix in which we live that affect them. In other words, we need to let go of the baggage that we are carrying that helps facilitate freedom from these subconscious thoughts. Your dreams can telegraph future events of your life too. If you pay attention, coded messages appear in your dreams that will leave clues to how to maneuver through future events.

Many people will claim that they do not dream. And if they do dream, they usually can't remember the dream they just had the previous night. Most dreams we do remember are the ones that we have close to the time we wake up. Sometimes sleeping 'in' in the morning (or during long naps in the afternoon), can precipitate more dream memories. At these times, we are in a semi-lucid state and this is when we experience more dream retention. When you are on the path of enlightenment, your dreams will be more vivid and also will have more meaning. Foreshadowing dreams are very prevalent in the 'awakened.' Somehow these people are able to see the future in their dreams and this is a way of helping provide insight and align to life's correct pathway. As an end note: Sleep naked. Sleeping naked (or with as little on as possible) is more natural and there are many other benefits to sleeping nude. By sleeping naked you will allow your body to self-regulate your temperature more easily during the night and provide a more restful, sleep.

EGO

BOOK 14

Your ego (super-ego) builds a tower for you to live in. It feels safe and protects you from dealing with certain people and situations. You are elevated in your mind, above the fray. You gaze down on humanity noting your separation. Ego is a sense of separation. Your destiny is somehow greater than others. You have been elevated and you are the chosen one. That is what our ego likes. It feeds on this attention and loves to distance ourselves from others. It loves to show off. This ivory tower we build is sustained by the electricity, our ego puts out. The more ego electricity the more stubborn and difficult the individual may be. Some famous people and pop stars crave constant attention and notoriety. They are "high maintenance" and enjoy being waited on 'hand and foot' by others. Our ivory towers create this isolationism and through this separation something horrible happens to the self. You actually become slightly 'mad' and it will require more and more ego and electricity to sustain this ivory tower so it will eventually consume, and ultimately kill, your inner spirit. Ego blinds you to common sense and reason and can make you moody, angry, sad, depressed, anxious, alone, unloved, regretful, uncompassionate, and will suck the 'life' right out of you. But for now you're "King of the Tower" and have virtually shut out all others in doing so. The competitiveness has made you win — but at what cost?

The illusion is that the height of this tower provides safety, security and protection by exclusion. But if one of the structural 'support beams' of your egotistical lifestyle is weakened (such as too much debt or a "fall from grace") the tower could collapse. Take a moment and realize that this tower must keep building upon itself to survive — a bigger title, a new car, bigger home, better clothes and more extravagant vacations. More and more is required to keep the ego façade going which in turn feeds upon itself. Not too dissimilar from a parasitic invader. What is your ivory tower really made of? Debt, stress, or both? The ego tower is made up of all materialistic items and once you can afford multiple homes and more cars than you can drive you may feel that you 'made it' but you have also taken many inherent ugly side effects with this success such as selfishness, jealously, greed, worry, paranoia and revenge. Ego-driven people are generally spiritually cold and have little compassion for others, but are really good at faking altruism. They have a very hard time putting themselves in other people's shoes and invest little or no time in esoteric thoughts. It is all about the wow factor. Some egomaniacs appear to be social and warm on the outside, but inside they are empty and find most people around them dispensable. They can treat others with disdain, scrutiny or indifference. The false ego has only one goal and that is to become more powerful than the true self. This illness causes us to be separate from nature and the natural rules of the world. The more we 'advance' technically and materialistically, the more the dependency increases on our ego and the farther we get away from nature.

There is a 'catch' to your ego. The catch is, you can't completely abandon your ego and survive here on Earth. You still need some ego to live and survive. The ego is a mechanism by which we are able to get up each day and conquer the tasks at hand. Simple things such as providing food, protection and shelter for yourself and your family are a part of our "ego trip." It is when we go beyond our 'fair share' of survival ego that most people lose control. Everyone likes attention. Everyone likes new things, but when the primary focus is on the accumulation of power over others and extraneous material items that is when we have 'lost control' in keeping our ego in check. Some refer to this behavior as "sociopathic" or even "psychopathic" since it is our own mind that causes us to 'cross the line.' Many very wealthy people have huge egos and just about any person seeking fame and unscrupulous fortunes may also have distorted egos. Professional politicians come to mind and certainly fall into this category of distorted ego (or unbalanced mental forethought) and are constantly compared with socio/psychopathic personalities.

Our ego is also a form of slavery in that once we achieve our 'magical goal,' we cannot let it go. It has consumed our motivation where we become a slave to pushing our ego bigger. All that hard work and time *literally* spent on grooming our ego when upon reflection all we really wanted in the beginning was acceptance from others. To be one with yourself you should monitor your ego and align yourselves with a higher level of conscious construct. Therefore, our ego or egotism and all the ulterior motives that many of us rely on must be let go...that is, if you are seeking true enlightenment in this life time. As impossible as it sounds to let go of that part of our ego, and the modern comforts of society that stem from it, individuals can still let go enough and be prosperous. It is when spiritual values are in harmony with the ego that we can survive and thrive.

This "gut feeling" (our intuition) helps guide and navigate just about everything and anything that we do. For example: When we do anything physical with our bodies such as climbing a tall mountain, we run through potential outcomes. In some cases, we conjure up a scenario whereby we see the potential for possibly getting hurt. Our intuition takes over and will guide us away from that scenario from that hurt occurring. Sometimes our intuition is wrong, but usually our first thought (what we initially feel) is the correct thought and is the correct decision. In completing any task, it is important that our energy mind and our physical body work together. Our intuition can only get us to the point of actually doing the task. Upon doing the task our mind/body interaction needs to work together to accomplish the goal as desired. If we are not in 'sync' with ourselves then accidents can occur.

Some people will boast they are enlightened when in fact they either say this for attention or are not enlightened at all. These pseudo-enlightened people believe they have been chosen like a demigod and know more than you. All this is just another construct of the ego. Enlightenment is a trap. Once you're 'enlightened' and you flaunt this, you are looking to feed your ego even more. The pseudo-enlightened, by means of their ego, look for outlets to tell people that they know more than you (books, movies) it's all rubbish. Be humble! The truly enlightened person does not want attention. They seek to retreat, go sideways — to become simple ... and nothing more. For example: If you had all the power in the world and were able to create anything you wanted — the truly enlightened would not want to show off — because once you did you would be like a circus act or a magician. The pseudo ego would strive for attention, notoriety and it wants fans, followers and worshipers. True enlightenment (true power/knowledge) is usually hidden for that reason. That is why many enlightened elite (oppressors) remain hidden and will purposely put out misinformation (fake knowledge) to keep us from becoming enlightened ourselves. If we want to serve humanity fairly, we need to learn, and not exploit, this knowledge of enlightenment.

What do you really want? What do you desire? If you really don't desire anything then 1) you either have it already, or 2) you don't know — just as why a knife can't cut itself...it is a mystery.

When you say you "don't know," that really means you can love... you can let go... you don't try to force...you have humility. Anytime you give up control (cease to oversee), you have accessed inner power. You have strengthened yourself by letting go on two levels: physically and mentally. You are wasting energy anytime you're in self-defense trying to manage things trying to force things. The moment you start 'stopping', that un-wasted energy is available to you. Having this energy available to you is being one with the divine principles. When you try to act like 'God' and you dictate how things are going to be, you, in essence, loose the divine energy. Because what you are doing is defending yourself.

The principles follow this law: The more you give it away the more it comes back to you (Karma). What if you don't have the courage to give it away? You can only overcome that by realizing you should give it away, because there is really no way to hold onto it; everything is discovering or denying and in a constant state of decay. We are all in a 'process' of constant decay. That is the great assistance in letting things go. Everything is in eternal decay. This allows us to provide an 'excuse' for all that happens to us. So you don't have to let go because there is really nothing to hold onto. It is just simply 'adrenalin' for you through the process of nature. But this is a process that gives you power when you really give it up. Give it all up. You will see that you have the power to access this inner energy and it will come to you not by forcing either. The power will ultimately come from the opposite direction or from an entirely new and different direction not even considered.

The ego will buy stuff we don't need — with money we don't have — to impress people we don't like. Give up desire. You won't suffer. But isn't giving up desire a desired outcome? Desire — less.

If you <u>have</u> to go on – if you <u>must</u> succeed – if you <u>have</u> to win at all cost, then you are taking yourself too seriously. In order to be truly liberated there is nothing you need to do. All your 'efforts' in the direction of being liberated are superfluous. They are based on your desire to boost your ego and that will never lead to true liberation. All you can do, is to be aware of what you're doing at the specific time you are doing it, without judgment, to see what the correct path is. If you can do this, you will have no future problems liberating yourself. Self-remembering is the key. At every moment during the day you should knowingly keep track of what you are doing. If you are picking up a stack of paper – realize and know you are picking up a stack of paper. Watch yourself. Don't be absent minded. Even simple tasks require your attention. Take things off your plate literally and theoretically. Focus on what is right in front of you. We have too many concerns during the day and we have become absent minded and that is how accidents happen. But they are not really accidents and are not really happening by accident. Don't be alarmed. These things are happening on purpose and are a part of the grand design to help you learn to slow down, pay attention and be cognizant of your surroundings.

Political Ego vs. Organic Ego: The political ego controls while the organic ego lets go. The political ego loves power and tries to control every aspect of the world around them. They are always involved in every minutia of detail and involve themselves even in other people's business. The paradox is that the most powerful and successful individuals are the ones that can just let go. The more responsibility you can relinquish and trust others to do the job by not looming over them is the one that can grow happily to gain more success personally and also financially. By not over- seeing a cumbersome process of endless oversight, the collective merits that are accomplished lay no claim to anyone. Yet, the more control you relinquish (and trust others), the more powerful you become, but in such a way that instead of tossing and turning having to lay awake at night (worried or concerned) going over and over everything a zillion times—you do it beautifully by trusting the job to everyone else and they carry it out for you.

Trust your nervous system. The power comes from overcoming yourself which is a more organic, natural way of achieving inner power. Coming to terms with unity and the oneness of the universe is not to try to obtain power over people, but the way to become one with the universe is to trust it and let go. The real secret to life is to be engaged completely with what you are doing in the "here and now." The future is a concept that doesn't exist. You only have now!

Don't hold onto yourself so tightly that you strangle yourself. Don't take yourself too seriously or you will suffocate in your own ability to make a smile. Don't look to others to make any significant change, the change must start from you and come from you. Don't just change for the sake of change. Change may not always be good and in that subtle hesitation will emerge the correct way we should change if we are going to change at all. All of these 'hot' buttons in the media are there to distract you from what is really going on or what is really important. Race, abortion, politics, healthcare and terrorism has everyone all distracted and fighting amongst each other. They want you to change to the "politically correct" way of thinking, but they also want you to fight with each other while doing it. Who does this really benefit? Perhaps the change you may need to make is to see through the façade and be able to make up your own mind.

We tend to notice things that we believe are noteworthy. When observing a photo we primarily focus on the main subject, but there is much more going on in the picture. People usually notice the foreground and not the background. Question: Do you see a circle or do you see a wall with a hole? The environment which an object is in is just as important as the object itself.

"To be... implies that there is a not to be."

-Not Shakespeare

You can go running on the 'wheel of life' (the rat race) as long as you want, as long as you like and as long as you think it is fun. But when it becomes time and you don't think it's fun anymore then you don't have to do it any longer...so go on fighting if you want, if you believe that this is the way, but by giving up the fight you will empower yourself in a much stronger way. Integrity is a person that is not divided.

We are always trying to find a way to 'one up' one another – even when it comes to benevolence and charity. Usually the giving comes by a more subtle means, but competition somehow enters the picture. How much did you give last year? The exact reason you want to be better is the actual reason you aren't. We are merely not better because we want to be.

As some say, "the road to hell is paved with good intentions." The do-gooders in the world are really trouble makers. On the basis of helping others they have, in fact, brought more negative and detrimental energy to the situation and should have left it alone. Just like the monkey who sees a fish struggling in the water and helps the fish by placing it in the tree. The white, Anglo-Saxon, Protestant, German, English American has been on a rampage over the past 100 years on the pretext to improve the world. Much that has been done is really at the expense of others. We have given the benefits of our culture, religion and technology to everyone who can afford it. We actually insist that they receive the benefits of this higher culture and society. Even our so-called Democracy is pushed onto other cultures. *"You better be democratic or we will shoot you!"* Having pushed this agenda so aggressively, and for so many years, we wonder why so many cultures hate us (America). Maybe because trying to do good for others or even good for oneself is amazingly destructive because its full of conceit.

How do you know what is good for other people? How do you know what is good for you? Especially if you don't know what comes before or after this life. You are just doing what you may be 'programmed' to do or think you know what is good or bad for yourself or others. When you say you want to 'improve' something you must know what you are improving. How do you know what you are doing is making a substantive improvement? What is the starting point and what is the finished goal? Sometimes we introduce an idea or concept into society that is intended to be beneficial when, in fact, it has the opposite effect. For Example: Monsanto has produced grain that is resistant to bugs, yet the downside of this process is that much of the regular grain now will not grow in the same soil. When we interfere with the process of nature such as growing manufactured plants and animals we will somehow, in the end, pay for it. We can see the eugenics-produced human beings are a horrible experiment on humanity. Perfection will eliminate all creativity and variety from this Earth. We need to leave well enough alone and let nature run its course and not interfere with it—because mother nature will come back one day and show you what karma truly is. An animal unto itself is virtuous, but when you put that animal into a crowded store of people it may become much less virtuous and just be a problem going on a rampage (e.g., bull in a china shop).

The most exquisite paradox:

"As soon as you give it all up – you can have it all...how about that one. As long as you want power – you can't have it. The minute you don't want power you'll have more than you ever dreamed possible. What a weird thing! As long as you have an ego you're on a limited trip."

-Baba Ram Dass

What may seem like a good idea today may not be so good of an idea tomorrow. We can easily see evil and heresy in people of societies retrospectively in the past, but we have trouble using these same 'critical set of eyes' to see the evil and heresy going on with societies in today's world. Today, people use different names and covers making it more difficult to identify the evil beneath. An idea may seem virtuous but, in reality, when you pull the curtain back, it is not. We see how evil it is…but we also have difficulty seeing it in ourselves. So beware of virtue. Ancient Chinese cultures say the highest virtue is not virtue at all and therefore really is virtue. The highest virtue is not aware of it virtuous quality. And lower virtue is so self-aware it is forced. Any ulterior motives are of or a lessor virtual quality.

When you breathe, you don't congratulate yourself for doing so. It is natural. Even though the act of breathing is 'virtuous' in its own right, we do not focus on it as doing a virtuous task. Some diabolical things are done and are packaged as virtue. A nation may convince its people that going to war is a righteous and virtuous undertaking while also convincing them that the enemy is really bad. Ironically, the other side feels the same way – just as righteous and virtuous in attacking and going to war with the other side. So who is right? Does it matter? Is there a right if it involves war? There will be a "plague on both houses." The 'moral' conclusion is that if you're aware of your own inner workings you can only try to go down the most virtuous path improving yourself as best you can even if you're surrounded by evil – and hope that everyone else will do the same.

Trying to improve things by tinkering with them or implementing many new laws and/or regulations will ultimately make things worse. In the same way, you cannot force righteousness or goodness onto others expecting them to be immediately reconditioned. This is a good guide to apply to relationships too. Our ego wants 'stuff' because we experience ourselves through other people's eyes. We want to be noticed, good, bad, or indifferent. Unfortunately, from being noticed, certain feelings of inadequacy, shame, embarrassment (or even pride) can knock our ego—and control much of our behavior. We want to look important, but what has ultimately suffered the most through all of this egotistical behavior is our relationships and family life, which are the things that can make us truly happy. Every human being is equally powerful to shape and create their own reality. You may ask, "If everybody is equal, how did some people gain so much more control and power over others?" In actuality, they did not grow or gain more power they just took it away from others. Nothing is lost. It is all redistributed (even monetary items) and as someone acquires more power/money others will lose that same amount of power/money. This is a direct inverse proportion equation.

The evolution that we are going through and experiencing now is a massive redistribution of power that favors the central government systems of the world. Central authorities have huge 'egos' and must feed them by taking our freedoms and power away from us. When the populace finally takes back possession of our lost power from our oppressive government then and only then, will we finally be free to move towards harmony throughout all mankind. To do this we must go back and 'reprogram' our ego-based belief and education systems to achieve a higher conscience for a better world.

"The things you own end up owning you."

-Tyler Durden

Illuminati (Occult)

BOOK 15

The "Illuminati" are a secret global organization of the most powerful and influential elite people in the world. You may have never heard of this organization per se or the individuals that control it for good reason, because it is hidden. They have existed and operated for centuries by maintaining secrecy and closely maintained family 'bloodlines.' They have influenced every one of us through conscious manipulation of every aspect of our lives (think "The Matrix"). They are a pervasive and corrupt fraternity whose sole purpose is to takeover and control all humankind by monitoring and regulating all aspects of our life. Some say that the Illuminati are controlled by G.O.D. (Gold - Oil – Diamonds). The Illuminati though does not call themselves the 'Illuminati' and are steadfast in not being identified by any name or any label. Although it may not have been called the Illuminati from the beginning, they have used the cover of many organizations and groups to affect and infiltrate our human conscience. Throughout history, many believe the elite have been associated with many groups such as The Knights Templars, The Freemasons, New World Order, Zionism,

Nazis, International Central Banking Interest, Oil Barons and Globalists. They set up many influential organizations such as The Council on Foreign Relations, The Bilderberg Group, The Club of Rome and the Tri-Lateral Commission and have infiltrated governments and regimes around the world. These groups, cumulatively, along with a few others, plan the fate of the world. They consist of International Bankers, top Government officials, leaders in world energy cartels and media monopoly owners and have control over the U.N., IMF, World Bank, U.S. military, Non-Government Organizations (NGOs) and many non-profit and charitable institutions. Their subdivisions reach into everyone's daily life without most people even being aware of it. They also manipulate all political parties, oversee the legal (pharmaceutical), illegal (heroin) drug trade and most federal agencies. They also have ties to the Masons, Skull and Bones and linkages all the way back to the Rosicrucians and the Jesuits. The ultimate goal is a one – world government, which they will control, along with a one-world currency and control and ownership of all land, property, resources and people. Finally, they want a one-world religion. This religion would be the 'State' whereby all citizens would look to the State for survival including all emotional, monetary and spiritual aspects of life.

Some who are familiar with the Illuminati will say that there is much evidence in the music, television and movie industry to indicate that the organization is very real, alive and current. Others will say that the Illuminati's power and influence has waned over time and has no real power or importance at this time. What many have witnessed is the 'pawns' of the real Illuminati who really don't go by or use any names to describe themselves. They are hidden. The real Illuminati use talented people in many industries to further the cause and establish a foothold in the consumerism of most of the Western worlds. Very well-known musicians and especially rappers today will flash Illuminati occult symbols at their adoring fans and they will regard these famous idols as the king and queen of Illuminati music, when, in fact, they are, literally, the figure heads to push the agenda. The reason they place the symbols in just about everything including videos, movies, advertising, and television shows using hand gestures or pyramids is to bring certain conscious attention to them to create a negative energy. The use of pentagons (stars) is clearly evident too. They harness this negative energy using modern technology and high-tech equipment since this works best to disseminate the message. They are paid tons of money, provided riches beyond belief and are held on a pedestal for this allegiance to the order and they get all of this for one 'small' price...their soul. These people among many others in the music, sports, movie and media complex are not the real elite powers or Illuminati. They are the 'front men' or the face to send out the message. It is no different than our 'puppet' presidents and politicians who are used to push political agendas.

What do we really know about our ancient history of the world? Have historical events been accurately told in our history books? Could there be a hidden history that has been kept from us in order to control and suppress people and knowledge? Could there have been a highly advanced civilization that once flourished on this planet long before recorded history and is it possible that elite global powers of today would like to 'restore' that high, lost culture in the form of a New World Order? Much evidence of the once-banished advanced civilization are fragmented all over the world and has been uncovered through writings, artifacts and most compelling the many monolithic structures that have survived over thousands of years such as the Pyramids of Giza. As farfetched as it may sound, perhaps there is a master plan in place to resurrect the great 'work of the ages' pursued by contemporary, modern, secret societies that involve a covert agenda to revitalize an ancient, occult, totalitarian order designed to once again reduce human population into a subservient role.

By tracing the origins of contemporary, secret societies and occult organizations we discover that there is a correlation between Free Masonry, Illuminati, Zionism (and even Nazis) and these groups derive much of their mystical lore from one common source, Babylonian Occultism. Could it be there is a master plan to resurrect this ancient occult high culture once again? Though, just because something is labeled as "Occult" does not mean it is necessarily 'evil' in nature. The word occult is derived from the Latin word 'occultus' which means hidden or clandestine. The occult understand many secret things and it is in the interpretation and whether the motivation of the actions is to be used for good or evil. Going back centuries the Occult has suppressed knowledge and technology such as mercury based flying machines and the destructive "Brahmastra" weapon that completely decimated whole civilizations with a flash of fire (which sounds like our modern-day atomic and nuclear bombs). It appears that there has been a meticulous secret operation to preserve the arcane knowledge of the science of the past civilizations with the intention to resurrect it again as a modern society 'dressed' as a modern utopia. It is from the area known as Mesopotamia (the Tigris and Euphrates Valley) which is the cradle of civilization that the origins of contemporary human history can be traced with the rise of Sumer which was a real, established and amazingly sophisticated human society that seemed to materialize from nowhere. The elite have knowledge about special physical phenomenon such as ley lines, numerology and ancient cultures and civilizations. These ancient civilizations have knowledge of "star gates," the use of certain shapes and also performing certain acts/rituals to gain access to the higher state of awareness. Knowledge has been passed down from the ancient cultures whereby the Illuminati (secret societies) have kept (hidden) to themselves for control over the masses.

There is a hidden hand working behind the scenes of all these unapparent and unconnected elite organizations as they advance the agenda (very quietly) for one world government, one world central bank, one world currency, one world army and a "micro chipped" population that has been systematically reduced to a manageable number. It is done secretly — because if it was done openly (and knowingly) then all the populations of the world would be rebelling in the streets. What is the truth of the secret society? Starting at the time of Babylon, Egypt and through to present history the societies have an unbroken span of manipulation. The Sumerians, 2500 B.C., were an intelligent and elite group who used secret knowledge that has been passed down very carefully. It seems incredible, but the fact is, that secret societies have been at the forefront of many agendas that affect our conscience for centuries. Most people who participate do not see, or are not consciously a willing part of the master agenda. The structure is that a very few people control this 'web'. The secret is now opening before our eyes through hidden clues placed there for the people (who are paying attention) to see and understand the secret knowledge. Ancient knowledge, if let out into the public, would empower all people and that would be detrimental to the controlling elite.

According to ancient legend, the advanced agriculture, architecture and science are attributed to teachings from extraterrestrials called the Annunaki. The Annunaki, which some define as "those who from heavens came" are the ones that came to Earth a long time ago and are the ones who are written about as 'Gods' in many texts.

Many believe these Annunaki are reptilian in nature. The Sumer or Sumerian civilizations evolved into the Empire of Babylon. The word "Babylon" means the "Gateway of the Gods." Babylon is the birthplace of all science, astronomy and alchemical sorcery better known as Kabbalah. One of the main objectives of Babylonian 'Maji' or magic is mastery over "Materia Prima" which is Latin and translates as the very fabric of time and space.

It is this type of hidden knowledge that the Illuminati elite have possessed and have integrated into their symbols of modern day. The modern day 'cabal' is more than just one group and comprises members of the three 'sister' organizations: the Council on Foreign Relations, the Central Intelligence Agency and The Military Industrial Complex who together have become a shadow government—of not only the United States, but much of the Western world. The goal is World Government control comprised of international entity members to form a cartel of people who are elected by no one and accountable to no one (stateless).

The esoteric knowledge exhibited in many of the stone masonry structures of the Sumer and Babylonian give clues of the knowledge and sacred geometry that these ancient cultures possessed. The "Mystery School" used these core teachings of sacred geometry and incorporated them into the design of buildings that enabled them to function as energy centers of the cosmos. At the beginning of the 6th century B.C., a large portion of the Jewish population was conquered and exiled into Babylon by King Nebuchadnezzar where they would remain for half a century. During this exile, a faction of the Jews adopted the Babylonian system of magic and sorcery rejecting the God of the Old Testament and embracing the forbidden knowledge of pagan Babylonian mysticism (known as Kabbalah). This Babylonian Magic was delivered directly from the Annunaki into the awaiting hands of the original 'priesthood classes.' The purpose of the secrecy was that this occult mysticism had the ability to control humans and keep them in perpetual ignorance and for good reason; because if the general population was aware of this, they would not be so easily controlled. The priesthood acted as proxies to the Annunaki so they could influence the course of human history or (more accurately) disconnect us from our true origins and knowledge thereof.

From here, over time, the Jewish Kabbalah was spread over new territories and infiltrated new cultures. One group that was the recipient of the mystical information was the original Jesuits.

Jesuit founder Ignatius Loyola was born of Jewish blood in the Spanish Basque country around 1491. He became acquainted with a group called the "Alumbrados" which was an emerging occult movement created by Spanish "Marranos" which were baptized Jews who secretly kept their Talmudic faith. Alumbrados is translated as the 'illuminated ones.' These illuminated ones were a heretical secret society of gnostic mysticism formed by people of noble blood who believed a person's soul could reach a state of perfection in a union with God in their present life and upon attaining this state could commit any immoral or criminal act without staining their souls.

If you go back far enough you can see how societal control and manipulation was started originally by the Knights Templar. History would have you believe that the Templars were a somewhat docile group of Military men and religious crusaders, but the truth is quite the contrary. Aside from creating some of the very first money lending and banking institutions, many of the Templar legends are connected to the Order's early occupation of the _Temple Mount_ in Jerusalem and speculation about what relics the Templars may have found there, such as the _Holy Grail_ and the _Ark of the Covenant_.

It is rumored that nine French crusaders (The Knights Templar) used a cover story for searching for something in Jerusalem; they found the Holy Grail which was either a chalice or a piece of cloth from Christ. This was supposed to give great power. There are also rumors that they acquired (stole) all of King Solomon's gold too. The Templars soon had gained so much wealth and power that it would use its force and coercion to gain an even stronger foothold in leading, controlling and issuing money even to governments. The Templars originating in France were brought to justice due to the 'secrecy' of their organization—and monopoly of controlling the money (think Federal Reserve). Most Templars were killed. A very few survived and made their way to Scotland and re-formed to become the (contemporary) Scottish Rite. The Scottish Rite created and expanded its control by forming lodges and spreading across the land. The more modern version of this is the Freemasons which are responsible for carrying the secrets and knowledge forward from the ancient times to modern times.

"The new Atlantis set forth an ideal Government of the Earth. It foretells that day when in the midst of men there shall rise up a vast institution composed of philosophic elect an order of illuminated men banded together for the purpose of investigating the laws of life and the mysteries of the universe..."

"The age of boundaries is closing, and we are approaching a nobler era when nation shall be no more; when the lives of race and caste shall be wiped out; when the whole Earth shall be under one order, one government, one administrative body."

-Manly P. Hall

Francis Bacon was an English philosopher who was to colonize the new Atlantis (America) with specific 'design' instructions from Queen Elizabeth I. But first she sent him to France to study science, language and high culture from the Knights of the Helmet. The French started improving language and Bacon observed this and wanted to do the same for England and the English language before going to America. The Knights of the Helmet were an interesting group that had secrets, cosmic knowledge and esoteric understanding of the universe. Legend has it if you wore the 'Helmet' of the Goddess of Athena you became invisible. Also, when Athena and Apollo 'shook their spheres' it represented a ray of light of wisdom; the ray of light of wisdom would be directed at the dragon of ignorance. Bacon was 'dramatically' influenced by this esoteric knowledge and teachings so he dedicated the remainder of his life, to the spread of culture, but also to understand some of the more powerful knowledge and hidden wisdom. His 'cosmic' event empowered him to create brilliant theatrical writings in order to progress and teach the English people and transform them into a nation that one day could dominate the world as an educated force. At one point, a heavenly voice told him in a dream to write behind the identity of a William Shakespere. This actually made perfect sense – since it was Athena and Apollo's "spere that was shook" at ignorance to translate into the word 'Shakespeare.' Note: The double 'A' Header for Apollo and Athena grace many of Shakespeare works. The double 'A' is shaded to show the light and dark sides of things and also shows 'both' worlds of Bacon and Shakespeare. Bacon eventually brought 20,000 new, revised and modified words to enhance the English language back to England and eventually on to America. The real Shakespeare of Stratford England could not write or even sign his name properly. Bacon had knowledge of the "courts," the "intrig of the law" and also the depth of language and words to write those amazing plays. This of course is not intended to prove William Shakespeare never existed. The Stratford actor's name and identity was used as a screen. It sounds preposterous because after all, who wouldn't want to take credit for such brilliant and gifted works - and writings...right? Shakespearian productions stamp their creator as one of the Illuminati of the ages — the plays possess both the secret teachings of the fraternity of the Rosicrucians and the 'true rituals' of the Freemasonic order, Bacon knew the true secrets – and revealed this knowledge in ciphers and cryptograms through his works.

"The Greatest strength of our order lies in its concealment; let it never appear in any place in its own name, but always covered by another name, and another occupation. None is fitter than the three lower degrees of Freemasonry; the public is accustomed to it, expects little from it, and therefore takes little notice of it."

-Adam Weishaupt

About two hundred years after Ignatius, Adam Weishaupt, a young Jewish boy of Ingolstadt, Bavaria was turned over to the Jesuits when his father passed to be raised and educated. A teacher named Calmer Joachim Levy, a Danish Cabbalist Jew, introduced Weishaupt to the secrets of "Osiris magic" and the Kabbalah. Weishaupt chose the Egyptian pyramids as the Illuminati symbol of power and he is believed to have been recruited by Mayor Rothschild of the Rothschild Banking dynasty to head up an occult group called the "The Hermatic Order of the Golden Dawn" with allegiance to Osiris, the Age of Aquarius and the New Atlantis. On May first 1776, Weishaupt founded his own Bavarian version of the secret society called the Illuminati and started infiltrating Masonic lodges and the Grand Orient for members. Because the nature of the organization was so diabolical in the Global takeover of the world (Novus Ordo Seclorum) at some point after some documents of the organization's plans had been taken and made public, Weishaupt took the group 'underground.'

The great strength of the order was its concealment and that it would never appear in its own name, but always covered by another name or occupation. The New Order of the Ages (or New World Order) had begun its final assault on the Americas which is a global program for world domination to be achieved by the abolition of all national governments, the abolition of inheritance, abolition of private property, abolition of patriotism, abolition of the individual home and family life, and abolition of all religions so that the Luciferian ideology of totalitarianism may be imposed on mankind. The Illuminati used occult ritual techniques in order to manipulate the collective social consciousness to covertly gain power for its evil practitioners from the life force energy of the unsuspecting masses. After Weishaupt stepped down, Giuseppe Mazzini an Italian 33rd – degree Mason, the father of the Mafia, came into power and soon after appointed America's Albert Pike as

Sovereign Pontiff of Universal Free Masonry and coordinator of the Illuminati in America. Pike was known as a Tennessee Ku Klux Klan; judicial officer and a satanist. Pike used the "KKK" as a tool to keep blacks out of Masonic lodges. This was the beginning of the modern era of the Illuminati.

The Illuminati outlined a future blueprint for "three world wars" whereby each war having the specific purpose of gaining 'more and more' control. With each conflict bringing the occult ruling class one step closer to their ultimate goal of totalitarian conquest by use of advanced weapons technology spawned by both American and German scientists during the Second World War.

"Since I entered politics, I have chiefly had men's views confided to me privately. Some of the biggest men in the United States, in the field of commerce and manufacture, are afraid of something. They know that there is a power somewhere so organized, so subtle, so watchful, so interlocked, so complete, so pervasive, that they better not speak above their breath when they speak in condemnation of it."

— Woodrow Wilson

People believe so forcefully that their 'just' ideas (laws/rules/guidelines) are correct that they are willing to hurt, disgrace and discredit other individuals who may not believe or are not aware of the situation. This is basic social programming. It is hard to attentively concentrate on any counter argument when the social programming has gone mainstream. At the same time, real knowledge and wisdom had to go underground to be protected by the elite.

"Anger and revenge are like a hot piece of coal. You're the one getting burned while you hold it waiting to throw it at someone."

-Anonymous

The people who created the State of Israel, Lord Rothschild, "Father of Modern Israel," and other elite families are the people who created Zionism. They are the same elitists who also created communism in Russia, Nationalist Socialism (Nazi Germany) and have been pushing for Socialism here in the United States. It is important to point out that the word "Nazi" is the combination of the word Nationalist and Zionism, not Socialism as you have been told. When you realize how sinister and serious these elite people are you will have a better understanding that any person who threatens them or their agenda must be dealt with harshly. The more powerful you are in going against the elite, the more severe the reaction. It was therefore essential to maintain control in America by eliminating threats such as Malcolm X, Martin Luther King, Jr. and the assassinations of President John F. Kennedy and Robert F. Kennedy to continue and ensure their control. The following is a powerful speech given by President Kennedy in April of 1961, before the American Newspaper Publishers Association:

"The very word 'secrecy' is repugnant in a free and open society; and we are as a people inherently and historically opposed to secret societies, to secret oaths and secret proceedings. We decided long ago that the dangers of excessive and unwarranted concealment of pertinent facts far outweigh the dangers which are cited to justify it. Even today, there is little value in ensuring the survival of our nation if our traditions do not survive with it. And there is a very grave danger that an announced need for increased security will be seized upon those anxious to expand its meaning to the very limits of official censorship and concealment. That I do not intend to permit to the extent that it is in my control. And no official of my Administration, whether his rank is high or low, civilian or military, should interpret my words here tonight as an excuse to censor the news, to stifle dissent, to cover up our mistakes or to withhold from the press and the public the facts they deserve to know."

"For we are opposed around the world by a monolithic and ruthless conspiracy that relies on covert means expanding its sphere of influence – on infiltration instead of invasion, on subversion instead of elections, on intimidation instead of free choice, on guerrillas by night instead of armies by day. It is a system which has been conscripted vast human and material resources into the building of a tightly knit, highly efficient machine that combines military, diplomatic, intelligence, economic, scientific and political operations."

"Its preparations are concealed, not published. Its mistakes are buried not headlined. Its dissenters are silenced, not praised. No expenditure is questioned, no rumor is printed, no secret is revealed."

"No President should fear public scrutiny of his program. For from that scrutiny comes understanding; and from that understanding comes support or opposition. And both are necessary. I am not asking your newspapers to support the Administration, but I am asking your help in the tremendous task of informing and alerting the American people. For I have complete confidence in the response and dedication of our citizens whenever they are fully informed."

"I not only could not stifle controversy among your readers – I welcome it. This Administration intends to be candid about its errors; for as a wise man once said: "An error does not become a mistake until you refuse to correct it." We intend to accept full responsibility for our errors; and we expect you to point them out when we miss them."

"Without debate, without criticism, no Administration and no country can succeed – and no republic can survive. That is why the Athenian lawmaker Solon decreed it a crime for any citizen to shrink from controversy. And that is why our press was protected by the 'First Amendment' – the only business in America specifically protected by the Constitution – not primarily to amuse and entertain, not to emphasize the trivial and sentimental, not to simply "give the public what it wants" –

but to inform, to arouse, to reflect, to state our dangers and our opportunities, to indicate our crises and our choices, to lead, mold educate and sometimes even anger public opinion."

"This means greater coverage and analysis of international news – for it is no longer far away and foreign but close at hand and local. It means greater attention to improved understanding of the news as well as improved transmission. And it means, finally, that government at all levels must meet its obligation to provide you with the fullest possible information outside the narrow limits of national security..."

"And so it is to the printing press – to the recorder of man's deeds, the keeper of his conscience, the courier of his news – that we look for strength and assistance, confident that with your help man will be what he was born to be: free and independent."

-John F. Kennedy

The power elite control our thoughts and actions. You will hear the same phrases in the news every night to scare us: 'If' an all-out war begins or 'If' they drop the bomb or 'If' they have nuclear capability. The fact is, that there is already an "all-out war," going on in America and it is on the American people. This war has been waged a long time ago. By saying an all-out war, it really means a 'total' war and not just a military war. Many of us are so used to thinking of war the old-fashioned way with guided bombs and sophisticated weaponry. World War III will be fought as a mind war, political war, economic war, food war, oil war, psychological war, spiritual war and may also be a nuclear war. But the military aspect is the least of concern. The only real military wars we have now are the 'guerilla' type whereby Special Forces go in to other countries and start a situation of social chaos, upheaval and unrest to create a condition, conducive for the elite few with power, using small groups of organized trained revolutionaries or insurgence. Most of these military campaigns would never succeed unless they were also waged along with manipulation and brainwashing of the general population by the news media to give the impression that there is support behind these aggressive movements. Weapons of socialist/communist conquest are not weapons of mass destruction, but enter propaganda as a slanted view of history. The preaching of hatred of a particular sector or groups to insight civil disorder has been used as a tool to control the way populations think. The tactics of subversion, threats of blackmail, political assassinations are all connected by soldiers that wear no uniform. Most of the "mind war" that has been used since WWII is based on the psychology of complete destruction.

People like Saul Alinsky, a 'counter culture' community organizer in Chicago who wrote <u>Rules for Radicals</u>, espoused psychological warfare on society and was a master of dividing people rather than bringing them together. He used the method of dividing people through driving wedges into any cracks in the system via race, income, age and gender. It comes as no surprise, Hillary Clinton and Barack Obama were both 'students' of the Alinsky teachings.

Things will happen, as the elite say it will happen, however, things currently are happening so rapidly in the world that the elite have been taken back (surprised) by this fast pace. They will have to accelerate their agenda to 'keep up' because so many people are waking up at this time. The 'real' news is getting out there (via the Internet) to the point it is even frightening them. The elite have planned everything behind closed doors. The elite are also getting older and are concerned about their children's welfare even though they are the ones that have caused the turmoil. The elite do have a "Code of Ethics" not like in the Bible and not like a regular moral person either, but a code whereby one of the facets is to 'tell the world' about everything they are going to do or what will happen before they do it. If the average person looks, he or she will find clues or buzzwords. The elite may use a movie to tell you what they are going to do. They use Hollywood and newspapers (*NY*

Times, Washington Post) to plant articles and national news stories using buzzwords to plant and provide hidden information (or not so hidden).

America is the only nation on Earth that could turn this around. We still have our freedoms, our independence and our guns which are more than most countries have. When America is pushed to a breaking point, it will revolt. But we need not be violent. Noncompliance is the best approach; the middle way. We are the only hope, the last frontier, and the last stand for the entire world. We must be strong. The elite are not God—they just might think they are. We have the numbers. The elite are working toward a date for the collapse of all world currency. They have put it in writing to tell us in advance. Unfortunately, the United States is broke—fiscally, morally and intellectually. The classifications of people are as follows: the very top elite; the supreme wealthy (not really a part of the controlling elite); then you have the wealthy; then the upper middle class; middle class; and the poor lower class.

They are not destroying anything; they are taking over and gathering assets. The gold and silver price for precious metals is 'slammed' intentionally for two reasons:

1) They hope to scare the small investor out of the raw gold market.
2) They don't want you to see the correlation between gold and real money. (Less than 1% of Americas own gold or silver printed before 1933 which is non-confiscation).

The economy will be 'crashed' deliberately in order to push the population of the world into such a state of desperation that they will ask for a new financial solution. The global elite will offer a solution with a one-world currency, controlled unfortunately by the same malicious oligarchs that caused the 'crash' in the first place.

After the economic crash, the globalists will be looking to fully implement The United Nations Agenda 21 by the likes of David Rockefeller, Maurice Strong, Henry Kissinger and George Soros. It was originally the Rockefellers who fathered the United Nations which is the epitome of a globalist organization. The ultimate goal of the globalists is to have a one-world government, a one world currency and a one world religion (the state) and they will stop at nothing to achieve this goal. In addition, other goals they have are to reduce the world's population to a manageable level and collapse the modern industrial world.

"Yet the individual is handicapped by coming face to face with a conspiring so monstrous he cannot believe it exists. The American mind simply has not come to a realization of evil which has been introduced into our midst."

-J. Edgar Hoover

The Illuminati are by no means strangers to controlling world events. In fact, they have done so for centuries. From the shadows they have engineered every major war, revolution and recession. They control everything you read, eat, hear and see. They have managed to indoctrinate an entire population to their way of thinking or how they want you to think about certain people and issues. They have infiltrated key positions of authority and it is from the 'shadows' that they have created a new political order, a new economic order and a new religious order. The ultimate aim is total global control/domination and they will stop at nothing to reach their goal.

"Some even believe we are part of a secret Cabal working against the best interests of the United States, characterizing my family and me as internationalists...and conspiring with others around the world to build a more integrated global political and economic structure — one world if you will. If that's the charge then I state that I am guilty and I am proud of it."

—David Rockefeller

The elite have created a totalitarian state built on egotism and material goods. They fulfill desire through Wall Street pedaling debt and mass consumerism. It has been an incredibly effective form of control that has convinced the masses to love their servitude. Somehow the system will get the populace to love it and go along with its own enslavement because the masses would be so 'doped up' and distracted and regimented that they would not even know they were being controlled. Consumer society with handouts going back to the 1960s with food stamps and FDR of the "New Deal"(and social security) and gave rise to credit cards in the 1970s with cheap accessibility to debt. All of this is coming to a head. It is mathematically becoming impossible to continue the debt and credit system, but society has managed to go along with it because for some reason people still respect authority and obey because they are afraid to do otherwise.

One of the most sensitive and taboo societal subjects is child pornography. There is a visceral reaction to it. Even the most hardened incarcerated criminals get impassioned about this subject and will ostracize their fellow inmates if they are guilty of this offense. Child pornography has been 'sold' to us as the most horrible and depraved human behavior and usually remains concealed at all cost on a very secretive level. Yet, it is practiced by many elite secret societies. The purpose is to show power and control over another individual. In the eyes of the secret society member, what better way to 'rule' over another than to take from them one of the most cherished gifts, their innocence. In the past it, was also a known practice of secret societies to actually sacrifice (kill) a young virgin and use the blood ceremonially. This, again, evokes great power and creates much 'dark energy' to the order. It is sacred to these organizations that this all remains hidden. Exposure of this usually means death. What really lies at the core of this? That the act is so horrible that most people understand that it is "off limits" for the average person, but if you're elite you are above the 'law' and literally free to – *"do as thou wilt."* Famed occultist, Aleister Crowley, who is said to be the 'Wickedest Man on Earth" and a firm occult believer—believed in these types of practices and partook in child pornography, bisexual relationships, recreational drug experimentation and Satanic worship. His influences are evident in British popular culture especially rock and roll bands of the sixties (e.g., Led Zeppelin) and there is a rumor that he is closely related to Barbara Bush, the wife of the 41st President of the United States.

Many modern occult teachings were presented originally by Madame Helena Blavatsky in her writings of the <u>Theosophical Society</u> and in <u>The Secret Doctrine</u> in the late 1800s. Blavatsky, of Russian decent, was an occultist, a spirit medium and an author of philosophical and esoteric teachings that investigated the unexplained laws of nature and the powers latent in man. Even today many occultists and satanists follow her teachings and continue to use various ancient symbols and symbolism that she outlined in her books including the swastika used by the German Nazis in the 1930s and 40s. The occult satanic symbolism is everywhere. You would not think that Satanic-Illuminati symbolism is being 'telegraphed' today, but it is prevalent in almost every hand gesture, every corporate logo and every social media symbol. By making the symbols omnipresent it places a lock on human consciousness. The elite have consumed our mind to get us to think a certain way and would like us to also believe they are so powerful that we are helpless and can do nothing about it. But like the Wizard of Oz, the 'man' behind the curtain…is just a man. No different than you or me. The only difference is the knowledge the man possesses and the use of it to control those that can be controlled.

Reality is not really supposed to be this way. Please understand that your life should have far more joy and far less conflict. The propaganda machine produces people to promote an agenda and just about anything you see or hear in the dissemination of information from authoritative sources is not true. It is all written and produced by professional liars and the amazing thing is that most of the people don't even know they are promoting the lies. They just want to be part of the majority so they don't stand out or 'buck' the trends of society.

Google along with YouTube, which it owns, are the most dangerous and secretive operation intelligence organization and strategic planning group of the New World Order. Google Earth literally has an eye on every building and intersection on Earth and can track anyone, anywhere, at any time. Google monitors all internet activity. I thought it strange that there were other websites at the beginning of the internet boom such as "alltheweb" and "Myspace" which looked better and did a great job when compared with Google and Facebook, yet a few years later just about all Internet traffic runs through these few sites. This is by design and has been structured this way by the government and the NWO.

Much information is disappearing on the internet too. It is important to save what you can since much of the information will not be available in the future. Most of the credible information that is vanishing is counter mainstream news that is truth. The 'powers that be' want to suppress any information that goes against the official 'script'. When we work at our jobs, pay our taxes, consume goods and services, deposit our paychecks in the bank, enroll in selected service, and apply for Social Security we are feeding the 'beast.' Ask yourself this question: Who took your freedoms away, Osama bin Laden or your own country (NDAA, Patriot Act)?

America is the new Atlantis... and will support the drive to control the world through the New World Order. America has always been destined to lead The New World Order's assault on humanity and Washington, D.C. is the epicenter of the occult and their symbols. In 1791, Pierre Charles L'Enfante, who was a French Freemason and architect, laid out the city streets and its buildings according to a specific plan and 'hid' certain occult geometry and many occult symbols in its design. The Pentagon (pentagram), the Washington Monument (obelisk) and the Capitol (lot 666) all have significant occult relevance. The exact location of these and other noteworthy buildings, including the White House in relationship to Albert Pike's Masonic Temple on Sixteenth Street, are all part of a specific layout design of the streets and intersections of Washington, D.C. Many of these buildings' locations form geometric patterns when connected with imaginary lines (including five and six pointed stars) which have deep occult power and meaning. When it comes to the layout of Washington, D.C., nothing was designed by accident with everything meticulously and specifically placed to harbor a certain negative, satanic energy over the city and the surrounding area.

Another very interesting and puzzling 'monument' is the Georgia Guidestones. The Georgia Guidestones, located in Elbert County, Georgia not far from Athens (and sometimes referred to as the "America Stonehenge,") is a granite monument erected in 1980 by an anonymous group/person named R.C. Christian which has inscribed messages of 'ten guidelines' (like the 10 Commandments) for future humanity in the New World. Engraved in eight different languages, including some of it written in Babylonian, Classic Greek, Sanskrit and Egyptian hieroglyphs, the messages inscribed into the large stones outlines that humanity (populations) shall be maintained under 500,000,000 people to be in perpetual balance with nature. Other guidelines cover uniting language, laws and other aspects of how humanity needs to be at balance with nature. Some of the guidelines sound reasonable, but we must look at 'who' is sponsoring the message and what the real meanings behind the writings are. Who really put this there and why? It seems clearly evident that the providers of "Guidestones" are also the providers of the New World Order. The one item that obviously stands out is the 'depopulation' of the world to be in sync with nature. Many agree that the world is overpopulated, and if we are to move forward in a harmonious world that overpopulation needs to be addressed. One would hope that with the awakening of our mass consciousness people around the world will become 'responsible' individuals and families and self-regulate the number of children being brought into the world.

The Denver International Airport (DIA), completed in 1995, was many years in the making, poorly located and 2 billion dollars over original budget and was brought to you by the New World Order. It is believed that the massive airport is a cover for an underground 'city' below which possibly could be used as a Central Government headquarters if Washington, D.C. is ever compromised or possibly something even more sinister. The airport is home to many unusual items such as runways shaped like swastikas, a Masonic dedication marker that mentions the "New World Order Airport Commission" (an organization that does not exist), 'creepy' apocalyptic murals painted by Leo Tanguma that foretell the world's future, an apocalyptic 32-foot tall horse statue "Blue Mustang" with red glowing eyes that actually killed its maker/artist Luis Jimenez by accident, and at least five high rise buildings that were built and then 'sunk' into the ground mysteriously. Some theorize that there is an underground tunnel from near Mineral, Virginia all the way to DIA that was designed as a "bug out" passage for the Washington elite. The CIA considered moving its headquarters to Denver at one time, and perhaps, at least in part this was done covertly when the airport was built.

Many awakened individuals could point fingers at certain groups they believe are the cause of all the problems and manipulation—Zionists, Bilderbergers, Council on Foreign Relations (CFR), International bankers, or The World Bank (or IMF), but the truth is that all of these entities are interrelated, possessing different mechanisms of societal control. Some speculate that the CFR is the most powerful organization of them all and the acronym

'CFR' really stands for Carnegie, Ford and Rockefeller and not Council on Foreign Relations. The fact is that neither Zionism nor any of the other organizations would exist in its current form without the 'medieval' politics fueling the intensity from the other supportive groups. It is all one system (network) integrated into the fabric of our society. Money, power and control are at the core. Like any criminal organization there are different levels of hierarchy of power within the pyramid, but all arms of the 'octopus network' connect to the 'body.' This conspiracy runs very deep and very wide and ties back to ancient Egypt and Babylon through generations of bloodline. This very old royal bloodline has 'interbred' with other elites that overtime have placed themselves in power positions of authority and have been able to maintain control. They have always ruled and controlled mankind during contemporary times with a hidden hand. The elite bloodline eventually aligned itself with the Bavarian Illuminati some 230 years ago to establish control that was headed to America.

These ruling elite classes are basically a secretive "Sun Cult." They worship and perform activities in relation to the sun god "Ra." They follow the sun, moon and the stars alignment during times of the year that provide energy. A little-known fact is that Christmas and Easter are solar cult holidays. Christmas aligns with the Winter Solstice and Easter with the Vernal Equinox. It is no coincidence that Jesus's birth and death align with these dates and that he was also the Son (Sun) of God. The word Israel is derived from three occult words of Isis, Ra and El from Canaan. These occult Sun worshipers have infiltrated and manipulated religion and certain religious beliefs as well as all other aspects of our life. They use religion to channel this energy to maintain control over this reality. Ideologically, the elite bloodline does share its goals with other non-blood elite. This network controls the world's resources by manipulation of the monetary system with central banks and global money supply. The fact is, we already have a one-world government and a one-world monetary system as mentioned in Biblical writings of end times. It is just hidden in the shadows through the world's covert systems.

Archeological evidence shows that there have been previous civilizations here on Earth. Some maybe even more technologically advanced than ours. Archeological evidence also shows us that a worldwide catastrophe has occurred several times, the most recent world catastrophe is the deluge with the flood of Noah. The deluge took place and has been recorded in many cultures some even going back before the Bible. The story exists with Native Americans so it is clear that this event occurred most definitely and encompassed the world. Evidence shows that an advanced culture and civilization was here before the deluge. During this catastrophe it appears technology was lost — but also wisdom, and an understanding of who we were through antiquity. What was lost were records and hardware of these people. It has been a long time and painstaking work to regain this technology. Keepers of the hidden cult now know this and have been attempting to control and regain this technology. This knowledge is power and the keepers of this hidden knowledge are the few controlling elite. These people understand that if you can control the emotions of the majority of the population, then you can control the entire species. With that you can, quite literally, control any reality you wish. They feed off this negative energy of reality in order to maintain it and perpetuate it. We must therefore understand our own potential, and seek to learn the true value of positive energy and vibration to counter these negative forces.

Secret societies have always played an important role in culture. At its core is the secret hand. This hand has manipulated, altered and directed our history to its own advantage and has very little to do with anything humanitarian, or national security, and mostly to do with money, control and power. The order of the Skull and Bones, at Yale University, is a platform for the world elite to be indoctrinated into the Illuminati. The problem with discussing this topic is that it so easily invites ridicule. It is very difficult for the general public to accept the fact that the super-rich leaders of the western world can be possibly as psychotic and deranged as they actually are. The public, generally speaking, are sensible level-headed people who need to balance their check books – so they inevitably tend to laugh at stories about secret societies, satanists or the occult. The elite have designed it this way and it aids them in their covert deception of what they are really doing. Historians will verify that throughout history that Secret Societies have played major roles in how history has been controlled and reported post conflict. Similar to the "Black Hand" of the Mafia where many believe this is all in the past, but corruption is very much alive and feeding off society today. When you analyze on a deeper level; you realize that between the "Dark Entities" and the "Skull and Bones" symbols that these elite people are really nothing more than pirates. They initially obtained money through their ancestors by being better thieves and criminals – better than the criminals who are behind bars.

At some point the judicial system can no longer police these people because they essentially own and control all aspects of society including the police and the courts. Those familiar with fraternal organizations can personally attest that keeping the activities of a secret organization secret is paramount. The secret societies will have its members do "unheard of and unspeakable things" (some sexual, including group masturbation) that can, and will be used in the future as leverage against anyone who steps out of the ranks or talks. This 'mark' is carried with you throughout your life as a reminder that your allegiance is to the order first and always. This mind trauma can obviously bring about psychopathic behavior later in life. Possibly the psychopathic behavior came first, but either way, it is with this 'breeding' that many of the world's future leaders are groomed and promoted to positions of power.

Clearly stated, if there are five people all qualified for a position and the person hiring is from a particular society, they will, in turn, choose the person with the same societal upbringing to ensure that they also can be depended on and controlled, if necessary, perhaps even to be a president. In the 2000 Presidential election, it was very interesting to see George W. Bush running against John Kerry, who were both members of "Skull and Bones" fraternity at Yale University — mention of which was 'severely' suppressed in the media during the election. So the illusion is that you had a choice to vote for either of two men that were white, connected, wealthy, Yale grads who were both in the same fraternity.

"Secret Societies have existed among all peoples, savage and civilized, since the beginning of recorded history...it is beyond question that the secret societies of all ages have exercised a considerable degree of political influence..."

-Manley P. Hall

HOLOGRAPHIC

BOOK 16

The entire universe and our existence here on Earth is a holographic projection which we all are a part of creating through our five senses. Quantum physics tells us that our reality is all conscience and there is no solidity to our existence and all matter is an illusion. This reality seems so real yet it is not. At one time in history many believed the Earth to be flat. Now we know better and the Earth is round. But we still have not progressed to the point of completely knowing what our true description of our existence is and have traded one set of false understanding for another.

Think about this: Your body is made up of atoms which look like 'mini solar systems' and these atoms consist of 99.99% empty space. And yet it is these mostly empty atoms that make up this seriously solid world both within you and around you. Each 'world' is a realm of millions of possibilities and at the heart of each atom is a magnificent amount of energy and power. This energy is consciousness. All that exists within this universe is consciousness. Conscience is pure energy and everything is a form of energy. Therefore everything is consciousness. If atoms are primarily 'empty space' the solidity of this world and our bodies is an illusion. This entire universe exists essentially as a hologram. The holographic nature of our existence is profound and significant. This means each atom could also be a microcosm of a seemingly endless universe. Could the universe we live in exist within the size of an atom?

Everything Is Energy...Energy Is Everything...

Society predicts that you're limited and that the solidity of the world around us is real, but this is a grand illusion. So, what makes this outward reality seem so real? We are expanding divisions in space. Space is real but the matter in the space is not. All matter is vibrational. You are vibrational energy. Even the Great Pyramids in Giza of Egypt were built to channel energy. The location and also the geometry are very specific. Each structure is like a book or a different learning experience of energy that one could tap into. The language of electromagnetism is the medium for the knowledge from these monolithic structures (a language of the heart). The 'powers that be' have painstakingly tried to withhold this sacred knowledge — to prevent us from accessing energy from these places and structures. These evil forces have trapped the energy and knowledge intended for all humanity – via the manipulation of our mind. Detaching human beings from our source of power through suppression of true knowledge, religion, patriotism, race, wealth and class has occurred.

We have established that atoms are 99.99% empty space. Therefore we can also conclude that solid matter does not exist. All physical matter is merely a product of perception. 'It is there' because human conscience perceives it to be there. This is what we are taught. If you gain insight into how reality works, you realize that it is all a holographic universe construct. Reality is a mathematical construct. But the complication is that the space between atoms is anything but empty. Even empty space is not truly empty—and is defined as a matrix as explained by 'Max Planck' and his, "Quantum Theory." He explains that each atom upon observation may be in one place—but they are moving, self-guiding entities that they are filling this entire field at any moment. A quantum hologram is essentially the mind of all matrixes. This is a conscience intelligence force that is the matrix of all matter. Perception of reality is influenced by what we see, touch, feel, hear smell, and taste. Perhaps our 'matrix' is a holographic projection and this could explain much of the unknown. The formula that exists is the foundation of everything. Quantum physics shows we can only assume there is an intelligent and conscience mind that makes up all matter. I am aware that I am one with the frequency of the universe and created in the divine holographic geometries of all. I am infinite light being capable of anything. I am strong enough to let go and patient enough to wait for what I deserve or want. I am not only human; I am much more. I am 'the works'! I am a water-based computer system who is having a human experience.

Quantum mechanics (physics) consists of entanglement particles which is a physical phenomenon that occurs when pairs or groups of particles interact in such a way as the quantum state of each particle cannot be described as independent. The system must be described as a whole. Smaller levels of the entangled particles somehow contain and transmit information yet without actual contact. Each object contains information about the entire entangled system; the only other structures that exhibit this phenomenon are called holograms.

Holograms are two-dimensional surfaces that show precisely detailed three-dimensional images and objects. To physicists, like Niels Bohr who pioneered quantum theory, this means that the universe before us could be one hologram. The great difficulty of science is that our understanding becomes increasingly abstract and can only be based on speculation. The discussions of the limits of science compared to the metaphysical which incorporates countless, spiritualist principles into quantum mechanics, as a support, exemplify how complicated our reality is and to which the naysayers' beliefs and the mainstream have been too quick to dismiss. Yet, we are made to believe there is 'conclusive' proof from science that our understanding in the world only applies to certain segments of reality. It should all apply to everything. We tend to draw conclusions about things—as opposed to inviting the possibility that our great advanced technology is indistinguishable from magic. As scientists move past the limits about our understanding of our reality - into a world where such things as teleportation as being possible and the entire universe being a hologram or holographic projection. We have to wonder if we have reached this point already. Our spirit is not from this Earth plane and we have chosen to come here to experience a life here on Earth, but more importantly to assist in the ascension of mankind. Picture this world. Dream it into being. I am a receiver and transmitter of higher dimensional communications—we are creator beings. We've had brief time periods of "Golden Rule" here on Earth whereby we experience incredible lives: peace and prosperity; love and kindness; joy and enlightenment; abundance and cooperation; service to others; unlimited health and well-being; ageless body and mind; telepathy and teletransportation.

We have the means to influence this field through our thoughts, emotions and our heart. What you think will influence this matrix (The Field) and will ultimately affect your reality. The art of positive thinking works in tandem with the electrometric magnetic fields that pulsate out from us. Our hearts are the strongest, magnetic field in our body—even more so than our brain. If you change the fields that those atoms are in then you change those atoms. When we have feelings in our heart, those emotions are changing the energy field of the physical world around us. If you change your self-esteem you will change your body. You are that amazing...

Your thoughts create the quantum possibility of what will happen. All scenarios of outcomes are "quantum possibilities" and what you think and what you believe influences the one that will play out for real. All the possibilities are already there and your thoughts choose which reality will be experienced. Our love (or fear) will bring that quantum possibility to this reality. All good or bad outcomes exist already. It is up to us to receive what we want as our reality. Self-esteem is very important and so is love—and confidence. It is a divine matrix. So when we wake up in the morning and see the news—fear sets in and we say "*I hope that doesn't happen to me,*" you will manifest that fear if you think, feel and respond emotionally to that negative situation. We live our lives 'as if' they, already happened and we invite this into our lives. The divine matrix field is the bridge between our inner and outer worlds, but we have been conditioned to feel or fear the things we don't want in life. The news and all media control us by controlling what we think and feel. The news tells you all the things you need to be afraid of. Why should we feel the things we don't want so much when we should be feeling the things we want to have—sync in with the positive vibration of what we want and don't focus on the alternate outcomes. Choose each moment of what you want and how you want it.

Most men suppress their inner feelings and emotions. Most Eastern cultures concentrate on thought, feeling and emotions—much more than Western cultures do. We breathe life into these thoughts. We tend to focus too much on the external, written words to feel power within ourselves when much of our inner power is untapped. When you ask others, "Do you feel you have the potential for so much more and we have not reached our full human potential (intellectually, physically)?" Most would say, "Yes." We have a feeling there is much more to us than what we are experiencing. We unfortunately need verification though the written word and our 2,000 year old text to predict how we are supposed to feel. The power is within you within your matrix and it has always been there. We just need to access our full potential. When thought and emotion become one, then you can 'move mountains.

You are that powerful—love can bring this feeling on and will provide for positive thoughts and emotions to our reality. Feeling is a language. Just by reciting a prayer or reading the words found in a book cannot give you the ultimate power or feeling.

Feelings are an entire language that have been suppressed by time and these innate feelings most physically account for how science explains everything. Compassion is a force that holds much of this matrix together. Compassion is a form of love. Having compassion for others and for yourself connects with the sub-conscious language of feelings. We have the ability to feel within our bodies and control the 'energy' that holds this universe together. By separating matter physically — you cannot separate them energetically. There is a bond, and there will always be a bond that exists. All particles of the universe are all part of one and have been slowly separating over time; many speculate that all world matter could fit into a ball (particle) no bigger than a pea.

'Is the external world a creation of our mind...?'

Everything you know is in your mind. The distance and the feeling of externality between you, other objects and people are also in your mind and a content of consciousness. The physical basis is all perceived. Are 'things' there if I am not witnessing them? Is anybody else really here or are you my entire personal dream?

Solipsists are people who believe they are the only ones in this world that exist and everything and everyone else is a product of their own creation. Question: How can a spiritual mind incarnate into a material body? Furthermore, what is the relationship between mind and matter — and is there a difference? When you start to differentiate between the two concepts on an analytical level you end up impoverishing both in that when you try to define or explain mind or matter alone, you are not able to explain either fully. Mind becomes vague because there is nothing tangible and matter just becomes mere 'stuff.' What enables us to make this transition is that any observation of anything must include the environment of which it exists in.

We have experienced a 'great forgetting' here on Earth. Man has been here for a very long time. Humanity could go back hundreds of thousands of years and man may have flourished in the past here on Earth for long periods of time. Our entire course of human history has been 'artificially' manufactured here on Earth and is largely due to the suppression of truth that we find ourselves today living within societies that are fractured. Destructive societies that are delusionary. If we investigate we can see how all educational and religious institutions are at its core misleading. That we are 'powerless people' and relatively insignificant is all lies. Each of us quite literally holds the key to the universe - a living library of information right here at our fingertips. We are not really spectators here. We are creating our own reality as well as others. This experience going on right now is the main event of creation and you are the participant. The macro-cosmos of the universe unites with the micro-cosmos with man himself and that which is above us in the heavens is also what resides within us in the human body (*As above, so below*) and all the quantum possibilities in between.

Together we are here participating in this creation at this time. We have a specific purpose — each one of us — to create this reality, perceive the experience and to gather knowledge. In order to achieve these tasks, we utilize thoughts, feelings and emotions. But the most powerful ability we have is our free will. Free will is the key that open the doors to understanding and knowledge. Free will provides us with choice and that choice controls the state of our consciousness. Freedom of choice decides which energy we want to put out there. It is this centered energy we choose to align ourselves with that goes into the 'collective consciousness' which we are all a part of. The free will of the collective conscious creates the reality that we live in each day. Our bodies are just vessels. It is what we see in the mirror — that is truly who, and what, we are as Quantum possibilities.

Listen to all, but follow none...

People want to ascend and achieve salvation without ever having to take responsibility for themselves or their actions. But this way of thinking possesses a problem. The problem is that no life lessons have been learned and there is no coming into a higher conscience of thinking. Even so, many of us see this as <u>not</u> a problem. That it is just the way things are. We are, in fact, allowing this to happen. In whose interest is it in to poison our food supply or to 'strip' our world of natural resources? Who is in charge? How do we harness this energy and control our holographic existence? Our holographic matrix is changing. At one time it was easier to control a million people than actually kill them? Yes, in the past it was, history tells us. But not today. Today it is easier to kill one million people than to contain them because of the shift in human consciousness. If the universe is a hologram, it suggests that there may be two significantly different levels to reality. The concrete reality we see when we look at buildings, furniture, trees, clouds and the other in how we see ourselves. Clouds are just one way that our reality manifests itself, but possibly on a much deeper level of reality where everything dissolves into an ocean of energy that's holographically inner-connected. Every portion of the universe is contained into a duplication of itself such that even the tiniest grain of sand possesses the same molecular structure (the atom) with the architectural structure of the universe. (*As above, so below*). A sand grain possesses all the information of the universe yet it only differs in size. The Earth is a large living body; we are a microcosm of the Earth and a sand grain is a microcosm of all things in creation.

Is there anything beyond the measurable confines of science? When science tells us there is nothing beyond a point (such as the end of the universe) they say it just stops there and there is nothing beyond which we can see. But that is simply not true. Everything is infinite. Science wants to quantify things and fit them into a box; to compartmentalize things, but that methodology just seems too easy and you're not really accounting for everything else. There is more to it when you start looking from a different perspective.

We are on the verge of a conscious evolution. Wars, terror, disease, corruption, central banking and religion are at the forefront. We need public awareness. We need to deal with all of these items but not with violence. Violence begets violence. The powers in charge want violence—they thrive on violence. It gives them energy, they want the polarized energy. The more people 'wake up,' the more the field is charged with positive energy and as more new energy is brought in the field the more will exponentially awaken through a peaceful rebellion and noncompliance. The powers that be understand that we also have power and a chance to ascend, but they want to control and try to hold us back.

Only conscious beings can be an observer. We are intentionally hooked into this reality and without us all of this would not exist. By use of our consciousness we create the things and events in front of us and thus no event can occur without our conscious involvement. Nothing definite is happening. Out of millions and millions of blobs of energy, light, photons, electrons that make up this imaginary 3-D world which doesn't exist at all according to the relativity of quantum mechanics, everything is occurring at once. Anytime we look at particles beyond a certain level the actual act of observation changes things. When you analyze this, you find that all matter dissolves because the particles are all vibrational energy. There are no objects anymore, only relationships. There is no locating and there is no "time" anymore.

The more you look at something in great detail, and you look at it as solid matter, the less and less it becomes solid. The only reality that we know is the one our brain manufactures. We create our own reality in the physical world and our mental one too. Our brain executes millions and millions of signals a minute and organizes them into a hologram (in our mind) which we, in turn, project outside ourselves – and call it reality. We are able to leap from one concept to another with the use of these holograms.

Holographic effects break down into simple numbers. Quantum physics explains that all matter is still 'joined' even when it becomes separated. The energy is still connecting it, and if we go back far enough in time we can trace back to a point where this expanding universe was originally just a small particle the size of a pea and through consciousness has expanded over time. All matter without the space/time relationship is nothing but a pea of energy of mass. That means all humankind is a part of each other. When we do harm to others, we (in essence) do harm to ourselves. The Parallel Universe Theory tells us that atoms exist in many states at one time. We are made of atoms so we therefore can exist multi-dimensionally and in many places at the same time. We can only contemplate one matrix at a time and that is how our DNA has been (re)designed.

Everything is connected and the biggest surprise of all is to the extent that individuality is an illusion. You actually create your own reality tunnel. All matter is just energy concerned by key vibrations and one consciousness experiencing itself subjectively. We must relate to the space between things since this is the connection to all mater. The 4th density (dimension) is 100 times more harmonious to us than our existing 3rd density (dimension) of life on Earth. Graduation into 4th density involves having at least a 51% service to others and this can be achieved by our mental conscience. The best way to service others is to love them and be there for them unconditionally.

To observe something, anything, takes conscious effort from an observer. For example: To observe the habits of a bird the bird doesn't know you're looking: but when the bird knows you're looking you are no longer observing you're interacting (interfering). The goal, ultimately, is to observe without interference. To really watch something it must not know you're looking. Try to observe yourself without you knowing or realizing that you are observing yourself. You would be able to see yourself as you really are, but this really can't be done. The ability to separate the two is virtually impossible and may only be achieved through a higher level of conscious awareness not part of our Earthy abilities.

There is an inseparability of man and his world. Does a tree falling in the forest make a noise if no one is there to hear it? Does a rainbow exist if there is no one there to see it? Does there need to be a neurological entity to receive the information (per these metaphors) for it to be there and exist? We believe that we are the 'ones' at this center of the universe and everything else is a part of it. So an ant is just an ant. Yet the ant also has its own ant universe. Whereby, it has its own world, concerns and conscience that contributes (albeit a small version) to the collective conscience of all creation. When we think of creation we narrowly focus in on our version of the universe. We never view it from another entity's perspective. It is fascinating to think that an ant's universe is really a sub-layer of the entire universe and just as important to them as ours is to us. Perhaps we are living in an ant's universe just as anything can be the center of the universal construct. Are we stuck in an 'ego centric' predicament that we are at the center of all of this? The holographic construct makes rational sense in how we can explain 'us' and our relationship to the universal world.

DNA

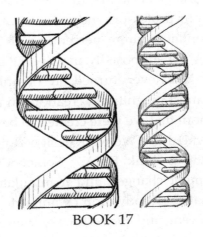

BOOK 17

Our DNA has been disconnected. Yes, disconnected. It is believed that the true nature of our DNA is a 12–stranded molecular structure that resides in our chromosomes of the cell nucleus, yet only a 2–stranded double helix is connected (presently). There are 64 combination sequences of 'codons' (codes) to our DNA structure that contain carbon, oxygen, hydrogen and nitrogen. We should have all of our codes 'hooked up' but typically we only have 20 of these 'turned on.' Humans, at one time, were operating on all twelve strands before the disconnection which means we are supposed to have 5 additional 'double helices' pairs 'lit' and all of our 64-code sequences activated. Imagine how amazing, beautiful and powerful our human capabilities would be in our fully connected form.

Our DNA contains all the knowledge and information of the universe. We are essentially the universe viewing itself from within. This disconnection causes a limiting of the full capacity of our minds and our connection to the higher realms. So the question is, who or what disconnected our DNA and why? And, if this is true, what would it be like to have all our strands of DNA connected?

To answer these questions, first we must look at what we have been told by our professors and our science books. They claim that our bodies contain a large percentage of 'shadow' or 'junk' DNA. "Junk DNA" is supposedly inactive DNA that has always been in our bodies yet never 'turned on' or utilized. The human body is one of the most magnificent creations in the universe and it is very hard to fathom that we were created to be anything less than what we were intended for. We were designed perfect. The fact is, there is no such thing as "junk' DNA." 'Somebody' at some point in our early development changed and manipulated the codes. The reason for this is that somebody didn't want us to know. If really we knew how magnificent and powerful we were meant to be and what our true connection to the universe was, there would be no controlling us. It is thought the entity that manipulated our early development is the same entity, a long time ago, that 'filled' one of the 'voids' in the creation of the Earth.

Since the Earth is a free-will zone and a living library of information, these malevolent beings thought that "Man" was best suited to take a subservient role here on Earth and be used to physically cultivate and work the land. Originally, man was here to find monatomic gold which is a very rich and exotic substance that has 'mystical properties' and 'magical powers' including healing telepathy and many other spiritual uses. These entities that controlled us are thought to be called the Annunaki or what many have come to be known as the Reptilian Gods. These 'Gods' are the same entities that are mentioned throughout the Bible and have been prophesied in many ancient cultures through writings and drawings.

We can activate and stimulate our higher DNA codes by knowing ourselves and asking for the connection. Physical reality is a conscious program created by these digital codes. These numeric codes define our existence. Our genetic memory is encoded to be triggered by digital codes at specific times and frequencies. If you ask to have your DNA connected, then this will trigger an awakening process whereby you are simulating an antenna that will 'start' to receive transmissions that will evolve human consciousness. Simply by 'wakening up' you are starting to reconnect your DNA. But you must ask for it. This will not happen if you are merely a spectator. Each day you must ask for your DNA to be reconnected. You will be amazed at what happens and how quickly those hidden aspects of your 'being' will be brought 'to the surface' for more transmissions and awakening. The truth is hidden deep inside of us. It is up to you, and you only, to free it during this lifetime.

We do not have to leave the Earth to be in the 5th dimension...and we can still have our life here and our memories. We just need to wait to 'shift' in unison with the Earth and all our past memories will be within us. If we have incarnated consciously from birth to death - memory transfer remains in cellular form in our DNA and surfaces when they are activated by certain triggers recalling these memories stored in the subconscious of our brain. We have 12 strands of DNA that correlate to multidimensional reality or 5th dimensional reality. We do need to eliminate all our past 3-D negative programming (old negative programming is brought to the surface of our consciousness and there we evaluate and make the decision to change these thoughts) we deal with those changes in thoughts as we become ascended beings here on Earth.

Therefore (to a certain degree) you can control your DNA activation. Individuals with negative fear-based consciousness are either unable, or unwilling, to ascend and prevent DNA activation connection. Low frequency fear-based reality is very strong (solid) and it sometimes takes an event or an "ah-ha" moment to get these reactivated. Low frequency individuals cannot be helped, healed, or regain a major connection to the higher realms unless DNA activation is stimulated. Some can ascend on their own if they walk in harmony with the ascending Earth pattern. This is done by working on your consciousness and being aware of the collective ascension of humanity. Our personal emotions have a huge impact on our individual lives. We can do this by helping others, but first we must help ourselves.

We are the designers and creators of this universe. Our highest vibration counterpart (ourselves) or future selves have created all this. There is no ability above us in that when we fully ascend we are the true light source of the universe and we are one. We are everything and everyone. All thoughts exist within us. But we are currently in a '3-D world' and exist on linear time so when we think of knowing the future it seems like a power or ability above us – but we have chosen to come here to assist humanity in the 3rd dimension. Understand we have wonderful abilities encoded in the knowledge that is already within us. Did we create ourselves? Yes. On the highest level of truth we created ourselves, but we also created others since we are all one related energy. When we say 'others' it is because here on Earth we can only think and relate to things in linear time. We are all amazing and we are all one…

Those others are just 'you.' From a higher density of existence which is the future (we created ourselves). Our ability is truly limitless when we lift the perception of limits from our consciousness then in fact we are limitless! But if you believe in limits then you will have limits. We manifest what we think.

Can we do anything we want? Yes! Then what guides us to which is the right and just way? It's our inner feelings and inner knowing. Intuition is at the heart of these inner feelings and must be in alignment with energies of light. The human mind must be used in balance with all of nature. When this occurs, the DNA becomes activated, and one can communicate with archetypes or angels from a higher consciousness and extraterrestrial civilizations. All new creation is not really new in that everything that is being created has existed before. It has always been here in some dimension. Question: Does right and wrong exist? Yes, and no. In our reality here on Earth there is right and wrong and this is part of the duality. We do have free will, and choice, and decisions to do right or wrong. In the truest reality there is only what there is. That is neither right nor wrong for in our true reality there is no duality – right is what we decide it is (nothing is wrong) just different hands of decisions and experience. No one judges, we shouldn't judge. We should just experience and through the expression of experience we will understand. But a lot depends on the level of consciousness of the person.

A planetary quarantine had been placed on us here on Earth. Our Earth consciousness requires frequency. A block or "666 seal" of dimensional frequency is happening within our genetic DNA. The diminished frequency affects our holographic 'material' architecture which has altered our planetary Earth body. This impacts every living thing on the planet. This quarantine (or seal) is slowly being removed now, as it is safe to do so at this time without 'disrupting' the Earth. The removal of the "666' seal," the person has achieved a process of ascension. Genetic miasma blockers affect all humanity. We need to clean this DNA blockage in order to 'go home.' Pay attention to this time. Go deep to clear subconscious patterns – pain, conflict, and suffering – bring balance to your body. Educate yourselves about healing consciousness for DNA.

"The law of one" and its healing principles into all aspects of our life will greatly accelerate one's consciousness. All damage to the cosmic fabric has manifested itself into all the problems living here now before us. A dedicated heart, will receive spiritual help to overcome these limitations. Declare your dedication to the creative 'spirit' of the sovereign law of one. Let your primal feelings and emotions flow naturally. All the necessary components to complete the entire DNA coded strands (connection) are already written in our body.   Fear will hinder this flow. Fear is a 'long slow' wave frequency that touches our feelings and emotions deeply.   Deep inside we fear many things, but in particular we fear death of our present existence the most.   In order to fully live, we should try not to fear death. Fear has few 'touches' on our DNA frequency. Love is a much higher frequency that 'touches' our DNA with much more frequency.   Therefore, feelings and emotions can affect our health and happiness through our vibrational relationship to our DNA connection and ultimately impact on our genetic codes and its connection.

We are guided to what is 'right' and 'just' by our inner feelings, our inner knowing, our intuition and our heart. But all of these feelings must be in alignment and balance with energies of light and with all of nature for the DNA to become activated. Our DNA and our conscience are connected. As DNA activation occurs, our conscience is shifting and increasing. DNA emits a certain level of light and the body's biochemical system receives these light waves. Light is responsible for the photo-repair of body cells so DNA (indirectly) is crucial to our health and keeping disease and illness at bay. Yes, you are that powerful!

The Pineal Gland is located just above eye level in the center of your forehead. It is light-sensitive (especially ultraviolet light) and is responsible for your DNA system activation.   When this gland is activated, you feel shooting rays of light pulsating through your body. Get comfortable, close your eyes and concentrate on the area behind your eyes (center forehead). By focus and concentration you can begin to activate this gland.   Your DNA carries a lot of energy and information throughout your entire body. Your DNA system carries information about who you are. You can 'heat up' your entire body from activating the pineal gland. This is why it is so vital that our Pineal Gland is malleable and not blocked. Fluoridated water (and other toxins we ingest) can block and negatively affect our Pineal Gland which ultimately impacts DNA activation.

On another somewhat related-topic to DNA is blood. There are several human blood types such as O, A, B and AB, but there is also another categorization of whether the blood grouping is Rh positive or negative. The Rh factor is a lab test to determine if the blood contains certain antigens which correspond to a rhesus monkey protein in your blood cells; Rh + (positive) means that you have the protein and Rh – (negative) means that you do not. Only about 15% of the populations have Rh – blood. The interesting fact is that if you're Rh negative, then you have a blood sequence that is alien to human blood. It does not share commonality of human blood with any mammal or know animal on Earth. This could very well mean that it is extraterrestrial and not of this world.

Most people are not aware of what purpose or why they are here on this Earthly journey. Some people have ideas – but don't know or understand it for certain. A lot of people seek answers to these questions. As we move further into the information age more and more people will be asking. When you focus on Pineal Gland activation it produces the codes to remember who you are. DNA is like a tubing system carrying white light (energy) inside of it similar to a garden hose. As the light comes in, it moves through your body but always comes in the crown (on top of head), gathers light from the sun and passes the (crown) light through your body. Imagery is being carried as this flows through your body; you have inner visions of what we are supposed to be doing. You see images of yourself and the powerfulness of your body healing. You will see clearly with intuition as a guidance system inside of you. When you look around, you see with your regular eyes but this will enable you to see better transcending time and space. Inner reality provides a sense of guidance intuition and begins to know and understand things before they happen. Many of us have had this guidance system deactivated here on Earth – it operates with magnetic power (magnetism). If the field of magnetism is interfered it will not operate well. Interference such as technology, food, water, can have a negative effect on the Pineal Gland – it can just shut down. Lose intuition and inner guidance and then you don't know what to do. You're confused and lost. And you don't know who you are. If you focus on this, you can reawaken and remember who you are. DNA activating will help achieve goals in your life.

All spiritual transitions stem from love. Love is a part of our genetic code and it is written into it. Love can change our DNA. DNA molecules can heal themselves in the presence of love and loving energy that is sent to us through intent. A change in the genetic codes to a New World of 4th and 5th dimension (2012–2018) is the time period transition for this quantum leap of energy.

'What level of DNA activation do I have?

It depends on your level of consciousness...'

We are water-based operating systems. Via cell membranes the frequency that is downloaded is dependent upon your DNA structure. Which makes you...*you*. When the collective conscious believes reality to be what we have before us, then that is, of course, what we experience. It is all programmed into the water via collective experience and beliefs of those who have come before. This hypothesis is supported by physical matter itself. Physical matter is made up of energy vibrating photon light and photon sound. How it is actually formed is all based on sacred geometry.

A person living in fear will also be only able to pick up a limited amount of vibratory frequency that our DNA is analyzing. Some are also fearful that the mistakes made to our DNA will persist, but this is not the case, this time around. Remind yourself of the decision you and others like you made before coming to Earth this time. There was so much creative potential in earlier times for utilizing DNA, but unfortunately the result of the disconnection left our DNA dark and aligned for negativity and ego-based desires. The spiritual overseers will not allow this scenario to repeat itself. Past lives want to reincarnate to Earth, yet previous experiences have left you hesitant about feeling that you can liberate yourself from the density of the earth experience.

CONSCIENCE

BOOK 18

"There is a higher court than courts of justice and that is the court of conscience. It supersedes all other courts."

-Mahatma Gandhi

Conscience: Is a moral judgment or intuition that assists in distinguishing right from wrong in one's conduct, motives or behavior. Moreover, a complex of ethical and just principles that controls or inhibits the actions or thoughts of an individual.

Consciousness: Is the quality of awareness and of one's own existence.

Conscious: Awake and able to understand what is happening around you (your five senses).

Sub-conscious: Is the part of consciousness that is not currently in focal awareness and a 'storehouse' of one's knowledge and prior life experiences.

Self-Conscious: Excessively aware of being observed by others whether physical or mental.

Middle Conscience: Is the center point of conscience which all other conscience is connected.

Super-Conscience: Is the untapped conscious mind that is capable of anything.

Consciousness is the created force of the entire universe. It has been given many names such as God, Yahweh, Krishna, nature, the field and divinity. The entire universe is a single, living organism with a complete awareness of itself. Some of this is difficult to comprehend because we are somewhat limited by our language and understanding and tend to compartmentalize things into categories whereby conscience is a concept that cannot be defined in one place, idea or thing.

There is a crisis today in consciousness. Many of us have not expanded our consciousness. There is an ocean of pure consciousness inside each one of us and it is right at the base and source of mind, at the source of thought and also at the source of matter. Anyone can tap into this ocean of consciousness. All matter originates and exists only by virtue of the force which brings the particles of an atom to vibration and holds this miniature solar system of the atom together that creates it into a conscious dimension.

We must assume behind this force the existence of a conscious intelligent mind which is the matrix of all matter. Modern science tells us that the solidity of matter (all things) is just a mirage.

It's all frequency. If you amplify the frequency then the matter will change. All matter is basically a semantic frequency of textured structures. Everything owns itself solely and completely to sound frequency. Sound holds it all together; sound is the base form of the shape of life. And in the beginning the first sound was "the word of God" (Yahweh) and that is how the world began and creation took place.

Most people would define conscience as being awake and or making an aware decision, but it is much more than that. Every moment that we spend in 'higher consciousness' helps uplift the consciousness of the whole world. There is a single field of consciousness. We are a part of everything that has happened, is happening and will happen; that is everything good and also everything bad. Each one of us created 'this world' that we see in front of us and from this creation we gain our experiences of life.

Just because ancient civilizations did not have electricity (as far as we know) doesn't mean that they were not advanced and civilized. We have been disconnected over time from knowledge. We are not observers; we are creators. By the act of participation we are creating. Wherever human consciousness looks we are creating the universe (reality). Every place we seek or investigate what is there (the act) of looking is a process whereby our consciousness creates what we see. We will never find the end of the universe because everywhere we look consciousness is creating something there. The power is within us; it does not take a majority of people to shift human conscience. It takes just a few people to 'think a thought' that can spread to the rest instantaneously. We are that powerful. The effect can be 'jump started' even by a minority. We can cross over these artificial boundaries put before us, which many of us create for ourselves, to overcome and connect to the one living code of life whose name is God the prime creator. God is encoded into our DNA – DNA the word God – 'YAHAY.' All things are made of intelligent energy and are a part of the 'Law of One.'

There are several subsets of laws that govern the mechanics of consciousness in the universal creation, but all will culminate in eternal truth and eternal love. Eternal love is the 'grass roots' of consciousness. Love is the inner 'light' of Christos and the 'soul' of Unity Consciousness. Hold respect for yourself. Love thyself. This is the natural state of "God's' eternal love" as a manifestation of the eternal spirit of life. Have courage to remove fear to become the embodiment of love. One has the ability to choose love and freedom without harming 'others.' Love Earth and love nature. Service to 'others' is paramount. Do it with unconditional love. Amplify the joy and service to others, and then, in turn, this will amplify the energetic flow of love back to you.

*"Ask me to do anything for you and I will, but if you tell me to do it...
I won't."*
-Anonymous

Being in service to others creates joy and harmony. Gifts will be brought into your life the more service and dedication to God's plan you have and the more spiritual support and conscience exchange of information too. The more ego you have, the harder this is to accomplish. If ego has authority over the body, this will be a difficult task, since the mental body creates mental obstacles and physical discomforts. We must be patient, but through spiritual identity and consciousness we can work through this. Learn to quiet the mind. Quiet the ego. Become still. Listen to your inner spirit for guidance. 'Inner' guidance will lead to the proper information and with the proper knowledge and understanding there will be less fear and worry. The Inner Christos is responsible for co-creation with God. It is the divine blueprint. We are all one. Knowing our purpose helps brings peace, joy and fulfillment. Any challenges will be overcome.

Man created electricity; electricity created light and light created the ability to extend the day (into night) and therefore expanding waking thoughts and waking moments of our conscience existence. All frequency is rising now as we enter into the "Age of Aquarius" and there is a 'cosmic shift' in consciousness which is affecting all humanity. The harmonic vibration of the Earth follows a time cycle of about– 13,000 years and in 1986, it was officially the beginning of the new shift. On this date, a new evolution started; an evolution in the rise in consciousness. The Earth is a conscious living being evolving together with human consciousness. We are on the verge of creating a new reality – human kind will be the victor. Long ago forces gained control of Earth and has worked very hard to maintaining ownership of its consciousness. These evil forces have descended down through the ages and have ruled through an elite bloodline of powerful families. We are the product of this manipulation of energy through undaunted propagation of fear by these families. Our mass consciousness has been negatively impacted through use of 'polarized energy' that instills disharmony by creating an atmosphere of tension, distrust, anger and fear. The ruling classes have been observing the shifts going on with human behavior over the past few hundred years, and this shift in energy fields has been increasing in frequency recently. They understand all humanity is a single consciousness and by controlling the collective conscience they can control humanity.

Light Workers came to the United States because here we could have the most impact. This is also a place where denial is pervasive. Americans believe we live in the land of the free and the home of the brave. Yet we live in one of the most controlled 'experimental' societies ever created. The United States has not reached a full conscious level and Light Workers are here to assist in elevating conscious awareness. Light Workers are not here to do this for us, but to help. We must do this (awaken) on our own. Most all people in the United States are having a difficult time giving up their conceded way of thinking. It may take a catastrophic event to 'shake America up' enough to elevate the consciousness and awaken the masses. So at some point, and not by choice, we will be forced to give up our privileged way of life. The current system in place is corrupt – it is not sustainable. It does not honor life and it does not honor Earth. Consciousness must change. This is part of the divine plan of all.

Our consciousness is more powerful than any science or mathematic equation. All matter exists in virtue of a force. Therefore we must assume that behind this force is the existence of a conscious and intelligent mind. This brilliant mind is the matrix of all matter and relates to the laws of quantum physics. Our current science cannot 'handle' consciousness because it doesn't know how to quantify it properly. A science experiment cannot be conducted accurately if a human being is involved in the experiment since the human conscious must somehow be accounted for as a variable. It does not even need to be human conscience since all animal species collectively have a mass consciousness. A wonderful example of this is the "100 Monkey Theory."

The "100' Monkey Theory," demonstrates how conscious-ness can be passed between groups and how social change can evolve. In 1952, on some remote islands off the coast of Japan, there monkeys lived who loved to eat the sweet potatoes that grew naturally. The problem was that the potatoes were sandy from growing on the ground and the sand made it unpleasant when eaten. One day, one of the juvenile monkeys took a potato and washed it off in the nearby water to remove the sand. The potatoes were much more pleasing to the palate since there was no sand or dirt to interrupt the taste. The one monkey showed this to another and before long several monkeys were washing their potatoes in the water before eating. At some point (when not even half of the 100 monkeys were doing this) all of a sudden the rest of the monkey tribe begin washing their potatoes before eating. They had reached a critical tipping point whereby once a certain percentage of the monkeys demonstrated the behavior it resonated to the rest without even showing them. Then the most incredible event was to occur. As this took 'hold' on the one island and the monkey count performing this task went from 99 to 100, it was witnessed by observers that monkeys on other islands were starting to do the same thing. Somehow the 'thoughts' and 'actions' of the one monkey tribe was able to transfer the act to another island some distance away. Miraculously, this practice started spreading to even more islands and before long the practice of washing sweet potatoes was a part of the rituals and culture of all the monkey tribes on all the islands. This shows the power of consciousness and how, when people (or animals) come together with thought, how social behavior can be affected even from distant locations on Earth.

We are all part of a universal energy field. We are not a 'separate' quantum entanglement theorized by Einstein. Nothing is separate. It is all connected through quantum physics. Everything we know is resting on a foundational structure which in turn connects all of us. Therefore, we have full knowledge of everything and the universe already in us, but we need to 'tap' into that energy frequency to fully 'get it.' So there is no separation; separation is an illusion and our thoughts and emotions can literally affect people we know living halfway around the world. Earth's magnetic attraction contributes to the change of the environment. When we create our own reality consciousness it is somehow linked into the quantum world. That is a participating universe and everything we do in it actually changes. There is interconnecting energy while we co-create with all the other living organisms in this world and the universe. Reality is not isolated; it is a relationship between all the parts and manifests its form when it takes shape by these relationships.

What could be used to elevate mankind has been used to enslave us. If we could 'mechanize' the knowledge and technology that has been hidden from us it would elevate mankind and help the quality of every individual's life. We function better in a state of happiness/empathy (positive harmony) than we do in a state of separation. The heart is the center of us (our soul), not our brain. We think using our heart through emotions and those feelings sends those to our brain. The heart actually controls the brain. We send and receive information every second in waking life and those signals originate in our heart. We sometimes feel what is going to happen before it happens. That is our heart thinking...

Our true conscious does not exist in our bodies or brains, but outside of our physical body. We have been told that we are separate individuals and that when we "think" it is completely independent of others. Yet, somehow people have been able to communicate through telepathy, telekinesis and clairvoyance with each other. All thought and emotions extend from us into the whole of the collective conscience. Picture your thoughts flowing through the 'air' just waiting for someone to receive it! In that regard paranormal behavior is misunderstood. The amazing thing is that we all have this innate ability. It may be hidden or suppressed, but we are capable of this – and a lot more. Since all thoughts are connected in the universe this could explain why so many amazing things have occurred simultaneously throughout history. Consciousness is molded by intent and therefore creates our reality. This is a difficult concept to grasp especially since many of us have been 'conditioned' to think a certain way. How do we know when we are aware of our emotions? Feelings and actions (or non-actions) are the physical manifestation of these emotions; love manifests itself in the heart and anger manifests itself in the ego. There are really only two emotions that we express, love and fear. All other emotions stem from either love or fear and that is all there is...

Consciousness through creation is one with Christ Consciousness. Christ Consciousness is the key. Understand that

Christ Consciousness is the consciousness of the Prime Creation and not of institutions of religions. Creation exists through love – the love of all, not separation. Love that is unconditional is the love that extends to all since all is a part of the one. Institutionalized religion hides you from the truth. Christ Consciousness lives within each one of us. Your inner thoughts affect the outer world. It is important to understand that your feelings and emotions have a distinct impact on what is going on in the world around you. This is nothing you control or switch on or off at will and is a part of the energy that flows from each person. It is ongoing. Every conscious decision is interacting with an energy field around you. You are shaping this physical reality with your inner thoughts and emotions. This information may be disheartening to many people the fact that your inner thoughts shape your world – there imparts a great responsibility. How will you accept this responsibility? How will you (now) choose to think and live your life? With this realization that whatever energies you put out for others to draw upon shapes your reality then understand that whatever you receive back from this energy (field) will be the same to what you have put out. Express nothing – you'll receive nothing. Express hate – you get back hate. Express love – you get back love.

Those who become aware of their full 'consciousness' existence is what the Buddhist call "Bodhi" (awakening). The Hindus call it 'Moksha' (liberation). Consciousness discovers the deep 'self' from who you really are, fundamentally and forever as the whole of being. You are 'what' the entire process is doing. But we easily forget that. We are unaware of the connections. We are 'the works' — playing it this way for a while (like a game or a show) and that is why we dread death because that is the end of the show. We are afraid of the potential pain, sickness and suffering that will bring about death. If you have no understanding that you are the works you may not have any <u>real</u> joy in life. You are mixed up with guilt and anxiety.

If it is the simple things in life that bring the greatest joy then should we not lead a simple life? We try too hard to change our surroundings too much and spread ourselves too thin with too many distractions and activities that we lose sight of the importance or what is right in front of us, our family.

I am sitting in the sun... nature is all around. I am at peace. I am (at) one with myself. I hear birds...I see squirrels...I smell flowers. I feel warmth upon my face. I close my eyes... my breathing slows. This moment is suspended in time, it is effortless. I am releasing the joy I have within to the external world that is without. I am a simple peaceful moment of now...the now moment of just being. I am in no hurry because I am already here...where I am now is where I can be...and where I want to be.

Give up the concept of God! Let him go in the 'traditional' sense. And after you stop seeking... God will come back to you in a new light. You will see and recognize that you are 'the works' – a part of the whole experience — individual, yet connected to everyone else. You can only have this experience 'one at a time' in this dimension. Remember...everyone is you.

Life is experience and you are smack dab right in the middle of it. No need to force things. Let it all come to you. Don't worry about planning for every detail of an imagined perfect future moment. If you do then your whole existence will be consumed on the future and you're not living in the present 'now' moment. 'Now' is really all you have. The past is but a memory. For example: Think about a birthday party you had as a child. When did the party take place? In the past? No, it took place in the present, occurring as a now moment. You're remembering it now which is also a 'now' moment.

Now think about an event in the future such as the upcoming New Year's Eve celebration. Picture the gathering of family and friends as the New Year's Eve "ball" is being lowered during the countdown - 10, 9, 8, 7, 6, 5, 4, 3, 2...1 *"Happy New*

Year!' This future event is taking place when? In the future?! No, again, it is happening (being constructed) at a 'now' moment and you're just visualizing it now. Therefore we can conclude that all past and future moments happen as a 'now' moment and anytime you think about the past or the future you are doing it 'now.' There is no avoiding the now moment because that is all you have. In the current moment you can re-live the past or contemplate the future, but this is not a time for regret or worry this is a moment of clarity. Why spoil this now moment. We are beginning to remember who we are though many try to hold onto the old beliefs of who we are. You should look inside for direction and not rely so much on what you have been told.

How many people need to put themselves into this mass conscience through their actions and speech before we hit the tipping point? The early ones to awaken will be leaders when we cross into new consciences from the old. You don't have to wait to do this in your next incarnation; you can do it right now. People are beginning to more easily articulate a higher level of consciousness than they could before by having a higher level of integrity of actions. Children ironically have this innate ability and it is 'taught' out of them. We need to learn from our children. The children are the wisest of all humans; they play for the moment and don't have worries, concerns or regrets. Their existence is filled with un-inhibited joyfulness by living in the present moment. We need to be more like children again.

Society tells us that we have to do X, Y and Z in order to achieve a result. But in actuality, it is the concentration on vibrational energy that will get the desired results. The inner soul cares not if you've paid your rent or if you're a millionaire. The soul is part of a living level of consciousness spirit awareness. The joy of being is merely what is in front of you. Whatever you put out emotionally and physically - that emotional frequency – is affecting reality and, in turn, that reality affects your emotions (somewhat symbiotic). The way you experience things is how you need to deal with it. The vibration or frequency you give off and generate determines ultimately, and absolutely, the experience reflected back to you from your reality. In other words, you go through the experience you're supposed to go through, to provide the lessons and teachings to assist learning through conscience awareness.

There should be a 'red light' that goes off in your head when something doesn't add up or make sense. When the news misleads us or there is a story that is conspiratory in nature, we should be able to question it because our intuition tells us to. But realize that the critics and debunkers will try to convince us otherwise, but they too face a problem; if they consider what we are questioning as possible truth about a 'conspired event' then it brings into question their own knowledge and acceptance of events. If they make a decision outside of their comfort zone they may have to give up a part of the foundation of their own belief system. They would have to let go of their very core conviction. But people usually don't want to do that. It is hard to let go. But by 'letting go' of the left/ right paradigm, where you belong to one group or another (e.g., Republican/Democrat), you're able to step back and look at all things more objectively. You will see how both 'parties' are essentially the same just with different agendas to achieve similar end goals. A 2020 political party ballot:

```
I am:
_  Democrat
_  Republican
X  Awake
```

When you 'wake-up,' you also start seeing holes in many stories. You'll see how things don't connect. You'll understand the level of lies that are being 'passed off' as truths. And instead of the "Conspiracy Theorists" having to prove the story as false the onus is placed on the debunkers to prove otherwise...and support their story as truth...if they can.

'You cannot save people ... you can only love them...'

We are the only animal species on Earth with a conscience of evil. An animal may kill another animal, but in doing so there is no sense of evil when the animal is harming another — the animal has no remorse and no conscience. Evil is a perception created by human conscience. Humanity is 'bombarded' with negative reinforcement from a very complex system (TV, movies, news) that breeds this evil behavior. The question is: What sort of mind could have thought this up? Is what we see a product of collective failure of human conscience or is there something far more sinister working behind the scene? The complexity boggles the mind and that is possibly why it is hard for so many people to see this and wake up. How did the human reality get into this state of conscience unless it has been conditioned by evil? And if we are so advanced as a species, why have we not been able to embrace the basics of human kindness?

If people ignore this important question then it will never be answered and humans will fail having never achieved any solutions to the problems that exist. When you create a solution, then you have acknowledged there is a problem. And there are definitely problems — the state we are in now is critical. All these problems will go away if we serve creation. We need to follow the "one law" of creation and stop serving the system. Stop supporting the corrupt network and support yourself and others, but not the system. Become free and serve the conscience of God. So if any legal or governmental entities are attempting to enforce manmade legislation upon you — and it goes against the "one law" of serving God or infringes upon the conscience of God — then just respectfully decline and say no.

We can't change the world if our conscience doesn't want to. We can't change the system if we operate within the same faulty parameters that the system has already been set. It must be revamped. The system itself is designed on self-preservation and there can be no fundamental "across the board" change unless we change ourselves. Remember the system is fictional (made up). We need to extricate ourselves from the system—and focus on solutions—and the solution is the community. An interesting study shows that city dwellers (on average) will have fewer friends than people living in the countryside. It seems the closer and tighter the space between people the more divided they are. In the countryside neighbors are further away from one another yet they are more helpful and friendly. We have innate fear to open ourselves to others. We wonder sometimes…what is it about another person that bothers us? The problem lives within us to know them better. Understand, the system creates psychopathic people; it is not the people, per se, it is the system that is maladjusted. People can change, but we must allow them to learn by their mistakes. Doing things wrong is a part of the learning process. People learn by their mistakes and we need to be patient with them. It doesn't matter what you did in the past, or what you got wrong; what's important is how you move forward from this point on. Emotions and intentions are the key to people 'moving' themselves into a more harmonious vibration. The more people that go into the collective conscience (ultimately) the more positive change can happen for everyone. This process filters out the extraneous and people will see the 'goodness' in the ones left to move on. We are generally so worried about what others are doing (and judging them) that we rarely if ever look at ourselves. Look at yourself…

We are transmitting conscience. When we believe what we are told, it reinforces that conscience. We give it more energy solidifying into our sub-conscience as we co-author the experience. We are responsible for it. Conscience is far more powerful then we imagine. Only a small portion of the world's population is really negative and the 'system' and 'media' dwells on just this small, negative portion. The higher levels of conscience fields contain all knowledge, all memories and all possibilities. We can access them with our mind. But human consciousness is at the same time a form of ignorance (too). The normal, everyday consciousness we experience leaves out more than it takes in and because of this we feel life is less 'profound' and 'mysterious' than we believe it should be; we feel something important is missing. Our everyday consciousness senses this shortcoming. The scholar in us learns something each day and each day 'man' unlearns teachings almost to the 'point of regression.' We cannot force ourselves into a certain frame of mind; it must come naturally. Many of us are intellectually smart, but have little idea of what is going on in the world. We are just plain ignorant. Free yourself from the intellectual mind and possess a humanitarian mind. When you are perfectly free to feel 'stuck' or 'unstuck' then you're unstuck and actually free. Watch the flow of your thought (your stream of consciousness) giving up control is a sign of control.

Every human being is born as a genius and every single one of us has untapped reserves of creativity energy which we either fail to realize or develop during our lifetime. We have this power within us. The basic assumption is that if you work harder you will get the desired results. 'Fighting' for that end goal of what you quest. And when you don't get the desired results – then you must work even harder. Stop fighting. Stop pushing (going against the flow) of what lies in front of you. There is a better way and that is through the use of your conscience, sub-conscience and super–conscience abilities.

Much of what we have today, as far as invention, is the result of using our minds. Children are very creative and imaginative especially early on before they are exposed to rules and regulations. Their capacity for abstract reasoning, creative imagery and curiosity is "off the charts" before the age of five. Ironically, it is at this age we tend to enroll our children into some educational system that will ultimately extract the creativity out of them by the age of 7. This, of course, doesn't happen to all children, but at some point we all succumb to a diminished creative mind. The good news is the creativity in each one of us is still there – it is just dormant. It is up to you to remember and 'tap back' into this creative energy through your super-conscious mind. Somehow this creativity is hampered by the suppression of independent thinking and the freedom to 'experience' by letting our imagination run wild. Most children are told that their actions are foolish or silly if they deviate too far away from the norm—when, in fact, this process is vital for us to experience who we really are. As a child, we are told a million things not to do (most of them for the sake of safety), but there is a happy balance that allows children to explore their creative freedom in a safe, loving environment.

Children learn on a sub-conscious level early on in life that it is 'less hassle' to just stay on the path that everybody else travels rather than forge a new creative path. Unfortunately, this is the first indoctrination into the structured world that directly stifles the creativity and innovation that is innate within all children. It is not necessarily "use it or lose it" in that if this creativity and innovation is not used, it becomes a 'latent capability' that we can still tap into at any point later in life. It never goes away. The reason we still have the ability to access this energy, anytime, is that it is a part of the "collective unconscious" or what some call the "super-conscience mind." The super-conscience mind is 'the' living library of all knowledge and information that is the Earth, the Universe and God. The super-conscience mind is working when you try to solve a problem and all of a sudden the solution comes in an instant; it literally 'pops' into your head, or when you receive a call from a friend that you just happened to be thinking about at that exact and precise moment. This reinforces that we have the ability to tap into a higher intelligence and energy that is the super-conscience; the collective cosmic conscience of the universe. It is a connection to everything and everyone. This higher form of conscience is the prime source of all pure creativity and breakthroughs in human inventions. This has nothing to do with born intelligence and has absolutely nothing to do with the measure of acquired intelligence through our everyday schooling via grades or fancy degrees. Everyone at some time or another has come up with a brilliant idea or invention, whether it is a product or just a concept, which could improve the quality of our lives. We usually don't immediately act on these 'ideas' (if ever) and sometime later we may see the exact idea that we came up with, in concept, made as a real product. The concern is not that we don't come up with these great ideas, but rather we don't usually trust or believe we have the capability (to act) with in ourselves to make and implement the product/idea into society. Many times our response to a new idea or product is, "boy, I wish I had thought of that." By thinking this response means we have a relationship to that idea. We think of many reasons why we can't do something and yet very few reasons why we should move forward creating them. Many times it is money, access and time constraints that limit our ability to process these ideas and concepts into the real world, but by just thinking of them you are part of the creative process even though you did not actually go to the trouble of creating it into a tangible product in reality. You don't have to be a painter, poet, writer or musician to be creative. All you have to be is you.

Think of it like this, every time you think something it is like pushing a 'button' on a 'conscience machine.' By pushing the button it will affect the balance and trigger a response. Understand that our thoughts (just like our actions) have an impact on other people and other people's thoughts. Your thoughts just don't go anywhere or nowhere, they move into the collective conscience where they interact with other thoughts. Each thought flows into the stream of consciousness making room for other thoughts and ideas that may have some relationships or attributes of similarity. This is how ideas can, virtually, come into your head even though you have never thought of them previously. Your brain has access to this vast sea of collective conscience and it is up to you whether you tap into it or not. You physically cannot see this stream, but many awakened people can feel the pulse of the collective, conscience vibration. Now imagine the power and impact it could have if everybody thought the same thought at the same time. We could move mountains! Or, better yet, solve any problem on Earth with just our thoughts. All hunger, sickness and overpopulation – all of it could be eradicated by mass conscious attention. The problems would not be instantaneously solved, but with all of humanity's attention focused it would be solved quickly and correctly. Conscious thought is the ultimate energy source and it is the essence of God himself.

The sub-conscious mind is what you 'pull' information from every time you think. It is 'below' the conscience mind and is not in focal awareness, but lies underneath the layers of critical thought which is consciences. There are times that we desire something so much that we formulate and concentrate on it in our mind with such focus – that we lose track of our surroundings – we lose track of time – we lose track of our purpose and we lose track of ego. It is the moment we become so involved in that experience that we lose ourselves and our identity. It is this experience that everybody has gone through and it is occurring on the conscious, but mostly sub-conscious level. The manifested reality that is being created by you the observer, is in full effect your consciousness influencing others around you. It can influence material properties and it can influence your future. You are co-creating your future.

The sub-consciousness is one-thousand times (1000x) more powerful than the conscious mind. The sub-conscious mind is 'programmed' and adapts to the situation you're experiencing.

These programs are generally limiting and sometimes can be bad, but it is from the sub-conscience mind that we access actions and emotions that predict what we do.

"Forget all the reasons why it won't work and believe the one reason why it will."

-Anonymous

When we program a problem into our sub-conscience mind and ask ourselves to solve the problem, the mind will pass this onto the super-conscience. To solve the problem the super-conscience takes all the stored data that we have acquired during our lifetime in our sub-conscious mind and sorts out the valid information that applies to the situation and discards the rest. Our mind is *literally* accessing a giant "super computer" that exists outside our body and is 'plugging' into not only our information of experience, but also all the information we have not yet personally experienced. In that way, we are able to come up with a solution to whatever problem we encounter even if we have never experienced that situation before. Not every solution is a palatable one, but 'perfect' or not, solutions will come to us that are germane to the problem at hand even if the situation is foreign to us. Many original ideas, insights and breakthroughs come to people that are completely unrelated to the field or environment that they are familiar or knowledgeable about. This tells us those ideas and thoughts are out there for anyone to access in this huge ocean of the collective conscious.

Super-conscience is the source of all intuition, all flashes of insight, and all hunches. It is the source of inspiration and motivation and the ability to see things in a new way and help us to achieve our goal. Our super-conscience mind is always working to resolve the problems given to the sub-conscious. The 'trick' though is that we need to be very specific. If you cannot clearly explain or define the goal you want to accomplish, the super-conscience mind cannot perform. The super-conscience mind is activated by clarity and the decisiveness from which you define the goal. If you set no goal, or are vague as to the details, you will never achieve what you seek or the longer it will take for the goal to be realized. The super-conscience will release the tools needed for you to obtain that goal. These tools come to you as a continuous flow of ideas and concepts that are pure energy that trigger even more 'free energy' from the atmosphere which we can channel. The other aspect of our super-conscience is that it responds to clear, positive affirmation. Every time we affirm ourselves in a positive, constructive manner we are sending this 'vibrational' energy from our conscience mind to sub-conscience mind and ultimately engaging our super-conscience mind into action. Positive reinforcement is as simple as repeating simple words (or a phrase) to yourself to reaffirm your desire for something. I would often repeat to myself, over and over again, that *"I want my DNA to be connected...I want my DNA to be connected."* These strong emotional affirmations are directly linked to the super-conscience and those with a positive, excited and enthusiastic attitude toward accomplishing a goal will, in fact, do so quicker and with better results. It is the power of positive thinking. This really works and if you doubt it – then you have never tried it.

The positive attitude breeds upon itself. The other amazing aspect of the super-conscience is that it will always provide the first correct step to take when you are trying to accomplish something. As you proceed on the path to your goal it will inevitably show you the correct next step, and direction, at the precise time you need to know. Each step will appear and be solved by accessing your super-conscience. Again, the trick here is to not push. If you are spending all day to solve a problem the solution may never come. The more you force the process, the harder you try, the slower it will materialize. Let it go and trust in the belief that it will come to you. Creativity cannot be forced. Creativity favors a relaxed mind.

If the mind is full of confusion/fear then it will never be able to relax and access the higher vibration of the super-conscience.

"It is done!" Picture what you want to accomplish each day and you will mentally attract that outcome. There is no sure thing as fate or destiny. You create your reality. There are no negative experiences, just those that you categorize or interpret as negative. It is all perception. Something perceived as 'bad' may have a "silver lining" and could be good. There are no mistakes – just lessons – and these lessons will help expand your mind and consciousness. Accept them, be grateful for them, and say thank you. Even though it may be difficult at times, these are life's lessons – so grow and learn from these events.

This goes back to the idea that if you clearly define what you are seeking, it will manifest itself. Close your eyes and picture 'it' in your mind. Picture the finished product or idea that you are trying to create. This is the essence of the creative process. Many of us never fully 'materialize' the finished product in our mind and if you don't see it, and construct it in your mind, then it may never happen. It is very important to stay positive and focused because if you dwell on the negative, or the reasons you can't do something, then it will never be achieved. Have the confidence that each step will come to you at the precise moment needed as long as you clearly define the end goal. Some of you will be 'smart' and say I want to materialize a Bentley or a mansion in Beverly Hills. If you want these things so much they may come to you, but there is also a 'karma effect' that guides the flow of all this energy. If all you want (or care about is money), then money is what you may create, but there will be a cost or price from that which this 'destiny' will come.

Create and invent for the sake of joy and inner peace and then the rewards of your inventions and convictions will come to you purely and harmoniously. Don't just invent money, because it has already been invented. If you stay the course and do what your intuition tells you, then you will be provided for, period.

The difference is that if it is forced, the path may take you through mistakes, stumbling blocks and hardships. Learning, teaching and growing will occur through these valuable lessons. You will recognize that any failures along the way are part of the growing process and you will not be discouraged.

Many times in retrospect we look differently at past unhappy events that we thought at the time were 'unfortunate' and later realize the positive nature of them. For instance, getting fired from a job never immediately appears to be a good thing, but when we look back at a later time, we realize that there was a reason it happened and we are in a better, happier and more successful place now. We must see that it was good fortune (or perhaps karma) to create a situation that opened us up for a new opportunity that may have not been available to us before. We must understand that 'right now' is where we need to be. For every obstacle or setback in life there are equal or opposite advantages or benefits and the successful person will always look for the positives in every situation. Sometimes we do lose a position we really like and we are sad. We must understand that things happen for a reason and there may be a more important calling for you during this lifetime and that position was not meant for us. A path change is required for you at this time to be able to 'wake up' or achieve your real destiny. Again, focus on the advantages and discard the negatives.

There is a certain "synchronicity" that occurs with the super-conscience. The common definition of Synchronicity is when seemingly unrelated events have a 'meaningful coincidence' and occur with no apparent causal relationship, yet seem to be meaningfully related. Many feel that synchronicity has nothing to do with coincidences and everything to do with certain energies coming together to provide you with coded messages. Synchronicity occurs when you are tapping into the super-conscience and reminds us that we are on the correct path. Nothing happens by accident. There is always a reason for something happening and we either brought this on through our sub-conscience or it is clues being left behind for us to adjust our heading and navigation. Those who pay attention can decipher this to their advantage and will prosper in whatever they're trying to create.

Remember the super-conscious mind works best when you are either relaxed or when you are doing minimal activity such as meditation. The super-conscience mind will not operate under duress. Let yourself flow by 'doing nothing' and let the ideas arrive naturally. The super-conscious mind has many incredible attributes and all you need to do is believe and participate. Another example of accessing the super-conscious is something we do each day and that is waking up in the morning. Some people do not need an alarm clock to wake up. They program and set their mind to what time they need to wake up the next day and their super-conscience will do the rest. You will wake up within minutes of when you set your internal clock. If you think you need an alarm clock to wake up then you will need an alarm clock to wake up. You are having doubt that you have the ability. Don't doubt! The power is within you. The take-away point is this; the degree to which you believe and the confidence in that belief, is paramount to the functioning of the super-conscience. The super-conscience functions in accordance with 100% total belief. If you believe you will never have this ability…you won't. It is important that we react to what our intuition (super-conscience) is telling us and do it quickly, *"Do it now, right now!"* The Nike apparel slogan, "Just do it" is a form of positive affirmation and super-conscience thinking. If you wait, the energy will subside and you will miss the energy flow or wave of consciousness that is coming through you. Any earlier (or later) will not be in the 'sweet spot' and those who delay will not benefit from any aspect of this enlightenment and energy flow.

Again, it is very important to pay attention to what you're thinking. Be aware of being aware and always keep your mind focused on what you want to happen. Always think and visualize what you seek...imagine it in your mind and focus on that happening and the desired outcome. You will experience what you visualize and project, that is why it is so important to focus on the positives and not the negatives of life. We must not dwell, talk, think, write or complain about things we fear or do not want to experience in our life. We must deliberately and systematically exclude our thoughts from our conscience mind that we do not want to bring into our reality. Remember, you are dealing with the most powerful force in nature, your conscience.

Our super-conscience can record all waking conscience moments of our entire lives and even record all dreams. If we were fully connected we would have the ability to access into the recordings and replay any moment of our life that we desire in our wakeful conscience state just like watching a video. Your super-conscience is like a living library of information and events. It occurs outside of your body separate from your brain. Conscience thought is 'picked up' by our body's antenna. That antenna is our brain in conjunction with our Pineal Gland. It is possible to connect with someone else's conscience too.

Somehow cells can communicate with each other even over great distances. Each one of us has a unique identifying frequency. The vibration field around us extends out to all living things and influences our behavior and movement on the surface of the Earth. During our lives, we come in contact with other individuals and inevitably (at some point) you will come into contact with others that share a common frequency. If we continue our movements we will ultimately meet up with people that share our exact vibrational frequency. This is very exciting because at that moment you encounter the person that has complimentary frequency to you and the harmonic resonance actually empowers your own vibration.

This is often referred to as "good vibes." Somehow we are able to see at a higher level that people are related to us by means of these vibrations. When two people come together who share the common vibration, it is constructive interference. When we encounter people that detract our energy that is destructive interference and these are the people who steal our life force or what's called "bad vibes." This energy precedes any type of verbal communication. With this level of super-conscience energy we are able to co-create our own reality and be able to communicate in this present moment with our ultimate (future) soul-mate here on Earth.

Everyone is constantly sending and broadcasting their energy vibration signature into the field or 'matrix' as well as receiving messages so we can focus on who our future life partner, business partner, mentors or even our spiritual teachers will be. They are here to help guide us on our journey and help us resonate where we want to go in life. We can even communicate with the universe itself through our super-conscience thought and (of course) God regardless of what religion you are. Through this connection we can access information and retrieve answers to any questions we may have. All future inventions and knowledge are already within us and we already know and understand how to cure every disease on Earth by means of accessing our super-conscience if we can tap into it. We can also tap into our inner genius. We are limited by our perception of things by measuring them by their quantity or quality. If you start to measure things by pure energy, then you, in turn, will become more intuitive and have greater awareness of your surroundings.

Prayer is one way to 'tap' into a type of consciousness, but prayer is not the answer to achieving desired outcomes. When you pray or wish for something you are asking for something – this is not how you get what you desire. When you pray you place yourself in a subservient role. And if you pray or wish with only partial belief, then you will set your intention only in partial motion. Therefore you in essence 'erase' intent because if you have doubt you neutralize it with the opposite thought. Belief, as soon as you create it, is the secret to the formation of reality. You have to realize that your reality is already created the moment you visualize and emotionalize it in your mind and heart. If you change your mind/heart you change your reality. Everyone has the capacity, at some level, to shape reality. This ability is dormant in most people. The people are known as sleepers, whereas 'awakened' people are enlightened. Because they are awakened, enlightened people can consciously effect change to their reality via willpower, beliefs and emotions. What we know as 'reality' is created by thought and consciousness. Just know that the desired outcome is already a fact. And repeat to yourself that, "It is done." Look only at what you want. Never give attention or power (basically ignore) to what you do not wish to experience. Reaffirm to yourself that the things you do not desire do not exist. Give your undivided attention to the desired outcome you want to experience. Focus on what you have rather than what you don't have. When you do this it will increase the quality and quantity of what you already have. If you only focus on what you don't have even things you already have are essentially lost. Be thankful for what you have and less consumed with wishing for what you don't.

What is the mind? What is the body? And what is the exact nature of our physical reality? As children we start to ask questions and many of us continue to ask as adults the philosophical questions such as, "Where was I before I was born? What am I doing here? What happens to me after death? Is there a God? What does it mean to exist? What is love? For what purpose if any are we here? What is the meaning of life...if any? Am I confined to this physical body forever? Am I just a skin encapsulated 'ego' in a bag of flesh and bones? What really is our purpose? Where do I live in the universe?" It is interesting that science today is beginning to ask these questions too. After all, science is the quest for the truth and these are becoming the most critical and important questions to us as we discover more and more about our physical reality. One of the most interesting aspects of science is what we call perception—what we see, hear, taste, touch, and smell. Ironically, they are the least reliable test of what reality is and demonstrates to us that we cannot trust our senses.

Pure non-corporate driving science is science that has not been manipulated by NGOs, governments or companies with specific agendas. This pure science searches for truth in our reality. What is really behind everything (The "grand design")? The connection (inter-relationship) between things, creates problems for physicists who study modern science in the attempt to explain our existence. Modern Newtonian physicists generally use math and equations to explain 'reality,' yet little or no consideration of 'consciousness,' 'spirituality' or even 'God' is used to derive the explanation of what it all means. Scientific people obstruct talking about conscience, freewill, energy connections, or intention or how all of this interplays into the equations of reality. Scientists do not, and cannot, introduce anything esoteric into our understanding of Quantum Physics because if they did - then just about all our understanding of the world would be drastically different from what we have been told for the past 100 years. It appears that some modern science is no more than an intellectual security blanket for the dumbed-down masses.

Question: Is there a God particle? Answer: No. There is no God particle. In fact, there is no particle at all because when you try to isolate a particle you end up observing a wave of vibrating energy that 'comes and goes' (or even vanishes) and cannot be isolated. It all comes back to consciousness because without the 'conscience mind' none of this, including all philosophy, physics and mathematics would exist. These concepts are observable and none of it would exist without the observer!

In 2015 a French news organization was attacked by a certain 'Muslim' group that was featured in the article written by the French making fun of them using satire. The news focused on the fact that these attacks will only increase over time as tensions escalate. The reporters repeated this over and over again until everyone listening to the report believed things could only get worse. It is drilled down into our conscience. Never once do any news reporters offer an alternative conscience solution to elevate the problem...such as suggesting that the French news organization should abstain from such satire in the future because it is wrong and hurtful. The report never focuses on solutions and only on the result. It is though one wrong action brings about many more wrong actions. Any answers to 'fix' the situation must now come from the opposite consciousness. Many people with the 'wrong' conscience that are vying to be in the new power/money paradigm of the "New World Order" are really only setting themselves up to be the next corrupt oligarchy; which is repeating the same problematic situation we are in now. How are they going to be any different conscience-wise? What are you doing to align yourself with the higher conscience that will be a part of the next paradigm and the solution to the world's issues and problems?

Can you see over the duplicitousness of our society? There are so many apathetic people that we may not be able to make a social change in conscience. We can do this, but how do we get enough people to make that social change? If just ten percent (10 %) of the population holds adamantly to an idea then that idea will take hold. As long as there is a core group that holds steadfast to an idea (similar to the "Group Think" concept) then it can happen. This is how so many 'theories' can remain in the conscience of the masses for such a long time period like The Assassination of President Kennedy. The event is still 'current' in that it has worked its way into the fabric of the mass conscience and as some doubters wake up to the truth more and more people will take hold of this idea. That is why the elite and mass media find it so important to keep telling the 'lie' since truth will eventually come out and possibly become the 'Group Think' of the collective conscience.

"Bi-Standard Apathy" is the situation whereby fifty percent (50%) or more of the people would like to act, but they find it easier to think that someone else is going to do it for them. They leave it up to their neighbor. But, when enough people take it upon themselves to educate, understand and pass this on to others then we all can emerge victorious and make a positive 'viral' change. It is honesty that prevents the blockage of flow from happening because you are not hiding yourself in shame and you're less likely to be apathetic. Honesty frees you to progress on your path and experience fully what you are and the choices you make...truth really does set you free. Honesty is the fastest way to resolve your problems. Those who encounter recurring problems over and over again in their lives are not being honest with themselves. Honesty is being clear and truthful to yourself, and others, and not hiding how you feel.

"A majority does not require prevailing, but an irate minority can set brush fires in the people's minds."

–Samuel Adams

From the beginning of creation (when conscience came into existence) it has never not existed. Everything is conscience...all time and all space which we are all a part of. In contrast, the unconscious does not exist. There is no such thing as the 'unconscious' since that is a nonevent. Many philosophers (Freud and Jung) have contemplated that part of the human experience *is* the unconscious experience. This is not so. Any experience is being experienced on a conscious, subconscious or super-conscious level. There are only experiences of when we are aware. So 'consciousness' started with creation of the universe and exists as far and distant as your imagination can fathom. One may use the term 'unconscious' for defining what conscious is not, for contrast arguments in conversation, as a medical term (i.e., unconscious) or even for, use of the term for reasons of convenience as being done here in these written pages, yet there is no real 'substance' to the word.

Question: How do you light a 5,000 s.f. house with one light bulb? Answer: The house has no interior walls. We perceive life per this clever axiom as if we are stuck in one room with light, but no knowledge outside of the room. Super-conscience can access the outside rooms and will show you the entire picture and the correct path to achieving a goal. It will also show you all the problems and obstacles you will encounter along the way and how to overcome them. Your super-conscience is the light of life.

Subliminal messages are 'consume' unrecognizable to the conscience mind and only recognizable in our sub-conscience...putting ideas into 'drink soda' consumers' heads has always been a marketing tool to sell products. But placing ideas or concepts into our conscience should be done slowly and subtly as not to 'jolt' or upset 'eat popcorn' people. If marketing of the subliminal message is inserted too abruptly into the public's mind the idea will be rejected.

We are all sharing – we are all one. The fact that one person is here and another person is over there is just a perception. We exist in one body. We exist in one breath. Our planet is our extended body. The Earth is recycling and we are contained in one consciousness. There is no difference between the creation, the creator (pure consciousness) and God. So we should learn to love everyone equally because (in essence) we are all one we are one... collective soul. Outwardly everything appears separate, but inwardly we are all manifestations of ourselves. When one is harmed, all are harmed; when one is helped, all are helped. An organism at war with itself is doomed. Fear is not cooperative. Choose love...

The evolution of our conscience should be our 'intention' here on Earth. We should all try to elevate our human conciseness to a height where even meditation is no longer needed; through less manipulation – less pushing – and a more harmonic existence.

The way to access your super-conscience mind is not like turning on a light switch. Rather, it is like superimposing a system of pathways that gets you further (deeper) into the thought process. This process allows the individual to see where they have been, where they are now and where they are going. Upon final analysis, one may find that this process happens all in the same place and it's perception of movement that (perceived as motion), is actually internal growth of the mind, spirit and soul.

A human being's greatest potential is realized by applying intelligence, emotion, and purpose in a manner least prone to error or illusion: philosophy. It follows that the highest form of consciousness enlightenment is born of a highly disciplined mind. The same principles apply to the average modern family when young children are being raised with conflicts, but with little discipline. The hope in achieving strength in character and success later in life is remote without having first experienced any "happy stuff" at home. Understand, children born today have the current world's conscience. They come from an evolved source of conscience (today's conscience) that's why they can pick up using electronics and computers so well. That also means they have inherited all the manipulation that has been thrust onto our conscience too.

The conclusion is that we are all interconnected to each other on a fundamental level through our awakened super-conscious mind. Our conscious is more powerful than we realize and it is through the power and connectivity of our consciousness that we are capable of anything. The Earth is a living organism which each one of us has a very deep and personal relationship with. Understand that the air your ancestors breathed, you are breathing today.

Understand, that the clouds celebrate by weeping tears of joy in the form of rain to the ground. Understand that the sun celebrates by shinning its rays of light so that we can reflect ourselves in the 'mirror' of nature. And understand that the soil beneath our feet is the same soil that we all grow from...

Everything is conscience. There is an ocean of conscience. Like a water droplet, you are an individual and the perception is that you have no relation to any other water droplets, but when you are placed in the ocean...then you become that ocean. Where does the droplet start and the ocean end? It doesn't. It is all one. The magnificence we feel and the greater intellect we sense all around... is us. There is no separation, there is no division, there is no isolation...this is all an illusion. Take back the most important thing you have...you...and move forward...

MINECRAFT is a brilliant computer game that is very much like real life. I believe it is a doorway to our creative spiritual world and similar to the matrix of our holographic existence. One could almost call it "Mind-craft." Below is the end poem to the game:

I see the player you mean.
Yes. Take care. It has reached a higher level now. It can read our thoughts.
That doesn't matter. It thinks we are part of the game.
I like this player. It played well. It did not give up.
It is reading our thoughts as though they were words on a screen.
That is how it chooses to imagine many things, when it is deep in the dream of a game.
Words make a wonderful interface. Very flexible. And less terrifying than staring at the reality behind the screen.
They used to hear voices. Before players could read. Back in the days when those who did not play called the players witches, and warlocks. And players dreamed they flew through the air, on sticks powered by demons.

What did this player dream?

This player dreamed of sunlight and trees. Of fire and water. It dreamed it created. And it dreamed it destroyed. It dreamed it hunted, and was hunted. It dreamed of shelter.

Hah, the original interface. A million years old, and it still works. But what true structure did this player create, in the reality behind the screen?

It worked, with a million others, to sculpt a true world in a fold of the [SCRAMBLED], and created a [SCRAMBLED] for [SCRAMBLED], in the [SCRAMBLED].

It cannot read that thought.

No. It has not yet achieved the highest level. That, it must achieve in the long dream of life, not the short dream of a game.

Does it know that we love it? That the universe is kind?

Sometimes, through the noise of its thoughts, it hears the universe, yes.

But there are times it is sad, in the long dream. It creates worlds that have no summer, and it shivers under a black sun, and it takes its sad creation for reality.

To cure it of sorrow would destroy it. The sorrow is part of its own private task. We cannot interfere.

Sometimes when they are deep in dreams, I want to tell them, they are building true worlds in reality. Sometimes I want to tell them of their importance to the universe. Sometimes, when they have not made a true connection in a while, I want to help them to speak the word they fear.

It reads our thoughts.

Sometimes I do not care. Sometimes I wish to tell them, this world you take for truth is merely [SCRAMBLED] and [SCRAMBLED], I wish to tell them that they are [SCRAMBLED] in the [SCRAMBLED]. They see so little of reality, in their long dream. And yet they play the game.

But it would be so easy to tell them...

Too strong for this dream. To tell them how to live is to prevent them living.

I will not tell the player how to live.

The player is growing restless.

I will tell the player a story.

But not the truth.

No. A story that contains the truth safely, in a cage of words. Not the naked truth that can burn over any distance.

Give it a body, again.

Yes. Player...

Use its name.

Player of games.

Good.

Take a breath, now. Take another. Feel air in your lungs. Let your limbs return. Yes, move your fingers. Have a body again, under gravity, in air. Respawn in the long dream. There you are. Your body touching the universe again at every point, as though you were separate things. As though we were separate things.

Who are we? Once we were called the spirit of the mountain. Father sun, mother moon. Ancestral spirits, animal spirits. Jinn. Ghosts. The green man. Then gods, demons. Angels. Poltergeists, Aliens, extraterrestrials. Leptons, quarks. The words change. We do not change.

We are the universe. We are everything you think isn't you. You are looking at us now, through your skin and your eyes. And why does the universe touch your skin, and throw light on you? To see you, player. To know you. And to be known. I shall tell you a story.

Once upon a time, there was a player.

The player was you,

Sometimes it thought itself human, on the thin crust of a spinning globe of molten rock. The ball of molten rock circled a ball of blazing gas that was three hundred and thirty thousand times more massive than it. They were so far apart that light took eight minutes to cross the gap. The light was information from a star, and it could burn your skin from a hundred and fifty million kilometers away.

Sometimes the player dreamed it was a miner, on the surface of a world that was flat, and infinite. The sun was a square of white. The days were short; there was much to do; and death was a temporary inconvenience.

Sometimes the player dreamed it was lost in a story.

Sometimes the player dreamed it was other things, in other places. Sometimes these dreams were disturbing. Sometimes very beautiful indeed. Sometimes the player woke from one dream into another, then woke from that into a third.

Sometimes the player dreamed it watched words on a screen.

Let's go back.

The atoms of the player were scattered in the grass, in the rivers, in the air, in the ground. A woman gathered the atoms; she drank and ate and inhaled; and the woman assembled the player, in her body.

And the player awoke, from the warm, dark world of its mother's body, into the long dream.

And the player was a new story, never told before, written in letters of DNA. And the player was a new program, never run before, generated by a source code a billion years old. And the player was a new human, never alive before, made from nothing but milk and love.

You are the player. The story. The program. The human. Made from nothing but milk and love.

Let's go further back.

The seven billion billion billion atoms of the player's body were created, long before this game, in the heart of a star. So the player, too, is information from a star. And the player moves through a story, which is a forest of information planted by a man called

Julian, on a flat, infinite world created by a man called Markus, that exists inside a small, private world created by the player, who inhabits a universe created by...

Shush. Sometimes the player created a small, private world that was soft and warm and simple. Sometimes hard, and cold, and complicated. Sometimes it built a model of the universe in its head; flecks of energy, moving through vast empty spaces. Sometimes it called those flecks "electrons" and "protons".

Sometimes it called them "planets" and "stars".

Sometimes it believed it was in a universe that was made of energy that was made of offs and ons; zeros and ones; lines of code.

Sometimes it believed it was playing a game. Sometimes it believed it was reading words on a screen.

You are the player, reading words...

Shush... Sometimes the player read lines of code on a screen. Decoded them into words; decoded words into meaning; decoded meaning into feelings, emotions, theories, ideas, and then layer started to breathe faster and deeper and realised it was alive, it was alive, those thousand deaths had not been real, the player was alive

You. You. You are alive.

And sometimes the player believed the universe had spoken to it through the sunlight that came through the shuffling leaves of the summer trees

and sometimes the player believed the universe had spoken to it through the light that fell from the crisp night sky of winter, where a fleck of light in the corner of the player's eye might be a star a million times as massive as the sun, boiling its planets to plasma in order to be visible for a moment to the player, walking home at the far side of the universe, suddenly smelling food, almost at the familiar door, about to dream again

and sometimes the player believed the universe had spoken to it through the zeros and ones, through the electricity of the world, through the scrolling words on a screen at the end of a dream

and the universe said I love you
and the universe said you have played the game well
and the universe said everything you need is within you
and the universe said you are stronger than you know
and the universe said you are the daylight
and the universe said you are the night
and the universe said the darkness you fight is within you
and the universe said the light you seek is within you
and the universe said you are not alone
and the universe said you are not separate from every other thing
and the universe said you are the universe tasting itself, talking to
itself, reading its own code
and the universe said I love you because you are love.
And the game was over and the player woke up from the dream.
And the player began a new dream. And the player dreamed again,
dreamed better. And the player was the universe. And the player
was love.

You are the player.

Wake up.

UNCONSCIOUS
BOOK 19

What....

RELIGION

BOOK 20

It seems puzzling that there are so many different factions of religions that have coexisted through time, yet each one with a slightly different interpretation from the other. Which one is right? Which one is truth? Are they all right or are they all wrong? The thing is, they cannot be all 'right' and the more pressing point is that all these divisions of opposing religious viewpoints are causing separation and encourages fighting (friction) between religious groups and people. On every level of society people cling to their beliefs and will argue viciously to make it known that their point is the correct one.

There is a belief that 'religion' was all set up thousands of years ago for the sole purpose of keeping us divided. Moreover, off the correct path of wisdom and knowledge about our true origins. Maybe there is no one "right" or "wrong" religious experience because collectively they all have an underlying theme, and that is... goodness. No religion exists solely on the basis of hate. At the core of all religion is love, and at the core of love is a sense of a greater good, happiness with a direct connection to a 'higher being' that helps guide us through life's amazing journey. The higher being many call "God" or the "Prime Creator." But does God really exist? And if God does exist, what difference does it make to me? And which religion is he? The question of whether God exists seems to be either unanswerable by many or irrelevant to some. Furthermore, if there is a larger purpose to religion...what is it?

Each religious experience is unique to the individual that is experiencing it. As far as religions go, there is no one right or wrong answer...just the experience. The Golden Rule of Life tells us that we should follow a "moral code of ethics" and that we should *"do unto others as we would have done unto ourselves."* The point of life is the journey from which we embark and go forth and experience this world and all the beauty it beholds. However, if we wish to experience life the 'correct way' and would also like our religious beliefs to be just and correct too. We have chosen to come here to Earth to be able to live, breathe, create, innovate, see, feel, hear, touch, taste and smell everything; to experience it all...that is the point. Must we also have a religious experience to fulfill our destiny here on Earth? You must first ask yourself the question: Who am I? Then ask: Who is God? And then ask: Is there really a separation between the two? Is whatever I am thinking...I am feeling...and what I am seeing...is also what God is thinking, feeling and seeing? Knowing God is the religious experience and knowing yourself is the beginning of that relationship. Whether you want to accept this or not...God is in each and every one of us...

If in fact God does exist and we are unaware of it, then we are living without knowing the most 'fundamental truth' in the universe. Some may find it difficult to comprehend that there is a good and righteous God with all the suffering that we see worldwide. Why would such a benevolent and all-powerful creator permit such pervasive suffering and evil? The answer is that God never intended for you to 'suffer' or for a 'violent existence' to be a part of God's original purpose for mankind. God created us to possess and be able to exercise free will. Unfortunately, the first human couple decided to reject God's intentions and use their "free will" and be influenced by an evil and mischievous presence, Lucifer. Today we are paying the price and experiencing the painful consequences of Adam and Eve's actions by biting into the "apple of knowledge." Ironically, Adam and Eve already had all this knowledge within them (it was encoded in their DNA) and were enticed into believing something different than the God-given knowledge which they had.

I do not believe the average person wakes up each day and says that they are going to do evil. In their own mind, they are doing 'good' and they have ways of justifying their 'ill' intended actions. They convince themselves that what they are doing is for the betterment for all. Even if the actions are horrific, they are able to validate in their mind there is a higher purpose to what they are doing...even if it means killing another person to make a certain revengeful situation right. Of course, this thinking is flawed and has no rational basis for us. The evil that people are bidding is in a large part parallel to society which has trended itself towards evil. People are innately good at heart and it is our thoughts and ultimately our actions that are evil. One would assume that a newborn child doesn't understand religious wars or the difference between good and evil until they are taught these concepts later in life. These concepts are not innate, but as children become aware of their conscience, they pick up the difference between good and evil and from here they align themselves with one or the other. The way to direct a child toward good is to give them unconditional love and support. Most importantly, this is best achieved through example of the parent's actions during the early nurturing period of life.

Jesus was a Christ Consciousness projection. In a way you are a Christ Consciousness being (too) in a projection as thoughts in the mind of God. We are all a manifestation of an expression of the Prime Creator. Religion chooses to explain many things 'externally'

When, in fact, much that should be explained comes from within. There is no 'old man' looking at everything you do, but '*you*' look at everything you do. The difference is that Jesus understood this relationship. He was a prophet from a foreign land bringing a new perspective on our existence. While most people have not figured this out for themselves, all of us have this illusionary existence. Every person living on this Earth in a 3-D reality is a 'Christ trying being' – subjected to a third dimension mental illusion of materialism. On Earth we have limited senses and many inner senses we cannot normally access. Because of this we are only able to perceive a narrow band of information in this reality. The way to unlock these senses is to understand the law that governs this reality. There is only one true law. It is the "Law of Unconditional Love and Servitude" to the creation of the Creator.

Evil is doing, in practice, the opposite of what we should be doing in principle. Disharmony is evil. Whatever we do, if it is not in harmony then it is disruptive. It is a conscience choice you make – but be mindful that if you create disharmony that it goes against the one and only true law we have. This battle of Armageddon that religion tells us about is, in actual fact, already being waged. There is also a battle being fought in the higher realms. It is a battle fought on several levels: spiritually, physically and electronically. The weapons being used to wage this war are all around you: food, toxins, water, and electromagnetic radiation. The outcome is to be determined. Either Man will activate his DNA and awaken and realize his true potential or succumb to the final destruction of humanity as we know it. We teeter on this balance beam between salvation and oblivion. Again, the choice is ours. (This battle has been raging for many, many years.) People are kept distracted by design and they just don't notice. When you step back from all this, the distraction becomes very obvious. We are not in the final days or even the final hours, but the final minutes of this conflict.

The Bible is encoded with deep knowledge and depending

on your level of understanding you will either get the real meaning behind it or not. If you take the Bible literally that there is an invisible 'sky-buddy' looking down, then I can't help you. The Bible is not just a fairytale; it is a guide to life and full of stories and coded information. You were told by religion to worship a deity outside of yourself and during this time never realizing that you were already part of the infinite consciousness of the universe. You joined the rat race as no other option was evident or possible. You were trained to be a consumer and seek particular brands and products from big companies. You questioned things but many people say, *"well that's life."* But it isn't. Don't fall into the 'born-work-consume-die' paradigm.

You have been taught to disparage others due to their differences which have made you vulnerable in your own right. These differences you identified, are reflections of yourself and you must understand that these are only differences – not good, bad or indifferent, but only perceptions. Accept the 'difference' in others then you, yourself, will become more accepted by others. You let the 'past' (past = guilt/regret) dictate your present and you 'worry' about the future (future = fear/worry) even though the past and future moments do not really exist, in that you only have the present...so live in the present moment. Forget all of the distractions. Forget, and move into the present and start living again. We feel confused and the 'people in power' have been working very hard to make you believe that you have no power, and no control.

Our inner conversations we have with ourselves are really us talking to God...

The Gospel is an impossible religion and Christianity institutionalized guilt as a virtue. Jesus of Nazareth was a powerful "Son of God" who came to open everyone's eyes to the fact that you and everyone else are also the "Son of God." There is no blasphemy in saying this, but it is clear that we are all the same and come from God and this 'understanding' has been suppressed for centuries. One could almost say it doesn't matter if Jesus is genuine or not, but his story that is told to us in the Bible has a lesson that is specific for each one of us. God has given divinity to all religions. So which one is correct, all or none? Some believe theirs is the most correct way when, in fact, they are all equal revelations of the divine.

An interesting fact is that the Roman Catholic Pope Gregory the XIII pushed the use of the '12' month calendar as well as the mechanical clock in society. Man changed significantly when he started to keep track of time. But there is a fundamental error in our accounting of time that has created a disconnection. The error in time keeping created by the Church pushed us into 12 months with varying amounts of days and 52 weeks that start on different days of the week. A more harmonious structure to the calendar would be to have 13 months (moon cycles) that are all 28 days long with four weeks in each month with 364 days in a year (Aztec Age of the fifth Sun 3113 B.C.- 2012 A.D.) and having each week and month start on a Sunday and end on Saturday makes better sense. This would be so much easier to keep tract of and less complicated. The way it is now has brought time to something that is inorganic which is outside of our natural body flow.

"If humanity wishes to save itself from biosphere destruction, it must return to living in natural time."

– Pacal Votan

The Bible (lie) was written and rewritten by man to fit the needs and wants of man. The elite use the Bible to keep people in control and to make everyone subservient without them even knowing it. Knowledge is part of evolution and we must learn and grow from this enslavement so that we can better our lives.

Even if you're not very religious, you can be a person that follows a human moral code—a feeling of ethical codes by which man should live. Strive for peaceful coexistence and developing indifference for material items and things. It is strange to me that most churches do not tell their parishioners to read the Bible and only 'preach' at them with scripture and passages in church services. People should take it upon themselves to know what is in the Bible. Unfortunately, many become disenchanted with the church when they realize that the people running the place, are more often than not, nothing like the "good book" said they should be and are somewhat hypocrites. This seems to be true of many religious institutions. The religious experience though is still beneficial since it instills goodness and people's attitudes can be adjusted and made better through more understanding, loving, caring and giving.

Most all human beings are concerned about the potential prophecy of the "End Times." If in fact the 'apocalypse' happens differently than we have been told, it should confirm that nothing we have been told is correct. The fact that everything is basically a lie including our history, our origins and that all our major world events have been 'orchestrated' is unnerving. As we uncover and learn more of the elite's demonic plans for us, we should vow to never surrender to them or the things that they have planned for us.

There is a God, a good and just God. But we don't hear too much about him in the Bible. The authors have lied to us about this too, selling us an evil God to keep control and maintain order over us. So I asked myself this question: If the establishment has manipulated everything and lied to us (about just about everything) then why am I to believe that they gave us the truth about God and the Bible? So much of the Bible seems barbaric and not really the behavior of a "Holy God." Have the authors hid the real God from us and sold us a false, evil God? The purpose may be in that you cannot control people who are united, strong and happy! You can go to the four corners of the Earth, all-encompassing different speech, food, cultures—but instead of showing all our similarities, the authors have used these differences against us to instill fear. Fear of others and the unknown. Everyone in their own corner with their own belief and the beliefs of others we conclude are wrong.

The only person that is served by all this division and confusion is evil (Satan). We need to look beyond our programming and use our common sense. We have been misled and it all started at the Tower of Babel where the first great society was corrupted. And yet today the division rages on... nation against nation, brother against brother, Arabs against Jews (even though they share the same father, Abraham), white against black, Democrats against Republicans, Christians against Muslims and Muslims against Jews. The aggression between cultures and religions has been raging for centuries, yet after all this time we have not progressed to live in harmony with each other. If you take all the 'belief systems' in the world today and compare them, logic dictates that many religions are predicated on false doctrines. It may be that each maintains a piece (or a fraction) of the truth, but they all lead to a false prophet.

The energy of the world is moving and shifting westward and will continue westward until it is settled back in the East (China). The energy is the essence of consciousness and the vibrational energy of humankind. The "Ark of the Covenant" is a mystery of the world. Some say the path of the Ark follows this energy force and creates even more power for those that possess it. The 'energy' originated within the higher levels of consciousness manifesting and coming here to Earth, in the 3rd dimension, in a human-like form to have this Earthly experience. These 'human forms' were reptilian in nature and many inhabitants of the Earth thought of them as Gods. These 'fallen angel' reptilian Gods decided to procreate man as a hybrid of human and reptilian cross-breeding. Earth has always been a "free will" planet for creation so this 'invasion' was all a part of the creation that took place as these

Gods re-designed man's DNA and memory to impose control over him. It was Lucifer that originally came here to have a hand in creating 'man' and from this doing, other entities (some good and some not so good), followed and it is possibly these entities that we read about in many religious texts.

As a taunt towards God you see the occult members never deny the existence of God, but instead have chosen to follow Satan. Everything the Illuminati do is for satanic reasons. Their purpose is to serve him by the control and manipulation of the masses. Satan's goal is to deceive and corrupt everyone on Earth so they, along with him, all end up living in "hell." However, Satan has also deceived the elite. They believe in the Luciferian philosophy. That Adam and Eve were held prisoners in the Garden of Eden and that they were set free from the 'chains of ignorance' through the gift of intellect from Satan and thus, by the use of this gift of intelligence, man himself will become God. It's with these Luciferian teachings that these occult societies proudly challenge the established beliefs of modern day religion.

"Does God Dance? Of course he does and he is one 'heck' of a fox-trotter."
-Anonymous

We spend much time arranging patterns in our life (setting the table). Our existence is filled with guilt which we should not have as long as we are always on the moral side. Religious observance has God telling us what to do —as if we didn't know already. I think we've had enough of "throwing the book" at people and shouting at them the gospel word. Preaching is a moral verbal violence. Which excites people's sense of guilt? Guilt is not a constructive feeling and inside each one of us is the just and righteous path of love and creativity. And there is no more uncreative sense than guilt. You cannot love and feel guilty at the same time; just as you can't feel scared and angry at the same time. We lack something vital in our Western religious experience — the room for spiritual experience. The ability where the individual can realize his oneness with the internal energy of this universe (who some call God and others prefer not to name). Western religions are suspect of mystical experiences.

However, it was a mystical experience that led to Jesus believing he was God incarnated. Looking from this perspective, God appears as a monarch and anyone else claiming to be God is an act of subversion and would be guilty of introducing democracy in the heavens. It is ironic how Americans insist that a Republic is the best form of government when all their religion is a monarchy? Jesus was a person who had this philosophical mystical experience or a "Cosmic Consciousness Event." Many refer to this as Christ Consciousness or coming into Christ Consciousness. So according to many people the 'Christmas Jesus' is God, but no one else. People don't live the religion 'of' Jesus, but rather live the religion about Jesus. The true 'messiah' is in each one of us and when religious people talk about the "return of the messiah" it is not just one person returning, but is comparatively the point when enough people have 'awakened' to shift human conscious.

Every soul and projection in this reality is an expression of consciousness. Consciousness through creation is one with Christ Consciousness. Christ Consciousness is the key to many doors. Once you understand that Christ Consciousness is the consciousness of the Prime Creation and not the 'institutions of religions,' you are able to step out and be free to grow. Creation exists through love, not separation – the unconditional love that extends to all. Institutionalized religion is there to actually 'hide' you from the truth; the truth that Christ Consciousness 'is' within each one of us. It is not religious; it is spiritual. Your inner thoughts affect the outer world around you. It is important to understand that your feelings and emotions have a distinct impact on what is going on around you, and you create what you want to experience.

Anti-Semitism should be discussed. (This is no way an indictment against Jews.) We should in fact, promote the idea that Jewish people, Judaism and more – specifically Zionism (The Israeli State) should be openly discussed and examined as much as any other people, culture or religion. Despite the inordinate amount of control in positions of power and influence in our western governments, corporations and social cultures across the planet - Jews make up less than one percent (1%) of the world's population. It is considered 'taboo' to question the motives or why so many are in positions of power.

Being a Jew, I was always 'pleased' to see so many of my brethren succeed in so many capacities of business and government. That was until I 'awoke' to start questioning everything I knew, including my friends, my faith, my religion and exactly what Zionism represented. I began to see how the real facts of how America rules over the world and The Zionist state of Israel rules over America and its people's conscience. It has been chanted over and over again by politicians and the news media that we should embrace Israel because it is the only 'democratic' state in the Middle East.

The Jewish lobby in Washington has a disproportionate amount of power and control and stands above others with support, money and access. As many before me have been able to do and 'step back' and observe the situation with a critical eye, I also now see how the events of September 11th 2001 have been beneficial for the Zionist State of Israel. The attacks have 'swung' the American opinion as well as the world's opinion against Muslim countries while at the same time giving support to align with the actions of Israel. This is a clever deflection technique used to stifle any discourse that may cast the Jewish people or Zionism in a bad light. Many people are tricked into believing that all the Palestinians are terrorists and the "Israeli State" is just a poor, helpless, innocent victim where the truth is quite the opposite.

Judaism — shields the religion from being exposed of its true nature which is at its core a racist and supreme ideology (cabalistic — pagan) that declares Jews as the superior race chosen by God and all Non-Jews as sub-human.

In a 1942 essay called "The Jew does not fit in" Manly P. Hall suggests that anti-Semitism was the price Jews had to pay for being what he called "a peculiar race – of conscious people." The 'karma' of the Jews holds a gradual dying out of racial persecution of Jews as a class in the degree and with the rapidity that the Jew forgets he is a Jew and remembers he is a human being. The most important takeaway from this discussion is that there is a distinct difference between Judaism and Zionism. For the most part, Jews and the Jewish people, are innocent bystanders just trying to make good during their life, when in fact the real evil, the real danger is in the support of the Zionist state.

The Bible is a beautiful book and has many 'unbelievable' stories and writings. Does that mean it is false? No, but it does mean that some parts could be grossly translated as in the King James Version. This is reality. Ignore it or accept it. We must be aware of the signs and even in the scripture itself the authors have given you a warning. In Jeremiah 8:8 the Bible actually states and asks- all of you and the whole world a question: *"How can you say, we are wise for we have the law of the Lord when actually the lying pen of the scribes has handled the scripture falsely?"*

Prophecies of the Bible 'line up' with what is happening now in the world today. The Bible talks of good versus evil and how at a time in the future Satan will try to take over. People and politicians may not be inherently evil, but are following a definite, well-thought-out sinister plan that they themselves are not aware of. This 'force' that has set this agenda in motion has been executing the 'grand plan' for years, decades, and possibly even centuries. The grand plan seems like its message is 'packaged' in world peace and goodness. But there is something evil and suspicious about the plan and many people are now waking up and seeing it for what it truly is: Satan's plan. Let's not fool ourselves either. There is a plan. When first enlightened to the "grand plan," it seems the arguments stated are compelling, the steps outlined seem, on the surface, to benefit humanity, but that is the cleverness of a mischievous fallen angel – to have you believe in something that is not truthful. Trust the owners of the universe, don't try to control it... that will only disturb it.

The veil between Heaven and Earth – it used to be one and may still be...as above so below...

Adam and Eve already had exactly what the serpent (Satan/Lucifer) promised them. They were immortal, enlightened (wise beings) in the image of God and ever since Eve bit into the 'apple' man has lost his way struggling to get back home. Humans are not just a physical body...our presence, essence is mind consciousness. That part of us lives on, forever. Isn't it ironic that one of the most recognized symbols in technology today is the 'bitten apple' (Apple computer)?

One of the difficulties we have is to discern messages from God and data from other sources. This is one great challenge and discrimination is a simple matter — the application of a simple rule (mind) is always your highest thought. The clearest word, your grandest feeling, anything less is from another source and not God. The highest thought is always a thought that contains joy! The clearest words are those that contain truth and the grandest feeling is the feeling which we call love. Joy, truth and love are always interchangeable and neither is set above the other since they are all equal. Follow the guidelines when determining information and what true source it is coming from. We must listen. If you keep making the same mistakes or the resolution is always the same and it is not the desired resolve, then you are not listening. You will get the message sooner or later. You will never be coerced because you have "free will" and it is these choices we make that guide us along the path of life.

You have the power to do as you choose. Again, there is no right or wrong. Just the experience! These helpful messages that come to you are just that – intended to help and guide you. These thoughts and messages will continue to come in various ways until you call them your own. Messages will take on many forms, but all will be the 'same' when analyzed. You can't miss them if you truly listen and cannot be ignored once truly heard.

Go talk to God! Question: When you talk to God or you talk to yourself....is there any difference? The inner voice you hear is there to guide, assist and help you navigate life's journey...is that you? When people think that there needs to be a special time, place or person that God communicates with them, they are hindered from actually receiving the message. There is no special time, place or person that can receive this information. It's universal. For some reason people have the preconceived notion that they must hear things from another person when, in fact, the true word of God comes directly to you from within. If you listen, really listen, then you are 'growing' in the right direction. Should we keep listening even when we think we are hearing unfamiliar, scary things or even if the information appears wrong? Especially when it may go against our 'established' way of thinking? Enlightenment is exactly that...seeing and considering other options and pathways. One day, all of humanity will start to listen on a collective level.

Ask yourself this question: What if everything I believe or thought I believed is wrong? We must 'unleash' ourselves from our previous conditioning. After that, we can grow beyond that point and we can understand more. We must theoretically 'let go' in order to actually find anything of value in this life. All discovery comes about by the person having the openness to not be 'right' all of the time. If you always have to be right, then you may never be able to grow beyond where you are *right now*. What if everything I thought was wrong? How do I know that I haven't been brainwashed if I am brainwashed? God cannot tell you his truth until you stop trying to tell him yours. Many believe that truth has come from God through words spoken by our priests, rabbis and ministers. Even the Bible tells us that these words are from God, but are they? No, they were written by man.

"Words are the least reliable bearer of truth."

- God

Listen to your feelings and listen to your highest inner thoughts. Listen to your experience and let that experience guide you. When this differs from what teachers say or what is written in a book (even the Bible) you realize they are just words. Words are the least reliable bearer of truth because of the writer's interpretation and the reader's interpretation may be quite different. When people want validation and to see "proof" of God's existence, they look to see some amazing "miracle" occur before their eyes. The fact is, God exists in front of us each moment of each day. Our mere existence is a miracle. It is how everything in nature 'shows up.' God has no defined form- but exists everywhere in everything. So the miracle is already here. It really is the great unseen. If God had one specific form then all would only look for that one form...when, in fact, God's energy is formless. So anyone can see God as they desire and not just in one form. The message can come 'catered' to you in any form. This is a part of you since it is created by you. This is an inward experience. Never pray in supplication, but rather in gratitude. Don't ask for anything but 'thank' for what you already have. Never supplicate – appreciate.

Your mind knows the truth of your thoughts and God

knows what you know. The thought behind the thought, what might be called the 'sponsoring thought,' is the controlling thought. What you don't have now is what you seek and this seeking will not give you the desired results. The actual act of 'prayer' is redundant. You have already thought it before you prayed. Be thankful and your desired reality will be manifested. Have an attitude of gratitude.

There is no religion higher than truth...

If you think God is some omnipotent being who hears all prayers, says "yes" to some and "no" to others and maybe not acknowledge the rest, you are mistaken. By what rule of thumb would God decide? God is the observer and together with you are the creators. God created you in his likeness, but the rest is all you.

God created the process of life and provided you with free will and in essence – your will for yourself is God's will for you. You have the will to live your life and God really has no preference how you live it. It is up to you. This is the great illusion of existence that God cares what you do – God cares not what you do (but you should). He is not the micromanager of everyone. We should care about the process more and not the result. The result will be the (desired) intended result if we perform the process correctly. For example: It doesn't matter if you let your child play hide-and-seek or tag, what matters is that they are in a safe environment to flourish to play whatever game they choose. The wise and patient parent knows this. Unfortunately, too many worry about the outcome. It is this dichotomy not caring deeply about the process, but more focused on the outcome or result. The 2nd great illusion of life is that the outcome is in doubt. The doubt of an outcome has brought about man's greatest concern, fear. If you doubt the outcome, then you doubt creation and you doubt God.

The Prime Creator is full of power with intentions that create results. You live your life with the illusion and if you doubt you will also fear. There are just really two emotions, love and fear. These are the opposite ends of the great polarity of the universe and our world as we know it today. All human action is based in love and fear. 'Motivation' and everything else (all emotion) are derivatives of these two. You must trust God's love.

As soon as we love, we fear we will not be loved back. And as soon as we know that someone loves us then we fear that we are going to lose that love. If and when you understand that you are the most incredible being God has created, you will never fear again. Why do you feel (as many people do) that you are less than magnificent? Know who you are. Love is non-conditional. We have forgotten what it is to be loved without condition. You only have been taught to live and clasp onto fear. If you do the opposite (and let go) then you will do much more than just survive. You can flourish to understand who you really are and who you can be. The more you are now the more you can become. You are the process of discovery... Who do you want to be? You are not here to learn lessons, but to create who you are. Remember who you were before and who you want to be in this life. Your soul knows and there is nothing it really doesn't understand from a life's perspective. You go to school if you want to learn certain 'man-made' subjects, but you already know deep inside what this life is about and why you have been put here. You just need to bring it out of you. The soul seeks to experience. So experience...

What is Hell? It is a belief that we have been given free will and yet some claim that if you do not 'obey' God and have sinned, then you will be sent to a place called Hell. What kind of free will is that? Does this not make a mockery of God? Hell is not what most people think. Hell is the experience of the worst possible outcome of your choices, desires and creations. It is the natural consequence, that which derives to who you really are. Hell is the pain you may experience through the wrong thinking. The word 'wrong' is used liberally here and is meant to show the opposite thinking. A better translation may be... *not in sync* with the divine. Hell is not a state of everlasting torment of fire and brimstone like Hollywood movies would have you believe. The fire and brimstone is a completely self-inflicted concept. You have created this from the fears programmed into your sub-conscience. What kind of God would let us believe that? As long as one of us (you and God) holds the truth about yourself through time it will never be lost...the truth about you will ultimately prevail. If there really is no hell, like we have been conditioned to physically think, then may you do whatever you wish without repercussions? Must you be threatened to be good? Does there need to be a presence of hell to make you a good person? Can you act without fear of retribution? God may say...is it fear itself that you need to do what is intrinsically 'right' or just? Who is making the rules and guidelines on how to act? Since you are your own 'rule maker,' you should only be judged by yourself. You have to live with yourself in this life. Who do you want to be? How well are you doing? Yes, you may do as you wish without retribution, but understand that your consequences of the results will either align or not align with the divine universe. Strive to realize this while you are still in this physical body. Remember we are here to create and experience. To do this properly, we should quiet the outer world so that the inner world can think and connect to our higher self.

"We are all self-made, but it is only the successful that will admit it."

-Earl (Nick) Nightingale

Inner peace is what we seek. But you can't have this experience if you're concerned so much about your outer reality. *"If you do not go from within then you will go without."* Many have been going without for most of their lives. Our potential is unlimited.

Nothing happens in God's world by accident. There is no such thing as coincidence. Nor is the world buffeted by random choice or fate. All snowflakes are unique just like individuals of humanity. The process can be the point. It does all start with a thought which leads to everything else. Most people have a hard time adapting the grandest truth. Some may say that believing we are more than we have been told is blasphemy, but go ahead and try and see if this is the truth. If you don't try, you will never know it to be truth or not. The biggest fear is that the biggest promise might be the biggest lie (from God).

1) You can do and have whatever you can imagine.

2) You attract what you fear. Emotion is the power which attracts – that which you fear strongly is that which you will experience.

We should have the freedom to worship any God we wish or even no God at all, if we choose.

Unlike what many people think about the devil, he isn't entirely opposing the divine plan that God has for him. "Satan" was created for a purpose and he has a gift to offer. His original name is Lucifer, but was called Satan which means "<u>accuser</u>" when he accused the Lord of evil. The name Lucifer means "light bringer" or "light bearer." God created Lucifer to be the enlightened angel of the universe. Lucifer possesses the highest awareness of all universal truths and understood the nature of all, realizing his gift was enlightenment to all beings. But Lucifer rebelled. It seems the 'elite's' religion is dedicated to Satan (Lucifer) which they believe is good. This is the opposite of what we understand. This thinking is called 'Satanic Reversal' where evil is good, lies are truth, darkness is light and death is life. A lot of religions use the words obey, serve, servitude, and these just de-power your true potential.

Elohim is the religion of the New World Order and is a 'humanist religion' which is about man (only) no god. A One world totalitarian, socialist government is basically a One World humanist government. In a Marxist, socialist society the underlying theme is there is no true middle class. Man was not meant to be a puppet. He was endowed with free will. The elite hold a dim view of the lower classes of society and promote birth control as a means of reducing the number of what they deemed the mentally and physically unfit. But the result of this population—controlling heredity through selective breeding—would provide reincarnating souls with greater chances of being born in to wealthier, happier and more creative families.

The Jesuits (the Society of Jesus) is a male religious congregation of the Catholic Church that works in education, intellectual research and cultural pursuits. What is not usually told is that the Jesuit group has been involved in part of the molding and manipulation of certain events and the history that has been reported over the past 500 years or so. Much of our higher education and the network of schools and universities have been established and controlled by this group. Most 'books' especially historical records have been written by the Jesuits and are the same basically used by most of our schools today. The influence of the Jesuits upon modern society is somewhat hidden in that a lot of the foundation of our enslaved society has been structured by the original Jesuits. All of the 'push' is disguised with the façade of a religious group cover and have also infiltrated the Vatican.

The 'Gospel of Jesus' is the process of waking up and knowing who you are. You being a man – make yourself God. Is it not said in the laws that ye are gods? If that is what the scripture said it cannot be denied, so why is it blasphemy to say that I am the son of God? Certain words have been emphasized in the King James Version of the Bible. Jesus is "a" son of God – just as you are. (The word "of" means "of the nature of"). Those of us who know and understand that we are the same as Jesus are quiet about it for obvious reasons. Some of us have this cosmic conscience experience and have realized who we are. You feel completely within the universe – you feel profoundly rooted in it and connected with it. The whole energy is intimate with you. It is through your moving, your seeing, talking and anything you do is expressed of that which moves the sun and the stars. If you don't feel it you can feel alien to this world – and if you feel you are a stranger...you can feel hostile and alone.

"People who stick to their words will also stick to the problems that arise from those words."

-Anonymous

There is a 'new wave' of manipulated conscience that is telling all of us that God does not exist and is putting religion and religious people in a bad light. As we progress more and more into the modern paradigm of money, debt and consumerism the further we travel away from the goodness that is a part of all of us. The reality of this is that this trending is not natural and has been guided, cultivated and implemented by an evil, hidden hand that has affected billions of people here on Earth even without them knowing on a sub-conscience level. Simply, we have been programmed. The "Hypothesis of God" doesn't help us to make any predictions if he exists or not. There is no real difference to science. Science is essentially profiling. Science bases its analysis on what's going to happen—study the past and based on those events, derive what will happen in the future. But if all of 'this' is in the "Hands of God" then it doesn't make any difference, does it? You are not accounting for the unknown or for many of us...the known. The New Age movement is all purposely designed to separate us (they want you to believe that you can become gods). The 'evil' people of this world are fulfilling and pushing Bible prophecy to the letter. Satan (or Lucifer or the devil) is real and he is not some little, red man with horns and a tail. Yet, he can be evil yet he can also be beautiful because he is a fallen angel and he used to be one of God's favorites. Even so, he is not one to follow during this time. In a world of increasing depravity and diabolical new laws we still have to live our lives, right? But just what are we living our lives for... the glory of God, or for the worship of Satan?

MONEY

BOOK 21

What is money? It seems that everyone is preoccupied with the accumulation of money yet they know very little about money. People will beg, borrow or even steal for money and it can cause some of the highest highs or the lowest lows of human emotions. Where did the concept of money come from? Who makes our money today? Why do we need money? And who stands to profit in the end? The 'real' history of money may be quite different than you know or even could imagine. First, money is an illusion. You don't need money (per se) since money itself has no real tangible value. You can't eat it, drive it, or sleep on it comfortably (even though some may think you can). It has no emotions or feelings, yet people love it. It is an inanimate object that represents merely a symbol. What can money do for you then? It can 'buy' food, or a car to drive to get to work, or even a nice comfortable bed to sleep on at night.

In today's world, if you don't have money - life can be tough. Each day, most of the world is preoccupied with money and it is amazing how many 'money related' jobs and careers have been created to just keep the money illusion alive. Traditionally the barter system was the main method for exchanging goods and products, but at some point it became much easier to use a medium such as money (gold and silver) to buy and sell items.

There are really no more important 'pieces of paper' in a modern society than its printed currency, and in America it is the "Dollar Bill." It is just a piece of paper yet it represents so much about us, our country and what we stand for...especially in its coded messages. The value is not in the paper itself, but in its perception. The dollar is no longer 'backed' by gold or any other tangible asset - and in fact it is backed by nothing (maybe oil to some extent internationally), but the truth is that the value is perceived by us solely on faith. We have essentially traded natural capital for manmade capital. Money is a symbol. A symbol used to represent the method of exchange of goods and products in a free market place, yet money has its own symbols and each bizarre symbol represents a specific idea or concept that has deep meaning. Your physical paper money (i.e.,...United States' dollar bill and the hundred dollar bill) has many symbols, some hidden and some not so hidden. People have and will continue to analyze the dollar bill for its century old puzzle of hidden messages and meaning like the 'All seeing eye,' the pyramid, the One World Government, and the Masonic symbols.

Much time and effort has gone into the details of our occult Illuminati money. The specific words, design, artwork and security measures that go into the printed bills are unprecedented. With so much attention to detail of money, it may be important to look deeper into the symbols on the money. The dollar bill has many coded messages for the discerning eye. Let's start with the obvious, the pyramid on the back of the dollar bill with the 'eye' at the top. Most people casually accept there is a pyramid on our dollar bill without questioning it deeper. A pyramid is an unusual thing to be placed on American currency (don't you think?), but there is a specific reason of what it represents and why it is there. The pyramid represents society and its representative levels of hierarchy. The hierarchy is not necessarily wealth, but rather represents power and control; as you move up the pyramid the power and control over the previous level increases. Note that the top piece of the pyramid is separated from the rest. At the appropriate time, the pyramid will 'come together' symbolizing total control of the top elite section over the entire pyramid (the rest of the world). The eye represents the "all seeing eye" or the eye of Horus. This eye is literally watching over everyone and has been since its placement on the dollar bill. So how and why is there a pyramid on the bill? It was in 1935 and Henry Wallace the Secretary of Agriculture and advisor to President Franklin Delano Roosevelt (FDR), suggested that the "Great Seal" be placed on the back of the dollar bill. It was well known at the time that Wallace was deeply involved in the occult and had close ties to one of the most unique and intriguing occultist by the name of Nicholas Roerich. Roerich was a Russian writer and accomplished painter who had been used by the government to secretly assemble all the Asian countries of the world into a one-currency system. He was unable to get this done, but was able to get his occult friend Wallace to convince FDR to finally approve the esoteric, pyramid symbol seal on the bill. Roerich's role as an advisor to America was no doubt backed, blessed and financed by the 'elite,' global, central bankers who also believe in occult philosophy. They believed by placing occult symbols, it gave them power and energy and relished the fact that it could be done through the printed currency.

Around the pyramid seal are the Latin phrases "Novus Ordo Seclorum" and "Annuit Coeptis." The former literally means "of the Ages" or "One World Order" and the latter is "Our Enterprise is a success." The word "Mason" (as in Freemason) can be made by connecting letters in the phrase within a five-pointed star. The pyramid has thirteen levels (13 being symbolic) and at the bottom is the Roman numeral date of 1776 (MDCCLXXVI). 1776 could represent the founding of America, but in this case the date May 1, 1776 actually represents the (modern) founding of the Illuminati of Bavaria here in America. The dollar bill represents the 'new' money of the 'New' America which was to be the modern world leader of the push for the "New World Order." If you look at the seal on the backside of the dollar bill there is a bird many believe to be an American eagle. This is not an eagle, but rather a phoenix which is another occult symbol. The phoenix is cyclically reborn as a new life arising from the ashes of its predecessor. This is an obvious metaphor for how a 'new society' will rise from the ashes of a previously destroyed society. The phoenix is holding thirteen arrows in one claw and a branch with thirteen leaves in the other. Above the phoenix is a cluster of thirteen stars laid out in such a way that a 'larger inverted' star can be drawn between them. The shield in front of the 'bird' has thirteen stripes. Thirteen (13) is symbolic because it is thought that the original 13 bloodlines had descended from Jesus. Ironically, the one dollar bill has the words "In God We Trust" on the back between the two shields. This was implemented during the Eisenhower administration in 1955 for two reasons: 1) to ensure that the appearance of 'God' was being 'packaged' with our money, and 2) because the fear of 'alien' threat was high (manufactured or not) and his administration did not want people to lose belief in God during this early time of space travel. Another bizarre item on the front of the bill in the upper right hand corner near the "1" is the presence of a very tiny owl sitting in the left side notch. The owl is very symbolic of the Illuminati since it represents wisdom and knowledge and can see things at night when others can't. The owl has been a symbol of the Illuminati and the elite for centuries. The final item on the front of the bill is the words "This Note Is Legal Tender For All Debts, Public And Private." The bill shows us that money is 'debt' written in plain English. All money brought into circulation is brought in as debt since the money (the principal) amount is owed back along with interest.

The hundred dollar bill (affectionately called a "Benjamin") is full of symbols, messages and hidden codes. The front of the bill makes it clearly evident that an important message is being 'telegraphed' out to the public. The left side of the bill practically looks the same as the traditional style of the $100 dollar bill for the past century – but the right side is all new and there is a thick blue bar or stripe with little 'Liberty Bells' dividing both sides. No bill has ever looked like this before. The 'new' right side has a lot of gold color (as in "Gold"): a gold inkwell, a gold feather, a gold '100' on the bottom right and gold writing. It almost looks like two different bills have been 'spliced' together at the blue division bar. The new hundred dollar bill is like a 'story board' representing what may or will happen to our money in the future. The bill could very well may be a significant change to take place in our Fractional Reserve Currency System (FIAT currency), which means "Let it be so" where we 'return' to a monetary system that is wholly backed or at least partially supported by "Gold." Many believe gold is real money and throughout history its always had intrinsic value. This 'change' will occur when the people lose faith in the current system of paper currency and demand a sound money policy backed by something of real value...like gold or silver.

The cursive words written on the right side are 'penned' from the gold Liberty Bell inkwell and gold feather. These symbolize the power that Congress has to dismantle the FIAT money system with a 'stroke' of a pen. The words are a portion of our Declaration of Independence – quote: *"That whenever any form of Government becomes destructive to these ends, it is the right of the people to alter or to abolish it and to establish new government laying its foundation on such principals and organizing its powers in such form as to them shall seem most likely to affect their safety and happiness."* It is up to the citizens to take back what has been taken from them. This passage is neither ironic nor coincidental. The Federal Reserve is 'mocking' every American to pay attention to what is going on. There may be even more hidden messages on both the dollar and hundred dollar bill; some see a face of an "alien" on the dollar bill.

The object of working is to make money and the object of making money is to be able to go home and enjoy the money which can buy you things (essential and nonessential). The illusion is that money can, or will, buy pleasure and happiness. This is a complete fallacy. Money never brings happiness, because all happiness and contentment depend upon not putting down a symbol of power (money) but rather in discipline. For example, boat piers with many yachts that are always docked and seldom used because they have been bought on the illusion that if you buy 'one' it will give you pleasure. But at some point usually, early on, they realize that it is a lot of work, money and time to get that pleasure—the art of seamanship may be rewarding, but to get the full enjoyment takes more energy than most people have time for. So they just entertain on the boat and have cocktail parties, never really using it for its intended purpose. In a myriad of ways, most people believe that very wealthy people (are thought to) go home to salacious orgies and great banquets of food and wine, but no one really does and they (just like everyone else) go home to a TV diner and spend the evening looking at an electronic reproduction of life on a 'box.' The box I refer to is the TV or your computer which divides and separates you by a video screen – whereby you have no real human interaction. It seems so many of us are waiting for some illusive moment in the future where we will be able to catch the brass ring on the "merry-go-round" ride of life —and usually it never turns up the way we think. We condition ourselves (and our children) through a false sense of identity and the insolvable problem of constant frustration and the perpetuation of one living only for the future. We are not living for today—because if you live for today - the future will also be more enjoyable. Happiness exists now (not in a promissory note like the dollar bill). For tomorrow may never come like you think?

We pay money for things we value (usually some kind of material item). The paradox is that anything that is really worth anything in life came to us free; our minds, our spirit, our souls, our hearts, our bodies, our hopes, our dreams, our ambitious, our intelligence, our love of family and friends. All of these 'possessions' are free. So the things that really cost us money (material items) are actually very cheap in the 'spectrum of life' since these items can be replaced. A fortune, a mansion or a gold piece of jewelry can be wiped out or lost, but you can never quite replace the prized possession of love or affection from another.

Countries borrowing money is a racket. The banking overlords use a process whereby they create money out of 'thin air' – then loan a country a lot of the 'created' money. When there is too much debt and the money cannot be repaid, the bankers will demand payment in the form of real assets or resources such as land, ports, railroads, utilities or some kind of infrastructure. If you control the water (utility company) you can control the country. Why should governments be borrowing money anyway? It is not fiscally responsible and it is unfair to the citizens. How do we cure debt with more debt? You don't, and it can only get worse. When you're collecting taxes during good times (financially speaking) people don't pay attention to the details as much. War creates the same situation, but war can also eliminate people's rights. It is during war times that governments push through laws and legislation that they don't want to have scrutinized. Generally, the purpose of war is many 'fold,' but nothing changes society quicker than war. What would take 50 years in peacetime can be accomplished in 5 years at war. The war propaganda machine will trample your rights and place a country into debt quickly. The unfortunate lasting aspect of wartime is that your rights and liberties that were taken are never restored and the war debt continues to mount and is still owed. England just finished paying off their war debt, not from WWII – but from WWI. It is during wartimes that countries borrow a lot of money and it is inevitably that the same ardent Private Central Banking Globalists Cabal are behind the funding of 'all' sides of the conflict. Millions of Americans report their income and employment status to the U.S. government out of fear and for no other reason. Many owners of businesses, especially small business are terrified that they will be persecuted by some government bureaucracy for not following one of the many thousands of regulations that business must obey; many regulations exist for no good reason – and are there only to protect larger business's profits. This is counterproductive because fearful small businesses are hesitant to take risks, expand, and borrow money or even hire new employees.

We have been separated from our natural system of flow. If you look at money objectively (or even subjectively) it is not natural. Money destroys all synchronicity and no true blessings will arise from the great force of the universe if you solely chase money alone. No miracles will occur if money is involved. Money corrupts because people think they deserve the 'intangibles' that are associated with making money. There is a sense that you deserve something in earnest if you have earned enough of these 'magical notes' by working. Money is just a 'medium' and all the money you make in this lifetime cannot be taken with you beyond death. The right thing will happen to you if you allow it and that is your desire, but this will have no bearing on the amount of money that can be made or acquired.

America with its controlling private international 'banksters' has invaded governments, toppled regimes, gone to war and have manipulated markets in order to keep the illusion of the 'Petro-

Dollar' alive. The entire debt-based monetary system and our materialistic society is a 'false society' and is essentially one of the lowest forms of a 'developed' nation in the history of mankind. We actually have only regressed on the 'ladder of ascended enlightenment' and right now there is way too much violence, way too much greed, and way too much manipulation.

'Petrodollar' – When countries buy oil, they exchange their currency into American dollars and this is called the 'Petrodollar.' In the past, most of the world's oil transactions were conducted in Petrodollars, but over the past few years many countries are 'pivoting' away from exchanging their money into Petrodollars and have circumvented the system. When enough countries refuse the Petrodollar this will weaken the dollar and could even bring about a collapse of the dollar. The Petrodollar creates immediate investment into the U.S. economy, but if this ends then all that money (debt) will come back to America devaluing the existing money supply already here in America.

All of the wars, the assassinations, weapons of mass destruction and the guise of doing this with the purpose of Democracy connect back to the Western Central Bankers. All wars are banker's wars for the sake of money, oil, power and control. I realize this is difficult to comprehend and that there should be a more noble cause for all of these events, but there is not. All the wars benefit the central bankers in some form or another or they would not occur. Question: Why is the U.S. mired in so many military conflicts right now? Even going back in history to the very beginning there are numerous examples of wars starting with the American Revolution. United States fought the revolution primarily over King George's monetary policies. The Third Currency Act which forced the colonists to abandon their own government-issued currency and conduct business using only the printed bank Notes from the Bank of England. Borrowed at interest, they would not let the U.S. operate on an honest money system and policies which freed the ordinary man from the clutches of the money manipulators. This is still true today. Our public schools don't teach that the bankers were really behind the American Revolution. After the Revolution, the U.S. was able to issue its own valued-based currency so the private banks couldn't 'skim' the wealth of the people through interest-bearing bank notes. The American Revolution was fought to free the citizens from King George's Currency Act which ordered all people to exchange and conduct business using the English bank notes.

The Bank for International Settlements (BIS) established in 1930 is an international organization of central banks based in Basel, Switzerland which "fosters international monetary and financial cooperation and serves as a central bank for central banks throughout the world." It oversees The European Union (EU) which in turn regulates the "Euro" which is the currency being used in most western European nations. Countries like Greece do not have its own central bank, but are members of the EU. At this time, most European countries are in severe debt. The important correlation to be made is that the same private International Banking cartel (Cabal) is in control of our money system here in America. The Federal Reserve Bank has twelve district banks located in the United States that issue our money supply. It is this hierarchy of banking systems that should alarm the average citizens since it is so secretive and guarded. Who is the person that sits at the head of the table at the BIS and gives direction on monetary policy? Is it a Rothschild? Who are these illusive people that remain hidden yet control so much of the world's money and debt?

The Central Bankers were tenacious and knew that they could easily corrupt its nation's leaders. Mayer Amschel Rothschild uttered the words, quote: *"Give me control of a nation's money and I care not who makes the laws."* The Central Bankers started setting up a new private bank called the First Bank of the United States. They did this with the aid of the Rothschild agent – Alexander Hamilton.

The First Bank was founded in 1791 with a 20-year charter which by the end almost ruined the nation's economy while enriching the bankers. It was in the process of not being renewed since the U.S. wanted to go back to the value based currency on which the people did not pay interest at all and threatened the Rothschild banking entity and also the government. The elite made reference – to the effect that the United States will find itself involved in the most disastrous war if the charter was not renewed. The U.S did not renew and found itself in war in 1812 and afterwards even though it won the war Congress was 'forced' to grant a new charter for another private bank. The Second Bank of the United States created and owned by the same international banking interest as the first. Unemployment and debt prevailed through 1832 until Andrew Jackson used the slogan "Jackson and No Bank." Fast forward about 30 years and – a little-known fact about President Abraham Lincoln who spoke out against the Central Banking system and big corporations, saw him as a threat. It was Lincoln's printing of the interest free "Greenback" currency which may have got him assassinated.

"The money powers prey upon the nation in times of peace and conspire against it in times of adversity. The banking powers are more despotic than a monarchy, more insolent than autocracy, more selfish than bureaucracy. They denounce as public enemies all who question their methods or throw light upon their crimes."
-Abraham Lincoln

The real agenda of the Central Bank is to create more debt than money which there is no way to repay except with more debt (borrowing more money). Private central banking is not a science, but rather a religion that benefits the elite priesthood (bankers). The rules are arbitrary and the fraud persists with lethal, financial results. People are brainwashed into believing that this is the way banking is supposed to be and no alternative paths exist or should even be considered or investigated. The "Rule by design" is by design. Divide and conquer – and impose debt which is a financial form of slavery. The system is built to 'trick' people into obedience. The fraudulent money system exists because people believe 'it to be so' when, in fact, it is just a house of cards or an elaborate Ponzi scheme. Central banks do not exist to serve the people. They only exist to selfishly serve the owners.

The Federal Reserve is a private bank with its majority class 'A' shareholders owned by International Banking families such as the Rothschilds, Warburgs, Rockefellers, Kuhn Loebs, J.P. Morgan, Israel Siffs, and Lehman Brothers (which is now defunct). This private banking cartel called "The Board of the Federal Reserve" is not officially part of the United States Government. They are a private bank. They are never audited; they never pay taxes; and design and print American money which displays their 'Illuminati' occult symbols. They also collect taxes through the IRS which they loan back to us as debt with interest. The U.S. is not a country anymore – it is a corporation. The U.S. is really just another crown colony of the British Empire. On our money, it says *In God We Trust* but which God are they referring to? Today, ninety–eight percent (98%) of all monies held by the U.S. banking system are basically just five companies (banks): JP Morgan, Goldman Sachs, Bank of America, Citibank and Morgan Stanley. The architects of this plan are the globalists and from the manipulation of the banking cartel - they (will) control the complete breakdown of the current system. Their motto is 'chaos will come from order' (order out of chaos).

The history of the Federal Reserve System is basically a history of the greatest 'Ponzi' scheme ever created. A group of private bankers (mostly from Europe) agreed to take over the monetary and credit system of the United States which they finally did in 1913. All the money and credit they have kept private ever since. The stock of the Federal Reserve can never be traded publicly. It can only be handed down through banking families or through company partner ownership trades. It is a monopoly. The cast is a "Who's *who*" of banking names such as, Rothschild (Great Britain), Sieff (Israel), Warburg (Germany) along with their American counterparts J.D. Rockefeller and J.P. Morgan. Paul Warburg was the original designer of the Federal Reserve. Many of these bankers personally financed the First World War, The Communist Revolution, Hitler, and the Japanese in WWII. Central Banks main function, aside from general banking, is to finance wars. War finance is the most profitable business for a Central Banker. It was in about 1911 these men met for financial collaborations on Jekyll Island, Georgia, to form a new banking cartel with the express purpose of forming The Third Bank of America of the U.S. with the aim to oversee complete control of the United States money supply. Instead of calling the new formed cartel The Third Bank of America due mostly to hostility towards the Second and the First Bank, they chose to name it "The Federal Reserve Bank" in order to grant the new bank a quasi-government image, but, in fact is a privately (held) owned bank. The Freedom of Information Act does not apply to the Federal Reserve since it is not a government entity. In 1913, the 16th Amendment was implemented which was the Internal Revenue Service for Income Tax for which several states still have not ratified the Bill or Amendment. This was all voted on at the end of the year during Christmas Holiday and Congress passed (somehow) with Woodrow Wilson, president at that time and servant to the elite, signing it as he promised the Bankers for exchange for campaign contributions. He unwittingly ruined the financial system forever. Note: Prior to the Federal Reserve there were no world wars.

Fast forward about 50 years, President John F. Kennedy understood much of this and although he was under control of the elite early on in his term he 'gained a conscience' at some point and he wrote, and signed, Executive Order 11110 which ordered and allowed the U.S Treasury to issue a new interest-free public currency called the United States Note. They were not borrowed from the Federal Reserve, but were created by the U.S. Government and backed by stockpiles held by the U.S. This represented a return to the system and economics the United States had been founded on and it was perfectly legal to do so under the Constitution. 4.5 billion dollars went into public circulation which eroded interest payments to the Federal Reserve and loosened their control over the nation. Five months after signing the Executive Order 11110, J.F.K. was assassinated in Dallas, Texas. Not long after that, the new President, Lyndon B. Johnson in charge and on board with the 'Bankers,' pulled from circulation and destroyed all the U.S currency notes. John J. McCloy president of the Chase Manhattan Bank and President of the World Bank was named to the Warren Commission to investigate the Kennedy assassination. The Warren Commission was really there to ensure the cover-up of what was going on and McCloy was there to make sure the American public never got a hint of the financial dimensions behind the assassination. Another interesting fact is that Allen Dulles (who was on the Warren Commission) ironically, had just been fired by President Kennedy from heading up the CIA.

On another note: Any person within our government that goes along with this plan should be impeached. Anyone involved in a criminal conspiracy is in fact a criminal and should be arrested according to U.S. laws. They took an oath on the Bible before office and, no matter what, should continue to support and uphold the laws given to us by our Founders. Money is a symbol. It is not inherently good or bad, yet some perceive it as the root of all evil. It is the people that manipulate money that can be evil. There are no evil governments or evil currency, but the people that run those organizations can be evil.

The banking elite plan to fraudulently take for themselves nearly all the wealth that remains in the current financial system by design. They will collapse the existing "Bretton Woods Monetary System" to hide their theft of tens of trillions of dollars, and to implement a replacement financial system that gives them total unlimited control over every economic transaction on Earth. This is what is planned for us and the world's economies unless it is stopped. We are governed by corporations today that have very little interest in the welfare of the United States of America or its citizens except for profits. The original goal of the New World currency was to set up three world currencies; the 'Euro' the 'Asian' and finally a new American-Canadian-Mexican currency called the 'Amero.' If these currencies encountered resistance then a new One World currency would be introduced. Currently the IMF, World Bank and (to a lesser extent) the Federal Reserve are working on a new currency which is a 'basket' of currencies called the SDR (Standard 'Special' Drawing Rights). The new basket may have the Chinese 'Yuan' as part of the new basket as China continues to muscle its way in as an international currency. As the Bible and many philosophers have prophesized, there will be a one world currency in end times. Some even say that we are very close to this time now whereby most all our transactions are controlled by the same money manipulators and elite 'Banksters.' Money today has also become "electronic" by means of computers and credit cards - so we essentially have a one world digital currency right now. One could argue that we are at that 'point' right now (it's your interpretation). Whether this is occurring 'incidentally' or being done on purpose, either way, a cashless society is easier to control.

It seems that in order to make "peace"...we use war. It sounds like 'double speak,' but if you really want to make peace with a country then go to peace with them! You don't go to war with them! We should try to figure out common ground and work together, but killing someone else's children to achieve peace doesn't make sense to anyone. The other 'fact' of war is that opposing sides will 'borrow' money from the same banking institution even though they are fighting against each other. There are countless examples of this through history and during WWII American private central bankers financed Hitler as well as America. This is wrong, but for International Bankers there is nothing more profitable than war. With International Bankers controlling the oil, media and governments, it is no surprise to find that we are always in a state of war. War is profitable! Important questions need to be asked when entering into a conflict like who stands to profit and what is the end goal of the aggression being done? There have been no fewer than 270 military conflicts since WWII that America has been involved in and this number is probably conservative. This number represents more military conflicts than 'all' of recorded history combined. All of this conflict for the sake of control and profits and solely at the expense of the average American citizen who is paying for it all through taxation, blood and bodies.

Because every dollar that we get from the Federal Reserve to fund our government is borrowed with interest, there's no way to ever pay it off. So, it is a system that sooner or later will collapse like a Ponzi scheme (house of cards). Now, I believe we can turn it around and we can fix it, but what people have to realize is there is going to be a 'little bit of heartache' with that. But the question posed to everyone in America right now is, *when* do you wish that heartache to be? Do you want that heartache to be on "your watch" or do you want that heartache to be on your children's or grandchildren's watch?

The Federal Reserve policies such as Quantitative Easing (QE) here in America and internationally have 'flooded' banks with money to lend out. A lot of this money has made its way into the U.S. stock market through corporations buying back its own stock. There is a 'disconnect' between Main Street and Wall Street. We have seen rising stocks values due to this QE money printing even though 'main street economy' remains weak and is getting weaker.

This combination is fiscally unsustainable. Going back just after the 2008 crash, President Bush forced us to bail out the banks with government money via the backs of American taxpayers. Banks claimed that if we did nothing there was going to be a huge collapse – which may have been the case. Quantitative Easing (QE-1) gave money to the banks to keep them solvent and to assist the faltering economy. The claim was that the banks would have collapsed worldwide if nothing was done. Congress, in turn, flooded the markets with newly printed cash. On the surface, the purpose was to save the money system, but this unsustainable methodology was really executed because the Central Bankers were not ready for the dollar and the currencies of the world to collapse at this time. It was too soon. They still had not extracted enough wealth from the middle class. It was almost as if they performed a 'limit test' to see if they could collapse the markets while analyzing the current amount of world debt. The goal was (and still is) to create such massive debt all over the world, in every nation of the world, and to affect *virtually* every individual - every family - every state - every city - every country and they have just about achieved their goal.

In America we are too well off. The Central Bankers want to bring us in line with the rest of the world. They want to create so much debt that the dollar will ultimately lose most (if not all) of its purchasing power. The New World Order and Central Bankers want the citizens to ask them for help (another bailout). It will not be forced on us this time. They already have a 'master plan' for a new monetary system that is to be implemented along with the following guidelines:

(1) A call for a creation of a New World Order.
(2) New Financial Institution run by the IMF or another World Bank entity.
(3) New Global Laws and Rules — abolishing the Constitution.
(4) A level playing field whereby no countries are above the other (America equal to Mexico, Canada) etc...

We are always in a state of 'fake recovery.' The massive money printing is not sustainable. The only way you can keep interest rates this low (near zero) is to print more money; a lot of money. The purpose of printing money is to buy more (Treasury) bonds and keep the system going artificially. Through methods of 'artificial scarcity' and 'artificial surplus' the financial markets are being 'propped up' to seem healthier than they really are. Ultimately, that strategy will fail because if printing money could solve all the debt and financial worries, and not create inflation, then why not just print even more money and get rid of taxes? We could print as much as we want yet, printing money will devalue the current supply of money and will eventually lead to definite inflation of the monetary system. The Federal Reserve knows this and is doing this on purpose to squeeze the middle class.

The 100-million-plus horrible deaths from all of the lies worldwide stem from a single policy of financial dictatorship by the private Central Bankers. They set the rules. The Central Bankers don't fight the wars, their children do not either, but ours do. You are being told by the corporate news media that foreign conflicts are a clash of people and citizens based on humanitarian needs...when in fact it is a real war between banking systems (private central bankers versus the sovereign country's banking system). Muslims are the target by corporate media because they do not believe in charging interest on borrowed money (since they understood in Roman times, prior to the Knights Templar, how these banking practices can destroy a civilization). Our government-controlled media must insist and convince us that Muslims have to be hated and killed. When, in actuality, they just refuse to submit to currencies loaned with interest. They do not want to be debt slaves to the New World Order. So the Central Banks ask through the government to have our sons and daughters go spill their own blood for the greedy bankers. The path to true world peace lies in the abolishment of all private central banking – everywhere.

"The greatness of a man is not in how much wealth he acquires, but in his integrity and his ability to affect those around him positively."
                                                    -Bob Marley

Iraq went off the Petro-dollar and within months they were invaded and Saddam Hussein was dead. The Iraqi currency was immediately converted back to the American Petro-dollar. Any Nation or country challenging the Petro-dollar will be met with serious adversity. Paying off our debt without reforming the money system is impossible. Inflation steals the value of all existing currency. Inflation is not the cause, but the effect.

As soon as the Libyan government was defeated (Gaddafi), the global bankers quickly put the country under western banking and away from the planned gold dinar. The BIS will not allow an Islamic nation bank to issue money interest-free either. The ultimate goal of the Central Bankers is to lend money out that cannot ever be repaid (debt) for total control as they have done in Greece and Cyprus. The Bankers want the country to get to a breaking point so that they have to give up something of real worth and value and that is the natural resources of the land or the land itself. Central Banks could even crash the currency so that the debt would be impossible to repay and again the resources would supplant money as a form of repayment. Syria and President Bashar AL-Assad are also targeted because they have no debt from the IMF, and don't use western central banks. American and NATO aggression continues to persist, also stemming from coveted land that oil pipelines could be run. Syria also has embodied laws against Geo-engineered foods so that companies like Monsanto are not allowed there to sell their seeds. Making all the people 'the same' is the way the elite Central Bankers will achieve a One World rule and a slave to the system.

The reason Cyprus is of interest is because wealthy international businessmen and drug lords were laundering money through Cyprus. The elite Central Banks had to wipe out their money in these bank accounts. When the banks closed on Monday, the pseudo-wealthy lost vast fortunes. Most people in Cyprus were not affected because they did not have much—but the people (drug lords and corrupt businessmen) lost most of their money. The 9% that was rumored to be "bailed in" was a smoke screen and it was actually closer to 48% that was seized during The Cypress Affair. Experts state that a similar situation will occur in other nations of the world. Here in America, if things get bad they could 'go after' the retirement funds of Americans—and maybe even 401(k)s and IRAs. Regular bank accounts may also be at risk. The Cyprus Affair was a test to see if the Central Bankers could get away with stealing people's money by means of a 'bail in.' The entire plan of the Central Banks is about 'Forced Debt Creation' (disannul wealth) like they did in Cyprus. They want massive debt for each person so eventually we will go back and ask for monetary help. They want us to ask for help because that way the ultimate blame for the problem is not pointed at them (even though it is). All European bonds and derivatives are 'made up' debt. It is these derivative markets that may crash first and then bring down the rest of the monetary system.

There are two kinds of economic systems:

(1) Free enterprise capitalism—private
(2) Monopolistic capitalism—public (tax control regulated by government)

It was in 1944 that Congress removed part of our money being backed by gold and in 1971 President Nixon officially took us off the gold standard, which at the time was only to be temporary. The FIAT money system hates gold. Adopting a 'Gold money system' or a gold-backed monetary system will shut down the printing presses and would in turn stifle the ability of the Central Banks to manipulate the money system and supply. The fractional reserve scam is a form of embezzlement and thievery. Gold will be used as a 'propaganda tool' of the financial elite and bankers to prop up the perception of value of 'paper money' usually by suppressing its value. Gold and silver could destroy the current money system. The FIAT system sucks the life out of a productive, capitalist system. The current systems exploit producers, consumers and any independent entrepreneurial people.

The powers that be want us to believe that ISIS (modern day terrorists) is adopting a gold/silver/copper money system similar to the proposed gold backed Dinar several years back that Kaddafi was structuring in Libya. ISIS, the 'bastard child' creation of the CIA, Zionist, Intelligence, and the established Wall Street Bankers, are left free to internationally move money around because they really don't want to stop ISIS. If they wanted to stop them - they would 'track' and 'seize' their bank accounts (by following the money), but they would rather them continue to create the negative image of having them run wild wielding their violence and pushing the gold standard. By doing this they are possibly linking gold to terrorists. This campaign is being waged in part to destroy the true value of gold and silver.

Gold is unique among assets in that it is not issued by any government or Central Bank, which means its value, is not influenced by political decisions or the solvency of one institution or another. When you take possession of physical gold you eliminate the counter party risk as when you deal with paper assets. *"The Golden rule is that those who own the Gold...rule!"* Wealth is never lost but transferred. The word "credit" is derived from the Latin word "credere" which means "belief." Money traditionally was pegged to a commodity, usually gold/silver. Historically, the ratio of fictional dollars to real dollars controlled by the banks was nine to one (9 to 1). This ratio is now inflated and there are no honest markets left standing, just manipulations, and that means *all* markets, including the stock market. Since 1971, gold and silver has been 'beaten' out of most people. It is really not even talked about and (for the most part), down right discouraged in all western countries yet the IMF can draw on Gold reserves at $42.20 per ounce anytime it wants from the U.S gold holdings. That is, if there is any Gold to be had at Fort Knox. Gold may be the standard, but the fact is that silver has been used more often as money by countries throughout history. It is the 'people's money.' It is trusted currency and has been, and will always be worth something. At times of economic turmoil it is the safe haven commodity to hold. At some time in the future you will either have gold/silver or you won't. Other alternative currencies may be introduced such as Bitcoin at times of upheaval, but be cautious because these are all based on some electronic form of digital currency and there is no intrinsic value. It will be then that everyone will be looking to purchase precious metals and you will not be able to find them anywhere. At this point, the price will sharply rise and will eventually go through the 'roof.' No true, fiscally responsible economics is taught in school today and they do not tell you that Gold and Silver are 'real' money.

This is the first time in history that virtually all the world currency is backed by nothing. The paper in your wallet is being driven to 'zero' just as fast as the globalists can accomplish this. The people on the inside know this is occurring. A complete paradigm shift will occur. This is all unprecedented, but FIAT currencies always inevitably collapse. The only difference this time is that the collapse will be on a global platform affecting every nation on Earth. The impending collapse may start as a derivative meltdown or possibly by an interest-rate hike. Investors may not be able to grasp how big the derivative (futures, options and swaps) market collapse could be because just about every single 'paper' financial product is attached to them in some form. All derivatives are attached to an interest rate. If interest rates increase (even a little) it will change the valuation of every investment. When, and if, the derivative markets fail, the entire system can go down quickly. After the collapse every person with a bank account will be looking for a financial savior and begging for the handlers of the World Bank and IMF (New World Order) to step in and bail the world out. The date for the impending collapse could possibly already have been decided for all the currencies including the Euro, Yen, Renminbi and the Ruble. America will descend into an area of zero sum austerity and violent political conflict extinguishing even today's feeble resemblance of economic growth. As major conflict 'brews' in Washington and across the world, it could be the economy to falter first...and through this could be the next big collapse – and then the greatest bank robbery ever done in America.

There are only two ways to go with our current monetary situation. Either default on our debt or create more debt to keep it going. Many European countries are dealing with this now that are on the Euro. Compounding interest on this money is reaching a point of collapse, or what is known as hyperinflation. It should be noted that the official debt for America now stands at more than 100% of our Gross Domestic Production (GDP) per annum. That is about $130,000 of debt per person in the United States. Five places not to be when the dollar collapses: Israel, Southern California, New York, Washington D.C., London, England. 2008 was a corporate problem. This next time it will be a global problem. People in their Mercedes will be driving around looking for food until their gas runs out.

There is too much debt...too many takers...too few makers... too many bankers... too much delusion...too much collusion...too few resources to sustain the unsustainable... we have entered the end stages of a sick society. We should stop feeding, obeying, complying with this corrupt system - we need to see through the illusion. A system seeking power will continue to keep its power unless someone stops it from growing. The system feeds upon itself for power.

The entire system is based on faith and right now that faith is being destroyed. Would you let the people that brought you the previous collapse be in charge of the new monetary reset? You wouldn't. They lied to you once (that you know of) so what has changed this time? Do you think they have gained a conscience? These days, almost every market is undergoing some degree of manipulation to the extent that 'free markets' are nonexistent. It should come as no surprise that the 'troika' US/CIA/FED is directly behind most events whose outcomes are typically destructive. The elite have been terrified that everything they have been doing and working toward as in the New World Order is at risk, something unthinkable until they started messing with Putin and Russia.

The Federal Reserve doubled its holdings of U.S. Treasuries between 2007 and 2014, but more amazingly it took 216 years to amass about 9 trillion dollars of unsecured debt total for America and it only took about 7-plus years to double that to 18 trillion. In addition, the nation's Central Bank keeps increasing this debt at a faster pace. This 'ramp up' of open market operations to purchase Treasuries through Quantitative Easing was done to stimulate the economy by keeping interest rates low to avoid a recession. The Federal Reserve has been criticized for simply monetizing debt since these purchases are used with credit it creates out of thin air. In essence it is just theoretically 'printing money' when, in fact, nothing is really printed and the money is issued as debt on the outstanding balance sheet. This shows how our money system is basically debt. Debt equals money and there is no way to ever repay this debt without printing more money. If the interest rates are low that means it has less interest to pay on the outstanding debt. If the interest rates go up, which seems to be controlled by the FED, then payments may not be able to be made on the debt and the U.S. could default on the obligation. When other countries run into this situation, they usually have to give up some resources in order to pay down the existing debt. This is how countries lose control of their country. Some reports indicate that China is the leading debt holder of U.S Treasuries and although this may be true for all foreign countries, the largest holder of U.S. Treasuries (debt) other than our government accounts (such as Social Security) is the Federal Reserve Bank which is a privately held entity and not a part of the U.S. Government system.

Money is important and our personal 'welfare' revolves around it, but it should be honest – it should be true – it should be reliable – it should be constant. One hundred cents today should be worth one hundred cents tomorow...yet, since 1913, the dollar has devalued by more than 96% which means that the hundred cents is only worth about 4 cents in today's real value. A better example is a million dollars in your mattress in 1913 would be worth (in buying power) $20,000 today. Unfortunately, people are unaware of the devaluation that is happening and are led to believe something that is not true or real. All money is tangentially interconnected and the 'big lie' is that you can get something for nothing and people are waking up to the fact that there is an elite class that 'prints money' from nothing that we 'common folk' all have to go out to earn and even give a portion of it back through taxes. People are getting "Fed Up" and are starting to know the real story of how this Ponzi money scheme works. Many people live their entire life based on the false belief system rather than understanding the truth.

The poor are honest. They will try to always pay their debts. They are charged more interest on the money they borrow on a percentage basis. Our democratic money system is an unlevel playing field. "Trickle-down economics" does not work because by the time the money actually reaches the bottom of the 'pyramid' it has lost its purchasing power. Our politicians will not change this either because they are dependent on lobbyists and big corporations for campaign contributions. They are beholden to corporate interests. When businesses and businessmen get together they do conspire against the general public by first focusing solely on profits from the consumer and then, second, by providing whatever products to fill their needs. This ideology should be reversed. Businesses that only provide money services to consumers are so decisive. They never provide a 'hard' product, yet through rigged Forex, Libor, bond, derivative, stock, gold and silver and money markets are making money off you through the corrupt illegal system.

The depth of criminal activity within the banking industry and the lengths to which they will go to conceal the evidence is unprecedented. These banks are the arm of the "New World Order" run by elite people who are the richest in the world. But you won't read about them in the news nor will they be on a list of the Forbes wealthiest since they are purposely left off the list to remain anonymous. They are intent on controlling the world, its people and the natural resources by placing everyone and every country into an unrepayable debt. They do this by lending money, whether you need it or not, and not only indebting you, but your children and your children's children. Initially, when elite global powers and bankers see resources they covet (such as oil or gold in a third world country), they will arrange for a huge loan to that country from an international bank like the World Bank or the IMF. However, the money never goes to the country per se it goes to the western corporations that will build infrastructure (roads, bridges) that they really don't need right now. The improvements only benefit a few better-off citizens that may have a car, yet the vast majority of citizens who need food and clothes for survival will never have access to any benefits. The debt will be paid back, with interest, by the poorer-class citizens through taxation, regulations and austerity. The real winners in all of this (if you can call them that) are the Central Bankers.

Even in the fight to eradicate terrorism...it's the bankers who profit by lending money to governments to provide income to

Companies that make weaponry to fight wars. You can 'flush' out trace and capture any so called "terror group" by following its electronic money fingerprint. Not by chasing them into underground bunkers or caves. Always follow the money. And this problem will only multiply with adverse effects since each time you eliminate or kill 'terrorists' (real or imagined) you create 'ten' more in their place. The citizens of the invaded country will rise up to see the injustices which are being done to the native people of that country. People are driven to "terrorism" because they have lost so much. It has little to do with them beholden to certain cultural or religious beliefs. When the media discusses terrorism – they always describe it as 'what they did to us' - yet they rarely, if ever, mention what 'we have done to them.' However, the media won't ever show those injustices to us.

"You have meddled with the primal forces of nature, Mr. Beale, and I won't have it! Is that clear? You think you've merely stopped a business deal. That is not the case! The Arabs have taken billions of dollars out of this country, and now they must put it back! It is ebb and flow, tidal gravity! It is ecological balance! You are an old man who thinks in terms of nations and peoples. There are no nations. There are no peoples. There are no Russians. There are no Arabs. There are no third worlds. There is no West. There is only one holistic system of systems, one vast and immane, interwoven, interacting, multivariate, multinational dominion of dollars. Petro-dollars, electro-dollars, multi-dollars, reichmarks, rins, rubles, pounds, and shekels; It is the international system of currency which determines the totality of life on this planet. That is the natural order of things today. That is the atomic and subatomic and galactic structure of things today! And YOU have meddled with the primal forces of nature, and YOU... WILL... ATONE! Am I getting through to you, Mr. Beale? You get up on your little twenty-one inch screen and howl about America and democracy. There is no America. There is no democracy. There is only IBM, and ITT, and AT&T, and DuPont, Dow, Union Carbide, and Exxon. Those are the nations of the world today. What do you think the Russians

talk about in their councils of state, Karl Marx? They get out their linear programming charts, statistical decision theories, minimax solutions, and compute the price-cost probabilities of their transactions and investments, just like we do. We no longer live in a world of nations and ideologies, Mr. Beale. The world is a college of corporations, inexorably determined by the immutable bylaws of business. The world is a business, Mr. Beale. It has been since man crawled out of the slime. And our children will live, Mr. Beale, to see that... perfect world... in which there's no war or famine, oppression or brutality. One vast and ecumenical holding company, for whom all men will work to serve a common profit, in which all men will hold a share of stock. All necessities provided, all anxieties tranquilized, all boredom amused. And I have chosen you, Mr. Beale, to preach this evangel."

-Arthur Jensen

In the end, our economic markets will go through three phases during the collapse: 1) The Great flushing, 2) The Great leveling, and 3) The Great reset. The 'socio-path' mentality is running our country; it is the attitude running Wall Street and it is the attitude running Washington. A 'socio-path' doesn't know how to feel other than the way they feel: competition and success is the rule, *"I deserve it all and I am going to get it all."* The President's Working Group on Financial Markets or what is more commonly known as, Washington's 'Plunge Protection Team' (FED, CFTC, SEC and U.S. Treasury,) are hard at work manipulating the stock market, but it can still be 'overrun.' Real markets can and will overrun the manipulation of currencies, metals and the 'false' strength of the US dollar. But who is going to 'margin call' the US government? In the future, you will pay the bank to hold your money. The 'dollar' may not go completely away. It won't be replaced by a 'basket of currencies' (SDR) either because a 'basket of junk' cannot cure the problem of 'junk.' The Fed must maintain control or they will be exposed, especially if the public's confidence is lost.

GOVERNMENT

BOOK 22

We are the first, perhaps the only nation that holds as self-evident truths that all men and women are created equal and are endowed by their creator with certain unalienable rights; and that governments are instituted to protect those rights and derive their just powers from the consent of the governed. Our nation was founded on certain principles and the first is the principle of rule. Because we the people do not consent to be lied to by a government that lays rules without consent of the governed, and ruling without consent of the governed, is slavery. An enslaved society is achieved at the point the government becomes tyrannical and oppressive. Unfortunately, we are at that point now. You should be outraged by the mere fact that so many of our young military men and women have sacrificed themselves in these 'bankers' wars' all started on the pretense of a lie. And they continue to lie today. A government that lies, and performs tyranny on its people, cannot be the legal government of the land. It is up to the people to stop this and stop this now.

"Ask the government why totalitarianism dictatorships find it necessary to pour money and effort into propaganda for their own helpless, chained, gagged slaves, who have no means of protest or defense. The

answer is that they would rise in blind rebellion, if they were to realize that lies being immolated and perpetrated, not to some incomprehensible noble purpose, but to plain naked human evil."

-Unknown

We think of government as something we need. Our society and modern civilization depends on it. Why? The fact is...when we do depend on government it starts to rule our lives. When a government owns everything of yours, it is called socialism. Government should be the last resort to solving issues and problems in our society and not the first resort. Is this your government...an elite, ultra-secretive, Neo-fascist, masonic cabal, involved in money laundering, assassination, drugs and false flag terrorism? It is written that the American government shall uphold the Articles of Confederation whereby each individual state cannot be overruled by the government. All government programs are basically illegal since only the state has the power over its citizens – Washington government only has power in the 24 miles that Washington, D.C. sits on.

The world has seen nothing but conflict and war since the First World War with a constant stream of war—everywhere on Earth. Western intervention is packaged and sold to us as a way to ensure peace. Peace is war. The CIA and Mossad undermine other nations with propaganda and terrorism. These departments were basically created by the Nazis. CIA is not just an intelligence agency, but allegedly also the number-one trafficker of drugs in the world mostly through Afghanistan. CIA and Mossad could very well be behind all terrorist events in the world for over the past 60 years and be the strong-arm of the global government and global monetary system. Unbeknownst to the American people, the "Third Reich" just moved to America and operates hidden as a shadow government. It has either created or infiltrated into NASA, the military, the government and controls propaganda for the media for the entire world. If a global conspiracy does exist, then it affects every person on Earth—including you—on a personal level.

Governments were supposed to serve and protect us—not own us. In dystopia, science fiction movies, man creates machines to make his life easier/better and of course the machines eventually take over controlling man—not too dissimilar to what is happening with our government situation now. Governments were created to make life easier and safer, but they always end up enslaving humanity. That which we create to serve us ends up ruling us. The U.S. Government by and for the people imprisons millions, takes a large portion from your wages via taxes and other fees, over regulates, invades other countries, kills thousands of foreigners, manipulates governments, tortures, slaughters others, imposes over 700 imperialistic battles over the world, inflates currency and creates massive debt for future generations. You can get more work out of person with the illusion of freedom. But giving people the perception that they are free (and taxing them) is just another form of ownership and slavery. Freedoms increase productivity.

Each person should have the right to read without restriction and speak freely without exception. This is not breaking any law anywhere. We are free to read what we want and say what we believe. Support and uphold the U.S. Constitution since this is the best thing we have that protects us from tyranny. And when you look at this objectively, it appears that all politicians are violating their oath to office and this is an impeachable offense.

The phrase "Group Think" may best describe what is going on today with how people think. Group Think is the inability of individuals to think beyond the consensus of a group. Much of Group Think is controlled by the Media Industrial Complex (radio, TV and film). One of the best examples of Group Think is the way in which people react to the words "conspiracy theory." Is it really wrong to question things? Is it heresy or unpatriotic to question the actions of our leaders? Our leaders are the first ones we should question. Politics is heavily influenced by Group Think (*think* – 'think tanks'). So the fear of standing out or being different influences many to conform to a mold of the Group Think mentality. Group Think gives a stigma to conspiracy theories. The phrase 'conspiracy theory' gives a negative connotation because you question significant events in history such as the JFK assassination or 9/11. Some people have the inability or motivation to ask tough questions of the government. For the aware person, government 'cover ups' seem more like a fantasy or a Hollywood script than reality. Much of it sounds made up. This is understandable – it's supposed to sound 'made up' through embellishments over time and misinformation; these stories have (dis) information added, omitted or changed and becomes nothing resembling the truth.

What better way to control people than to make news stories sound unbelievable? The mainstream media is there to persuade the majority of the population (and sets precedence) that you're ignorant to believe or think with an open mind about conspiracy theories. Everything happens when, and only when, someone conspires to do so. Movies, books, TV, fairytales... are all program tools to make the average person feel 'insane' for supporting, believing, suggesting or even thinking about a conspiracy theory. They always seem to portray conspiracy theorists in movies as crazy individuals with many peculiarities and paranoia (e.g., the cabbie character Jerry Fletcher played by Mel Gibson in the movie "Conspiracy Theory").

"Let us not tolerate outrageous conspiracy theories...concerning the attack of September 11th. Malicious lies that attempt to shift the blame away from the terrorist themselves."

-George W. Bush

All teachings of history lead us to conclude that all events happened because they conspired to happen. Nothing happens just by chance. You don't start wars by accident. A person or group of persons make decisions to attack, therefore by definition, they have 'conspired' to perform some aggressive act or tactical plan. To gain support of this aggression they alter the thoughts and beliefs of people in order to persuade the perception even (especially) if they don't understand the situation. Any time two or more persons make a decision in secret that would affect another third party it is clearly a conspired event. Just about all business transactions are handled like this (think buying a house). Any strategic move is never told in advance. You want to get the best price. Another example on a larger platform would be a company takeover. The less people know or understand about the event (or deal) ahead of time, the less likely there will be road blocks to 'seal the deal.' To get an 'edge up' on your competition, decisions and meetings must be made in secrecy. Businesses must protect themselves in order to compete with each other. Governments work in similar fashion, though we don't want to publicly admit it. Governments covertly transact hundreds of secret missions each day, all done in secret that were conspired.

"It is time to fire the liars. The only thing necessary for the triumph of evil is for good men to do nothing."

– Edmund Burke

Organizations such as the CIA, FBI, NSA, and Homeland Security must work in secrecy and therefore by nature conspire to either create or alter events occurring in the world. We would never want or wish to believe that our government (per se) is doing anything disruptive or manipulative to other people, nations or countries. But the fact is these government organizations act as though they are not a part of our core government and operate almost exclusively autonomously; almost like a shadow government. The 'pyramid of power' shows us this delineation from one power level to another and demonstrates that the people operating within the organization on the bottom know nothing of the agenda or specific goals of the people at the top. Very little information is shared between organizations or the levels of the power pyramid and as you 'go up' the pyramid each level holds its agenda quietly and does not disclose much to the level below them. When communication does come, it is usually in some form of formal order. If you're familiar with the military then you know orders are given, not questioned. People in the military are punished for asking questions or asking the question, "Why." Asking 'why' is depicted as being insubordinate. Questioning authority is not allowed. If we question anything, others around us have been conditioned to criticize and think less of us. When you stand out, you can be singled out or just completely left out. You're looked at as a lesser person or a third-rate citizen if your views and thoughts are outside of the mainstream mindset. Never is a non-biased independent investigation done to quell any questions from the left or right field. All aspects from beginning to end are controlled, if you own the mass media – you can control all information on the event that occurred. Much 9/11 news has been offered by this 'modus operandi.'

"There's no way to rule innocent men. The only power government has is the power to crack down on criminals. When there aren't enough criminals, one makes them. One declares so many things to be a crime that it becomes impossible for men to live without breaking laws."

-Ayn Rand

The first step is to free yourself from the mechanics of the physical world. Reclaim your birthright. Do you think that the manipulation that is happening in the world today is normal? Is the war on terror real or is most, if not all, of it made up? What would be the purpose of convincing us of lies? Open your mind and look at this analytically (e.g., Building 7). Take notice of the continued illegal invasions of other people's home (land). Take notice of the continual removal of all your rights. Take notice of the anti-humanitarian aggression by our government. Take notice of how 'evil,' toxic vaccines and debilitating polio shots are forced upon the Third World nations that are being masked as humanitarian efforts. This situation cannot continue without our letting it do so.

Police officers are turning into hired hands for our government. They do not serve or protect us anymore. They serve and protect the elite. Military and police are 'ordered' to virtually carry out any legislation, just or unjust. Has the modern officer forgotten that they are human too? They have been controlled for what; a paycheck, some health coverage and nothing else? Maybe 'pseudo' power, but power doesn't feed their family. There is very little resistance – we are just "Sheeple" (Sheep People). We are not 'just' numbers – we are sovereign people. The government serves the people – the people do not serve the government! Our entire system is backwards and corrupt. Government should be the last resort not the first resort to solving anything. The entire monetary system is not fair. War is used like it is a first option. Corporate interests are unjustly supported. Countries are brought to their knees all for the sake of profits. We need to concentrate on the foundation that shows our similarities. We need less division to each other and a better connection to one another.

Are you proud to be an American?

- Slaughter of the American Indians
- Invading foreign lands for control and oil
- Suppression of true religion and freedoms
- Assimilated all people for the benefit of the state
- Suppression of the home and the family environment

- Pushing a homosexual/transgender agenda onto every citizen
- Forced debt through consumerism
- Punishing citizens/individuals for free thinking and questioning authority
- Stripping the last threads of our Constitution and liberties
- Changing the definition of "Free Speech"

"Individual rights are not subject to a public vote: A majority has not right to vote away the rights of a minority: The political function of rights is precisely to protect minorities from oppression by majorities (and the smallest minority on earth is the individual)."

-Ayn Rand

The Birth Certificate: *"Straw man"* – he/she is a 'legal you' as opposed to the 'natural' you. It is the entity that enters into written or legal contracts. When you register a new baby in America, the parents sign a birth certificate and on that certificate the baby's name is 'typed' in all CAPITAL letters. This is the very first indoctrination into being owned by the state. From then on...all bills, certificates and legal documents appear in capital letters for that person. Whenever someone gets registered for anything 'official' by the government such as a marriage certificate, business license, Social Security card or even a driver's license your all – capital legal name is used. This is your 'straw man' person as opposed to your natural self-person. Your 'straw man' is technically 'dead' – in that it is not you the living person, but you – maintaining and representing the 'straw man' by continuing to sign 'identification' documents all created and stemming from your birth certificate. Back in 1933, the government started to 'hatch' a plan to legally incorporate a fictional character (you) where they have essentially registered and monetized a 'human soul' (a spiritual being). You have become a corporation with all monies you will earn during your lifetime calculated and issued as a bond. That bond (or debt) is paid back as the person gets older and generates 'income' for the state through taxes; it has been said that every American citizen has a bond on the stock market using their social security number. Based on the current debt level and population statistics the current outstanding debt is estimated to be calculated around $147,300 per American household or about $57,000 per person living in the U.S. Our future has been sold and your certificate is a share by which you are held as collateral to service a debt owed to international bankers. We are collateral 'chattel.' We don't own ourselves. America is a corporation. In 1871, our Constitution was changed and incorporated America, and at that point, all citizens became like employees of the state.

Any 'violence' or resistance by a large population doesn't mean they are any more violent than any other population in the world—it just means it is an 'alarm' or a signal that something is wrong in the treatment of that population. It usually stems from oppression from a centralized government and unfair care of its citizens. Many times governments will say one thing and do the other (the opposite) to try to hide what 'true' agenda is at hand. Peace equals war and war equals peace. When authorities say they are trying to negotiate for peace, which really means (the opposite); they really want war.

...History is not the version of past events that people have decided to agree upon...History is decided by the winners."

– Napoleon Bonaparte

Women wanted equal rights so they went into the work force. Now women work and get taxed just like their male counterparts. It may surprise you that the original push for the women's equal rights movement came from the backing and financing of the 'power elite.' It was an underhanded way to get all citizens' wages taxed while having your children's upbringing and indoctrination into society forced onto them by the government via the public education school system. A socialist government always wants to step up its control of its citizens through more taxes, but also through propaganda, lies, manipulation, superstition, wars, fear and paranoia.

"An evil exists that threatens every man, women and child of this great nation. We must take steps to ensure our domestic security and protect our Homeland."

-Adolph Hitler (1922)

Globalism, for many, is the desire for the installation of a one world, totalitarian government. On a broad, philosophical basis Globalism doesn't sound that bad, but the problem is that we are being pushed into this globalization in secrecy and by deceit! When you consider the ramifications of the methodology being used it is diabolical. Many global groups make no secret or hide their desire about wanting this. If you control central authority then you can control all aspects of everyone's life. Globalism is a form of socialism where the government will take care of you from cradle to grave, provide your education, your health care and all this requires central administration and authority. The wealthy and the powerful strive for this type of control because otherwise large populations become very powerful themselves since they outnumber the government. The goal is total world control, total domination and elimination of any governments that are independent of American's western banking cabal. It is all geo-political.

Our Republic is gone and it's because of the corrupt actions of the people who have conspired to do so and the public that is too asleep to realize it. We have become a Socialist, Fascist and Zionist nation that would rather be "politically correct" than do what is correct. When it comes to any issue nowadays people don't want to face the truth (the real truth behind the fabricated truth that has been told).

'They' would rather lie than be honest with the American public. Don't fear what you have been told. Remember the Holocaust happened to people just like us. Many will say we are overreacting, but when is it a good time to react? Now or later? Stop and question things before it is too late. Though, according to many, we are on the doorstep of "too late."

Robert Welch, founder of the John Birch Society, mentioned these following bullet points for the road map of how society was trending back in the 1970's:

1) Greatly expanded spending for every conceivable means for getting rid of large sums of money and creating debt. "Be as wasteful as possible."

2) Higher then much higher taxes.

3) An increasingly unbalanced budget despite the higher taxes.

4) Wild inflation of our currency.

5) Government control of prices, wages and materials.

6) Greatly increased socialistic controls of every operation of our economy and every activity of our daily lives. This goes with a huge increase of government.

7) Centralization of power in Washington and elimination of state lines and borders.

8) The advance of federal aid to control our educative system leading to complete control of public education.

9) A constant hammering to the American consciences of the horror of modern warfare. Hidden as "Peace" — this really means war (peace in communications).

10) The willingness to allow the steps of aggression upon government (socialism) which amounts to a peaceful surrender of the United States itself.

Is the story true or not? We internally ask this question when we hear of current events. Especially events that do sound incredible like flying planes into buildings. If you doubt the official story and go against the 'grain' then critics will ridicule you and ask you to prove otherwise. The onus of proving 'it' becomes the burden of the one questioning 'it' when the entity telling us the way it is should really be the one proving the "official story." Why do we, the questioning, have to prove it when it is their story? – They (the government) should prove it. Investigate it! But they never will. How can I prove anything if I do not have access to anything in the case? I am virtually powerless. And they know this...

"You cannot expect or demand freedom for yourself if you deny it to others."

-Anonymous

The Military Industrial Complex needs to have war. War is what makes many of these corporate companies survive and keeps most of our government and military busy. All of these businesses depend on government to survive, and needs conflict to feed the bottom line and show profit – which in turn feeds Wall Street. A lot of it has to do with profits on the backs of innocent Americans who really don't know the truth of why they are fighting. Stockholders (Wall Street) survive on the manipulation of other countries. This policy of invasion into other countries is originally the British Agenda and not an American Agenda – that only has come about after our banking system had become infected by the globalists. That agenda has soiled the American reputation around the world.

Our aggression into other countries is all 'backed' on the lie of spreading democracy and freedom. All the hard work and integrity that we built early – on last century has been wiped out by our endless involvement in wars and military aggression into other lands and the news media wonders why "they" hate America – it is not because we are free. We are, in fact, the most controlled society. We have been brainwashed into thinking we are free and don't realize this because we have been brainwashed. But we are supposed to be productive and taxed so that we can fund the Military Industrial Complex to do what it was set up to do and that is police the world with a hidden hand from the British Empire, Zionist Bankers, etc. America has been usurped by the globalists.

"We are fast approaching the stage of the ultimate inversion; the stage where government is free to do anything it pleases, while the citizens may act only by permission; which is the stage of the darkest periods of human history, the stage of rule by brute force."

-Ayn Rand

We need a revolution in the way that Americans think about things: money, politics, and government. The rejection of the same way we have been thinking, sustained opposition. In this type of 'surveillance state' fewer and fewer people will be creative because they are afraid of their ideas and inventions being stolen.

The government cannot protect my property by taking half of it first. It cannot protect your life by threatening you with endless violence. It cannot protect your money by using currency that is counterfeit. It cannot protect your children by sealing them up in a school (prison) for 7 hours a day. "Statism" is just like a religious cult.

The so-called "war on terror" is a cover for military aggression to gain control of the resources of western Asia and the Middle East. It is a calculated war against Muslim countries trading blood for oil. To most of the world the U.S. is the terrorist and that's why your own country wants to control you so badly because when you find this out, as many are awakening to, they will lose control. They are laying the foundation for all these military bases and when the military occupation ends (if it ends) the economic occupation will be there to control businesses' money, commerce, guns, drugs, and surveillance. Your government, politicians and military personnel stand to profit when they go back to civilian life and set up 'shop' for corrupt businesses in these foreign lands.

" — *Government is collectively guilty*" – government is the number one threat to people. Our Constitution specifically states there shall be no standing army in America. Although, maybe on paper we don't have a standing army, but one could technically say that the Department of Homeland Security is, in fact, a standing army. Many military drills that have been exercised over numerous states in conjunction with the militarized police force also give evidence and credence of a standing army that could be used on the American people. After Martial Law has been implemented on the American public (or when a collapse of the current system has occurred), everyone can sit around then and talk about who should have done what. Unfortunately, at that point it just won't matter. It will be too late. It will be too late to fight for your ideologies and your guns. The only thing that stops a bad guy with a gun – is a good guy with a gun. We need to stand up now and say "No!" to any type of gun control. We need to stand up, now, for our ideological and expose the ploy by this administration that they are not being authentic to America and really just want to take our guns away under the guise of "common sense gun control." The purpose is to garner an emotional response via a national (emotionally charged) crisis, and to further their ideology.

The agenda is being imposed now which involves the evaporation (or a slow disintegration) of your civil liberties and rights and your ability to live and let live in the here and now. It is a disturbing pattern. Gun control has no effect on violence. Outlaws don't care about the law. So ask yourself, "What is the purpose of all this gun legislation to disarm law abiding American citizens?" Men and women just want the ability to defend themselves and their families. Even Veteran's gun rights are threatened. It is morally unethical to disarm us while allowing others – and organized criminals – to impart violence on us knowing that we will be defenseless and not able to carry any weapons.

A 'False Choice' whereby you really have no choice between two options or both choices are basically the same under the surface such as the two-party political system in America.

Many people think like this: As long as I am not doing anything wrong, why should I worry or concern myself with what my government is doing? The biggest problem with this thought process is that governments are working really hard in developing legislation and techniques by which you will be controlled (even without your knowledge). The end goal is for the controlling oligarchy, which has existed and presumably will always exist, to get people to love their servitude.

*"First they came for the Jews
and I did not speak out because I was not a Jew...
then they came for the communists
but I did not speak out because I was not a communist
then they came for the trade unionist
and I did not speak out because I was not a trade unionist
then they came for me
and there was no one left to speak out for me..."*

-Pastor Martin Niemoller

Question to Police: "Will you do anything that your 'superiors' tell you to do? Anything? Such as applying force to innocent protestors. Or will you, at some point, see yourself questioning if what you are doing is the right and just thing to do? At some point, could you see yourself saying no to wrongful orders! I will not do that...! Could you kill a fellow American citizen? If it came down to doing the right thing would you disobey the politicians?"

There has been a militarization intervention for well over a decade by the western powers into the Middle East and now it's spreading into North Africa. America has created the problem and has made it worse by our involvement. Before 9/11, there was no Al-Qaeda in the Arabian Peninsula—now there is. We must realize that western intervention is not a solution. In addition, bin Laden was a product of a monumental miscalculation by western security agencies. Throughout the 1980s, he was armed by the CIA and funded by the Saudis to wage Jihad against the Russian occupation of Afghanistan. Al-Qaida means literally 'The Database' and was originally the computer files of the thousands of Mujahedeen who were recruited and trained with the help from CIA to defeat the Russians.

The government always seems to have a dual agenda. The real enemy is outing our own people. Militarily, diplomatic, intelligence, economically, scientifically and politically is how they do it. It has been scripted. The U.S. is 3% of the world's population yet we have 25% of the world's incarcerated population. We are only as free as we believe we are. We are in denial. We do not see the signs that are staring directly at us, keeping our minds turned off and busy with mundane affairs of daily life. If you would like to know the truth and wake up, it's not too late. Removing the blindfold that has kept you from seeing reality is the first place to start. Every few years the U.S. Government props up a new 'bogeyman' for the masses to fear. The most recent group is called

ISIS. ISIS, which has deep occult meaning, is used to wreak havoc on the masses. ISIS was also the name of a Egyptian Goddess. ISIS wages a psychological agenda put upon us to instill fear in anyone who is an observer of the corporate, mainstream, media paradigm. The elite, government entity can and will sell us propaganda through the National Defense Authorization (NDAA) to make us believe their New World Order agenda. Al Qaeda was a CIA creation and all the bogeymen including Osama bin Laden (aka Tim Osman) whose death was a hoax. No evidence has ever been provided to show his death. 9/11 was also trauma-based event. The ultimate tyranny is total control and does not come in the form of Martial Law, but rather from the control of the psychological manipulation of human conscience through which reality is defined. Here the victims do not know that this is even going on. Most of the propaganda is to promote the narrative for the war in the Middle East. They want to scare and influence you (America) into thinking that this is a great terror and that it's real...which it is not. The government wants you to ask for protection against the boogeyman and have them invade foreign lands because you're scared when the real reason we are over there is for oil, control and to set up western banking cartels.

They told us we were attacked because of our freedoms...what freedoms: 1) Patriot Act/Freedom Act; 2) NDAA; 3) TSA; 4) Police militarization; and 5) NSA/CCTV spying. 9/11 was the biggest psych-op operation in human history. Why would they do this and lie to us? They did it to create a perception in the public mind that western democracies were under attack from Islamic terrorists so that the public and their troops would support invading sovereign countries in which they want to establish a foothold (military bases) and, in turn, control the natural resources, implement a western banking cartel, and do trade in Petrodollars. Also take control of any drug/heroin or oil production and steal any gold the country has in its vaults. Our country is a thief.

The U.S. has made a complete mess of the Middle East and specifically Benghazi. The American Embassy in Benghazi was a logistic hub for so called army, elite sub-antiterrorists created by your own state department covert operations. They were shipping tons of weapons to Syria via Turkey to the U.S. proxy army. Russia was aware of this and put a stop to it by exposing it – ironically on September 11th, 2012. The real truth can be so depressing and overwhelming at times. In America, it is easier to blend and conform (play dumb) than to be smart. If you question anything the government does you're accused of not being patriotic. Question: Has the thousands of laws imposed on you made you a better person? Are you a more lawful person or just scared to death of doing something wrong because of all the rules, regulations and laws that the government implements?

"The Best way to take control over a people and control them utterly is to take a little of their freedom at a time, to erode rights by a thousand tiny and almost imperceptible reductions. In this way the people will not see those rights and freedoms being reminded until past the point at which these changes cannot be reversed."

-Adolph Hitler

Throughout history, countries and nations have a tendency to shift into a totalitarian control. Most Americans refuse to believe it could happen here. But it is happening right now. There are three ways of dealing with this:

1) Pretend this is all a "Conspiracy Theory" and mentally and willfully ignore it.

2) Do everything to avoid the government from identifying you and stay low.

3) Move to stop this and raise awareness to others of what is happening.

It will be either a prison planet or an awakening of consensus, but both may actually be the same because the powers that be will make it seem like the 'Awakening of Consciousness' is for all to come together under a "New Age." The New Age is a New World Order. The Solution is by warfare - fooling you into accepting the very thing we are fighting against all along. In any scenario, the goal would be to control the people and the best way to start is to disarm them. It may be difficult to take away all our guns, but they can still control the amount of ammunition that the public has access to. The right to bear arms is our last line of defense against tyranny and protection from a government that has gone wrong. Guns are really not only for hunting. It was on November 11, 1938 that Wilhelm Frisch, master of the Internment, passed Regulations Against Jews' Possession of Weapons. The parallels that can be drawn from what happened in Germany to what is unfolding today are amazing. Compare the years leading up to World War II with the implementation of laws and the German's loss of freedoms and gun confiscation with what is going on now in America. The resemblance is uncanny, even down to the executive orders that are written into law just as Hitler did. Perhaps a more critical eye needs to correlate if the same group of elites that masterminded Germany is masterminding America now.

The most powerful Nazi supporters in past history were not only in Germany. Many were right here in the USA. The Rockefellers, Harrimans, Fords, DuPonts and even the Bush ancestors helped 'create' Hitler and the Nazi empire. They helped promote him, arm him, support him and even finance his campaigns. It has also been speculated that there was a significant relationship to the Rothschilds (Hitler being an offspring of that family). The Nazis did not lose World War II; Hitler did, the German people did, and the Jews did, but the Nazis did not. The true Nazis escaped to various parts of South America such as Argentina, but most of the real brain power came to America through 'Operation Paperclip.' Operation or 'Project 'Paperclip' has created a situation where we have Nazis, essentially, running the CIA, all our intelligence, NASA and most of our foreign policy. Also around this time, in 1947, touted as the world's solver of conflict, the U.N. was created supposedly to protect the safety of the world and its people and ensure that nothing as horrible as WWII ever occurs again. The U.N. is just another extension of the same monster creation that is our own shadow government.

After eight years in office, President Eisenhower figured this out, but he did not call them Nazis, but rather the "Military Industrial Complex." Eisenhower was surrounded by 'them' and he tried to warn the new president, Kennedy, that the "Shadow Government" was trying to take over the government and diminish freedom. They also came over to loot the U.S. treasury and take whatever gold they could lay their hands on.

"In the councils of government, we must guard against the acquisition of unwarranted influence, whether sought or unsought, by the military-industrial complex. The potential for the disastrous rise of misplaced power exists and will persist."

-Dwight D. Eisenhower

Today America can be defined as – a new order of world ethics firmly established on a foundation of democratic idealism. The operative words in the previous sentence are new, order and world... *'A New World Order.'*

A totalitarian government records and stores all communication on its citizens. Totalitarianism is: *"A society living by and for continuous warfare in which the ruling caste have ceased to have any real function, but succeed in clinging to power through force and fraud."* Plummeting digital storage costs enable the feasibility to record and store every phone/email and this will make it possible for authorities to not only monitor malcontents, but to store a complete set of digital data on everyone within the borders. The arsenal of data and material video footage of public spaces linked with calls being monitored can process this info in real time (think "Minority Report"). This could be correlated to a regime facing dissent and will expand monitoring which amounts to 'a time machine' of sorts, allowing an authoritative government to perform retrospective surveillance. Now they are trying to 'back pedal' and legalize what they have already been doing illegally for years.

"You're not to be so blind with patriotism that you can't face reality. Wrong is wrong, no matter who does it or says it."
                                        - Malcolm X

No 'autopsy' required...because most of the public doesn't know what is going on and they really don't care to investigate it either. They just know and only care about their own world. It was said that a public who doesn't watch its government will soon be under tyranny. You're encouraged to "not ask" questions of your government. Go out and enjoy your life while 'they' go about mining the store, and if you're not happy – get some pills from your doctor – but don't get too involved with your government dealings or foreign affairs. The establishment may tell you that you're small and insignificant, but they need you to be in denial and believe all of this forced propaganda to progress the corrupt ideas throughout society. If you believe to the contrary, then you're dangerous. They are taking away your freedom to express yourself and are trying really hard to control even what you think. For this reason the United States is no longer the land of the free. Americans live within a debt-based system of literally a million, unnecessary government regulations and laws that has essentially destroyed the free market and sent tons of jobs overseas. Americans today are constantly watching their 'speedometer' and trying to abide and conform to every rule and law. There are so many rules and laws today that it is impossible for most honest, law-abiding and hardworking citizens from breaking some kind of law every day.

There is also a major disconnection from our government representatives. It seems like it is a specifically designed deception too, whereby each politician and public servant swears that they will uphold the Constitution and then goes out and breaks every possible law and rule there is on the books. There is a fight going on and the title bout is 'Freedom vs. Gov. Control (World Government)'. It is the focus of Good vs. Evil. Sun Tzu said, *"If you know the enemy well you know yourself, you need not fear the result of a hundred battles."* Our enemy is from within and has great power (through deception). All warfare is based on deception. If someone can control you, but with the illusion that it is good for you or in your best interest and it is (really) not, that is the ultimate type of deception. We need to break down and expose this wall of deception.

There is little doubt that those who have seized control of our government have been lying to the American people for decades to create an artificial reality. Anyone who opposes the (NWO) is a terrorist (as outlined by Henry Kissinger). Ironically, it's the NWO who fund and create 'real' terrorism. Every U.S. president from George H.W. Bush to Bill Clinton to George W. Bush and now Obama has committed crimes against humanity and even treason against the United States. On a further note, it is also ironic how you need to have a background check to buy a gun today which is our civil right, yet it seems you don't need any type of background check to be President of the United States.

Are we being desensitized to the overbearing police state that is evolving with the military now? People should not be categorized as anti-government if, in fact, they are only looking for legitimate and lawful government. In order to be truly free one must think for themselves. Become independent. Remember ...No one cares about you as much as you.

"Agenda 21," (now Agenda 2030), is a 40-chapter document about smart growth brought to you by the New World Order. It sounds harmless from the casual observer, but Agenda 21 will restrict choice by individuals and take away freedoms by using the cover of environmental concerns to control every aspect of human's lives. It is based on underlying socialistic principals. Our private property rights and our civil rights will be diminished or eliminated. "Green" is just a guise for control and they will tell you things like nature above man and that you're guilty until proven innocent. Agenda 21 is control of human beings across the globe under one set of rules provided by a small group of elite people.

What is going on across the world is the same thing going on here at home. A 'Marxist' state will be forced upon us whether we like it or not. It will seem strange and foreign to us, but that is the direction things are moving. In America, we are supposed to have a 'Republican' (Republic) government, whereby the state represents the interests of the individual and the small businessman and it does nothing of the kind. Nor does the Democratic government provide this either. They appear to be different but they are really both the same. There is no way of choosing between the two. Which group of corrupt gangsters are you going to put into power?

He who controls the past controls the future. He who controls the present controls the past...and the future. Much of the language we use has been adulterated i.e., Republic versus. Democracy – there is no mention of the 'republic' in any text books showing that America was a 'class conflict' between the rich and the poor (advocacy of a world government). World government was always the goal of Communism. The Bolshevik revolution was financed by the richest men in the U.S. and the U.K. Communism was forced onto the Russian people - mostly from the outside of Russia. Communism was controlled and manipulated by some of the wealthiest men and families in the world in order to gain better control of the populace and the world. A total managed and controlled society by a few, very elite and wealthy industrialists and families. Centralization takes government away from the people.

The key factor is control. Behavior and objectives designed to capture the decision-making process of government. A system of central government replaces 'self' government. The use of social engineering to control what people think is apparent today and the obliteration of the free-thinking ideas which is the cornerstone of our Constitution. The conditioning of the mind is not a byproduct of government inherently, but it is of tyranny or a tyrannical government. It is the hallmark of tyranny. What is going on now is the continuing of both Eastern and Western cultures to accept a one world government system. All made to look like it is for global peace...when, in fact, it's all to do with enslavement of the world population, for the global elite, and loss of sovereignty of our cultures. They want to infiltrate all aspects of society and destroy civilization from within. The public is delusional to the extent for which only a few privileged people want full control of the planet and all its resources. Hidden rulers believe they are the lords of the planet. If the people of the world do not know or understand the objective of life, then they are not capable of administering a peaceful society. By not understanding (no explanation) what is happening in the world is a deliberate attempt by the elite to undermine the primary objective of life. The New World Order will be run by those in the pinnacle of power and are unfortunately connected to the current system of government. The sum total of a decent government is tied to the preservation and purpose of life...which should be the goal of any administration.

The consumer slaves need to pay taxes to their government which funds are used for more control and weapons against the masses and involvement into other countries in illegal wars. Since 1945, America has tried to 'overthrow' at least 50 governments. The grotesque task of invading other countries claiming them as your territory and stealing their resources is called "Empire Building" (in modern terms – Globalization). Globalization or 'Unification' is, in essence, the acquisition of other people's resources…at any cost.

The Prism Surveillance Program (NSA) is watching you. Big Brother is alive and well, thriving on your ignorance, but this did not happen overnight. What has happened is the gradual habituation of the people, little by little, over time, to the point where everything you do is being watched, documented and recorded. It also seems we are being governed by surprise and important decisions are deliberately made in secret without any foreknowledge by the public. We are usually told that the 'situation' was so complicated and that the government had to act on information which the people could not understand and it could not be released due to 'National Security.' The separation gap of government and the people is widening. This separation has taken place so gradually and so persistently, each step disguised and implemented as a temporary measure that will become permanent over time. All the causes and reforms occur so the people do not see the 'slow motion' movement of the whole process of government growing more and more remote. Like the iron fist of the Nazis, America must submit to 'revolving surveillance' and warrantless searches, without the requirement of a judge's authorization. Surveillance laws are part of a larger arsenal of weapons against political dissidents and whistleblowers.

"Fusion Centers" are windowless non-descript buildings in every state across the United States and are used for spying on you. Information and data are being collected, assembled and analyzed on every American citizen. The government says that, "We don't spy on Americans, just anti-government Americans"…but doesn't that mean it spies on everyone? The narrative on many major events (e.g., 9/11, Sandy Hook) has changed due to everyday citizens investigating for themselves, questioning the 'mainstream' version of the story. A list of all political dissidents is maintained by the Department of Homeland Security (DHS). Yes, these lists really exist along with "no fly lists." On a personal note, when I heard the term, 'Homeland' being used in reference to America, I immediately connected the term to Germany usage of the term during WWII.

The vocal opponents that are speaking out against the New World Order are at the top of the list of people that will be 'handled.' At some point in the future, anyone standing in their way will be either, detained, imprisoned or even killed. As more people 'wake up' and the dissident lists get longer, the government will be unable to control the masses of citizens who will be rebelling. There will be a time in our future that it will be safe again to speak and think freely as our First Amendment has always provided.

"The one thing every man fears is the unknown. When presented with this scenario, individual rights will be willingly relinquished for the guarantee of their well-being granted to them by the World Government."

-Henry Kissinger

Our government is the greatest purveyor of conspiracy theories. The greatest irony is that for the past 20 years (and maybe more) the biggest pushers of conspiracy theories have been the very same Western, elite politicians and establishment gatekeepers so quick to accuse others of peddling conspiracy theories. When people challenge the dominant, establishment narrative are deliberately marginalized. They were the ones who pushed theories such as Saddam Hussein had weapons of mass destruction. It seems OK to make outrageous claims of other countries or enemies of America without much evidence (or even any) and the claims don't even need to be logical, but they are directed towards our own government you are called a "conspiracy theorist." Does this make any sense? Is this fair?

There is no 'bigger' or more important 'story' as far as the U.S. Federal Government is concerned than 9/11. Simply put, it is their lynchpin for the reason we have invaded so many countries and the illegal creation of a surveillance state here at home. When the American people come to understand that the attacks of September 11, 2001 were in fact, a *false flag operation* carried out by proxies of the U.S. Federal Government and Mossad (Israeli Intelligence), everything will change. It seems that the timing of all world events corresponds to a pagan or religious date of importance (i.e., May 1, Sept 11). It is difficult to think that every political/military event links to a pagan or religious date or numerology, but they do. If you question just one thing – like 9/11 – then you can certainly question everything that the government has done. By questioning, you can get out of this controlled paradigm and be free. Free to think your own thoughts. Published material and facts can prove the U.S. Government complicity in the 9/11 attacks for the successful manipulation of public opinion. The attack was planned so that an assault on America and its citizens looked like an act of aggression of international terrorism. Once a well-respected and connected authority figure comes forth publicly and explains what really happened on 9/11, the truth will spread amongst the masses from one person to another very quickly. The media will not be able to contain the truth; the truth that we have been living our lives, for the most part, in a false reality.

"The most foolish mistake we could possibly make would be to allow the subject races to possess arms. History shows all conquerors who have allowed their subject races to carry arms have prepared their own down-fall by so doing."

-Adolph Hitler

How Hitler and the Nazi Party got most of their funding is a 'little under-reported fact.' The American-owned Union Banking Corporation helped finance Germany's Nazi Party. It's all connected in this incestuous, global, banking web. Political campaign debt is always amassed during elections and Hitler's Nationalist Socialist Party was no different. After the Nazis had started to claim power throughout Germany, with that power, of course, came debt.

A partner in Hamburg America was Samuel Pryor, who was on the executive committee and chairman of Remington Arms. It is commonly known and accepted by historians that the guns used by Germany were American-made. It has also been known that some of the tanks the Germans used were American made too, by Ford Motor Company. Samuel Pryor was also the founder of the Union Banking Corporation in New York. Kurt Baron von Schroeder was a German who had ties with Thyssen foundry that was owned by Friedrich "Fritz" Thyssen who was a German steel entrepreneur and had banking operations affiliated through a subsidiary called W. A. Harriman Company. The company was changed to Brown Brothers Harriman in 1933 in New York. This company controlled the Union Banking Corporation and the other co-director of Thyssen Foundry was the Union Banking partner Joanne Growing, who was also partners with another Union Banking Corporation Prescott Bush. Prescott's father, Samuel P. Bush, was also involved in running arms with Remington and developed a relationship with the U.S. Government. It seems that over the past century, the Bush family has either been a part of the financing and supporting of fascism or pushing its agenda on America and the rest of the world.

"When Fascism comes to America it will be wrapped in the flag and carrying a cross."

-Sinclair Lewis

Fascism is ownership of a government by an individual or by a group. Corporatism is Fascism in that it is a merger of corporate and government powers (in bed together). Power-Fascist regimes are often run by government leaders in core positions placed there by industry and business associates. These associates appoint others with 'like-minded' thinking to positions of power to protect their assets. This is what is happening today in America.

Morpheus shows Neo in "The Matrix" film that the human race has been turned into a battery; this is not far from the truth. The matrix is only generated by the power that you give it and when you step out of the line, like many have done, you weaken the power it has over you. What has happened in our society is that it is a crime now to be different. There are many people who are stressing 9/11 was an inside job...the Reichstag was an inside job. But many people say, *"No- no- no...Osama bin Laden did it. I've seen on the news, it must be true."* The people who have stepped out of the 'matrix' come to a point in their lives when they must take that next step on the path of enlightenment and awakening – or step back in line and conform. Your next step is obviously very important. It was written, *"The most dangerous man to any government is the man who is able to think things out for himself - almost inevitably he comes to a conclusion that the government he lives under is dishonest, insane and intolerable."*

In my lifetime we have seen a massive centralization of power. This power is being assembled like a giant pyramid; business, money, military, politics and all parts up the 'agenda' are at the top and the people, who go to work, who pay their taxes and don't ask any questions are at the bottom. They own their ignorance and are easily controlled. As you ascend up the levels of the pyramid the more one advances the knowledge within the institutions. You would think that when you reach the President and Prime Minister level that you have reached the top of the pyramid, but you have not...that is why Presidents and Prime Ministers in power do not seem to care about what the people at the bottom say or think about them. They are being controlled from up above by the higher levels on the 'pyramid of power.' It is the people on these highest levels they fear. But if you step out of line you are dealt with in a very serious and public way (e.g., John F. Kennedy).

Some guidance: don't be frustrated when uncovering truths.

Many of us will latch onto a conspiracy topic like '9/11' and must investigate every shred of evidence. This is very time-consuming and also mentally debilitating. I believe a better, more centered approach is to look at the bigger picture and ask as to who benefits and ultimately who profits by such events – and place these events into a larger category that are either suspect or not. To argue or debate endless hours with another person on whether or not 9/11 was an inside job will neither convince the other person that it was, nor improve your 'standing' with them. To drill down on every detail is exhausting and, at some point, you just know that it was a manipulated historical event and you can move on from there. Placing a mental 'footnote' on each topic of theory and labeling it as such is a healthier method to connect the dots. If a purported 'story' does not make sense, does not add up or has too many unexplained, sub-events then all you should do initially is acknowledge and place the event into the questionable category. As you move on with your enlightenment process, if this topic is important, then the additional supplemental information will come to you as needed and as required. As you connect more dots through the wider range of knowledge you gather, you will bring more validity and confidence to your position.

It is from these three 'City States' Washington, D.C. (military), The London Square Mile (financial) and The Vatican (spiritual) that the New World Order government is controlling the consciousness of the world. These three 'City States' are sovereign areas under no laws or regulations and pay no taxes, yet from these locations the elite have painstakingly designed a system to have dictatorial powers over the rest of the globe. Each day much of the world's events are channeled through these energy centers. These City States have much in common including the very telling symbols of the New World Order. What is clearly evident is that the 'Fascist' symbols can be seen being exported through the 'fasho-bundle' symbolism. The German stamp 'fachet' and the Eagle are prominent visible symbols used by the socialist group as representations, but who would have thought that the same symbols would pop up in America on the Mercury dime and on the current Roosevelt dime issued in 1946. There are many Fascist symbols in Washington, D.C. and if you take a trip to visit any of the monuments or popular attractions, you will see statues of the first president resting his arm on the Fascist symbol and most notably the Lincoln Memorial with 'Honest Abe' sitting in a chair with two fascist bundles as arms of the chair. And while you're in Washington, D.C., observe the congress building which is called the "ceremonial maze." This maze is 46 inches high and consists of 13, ebony rods which represent the 13 original colonies. They are bound together in this maze by a silver band. The similarities between Fascist symbols from Germany and America are strikingly the same. Over the past 60 years America has slowly been sliding into a Fascist state. Is it perhaps that the same handlers (families of elite) of (Germany back in the 1930s) are here in America now doing the same corrupt plan?

The way to 'collapse America' is to overload the government with all the entitlements and a ton of debt to bring it down from the inside. The elite powers understand this. The entitlements are merely just a redistribution of money and resources from one group to another. It is not up to our government to redistribute wealth, but should rather provide and concentrate on opportunities for those people that want to prosper. Redistribution is not in our Constitution. Neither is 'democracy.' Our Founders set up a Republic so that we would not have "mob rule" since all democracies throughout history deteriorate into a two-class society (the haves and the have nots). The reason is, that a group of people cannot promise someone else's money to other people. This type of governing and redistribution will eventually destroy the very principles it was built on. That type of system will also 'pit' one group against its brothers and take the focus off the real problem, the 'Banksters' that created it. The difficulty is that we can't attack the current system 'straight on' since America is led by not only psychotic traitors, but is also backed by a very strong and brainwashed military. The way to combat this is by being true revolutionaries ourselves and to stop complying with the system.

This is occurring now on a global basis with the creation of the BRICS (Brazil, Russia, India, China and South Africa) nations, the AIIB (Asian, International Investment Bank) and the pivoting back to a sound money system that is fair for all (perhaps backed by gold). If you destroy the U.S. dollar, you destroy the United States Federal Reserve (FED). If you destroy the FED (the buyer of last resort) then you have weakened the control it has over its citizens. In a way, we all need to be anarchists – in the philosophical sense. No guns need to be fired and no bombs need be thrown...we just need to stand our ground through peaceful non-compliance and non-cooperation. All governments over time become self-serving corporations with only its interest at heart. It is up to the citizens to reject 'the status quo' and in a non-violent manner take back our government.

Maybe there isn't a gun ban agenda. And maybe the Iraq war didn't cause over 1 million innocent people to get killed, and maybe the Palestinians haven't gotten murdered by Israelis militia, and maybe U.S. banks aren't corrupt, and maybe there is no LIBOR scandal, or Foreign Exchange rigging, or gold manipulation and maybe there are crazy terrorists out there that want to kill us because of our freedoms, and maybe the Patriot act, and the NDAA act don't violate our rights, and maybe the TSA should touch us everywhere, and maybe we need more close-circuit TV cameras, and maybe the media doesn't lie...! Maybe it is time to start looking at ourselves closer to see exactly what we are doing to ourselves.

"It is to be regretted that the rich and powerful too often bend the acts of government to their own selfish purposes."
-Andrew Jackson

So what can we do about it? Here are some key points: 1) Know the Constitution and understand which parts are being destroyed. 2) Connect with people in your community who might be interested in defending civil liberties and start educating others together – then create a strategy through that network and accomplish awareness through educating on a larger scale – such as your community. Civil liberties and rights must never be taken for granted, and 3) Network and outreach with other organizations and, if possible get media coverage.

EXTRATERESTRIALS

BOOK 23

Is 'man' alone here on Earth? Are there 'extraterrestrials' from different worlds amongst us? Has mankind's evolution been misunderstood? And if so - is the extraterrestrials' (ETs) presence on Earth today here to 'help' or 'hurt' us? We have no 'clear cut' knowledge or understanding of our universal beginnings or extraterrestrial origins so we can only theorize and speculate as to their authenticity. But the one conclusion we can derive is that for some reason we have been, to a large extent, 'misled' and 'lied' to about aliens. We would be naïve to think that we are alone in this vast universe with so many planets and galaxies full of potential life, yet nothing ever definitive or official has been presented by our governments or news media – and to my knowledge "little green men" have not landed on the White House lawn as of this writing. The extraterrestrial/UFO story has many complex 'layers' and agendas and is actually 'designed' to be confusing.

Much compelling information and coverage would have you believe that UFOs are real. Going back more than a century there have been writings of extraterrestrials visiting the Earth. More recently a bombardment of "science fiction" movies, television shows, comics and video games that have all 'imprinted' into our life's 'socio-cultural' fabric— a convincing argument that ETs are real. Even ancient artifacts and drawings have shown that earthlings previously had some form of interaction with an 'advanced civilization' from the sky. There is also a huge push by investigative groups such as the "UFO Disclosure Project" to enlighten us to the fact that there are all sorts of 'types' of extraterrestrials here on Earth and have inhabited here for a long time. Some say, it was perhaps, when we first set off the Atomic Bomb in 1945 on Hiroshima and Nagasaki that got the attention of extraterrestrials. It was around this time when we started to have more 'sightings' of UFOs visiting Earth. Many believe that they were coming to observe us to make sure that we don't really blow ourselves up. One of the more famous and controversial sightings was in 1947 near Roswell, New Mexico where 'allegedly' an extraterrestrial spaceship with aliens crashed in the desert. After what many call a "cover up" of what really happened, the Military officially reported that it was a "weather balloon" that had fallen to Earth and not a UFO crash. Then there are the skeptics and non-believers who say this is all lunacy and that it is all made up that there are no UFOs or extraterrestrials. Who is right?

Well maybe both groups are correct, and here is why. There are 'extraterrestrials beings' here on Earth and, in fact, you are one of them. We are all extraterrestrial and through our creative 'conscience' we have manifested here on Earth and created this world. We are 'multi-dimensional' beings of great energy that can exist in many locations and in many worlds. Yet during this life time we are only able to 'tune into' this 'one' frequency and that is the Earth's frequency. Just like a radio with different channels, you can really only listen to one station at a time, yet there are hundreds if not thousands of other wavelengths of frequencies (stations) broadcasting all around us.

In this dimension we are only able to see, hear and experience (tune in) this one dimensional frequency and we are unable to access any higher vibrational frequencies, therefore limiting our 'understanding' of this world to just this one channel. In the higher realms of the 4th and 5th dimensions, and above, you would be able to 'digest' a lot more input of information. Why is just about every form of entertainment nowadays, especially movies, fascinated with super- human powers and aliens flying around in spaceships? Is this to subconsciously persuade us that aliens, UFOs, crop circles and extraterrestrials really exist? Perhaps, the reason for all the alien propaganda is to influence us that extraterrestrials exist. But if they do in fact really exist, they are most likely not what you have been led to believe by Hollywood. Extraterrestrials come to us from a higher dimension and are highly evolved. They are not nearly as violent or menacing as the movies would have you believe. They are a more evolved culture. Do they have powers where they can fly spaceships 6,000 miles per hour and turn 90 degrees on a dime? My answer to this would be – who knows for certain, because whatever powers they do possess would be created from a higher level of consciousness. They may have increased abilities to access what many might consider as magic here on Earth such as telepathy, teleportation, psychic awareness, healing, and clairvoyance. More than likely, if they are real, we are dealing with an advanced culture capable of using a 'multidimensional existence' where they are able to 'pop in and out' of different dimensions that man (earthlings) is not able to see or comprehend.

   If you have seen a UFO and told your friends and family about it, you will get that look of disbelief or maybe even a 'scratch of the head' from them. I have seen one (or maybe even two) on different occasions and can personally affirm this is the normal reactionary response. For many personal sightings, the individual is fully convinced that what they saw was a flying saucer or a UFO. It is a powerful, ominous and scary thing to see. But most of the objects that are seen in the sky are probably from our own creations and inventions meaning advanced military aircraft.

It is hypothesized that we originally got our advanced technology from fallen unidentified objects (UFOs), such as "Roswell," and our military and NASA have "back engineered" much of the 'propulsion' systems and materials into our own modern-day flying machines. Whether or not this is the case, perhaps what people have seen in the sky were flying objects created in a facility right here in America. The "S4 facility" at Groom Lake (aka Dreamland) just may be that area where these aircraft are engineered or even where 'real' UFOs are being stored.

Conceivably the real reason we are misled to believe that aliens are coming here from millions of miles away is to scare us. The "UFO agenda" is to somehow cleverly convince the public that aliens are real and menacing to humanity yet at the same time suppress the fact they really exist. This way, everyone picks a side as believers or nonbelievers. Either way, why would authorities want to not only confuse us, but subconsciously have us believe there could be the possibly of alien invaders? It goes back to a man named Wernher von Braun who was a German Nazi brought over after World War II through 'Project Paperclip' to head up NASA and our new aerospace program. Before he passed away he confided with his assistant and told her that as a 'last resort' to control all the people of the world into a "New World Order" they will convince the public that there is an alien threat and that we need to implement space-based weaponry to fight the forthcoming alien invasion. It was Ronald Reagan that stated in a speech in 1987 before the U.N. "*I occasionally think how quickly our differences worldwide (all nations) would vanish if we were facing an 'alien threat' from outside this world.*" Many fear their own government and may fear other governments more, but the scale of fear from a threat 'not of this world' would be unprecedented.

If this threat was not real and was still sold to the public as propaganda, then it would still have the same effect. Think about the impact of Orson Welles's infamous "War of the Worlds" radio broadcast in 1938, and how everyone listening believed it was real. This is what he warned us about, a fake "false flag" invasion by aliens. Wernher von Braun never mentioned that it was going to be real aliens. This may tie into why so many people are waking up to the fact that we never made it to the moon. Because of interstellar distances and dangerous Van Allen Belts (or the firmament spoken of in Genesis 1:6-8), it is virtually impossible for man to have made it all the way to the moon and back in the capacity that we have been told. Not impossible, but most likely improbable. President Kennedy in the early 1960s initially challenged us to go to the moon and unfortunately the space program had to make this happen even if it meant 'faking' filmed moon landings in a studio in London. Stanley Kubrick used rear screen projection in a "2001: A Space Odyssey" movie which was filmed two years prior to us 'landing on the moon.' The resemblance is uncanny.

So where did we originally get this 'back story' of aliens coming to Earth? It all may have started with the ancient teachings passed down through generations that talk about reptilian god-like creatures coming to Earth and interacting with humans. These Reptilian Gods are 'one and the same' that many cultures talked about in ancient writings of "Gods" coming down from the heavens and skies. They are called the Annunaki, the ones who took part in creating us, and the ones who 'marked' the Earth with unprecedented monuments such as the Egyptian Pyramids of Giza and Nazca Lines of Peru. The Annunaki came to lay claim to the part of the Earth that was rich in monoatomic gold now known as the area of the Persian Gulf (specifically the mouth of the Tigris and Euphrates). Gold has always been valuable even to the extraterrestrials. Monoatomic gold has healing powers and is a great source of esoteric knowledge and power. The Annunaki assisted in the creation of ancient civilizations such as Atlantis and Lemuria. These real civilizations existed as did most of all the 'Mythological teachings' that we are taught of our past history here on Earth. The Annunaki, some of whom say were influenced by an evil spirit or possibly Satan, experimented creating great civilizations and playing with man's DNA, but ultimately it all exploded into destruction of evil, greed, ego, and by going against the laws of the Prime Creator. Since these civilizations self-destructed the Annunaki had to start over with a new 'unplugged' man with a disconnected DNA (dumbed down version) of species to see if they could achieve collective consciousness for all humanity. Some artifacts (not many) exist today from these ancient civilizations that have left clues to our previous ancestors: The Pyramids of Giza, Easter Island, Stonehenge, and Göbekli Tepe possess ancient knowledge of the universal architect.

These 'monolithic artifacts' are placed at powerful energy centers and help connect the movement of energy across the Earth. The energy wave moved through Iran first, then to Jerusalem, and then on to Egypt. Several hundred years later it moved into Europe to create the great civilizations in Greece and Rome. These sophisticated societies experienced utter self-destruction of some great cities such as Athens, Rome and Pompeii. Then hundreds of years later the energy wave gave rise to the Spanish explorers sailing the seas, then on to French culture which had influence over much of the world for a time. The wave of energy then moved onto England with the creation of 'monarch economics' and onto the inventive German culture emerging into more modern times. The energy then moved west to America which was the 'new' test or experiment in freedom and capitalism. America was designed to be an industrial powerhouse to take hold of the world economy and rise to greatness through the Industrial Revolution all the while still being controlled by the European Financial Cartel. Yet America excelled and became even bigger globally and stronger monetarily than the European elites could have imagined. The experiment of liberty, freedom, and justice for all thrived so well that at some point the citizens, by European standards, got too free and too wealthy. Now America is in decline and the energy is moving further west towards China.

The real evidence of ETs has been suppressed and (long ago) much of the knowledge has been lost. All informative knowledge of their extraterrestrials has been re-written or erased from our history school books that have been published by the elite. They want to keep us dumb and ignorant about our real history. The person with a history degree is perhaps the most uninformed person because the lesser-educated person may be more open and have a better insight of the world. The highly educated person has learned a false dialogue. Their belief is they are the expert on truth and 'look down' on other concepts or ideas if they come from a less educated or social class person. Our society rewards those who think the same as the perceived intelligent person when, in fact, this is not nearly the true data. Question: Did extraterrestrials build the Pyramids of Giza? It is these types of questions that are not being asked and the answers have been hidden because if the truth were to come out, it would change everything.

Many accredited scientists, societies and cultures believe that extraterrestrials are real. They claim there are different species of 'tall whites' and 'small greys' with many variations. We live in a cosmos teeming with life. To think that we are not only alone, but there are more advanced species than us is humbling. Other peripheral evidence like crop circles, alien abductions, animal mutilation as well as the unearthing of elongated skulls and bones of 'Nephilims' brings even more questions to light as to the real origins of extraterrestrials and their current involvement in our world. Question: Are the ones that have hidden the secret from us about extraterrestrials the same 'vested interests' that controls our destiny 'Who are these vested interests?' And what are they up to? The answer is "Yes," and it has everything to do with controlling you with fear.

"That was a UFO beaming back at you. They have bases all over the world now and they have been coming here ever since 1946 when the scientist first starting bouncing radar beams off the moon. And they have been living and working amongst us in vast quantities ever since. The government knows all about them. Well they are people just like us from within our own solar system...except that their society is more highly evolved...I mean they don't have wars they have no monetary system they don't have any leaders because I mean each man is a leader. I mean man...because of their technology they are able to feed, clothe, house and transport themselves equally and with no effort. Why don't they reveal themselves to us is because if they did it would cause general panic. Now I mean we still have leaders upon who we rely for the release of this information. These leaders have decided to repress this information because of the tremendous shock that it would cause to our antiquated systems. The 'aliens' have been mating with people from all walks of life in an advisory capacity for once man will have a guide-like control over his own destiny. He will have a chance to transcend and to evolve with some equality for all."

-Jack Nicholson "Easy Rider" (1968)

The extraterrestrial UFO question is quite an intriguing one to try to answer, but after all the deliberation one can only speculate that they do exist. Whatever means of travel appears to be either a 'hyper' or 'multi-dimensional' capacity allowing the ETs to circumvent the space-time medium of perceived great distances in relatively short or instantaneous time periods and materialize into our 3rd dimension. Most people don't see them, interact with them or feel their presence, yet they are here among us. Let us hope that if they are here, they are here for good and benevolent intentions and, at long last, to assist humankind at this perilous time in our history. Perhaps one day, if necessary, they will make themselves fully known here on Earth to show us a better way to take care of ourselves and our beautiful planet.

"The result is we live in peace, without arms or armies, secure in the knowledge that we are free from aggression and war. Free to pursue more... profitable enterprises. Now, we do not pretend to have achieved perfection, but we do have a system, and it works. I came here to give you these facts. It is no concern of ours how you run your own planet, but if you threaten to extend your violence, this Earth of yours will be reduced to a burned-out cinder. Your choice is simple: join us and live in peace, or pursue your present course and face obliteration. We shall be waiting for your answer. The decision rests with you."

- Klaatu

CANNABIS

BOOK 24

For most of my life, I believed what I was told...that marijuana was bad for you. The fact is when it comes to marijuana 'they' (our parents, teachers and governments) lied to us. This is evident now that 'local laws' against consumption and selling have slackened in many countries and more recently, here in America as more information is brought to the forefront. Marijuana (Cannabis sativa forma indica) whose active ingredient is THC (tetrahydrocannabinol) has many attributes and benefits. It is clearly one of the most 'magical,' natural plant substances on the planet. Among its many beneficial attributes as a medium to achieve a "higher state of being" are its too-numerous-to-list cancer fighting, preventative medicinal and restorative, healing qualities. Each day more and more benefits and uses are being discovered too, medicinally, socially and industrially. Cannabis 'works' and interacts on the mind, body and spiritual playing field. It places the body in a restful state while stimulating your thoughts, helping spiritual connection to your higher self (literally) and rejuvenates the 'self.' Every day millions of people use cannabis to 'get high' as a means to mostly escape the grind and lessen the stressful routine of life. 'They' call it a 'high' since when consumed (smoked or eaten) it takes you into a euphoric, levitated condition that generally relaxes and encourages a creative state. Sometimes this state is to do nothing or be consumed or amused by a seemingly useless activity. Even in the 'nothingness' comes 'something' to those that enjoy its use. It is used as a release from this reality into a higher conscience state of awareness that accentuates the "here and now." In that regard it is not too dissimilar from an intense meditative experience. The five (six) senses are all heightened during use whereby music can sound more alive, food can taste better and touching can arouse a sense of playfulness. As marijuana consumption increases around the world people are finding out more significant upsides to a moderate or even daily use it can have, such as lowering blood pressure; lowering intraocular pressure from glaucoma; a natural form of sleeping aid; a muscle relaxer; a mood enhancing aphrodisiac for sex. The chemicals in Marijuana, cannabinoids, mimic the activity of natural chemicals already found in the human brain – chemicals that help regulate sleep. The THC is the chemical in cannabis (marijuana) that provides a relaxing calming "buzz" effect to the body which aids in sleeping. THC can increase the amount of 'slow-wave' or deep sleep which is the type of sleep that plays a big role in repairing and restoring the body. A little THC before bedtime can help people fall asleep faster and stay asleep longer creating a more pleasant sleeping experience. The evidence is also far too overwhelming in helping with seizures, anxiety, Alzheimer's, Multiple Sclerosis, Hepatitis C, arthritis, Parkinson's disease, metabolism, nausea, stimulating appetite and the list goes on and on.

Though marijuana's benefits are multitudinous - it does affect people differently and it is certainly not for everyone. Either you like (love) it or you don't. Some people do not like the 'high' feeling and experience a discomfort with the 'loss of control' and suspended state of animation. If consumed in high enough concentrations even the most seasoned pot smoker can experience an uncomfortable 'high.' Yet very few adverse effects ever come from this and these events are always temporary. The experience of time slowing, dry mouth, red glassy heavy eyes, increased heart rate, lightheadedness, short term memory loss and laziness all subsides in time and whatever affects it has on the body as mentioned previously are temporary. Repeated use of marijuana can also desensitize cannabinoid receptors which means that the 'side effects' such as the increase in appetite (or dry mouth) subsides with use, but also the individual is not as consciously aware of it as they were as a novice smoker. Seasoned smokers actually experience a decrease of eating and have healthier figures than their sober counterparts or alcohol-consuming friends. Marijuana smokers have a 7% lower body mass and a 4% smaller waistline on average. This is because there is less unused sugar in the cells and pot smokers make better use of their insulin in reducing excess weight and decrease diabetes.

The big propagandized lie about marijuana's harmful effects has been told for a long time. But why would authorities lie to us if they knew about its proven benefits and uses? Why outlaw a natural plant, when it has more diverse uses than just about any other natural material on Earth? Aside from its proven medicinal benefits – perhaps the fact that it has real world use as material products such as oil, rope, lumber, plastic, paper, fabric, textile, fuel, diverse nutritional aspects and even external body care ingredients are the very reasons why it has been suppressed. What companies have patents for marijuana and hemp? Or have the power to suppress its uses and accentuate its supposed dangers? Did the threat of marijuana make it so dangerous to corporations or was there another even more important and underlying reason?

The Hurst Corporation (William Randolph Hurst) along with several other big corporations and Harry Anslinger, head of the Federal Bureau of Narcotics, sought to outlaw the hemp plant back in the 1930s. Because it threatened to be a cheaper alternative to what the oil corporations were offering. By sticking with the oil and oil by-products, the refining companies could control the use of just about any man-made product. Hemp is one of the cleanest and most useful renewable energies on Earth. It would be nearly impossible to control a plant that "grows like a weed" and could be virtually grown by anyone – anywhere. The other reason, and quite possibly the more important one to the establishment, was that the people that used, grew and understood marijuana at that time were mostly from third world nations (e.g., Mexico, South America and Africa). These people were labeled as undesirables by the establishment – and America did not want any part of them. 'Race' as being possibly a motivating factor, the powers that be did not want 'marijuana types' to commingle with the youth of America figuring it would be a bad influence on many levels (today, things are apparently much different and our borders are open to anyone who wants to come here legally or illegally). Hypothetically, by legalizing marijuana, for whatever reason, would have created a socioeconomic instability and made it much tougher to control these individuals and the youth of America. By simply banning the hemp part of the plant, made it illegal for any medicinal or recreational use too. So the corporate lobbyists for big oil and paper companies are to 'blame' for the many federal laws still in place (on the books) that keep hemp and marijuana use illegal for most of the United States. We have been sold a 'bunch of lies' and authorities certainly don't want you to self-medicate by growing your own 'medicine' in your back yard skipping over 'Big Pharma' and the medical system.

'We' smoke herb to ease pain, to raise our spirit, to stimulate the intellect, but also to connect with our physical being to reach heights of ecstasy which are unattainable otherwise. While the act of sexual intercourse is considered to be magical in its own right, it is with even greater intensity to experience the intimate encounter "high." As in the saying "sex is a drug" is indicative of feelings of being high. Marijuana users can all agree that when high, cannabis has many enhancement factors. Webster's defines enhancement as: "heighten intensity - raise - make greater." That is what happens when you experience sex, high on cannabis. Marijuana intensifies sexual experiences because the experience is connecting with your very soul. Everything we see, hear, taste, touch and smell during sex is amplified and this arouses the mind/body relationship. It is the melding of the 'mind and body' experience that can be so arousing and euphoric while you're high that people are able to increase a heightened level of excitement and achieve a better climax and orgasm. Marijuana use is highly recommended to couples who are lacking intimacy in the bedroom. Good, healthy sex has many benefits and can bring more vitality, youthfulness (make you look younger), and can enhance mental clarity.

The word "nirvana" means to "blow out." This is very much like what you do when smoking...you blow out and this practice is actually very therapeutic. The blowing of smoke is tied to many ancient practices. In a relaxed state a person can really be in the moment of 'now.' To put aside everything that we are thinking about from our busy life and just empty our minds is one of the best and freeing things you can do for yourself. Marijuana can help you achieve this. Cannabis is spiritual, natural and God's gift to us here on Earth directly from the Earth. Responsible use can bring introspective insight and profound revelations to our meaning of life.

"A certain amount of passivity would be an excellent remedy for our kind of culture."

-Anonymous

The other scare tactic used by the government propaganda machine is to convince us that marijuana is a "gateway drug" that can lead to heavier drug use. This is another 'lie' used to dissuade us from seeking the use of marijuana. Alcohol, cigarettes and marijuana can all be labeled as gateway drugs, but so can many other things. The simple fact is, that beer, cigarettes and marijuana can more easily be acquired by kids at a younger age. Just because someone enjoys smoking marijuana does not immediately mean that they are also going to like cocaine, heroin or any hard drugs. Quite the contrary, a person that is destined for harder drugs will get there despite any previous use of less 'hard' class drugs. Many people are content with just smoking marijuana and have no desire to use anything harder. Unfortunately the 'system' may cause people to be placed in uncomfortable situations. With marijuana still illegal in most states, users are forced to sometimes deal on the 'black market' to purchase marijuana and will no doubt run into a 'tougher crowd' to do so whereby exposing cannabis users to sellers of harder, more serious narcotics. It is usually peer pressure of a friend or the assistance of a drug dealer/pusher that will invite harder drugs into one's life. It is up to the individual whether they choose to accept that invitation or not.

The other aspect that makes marijuana so dangerous to the establishment is that it frees your mind. Free thinking people question authority. This became a huge problem in the late 1950s through the 1960s because so many kids were trying "pot" that a 'new' cultural wave took hold and spread across the planet. A stigma has been created by the 'powers that be' that if you smoke marijuana you're stupid, lazy and unproductive. It is amazing the power of the media juggernaut because this is the furthest thing from the truth. Marijuana smokers are some of the most creative and intuitively productive people. They are also some of the most astute observers of seeing the "big picture" and social trends in society. The wave of freedom and free thinkers was initially started by the "beatnik generation" (early bikers and musicians) and then carried on by the hippies of the sixties through the seventies. Smoking 'pot' became a symbol of freedom, free thinking and counter culture. The entire youth generation movement was based on freedom, creative thinking and love...all very dangerous concepts to the elite and authorities. If everyone was free doing their own thing then there would be no way to control them.

Understand that the "hippie" movement was started as a covert operation to create social discourse between the older generation and the youth, but at some point the movement got too big and too popular. The reason being, is that truth and love, which all hippies were seeking, was actually the correct path to a higher level of conscience. Hippies began to ask the questions of "Who am I" and started looking for a greater purpose of one's existence. Hippies did not desire the materialistic items that their parents accumulated and they rebelled against the ways of the establishment. At some point, as the hippies got a little older and had their own children, the elite controlling interest were able to 'reel-in' the free spirits back to the corporate environment by enticing them with affordable modern houses, shiny cool cars and well-paying corporate jobs. The 'change over' occurred in the late seventies, and by 1980 it was the dawn of the money-printing preppies of Wall Street who took over the consciousness of the youth and sold them the brand new illusion of the "American Dream" (of debt and slavery).

The (non) fact that marijuana is addictive is also a heated debate. Plain and simple...marijuana is non-addictive. You may really crave it and if you don't have it you may feel depressed or upset, but your body can function and survive without it. You may smoke every day for years, but you can actually stop for a day and be OK unlike more addictive substances such as alcohol, heroin or even tobacco that your body craves and goes through a painful 'withdrawal' process even after one day, or two days, of non-use.

Other drugs such as heroin and cocaine are essentially 'illegal' manmade substances that have many addictives qualities and dangers that can even kill you if enough of the substance is ingested. Yet, both are loved by many. Drugs (and specifically (cocaine) has been glamorized in the movies by celebrity models, actors, comedians and musicians. These illegal drugs have been the source of many wars, money disputes, gang rivals and even government takeovers. Historically, it is through the U.S. Central Intelligence Agency (CIA), and our military, that many of these harder drugs make their way from places like Afghanistan or Columbia to American street corners and eventually into the hands of our children. When the government said that there was a "War on Drugs" they actually meant the opposite; you saw more drugs on the streets than ever before during the 1980s. It is this type of hypocrisy that makes it so challenging to identify the real "bad guys" and our trust in government authorities has been tarnished.

Psychedelic drugs are of historical importance. Hundreds of years ago a natural form of hallucinogenic drug such as peyote, from the cactus plant, were used by Native American Indians in ceremonies and spiritual awakenings. It was these natural drugs that allowed man to explore the farthest regions of the mind and to connect to the spirituality that is within each one of us. In more modern times a manmade hallucinogenic substance lysergic acid diethylamide (LSD), that mimics the peyote hallucinogenic experience, was created and used by early governments as a possible aid to psychiatric patients. LSD is a drug that explores the inner soul and discovers, through self-awareness, the polarity of life. At some point, officials at the CIA thought the drug might have applicable use on certain mind-control patients. The MK-Ultra research program propagated the drug among young servicemen and students in the late fifties and early sixties in the hope to elicit responses of 'mind control' over them. The MK-Ultra program quickly went underground, but we can only speculate that on some levels the CIA was successful. Ironically, LSD made its way onto the streets and in the mid-sixties it became a part of the hippie and alternative culture. Many counterculture youths used LSD as a means of experimentation, escape and entertainment. Even Cary Grant, the famous movie actor, experimented with LSD and just like him many people 'dropped LSD' searching perhaps for some higher level of truth or clarity of life.

DMT (*N,N-DiMethyltryptamine*) which is a human neurotransmitter is the most powerful psychedelic known to man — and your own brain makes it. DMT is released when you're in heavy REM (Rapid Eye Movement) sleep and at times of extreme stress like when you believe you're going to die. DMT has some commonalities to serotonin and melatonin and is released by your brain to assist a person during the transition from the living conscious state to the resting conscious state. This is evident in near–death experiences when large amounts of DMT that are stored in your Pineal Gland (aka "Third Eye") are released. DMT has been reproduced into a crystalline form and can be consumed as a drug. The DMT experience is like having a meeting with God. It is profound communication with the divine and an incredible loving energy experience that is at the source of everything. It leaves you so humble that after the experience you are still *you* (and you still look the same), but you are not 'really' you anymore. You have been changed from the inside out; in essence you have been 'reprogrammed,' but in a positive way. You won't look at life the same way as before and will have a better understanding of how you fit into this world. You have experienced what very few people have experienced because DMT — removes your ego. The experience may only last a short time, but it will forever be with you. The drug is most commonly produced inside the human brain stem in the first 28 days of life as a baby. After that point, it is stored in the brain's Pineal Gland and is only released upon brain/body communication stating that the body is sleeping (in small amounts) or is dying (large amounts). During death DMT is released throughout your brain and nervous system, numbing pain, freeing the mind and drifting your subconscious off into the land of death. This is perhaps why some people make claims to having seen the light at the end of the tunnel or having an "out-of-body-experience" during near-death experience. When DMT is consumed, the trip usually lasts about 15-20 seconds (much like the lesser-extreme psychedelic, Salvia) but it seems like much more. The drug separates the wall between your subconscious and conscious mind, essentially causing you to dream while wide awake. Upon 'waking,' you feel like a million bucks, better than any commercial or non-commercial drug you could ever find because it is natural. Essentially, you are re-born.

Pharmaceuticals: You are sick and you need to take something to get better. This is what you have been told your entire life: Pop a pill and you will feel better; Pop a pill to be thinner; Pop a pill to be smarter; Pop a pill to have sex. The solution to all your problems, whether they are imagined or not, are in a little, colored pill and the "good news" (sarcasm) there are tons of companies lining up wanting to sell them to you. Not all pharmaceuticals and medicines are bad. Drugs (especially natural ones) have their place in our society, especially if they can be distributed affordably and used responsibly.   The problem is when you are 'pushed' into thinking that the only solution is what the pharmaceutical companies are telling you, or rather, what they are selling you. Many people "get hooked" on prescription drugs that are made for imagined ailments; such as the many advertised…"As seen on TV" or heard on the radio.

The fact is that your body is an amazing machine. You are capable of healing and nurturing yourself. When you have been told that you have a problem, over and over again, you start to believe what you hear. Much of the difficulty that you may be having is in your head and that may actually contribute heavily to keeping you sick and dependent. You know yourself better than anyone else knows you, so what you have done is 'disempowered' yourself to the marketing campaign of the pharmaceutical company's propaganda.   Why?   Because the healthcare and pharmaceutical business is a multi-billion-dollar industry that needs your money to survive and the way to do this is for them to tell you that you are sick, even if you're not. You will start to see, at some time in the future, the pharmaceutical companies finding a way to work themselves into regulating the marijuana business...because there is too much money in it...to not be in it.

UTOPIA

BOOK 25

"Utopia"...this unique word looks and sounds intriguing, but what really is Utopia? Utopia is a community or society possessing highly desirable or near-perfect qualities. It is the epitome of existence where all people are happy and thrive, where all desires are satiated, and has been written about by scholars for centuries. The New World Order (NOW) 'Utopia' though is not designed for the common person. The fundamental difference is that where in the Ideal Utopia all men are created equal, in the 'New World Order Utopia' most of the population is enslaved serving a small elite group of people who have power, access and money as 'over landlords' controlling all the worlds' resources. The fact is, that their version of Utopia is only to be enjoyed by the few, the elite, the privileged. The rest will work, serve and obey in order to provide that Utopia world for them. Their goal, as it has been for centuries, is to reestablish, here on Earth, through a secret agenda of malicious hidden intent the ancient Babylonian civilization of long ago whose society was ruled by a small council of wise men – benevolent overseers of a one world totalitarianism socialist government that aspires democracy and protection. The Twin Towers, that came down on 9/11, were a 'recreation' of sorts of the Tower of Babel which was rumored to be so high it touched the heavens. The 'Towers' were collapsed to signify the end of the western world's rule and to freedom in America. If you love 'freedom' then this Utopia is not for you. Today, the global elite are pushing us into this false Utopia of the future by means of non-profits, corporations and organizations that say they are helping humanity– masked behind hidden agendas such as global warming, climate change, gun violence and the U.N. Agenda 21. They make it seem like they are doing good for the Earth and humanity, but this is not the case. It is, in fact, the opposite. The benefactors of the NWO will be the small elite group of people that actually already control (or own) most of all the world's companies and resources. By pretending to do good, they extract more money and resources for themselves. When they talk about a perfect society with no war, famine or disease they are defining their own world vision of Utopia because they are to be in total control.

Living in the New World Order will essentially be slavery for the average person. You will be a "worker bee" not able to get ahead or make enough funds to enjoy yourself or even be able to adequately retire. The system won't allow you to amass enough wealth to be self-sufficient or do what you want in life. You will work for "the man" and be monitored "by the man" *literally*, in everything you do. They want you just smart enough to do your job, but not too smart to question it. In '1984,' it showed a two-class system. There are the ruling elite and all the rest of us, and 'you' are the rest of us. Even today the implementation of 'Global Technocracy' by the elite significantly assists in control and monitoring of the populace whereby civilian people are treated like the enemy and are listed as terrorists. Examples of this would be how the Department of Homeland Security is targeting citizens who think counter to the government by discussing the New World Order, Christian identity, anti-immigration, guns, opposition to the Federal Reserve System, freedom of speech, gold or

Constitutionalism. This overreaching authority, literally, sets just about everyone up as a terrorist. It demonizes America and its citizens while giving Draconian power to the state.

The blueprint for world peace by the United Nations (U.N.) is to progressively strengthen the international peace force while citizens of the world are to lose freedoms, rights and sovereignty. This will ultimately bring about the scenario where no state (or country) has the ability to challenge the U.N. or have the power or ability to override it — all international disputes will be handled by the U.N. and through Agenda 21 all aspects of human existence will be monitored and regulated by this international body. Even though currently "we the people" have the right to keep and bear arms and this right "shall not be infringed" in the future all arms and ammunition will be outlawed or regulated for your average citizen of the world and they will not be able to protect themselves or their families from any future threats (including a tyrannical or rogue government). Agenda 21 (2030) is a 'stepping stone' toward world government and one step closer to the world Utopia control of the elite.

The only way a society can remain free and independent is to hold in their power the weapons necessary to secure their internal security from its own government or from any external international force. The Second Amendment was created to secure freedom from an oppressive government takeover; it is not there so you can go hunting. The Second Amendment is there to prevent the U.S. Government from becoming a dictatorship either by treason or betrayal of the Constitution. Those who are attempting to change, alter, or even eliminate our 2nd Amendment rights should understand that our 1st and 4th Amendments are directly correlated to the 2nd Amendment. Society must also be wary of merging the U.S. (via the "Iron Mountain Report") into the U.N. The United Nations is a corrupted international organization/ dictatorship with no freedoms — hence they must get the guns from the citizens of any participating nation. The Iron Mountain Report from in the 1960s covers the handling of all men, women, children and babies on the basis of a herd or animal management without regard to morality. It reduced people to objects, classifying all humans as non-entities with no rights or self-worth. Many may find it ironic that with all of these thriving international, non-profit, charitable foundations and organizations which are supposed to protect the individual person, that we don't see any major improvement in how society treats people.

In a perfect Utopia, there would be many wonderful inventions and creations to benefit all the people. All disease would be gone. All money matters non-existent. All your essential needs are... taken care of. A Utopia society actually exists today in subtle forms, but you have to look carefully. There are super foods that can nourish and heal our bodies; medicines that prevent sickness (even cancer); technology that can provide free clean energy and electricity for houses; buildings and businesses; cars and trucks that run on nonpolluting gallons of water not gallons of oil or gasoline; underground high speed rail systems called 'Maglev' trains (magnetic levitation) which can transport you from Washington, D.C. to Denver, Colorado in less than a few hours safely; and deep underground cities (Deep Underground Military Bases –D.U.M.B.S) that can house thousands of people for long periods of time in case of a natural or unnatural disaster were to happen on Earth's surface. All of this exists today, but the problem is that your average person does not have access to it. The elite have hidden this technology. Specifically, the 'Electro Magneto Levitron' track system (VHST) created by the RAND Corporation should be used by the general public and could save us a lot time. It is a frictionless rail system that allows an aerodynamic train to access speeds of over 400 miles per hour (as fast as an airplane) and does this safely, cheaply and without the consumption of fossil fuels. These technological advancements have been suppressed, but for what reasons?

"If you stick your head in the sand…the world is still going on around your ass."
-Anonymous

The entire world is a stage—Obama is basically a puppet—and his job (as all presidents of the past 20 years) is to read teleprompters and make no decisions alone—taking specific directions and moving us towards global control. The power elite and international banking interests have the majority of power in this world. Those that control the financial systems are also the engineers, criminals and ultimate fraudsters of the world—the Federal Reserve, IMF, World Bank, European Central Bank; they are the real, string-pullers of power. The power elite send your sons/daughters to do the dirty work in foreign lands and you're paying for all of it too…through taxes. War and deception is out of control. 9/11 was the false flag operation that was used to justify the invasion of Afghanistan, Iraq and other countries. Osama bin Laden stated in the aftermath of 9/11 that he had nothing to do with the attack. Bin Laden, who may have died of renal cancer back in 2001 and was most likely a CIA asset, was never charged and no case ever has gone to trial convicting him and/or any of the other so called 19 hijackers.

A Utopian society can only exist with peace. It solely rests on the shoulders of all the individuals in the world to achieve this peace. The power is with the people and all we need to do is awaken the power in the people. People need to realize that they have the majority rule by means of collective power.

"New Age" spirituality is not what you may think. Anything with the label 'New' is not a part of our true nature. It is part of a new wave of misinformation. Do not be foolish or gullible to think that in the 'New Age Consciousness' awakening – that everyone is pushing on celebrity talk shows will benefit the average person. Do not be fooled when they say that coming together in one system (monetarily, politically, educationally or spiritually) is going to be beneficial for all. The New World Order is right in front of us now. This is the agenda, to have all nations come together in a peaceful 'Utopia' existence with no war or conflict, but this will be disguised as a 'conscience shift' and it will be the wrong conscience, a conscience of evil. Be careful because it sounds good, but it is a "wolf in sheep's clothing." Countries and individuals should not have to give up their individuality or independence to be safe, secure, or free, to live as they want.

This is the 21st century. If we use our resources wisely and responsibly, there is no reason everyone can't have what they need to survive.   There is no reason people should be starving to death (especially with how much food America wastes each day). There is no reason people should be homeless and not have a proper place to sleep or family housing. The common man and woman just want to live in peace in a clean, safe environment. When you look around the world today, you can see this is not the case for many. Understand that the will of the majority is not being heard and this is the first (not the last) sign that our system is breaking down.

I AM FREE

I am free to pay taxes…..
I am free to get a marriage license….
I am free to work…..
I am free to pay interest…..
I am free to choose between the two political parties….
I am free to get a driver's license….
I am free to use credit cards…..
I am free to use a bank….
I am free to have healthcare….
I am free to buy anything I want….
I am free to be 'patted down' when flying….
I am free to watch the news….

I am free to have a business license...
I am free to own a home....
I am free to pay for my education....
I am free to get vaccinated....

I am free to....

There is a purposeful attempt to collapse the American economy and redistribute the wealth from the 'middle class' to the poor through subsidized, government programs and to the corrupt and greedy, super-rich who are beneficiaries of favorable corporate treatment by governments. This will wipe out the middle class whereby we will be left with just a two-class system: the super-rich and the poor. This socialist system is the best for controlling populations. The elite feel that America has gotten too wealthy and we are too free. The elite feel they need to bring America 'in line' with the rest of the world in order for them to fully implement a one world political, monetary, economic, governmental system. The New World Order. But, they still have to get our guns to completely control us.

The two class society system that has been created and implemented by Communist, Socialist and Fascist governments is finally making its way to America. Everyone is under control in a two-class society. The poor are dependent on survival from the government through subsidy checks, food stamps and health benefits and the super wealthy are also dependent upon the central government through government contracts, carve-outs, tax policies and regulations and laws that only serve the super wealthy. The super wealthy will continue to prosper. Those in the 'upper middle' and 'middle' class have been ratcheted down. Everyone in the 'middle' classes is getting squeezed hard financially. The middle class that is being obliterated are the true patriots of this country. They are the faithful ones who pay most of the taxes, support the public schools, go to church, believe in God and help others within their communities. They are the law-abiding citizens that made America great in the 'heyday' and, when they finally have had enough, they will come together to revolt. That is why the government has taken so many precautions to plan control of the middle class by limiting our freedoms, extracting money out of our pockets and control of weapons and ammunition. They (the elite, central bankers/government) cannot afford to leave us with any means to rise up and take over the tyrannical system. The true middle class power is not a group that you can pay off like the poor or the super wealthy.

The super wealthy have no conscience and will virtually do anything for the next million or billion. As long as they are on the 'right' side of the money chain, they seem to not really care what happens to most of us. Even if they are dependent on the middle class for 'consumerism,' they will always be on the correct side of the equation for power, resources, money (wealth) and control. The way you control a population is to overwhelm the system with entitlements, taxes, regulations and spending. This is not the type of Utopia that the average person would dream of. The "American Dream" is now turning into the American nightmare for most Americans.

Much of the new push for the foundation of America is based on fairness for all. But America was never based on fairness in that America prospered with the ones who wanted to work hard and make honest money doing it. If everything is collected and redistributed, then you will never have that entrepreneurial spirit for true capitalism which is what drives success in business. America was not based on happiness for all, but rather the pursuit of happiness. Those who want more can attain it if they so desire. But it is not merely up to the government to predict who gets what and how much. Equality and social justice is what is deteriorating the system from within. If you let people have some freedom to create and invent, then jobs, income and happiness will flourish for all and not just a few. America's wealth is being destroyed with lower income, more taxation and more debt than any one nation has ever seen.

The "key" to a true future Utopia is the police, military and the hired security forces that personally protect the elite. The key 'unlocks' the security chain that protects the corrupt, global, corporate bankers from the people. At some point in the future, the citizens will demand access to these elite people's homes and offices. When the elite have no security to protect them, then we could have access to sit down and talk with them and ask them questions. They will be held accountable for what they have done. If need be—detain, arrest or even incarcerate them for the crimes against humanity they have caused. I do not believe a lynching is in order. It will be up to their 'security' to decide to put down their arms, step aside and grant us permission to access the elite. All the security has to do is say "No" to their bosses step aside and join with the people. So I appeal to the police, the military and the security forces around the world (and here in America) and ask them to think about what is the right and just thing to do. What would their own families and children want them to do? Continue to protect the real criminals or side with humanity? I ask, no...I plead...that when the time comes, they will put themselves in our shoes to see the situation clearly; that it is the manipulators and not the good citizens of this country who have caused us this great unease. There is a big evil lie of the New Age Movement and it is up to our protectors to also use non-compliance and do the right thing when the time comes. And the time is coming soon...

"If it once became general, wealth would confer no distinction."

-George Orwell (1984)

Imagine a real Utopia where every official in our government resigns if they can't uphold the Constitution. Those who can serve should do it for free and receive no benefits. All debt erased from the balance sheets. If you owe money on a house or a car the debt is gone. If you own a business, you own it outright. A new monetary policy shall be implemented based on no interest loans and sound money backed by gold. All taxes on income are abolished. The only taxes are levied on either consumerism or anyone (company) producing or manufacturing products whereby they use anything taken from the Earth (oil, coal, silver) and this way we are able to keep and manage our natural resources for future generations. All electricity to our homes is provided for free by use of Tesla's alternating, ground, current system. All food would be grown without the use of any genetic mutations and be done naturally. All Geo-Engineering and weather manipulation shall stop. All fluoridation of water shall stop. All addition of chemicals in our products shall stop. All pharmaceuticals shall be evaluated with at least 80% of them (the useless and deadly ones) eliminated from the market. Lastly, all manipulated markets are stopped (stock, gold & silver, oil) and are made just again.

Attention! All you rule breakers, all you troublemakers, all you free spirits, all you pioneers, all you visionaries, and all you non-conformists – everything the establishment has told you that is wrong with you – is actually what is right with you. You see things others don't see. You are hard-wired to change the world. Your mind is irrepressible and thus threatens authority. You were born to be a revolutionary. You can't stand 'rules' because you know in your heart there is a better way. You have strengths dangerous to the establishment and it wants them eliminated because your whole life you have been told your strengths are weaknesses – now, I'm telling you otherwise. Your impulse is a gift. Impulses are your way to the miraculous. Your destructibility is an artifact of your inspired creativity and your mood swings reflect the nature pulse of life. They give you unstoppable energy at a high level, but can also provide deep soulful insight at a low energy state (level). Society has told you that this is a disorder and that you need medicine or drugs to keep you at 'one level' – a level that doesn't feel anything and is numb – but your addictive personality is just a 'symptom' of your vast, under-used capacity for creative expression - spiritual connection – and your open-mindedness and unrelenting thirst for truth and knowledge. Those are the truths of some of the greatest minds of our time...pioneers, visionaries of creative inventors, revolutionaries and even procrastinators – and we are all connected. We are the same. We are one. One idea, one entirely original thought – whether it is good, bad or indifferent – is in all of us, so we must choose how we want to conduct our life independently, but collectively as one. Society is filled with so many distractions that people are overwhelmed. They are confused. And inherently, they do not want to revolt, but the rules and 'laws' that have been set to protect us in theory will ultimately destroy anyone or anybody who violates them.

"We need to treat our whole planet like it is our homeland."

-Anonymous

Question: Has our modern, consumer-based society made us any happier? The better question is...if '100' years ago you told a person that they would have a home with central air-conditioning and heat, a supermarket with vast selections of food, healthcare, modern transportation and technology that delivers 24-hours-a-day entertainment, they would think that you were describing heaven – a state of extraordinary societal harmony and everything would be grand. Yet, with all the material wealth, progress and modern comforts of today, we (humankind) may not be any happier. Sales of anti-depressants are at an all-time high. We have had great advancements in the quality of military, technology and industry, yet not any advancement in the quality of our inner happiness.

As we search for our Utopia here on Earth, it is important to point out a very vital aspect of our real future. Tough times may be ahead for us. These tough times will be exacerbated by the fact that we here in the United States don't manufacture anything anymore. All of our manufacturing capabilities have been shipped overseas so very little, real, usable products are made here in America anymore. Question: What good is a society that is great at 'pushing papers' around when all you really need are a pair of shoes? If we can't make anything for ourselves, we are dependent on other countries for products that are essential to our welfare. If those products slow or cease to be imported to America, then America could seep into a "third world" status. This could happen if the credit markets 'unravel' or collapse where all business would just stop since there would be no central means to pay or trade goods. We still have agricultural production here in America, but we have no factories or manufacturing equipment left to make anything else. It seems that by 'selling off' our manufacturing in the 1980s to China, and other nations, that America has been driven into a ditch...on purpose. The international elite don't really care about America and they certainly don't care about you. It is time for us Americans to "pull ourselves up by our own bootstraps" and get busy starting to make things here in America again or we will always be dependent on others for survival.

Would you consider yourself an anarchist? Not an anarchist in the traditional sense of throwing bombs, but a 'philosophical' anarchist who would leave things very much alone to take their natural course. Everything will sort itself out, in time, and sometimes our intervention makes things not only more complicated, but (generally) worse.

All civilized societies depend on trusting one another. Now, we are all somewhat untrustworthy, but there is really no other option than to trust each other moving forward into the future. Our conscience must prevail. We must make this gamble for future societies because the only alternative to trusting one another is a police state. And who trusts a police state? Would the police have your personal interests at heart? All governments   become self-serving corporations with their interest at heart, not yours. So you see it is crucial to begin to trust others and trust yourself to do the right thing. Most people are not in favor of what we are doing here in America. A Republic is supposed to represent the individual, the small businessman, and it does nothing of the kind. Neither the Republican nor the Democratic Party supports the independence of the individual. They are, essentially, both the 'same' and trying to choose between the two political parties is like deciding to choose between which group of gangsters you're going to place in power.

The natural human condition is optimism. As long as there is a shred of hope then we will go on, but as soon as we realize that there is no hope, we will rebel. People will tolerate a lot as long as the deterioration of their society is implemented in a slow methodical fashion. This provides control for the people in power, but at some point, they will lose control and from this a more just society can emerge. A perfect Utopia is within our grasp. It will rise up from local communities whereby citizens will empower themselves to take back what centralized governments have taken from us. The farmer, the doctor and the store owner will go to Washington to represent the needs and wants of their community and then go back to their communities to live and work among their family and friends. There is no need for full time politicians and certainly no need to pay these representatives with outlandish salaries and free lunches. The Utopia civilization is here now, we just need to create it now...

NATURE

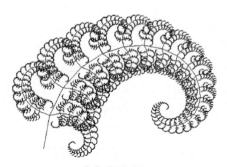

BOOK 26

When was the last time you really connected with nature? When was the last time you 'consumed in' the wondrous, natural beauty of the mountains, rivers, flowers or trees? Ancient cultures have traditionally honored and observed nature — especially the changes of the seasons and the procession of the sun and moon. We have been so distracted in our modern-day lives that we have almost forgotten where we come from and that our true essence is nature. Nature is what is natural. If you look around, you will notice that the composition of everything is becoming less and less natural and more and more manufactured. We have distanced ourselves from the true source of life by inviting the 'ease-ability' of everything we 'need' to be manufactured in a factory and purchased in a store. True, we all have grown accustomed to modern conveniences and we should not shun progress just for progress' sake, yet there is a proper balance that should take place in our life so as not to completely lose our connection to nature.

In ancient times this knowledge was not in conflict with the modern trends as they are today. An intimate relationship with the natural environment is 'built' into the human psyche and always has been. The sights, the sounds and even the smells of nature are interconnected to our vibration that makes us feel whole, good and just. All aspects of nature are beautiful...even the destructive ones. The unique trait of nature is that it always shows up beautiful. There is beauty in every sunrise and sunset. There is beauty in every mountain range and pastoral valley. There is beauty in every lake and shoreline. There is even beauty in the sounds of nature. The birds and bees on a spring day are the background music score to our life as we enjoy a walk in the woods. Did you ever notice that the sounds of a waterfall, a storm or even rocks falling are always somehow pleasant to the ear? This is because nature makes 'noise' as if it were music...music to our ears...that resonates and rings in perfect harmony with our inner self. The sound that a simple falling rain makes as it hits the Earth has a calming affect and resonates naturally through our body. The beauty of a nighttime thunderstorm that is scary and calming at the same time, is a symphony of sights and sounds as flashes of lightning and rolling thunder dances magically across the darkened skies before our eyes. Nature's frequency is our frequency and this demonstrates unequivocally that there is no real separation between us and our natural surroundings.

Nothing in nature takes more than it needs. And when it does, it becomes subject to the 'laws of nature' and the strangest thing happens ... it dies off. Animals do not drink all the water in a stream or take all the nutrients in a forest, but only what it requires to survive. Therefore the forest can thrive as well as the animals. Even a predatory animal does not kill other animals unless it is for survival and will not kill more than it can eat at one time. When the body takes more than it can handle it will respond with illness or disease (dis-ease). We, therefore, are as much a part of the society of nature. Nature always improves. Nature will not support plants that do not grow. The more we (humanity) stray from our origin, the further we get from the bond with nature and we cannot grow.

And, much like nature, humanity will not survive if we

distance ourselves too far from this bond.   It is a shame that we cannot apply these same 'natural principals' to our personal material life and fortunes to see that by taking on more than you can enjoy at one time (in one moment) is truly a waste...

The Earth is a living library of information and is accessible from many interstellar avenues in our astral plane. The original 'blueprint' and design of the Earth, and more specifically, 'man himself' has been altered by the elite, reptilian agenda which has imposed serious harm to the Earth's natural growth. These entities knowingly understand what they are doing to us and have placed a quarantine. Our natural kingdoms want to grow, live free and evolve unmolested, but cannot until the quarantine has been lifted. The quarantine is on our ability to access the higher realms and to be able to understand all of this. This quarantine has spread negative energy across the world and these entities, the ones we call fallen angels, thrive on this negative energy.   These natural kingdoms want to evolve, connect and work with humanity and as conscious humans accept their responsibility Earth's nature will begin to co-create resolutions of better and more harmonious ways of living. We have much to learn from nature and all her creatures. Our purpose, and why we are here on Earth now at this dynamic time alongside other humans, is to participate with evolution and to turn the planet back to Nature Laws. We should love nature and the more we love, the less the Earth will be enveloped in negative energy.

There are a lot of lost and confused people here on Earth at this time. If you don't know what is 'going on' the more anger and confusion will arise within you. Today we have some awareness of the events that have impacted our lives and this is a good place to grow from.   This will assist in helping lay the correct path and spiritual embodiment potential that we all possess. We must get past this 'mind control' of the negative energy to experience our true spiritual consciousness. We need to communicate more compassionately with others around us. We are here to assist in the un-bondage of suffering from unconsciousness. As one becomes 'awakened' to nature, they are re-made in the external image of light, of God and of truth to live and flourish by these Natural Laws.

The Fibonacci number sequence is found in just about everything we see, touch and hear. Sometimes called the "Phi Ratio" or the "Golden Rule" is the fundamental way in which everything grows in nature. There is truly nothing more important than this number sequence which is not taught in our public schools and for good reason. If it was taught, then people would have a much clearer understanding that the universe, the Earth, all of nature, all animals and all humans, are a part of an intelligent design with a direct correlation to God as our prime creator. This dangerous information would disrupt the establishment's control of your false understanding of evolution. All of nature follows and grows according to this supreme set of rules and numbers. A single flower seed will grow by dividing itself by the Fibonacci number sequence and ratio. A pinecone, a sea shell and even your human body are the best and most apparent examples of the Fibonacci sequence in nature and demonstrates how everything grows from one.

Leonardo de Pisa is the creator of the <u>Fibonacci Number Sequence</u> (Phi Ratio or Golden Ratio) which occurs in nature...naturally. The mechanics of the Fibonacci sequence is the next number in the sequence and is always the sum of the previous two numbers. The most interesting factor is that <u>all</u> the numbers in this sequence have the same ratio to the preceding number (the one before it). For example: starting at 1 add 1 to make 2. Then add 1 plus 2 to make 3. Add 2 plus 3 to get the next number in the sequence 5. Then add 3 to 5 to make 8 and so on and so on. The result sequence (1, 1, 2, 3, 5, 8, 13, 21….) yields a ratio that always equals .618 (or 1.618 inversely) when dividing any number in the sequence by the next number in the sequence. As you go higher up the Fibonacci sequence, the resulting numbers get closer and closer to this exact ratio number of 1.618 (3/ 5 = .600; 89/144 = .6181). By definition, the first two numbers in the Fibonacci sequence are 0 and 1 (alternatively, 1 and 1), and each subsequent number is the sum of the previous two.

Leonardo de Pisa also posed, and solved, a problem involving the growth of a population of rabbits based on idealized assumptions. The solution, generation by generation, was a sequence of numbers, later known as **Fibonacci numbers**. The number sequence was known to Indian mathematicians as early as the 6th century, but it was Fibonacci's *Liber Abaci* that introduced it to the west. In the Fibonacci sequence of numbers, each number is the sum of the previous two numbers, starting with 0 and 1. This sequence begins 0, 1, 1, 2, 3, 5, 8, 13, 21, 34, 55, 89, 144, 233, 377, 610, 987 ... The higher up in the sequence, the closer two consecutive "Fibonacci numbers" of the sequence divided by each other will approach the golden ratio (approximately 1 : 1.618 or 0.618 : 1).

Phi is the basis of all resonant vibration e.g. music. The music scale is based on mathematics and ratios (1, 3, 5, 8, and 13 as the primary notes for major cords). Music that adheres to this ratio of vibration frequency is appealing to our ears. Noises and sounds outside of this frequency are foreign and sound dissonant. Art follows the Phi ratio of 1.618 as the perfect 'parts to the whole' and is used to create beautiful proportions of human body form such as demonstrated by Leonardo DaVinci's Vitruvian Man. There is a certain unexplainable beauty in symmetry and proper proportions that achieves perfect harmony when creating using the Phi ratio. Whether the medium be a drawing, painting, photograph or sculpture, an artist's composition representing the Phi ratio best will be most appealing to the observer. This ratio is (also) naturally occurring in <u>all</u> animals, insects (bees, butterflies) and <u>all</u> living plant material including coral and rocks.

Note: The length of your entire arm from shoulder to finger tip compared to the length from your elbow to your finger tip is approximately 1:618.

Our inner and outer physical body has countless examples of Phi. Most profoundly, this ratio is within the building block of our life, DNA (Deoxyribonucleic Acid), occurring naturally in its spiral formation of the "Twisted Double Helix." This natural 'spiral' formation is, 'literally' and 'figuratively,' the smallest and the largest concepts that we can imagine. The smallest thing we can comprehend is the atom, which can only be seen using an electron microscope. Everything is made up of atomic particles and follows the same 1.618 ratio principals.

The largest thing we can comprehend is the universe, which for the most part is unknown. But from what we can deduce from our high-powered planetarium telescopes is that the visible universe and all the solar systems that it encompasses are a "self-spiraling," expanding, living entity. Ever expanding, never ending only to be limited by one's conscience thought. Observe the similarities of our solar system with that of a storm cloud. Phi patterns exist within all weather systems such as hurricanes, tornados and even natural storm clouds. The more compelling question is: If the largest and the smallest things that our conscience can identify follow this principal of Phi ratio and all that encompasses in between (man, plants, animals, weather, music, art and the Earth) then what does that mean? We must conclude that there is an undisputed, underlying and universal relationship between all thought and all matter (as above so below) and this Fibonacci sequence of numbers plays a vital, if not crucial, role in 'what' we are…and therein lies part of the answer to the question of, "Who are we?"

The Phi ratio also plays a huge part in our conscience and sub-conscience and can predict trends in our actions, emotions and behavior. Music and art, as demonstrated previously, are examples of Phi in man's creation. All architecture and literature are extensions of expressions that have been directly or indirectly influenced by Phi ratio. It is innate within us. It is us to be more exact. And if it is us, then all that which we create is governed by this supreme law and follows the Phi ratio of life.

Plants respond to people who have them. Attention and love makes them grow better. Emotion is energy in motion. When you move energy you create effect. If you move enough energy you can, in effect, move matter. Matter is energy consolidated – alchemy of the universe. Thought is pure energy. It never dissipates. Thought is creative energy and your thought never dies. It leaves your body and goes out into the universe extending forever and ever. All thoughts play into a complex 'web' of energy. Like (kind) energy attracts other like (kind) energy. If enough similar ideas and thoughts are 'put out there' then they clump together to create a bigger energy idea that can manifest into matter. For example, if the masses believe that "Paris, France" exists, then in fact it exists. Once energy becomes matter it stays matter for a very long time. Adam and Eve may have been a little naïve, but they really did not make any bad choices. In fact, nothing would really exist without them making a choice and trying to experience something new or different. If you ignore something on a conscious level it will go away. Thought is creative and fear attracts like energy. Love is really all there is. Love is the ultimate reality. Love is the experience of knowing God in the highest truth. Love is all there is was… and will be….

"The best time to plant a tree was twenty years ago. The next best time to plant a tree is right now."

                                                              -Chinese Proverb

Humans did not evolve from apes. Humans did not evolve from monkeys either. Man was made just as he is today, but perhaps with a few more wires connected. To think that we evolved over a long time period emerging and crawling out from the 'primordial soup' has to be one of the hardest stories for us to really digest as humans. To think that something as complex or sophisticated in design as the human body (or really any animal) could come about over time from literally the sludge on the Earth's surface is insulting to our intelligence. Nothing so advanced as the human species could be created by anything else except an intellectual mind that would have knowledge of all the universe and creation. Man has a soul and that in itself speaks volumes to the fact that we are created by a prime creator with intent, intellect and insight.

Since man is classified as an animal (part of the species genome), it is important to differentiate a clear distinction between the two. The primary difference between man and animal is our higher conscience and our ability to think abstractly (into the past or into the future) and manifest this into creative energy here on Earth. Animals can build structures for a home or survival such as a beaver, but man is the only species that will build structures for the benefit of obtaining material items, such as wealth. Wealth and money among many other tangible items is what man seeks, but animals have no desire to accumulate extraneous items of a materialistic nature. One commonality between man and animal is emotions and feeling such as love or hate. Both man and animal are also territorial and have "pack-like" tendencies and will kill each other if we invade each other's space, try to take each other's food or harm one another. Man is so much more complex when it comes to how we interact with each other and our relationship with mankind. Animals are essential to man's survival. Without animals and insects we would not be able to sustain ourselves here on Earth. I don't mean in a consumption capacity either (eating them), but the keep the balance of nature. For example: Without bees most plants and fruits could not pollinate and therefore, would not able to grow. Our bee population has plummeted over the past decade and studies show that this may be due to very high concentrations of aluminum found in them. Animals are in tune with the Earth's vibrational energy and they can sense danger and weather patterns before they happen-solely by vibration. This is innate and humans have this ability too, we just cannot connect to this vibration.

A better question to ask is: "Why is the traditional Darwinian evolution theory taught so extensively in our public school systems and supported by the mass media and governments?" No other explanation of our existence is even entertained (in the mainstream) and if you come at this with either a religious/creationist slant, you're looked at as crazy. What is crazy is that nothing adds up in the evolution theory. Where is the missing link? They can't find it because it does not exist. All bones found are either primates or man. The two have existed side by side for centuries and if we did evolve from apes/monkeys then apes and monkeys would have also evolved into man at some point... and they have not. The best, and possibly only, reason that critics can explain this is that our entire history and timeline of man has been covered up. If the truth were announced, then you would immediately know that you are much more than you have been told. What I mean by that is, you are "The Works." You have been created perfectly just as you are and you possess full knowledge of the universe, but you have been disconnected. Disconnected from the truth that man has been here on Earth for a lot longer than you have been told, but also disconnected in the physical sense whereby your DNA and the encoded memory of all existence is not accessible here in your 3-D body. If your DNA was fully connected and you could utilize your full brain capacity, you would know who you are, where you came from and why you are here. The proof, or more specifically, the science, is showing us that all ancient artifacts that are dug up such as bones are not nearly as old (relatively speaking) as they tell us, and that man also lived along side dinosaurs/dragons and advanced civilizations existed here on Earth prior to modern times.

till soils... not bullets

plant trees... not bombs

build gardens... not wars

sow seeds... not uniforms

harvest crops... not people

grow flowers... not arsenals

multiply foods... not famine

blossom buds... not hostility

widen landscapes... not roads

cultivate lands... not nations

spread fragrance... not fear

raise flora... not aggression

produce fruits... not deaths

amplify colors... not noise

sprout life... not conflicts

flourish love... not hate

obey nature... not laws

KNOWLEDGE

BOOK 27

Knowledge is power. Knowledge is strength. Knowledge is freedom. Knowledge is more valuable than just about anything because with knowledge you have the information required to know where you 'stand' in the world. Knowing where you 'stand' is essential to creating a happy and healthy foundation to your life. Knowledge is awareness, consciousness, realization, and familiarity gained through facts and information acquired through experience. Knowledge is gathered through past or present experiences that ultimately help one make decisions based on that information.

Unfortunately, many 'sinister' forces understand the power of knowledge too and have used this against us by hiding specific knowledge in order to control and enslave us. Nothing can replace knowledge...not even money. Today, most true and vital knowledge is privately held and is shrouded in secrecy. Important, 'secret' knowledge is passed down by the elite from generation to generation. Information about the origins of the Earth, our true beginnings and all past history of antiquity has been hidden from us. This method alone has been extremely effective in controlling the masses. If all knowledge of everything was given to 'the people' then there would literally be no controlling us. That is why it is so essential for elite families and secret societies to protect this knowledge. Most sophisticated class systems have been structured with "haves" and "'have nots" by design. The delineation between these two groups is essential for the elite to continue the separation of hidden knowledge. The secret knowledge acts as a barrier between the true accounts of past history and influences our real knowledge of what is happening in today's world. This not only pertains to our past history, which has been sanitized to prevent us from being enlightened, but also our current affairs through a methodical 'dumbing down' process of knowledge, suppression and misinformation. There is so much misinformation and disinformation that it is nearly impossible to know which is up from down nowadays. This is all being done deliberately, systematically and with great precision.

The scientific knowledge that we've been 'operating' with for many centuries, and more specifically the past hundred years, is not found to be 'valid' which means we've been living with misperceptions and misbeliefs. If you don't understand and have a misperception of the world it can severely affect your wellbeing. For example: A person that believes they are ugly may in fact be attractive in reality, but to them their perception is that they are ugly. There is nothing wrong with their biology, but rather their perceptions are mistaken and have overwhelmed their interpretation of the situation. This false perception may 'hold them back' in some capacity (confidence-wise) during their life and may change how they choose to interact with other people. Applying the same thought process to our existence, there are three misperceptions that are causing our own demise: 1) is the belief that the material realm is all there is and all that matters is 'stuff,' 2) is the belief that 'genes' control our lives which makes us the 'victim' because we can't pick or change our genetics therefore we are powerless, and 3) is the extension of Darwinian belief that says that the world is based on a "struggle for survival" and only the fittest will endure. The idea of the "rat race"' is pervasive and our fundamental beliefs are that if we don't go out there and fight for our 'fair share' or to 'stay alive' you'll be trampled or worse, annihilated. So we see a world based on this "Darwinian philosophy" is a nightmare world of struggle for survival that involves war, competition and having to fight and climb on the backs of others to stay alive.

So what's wrong with these perceptions? The belief that matter is 'all that matters' (which is a Newtonian belief) is a false assumption because what we have learned from quantum physics is that not only is the physical matter important it's the non-visible matter you can't see that is also important. Because it's the non-visible energy fields that 'shape' the matter we see. So if you look solely at the "material structure" of things you've missed the greater point. Direct your focus on the 'non-visible' for the biggest part that contributes to the structure which is our creative mind. Our minds are holographically, shaping the world so whatever we believe influences energy fields that shape our biology and our life's reality.

The other misbelief is that "genes" can define who we are and 'set' our destiny. For example: If a certain type of cancer is prevalent throughout my family that, "*I will play the victim*" and assume that because of my genes, there is nothing I can do to change my fate. Many become despondent of life because "*if I can't control my life, why should I care?*" But this is not correct because nature leads us to the scientific conclusion that genes don't control your life. Your heart, your mind and your emotions do. It is an epigenetic control mechanism by which the environment, or the perception of the environment, controls our genetics and ultimately controls heredity and all our senses. That means, if you change your mind to your perception then you change your biology. So you are the master of your life rather than a victim.

The last myth says gather all the stuff you can take from the Earth and gather it all in your yard or garage because that's the measure of your success. This is not correct. The competition you use to gather all this matter is actually found to be destructive because evolution is based on cooperation not competition; when we look to the higher realms, cooperation in the sense that there needs to be a balanced approach to the acquisition and accumulation of material items. When we take on more than we can physically use, then we can become burdened or even worse, unhappy. Plants and the animals are not in competition with each other. Rather there is a sophisticated level of cooperation between the ecosystems. The plants don't look at this world as a huge garden for themselves nor do animals think that it is their entire, personal playground. These are misperceptions and it is these misperceptions that can seriously affect you if you're not careful. Recognize fundamental misperceptions on which we base our civilization as the destructive elements leading to our extinction. It's all a balanced, harmonious community and we should take note.

Essential is our foreknowledge of our origins. All human species strive to suppress the negativity here on Earth. The Earth is full of many beings from different levels of dimensional knowledge. Established governments and organizations ridicule any esoteric topics that further develop your consciousness awareness. The people in power have been lying to us for thousands of years about knowledge of extraterrestrial and cosmic gods. Investigate the facts yourself if you care to know the truth. But this journey is one you must take for yourself. The truth exists, but no proponents can force it upon another. There has to be some inner need, some inner desire and some inner thirst to learn the truth. Many people have a suspicion that something is not right in the world and the curiosity for investigating is strong enough for the person to consciously 'stop' and concentrate on the research to reflect and think with an open mind. But there is a 'shroud over us' that has been created of negative energy – which encompasses your consciousness through wars, taxes, and fear to make it difficult to find truth and knowledge. Investigation and seeking knowledge is a part of growing. Growing is part of the human experience that we all share.

In the past century we have experienced some hard times as a civilization. Even with a positive attitude there is so much uncertainty that it makes it difficult to thrive. Many who have taken the time to investigate these 'things' of life – will end up reaching an overwhelming conclusion of manipulation by an autonomous entity. Many feel 'powerless' in relationship to the "New World Order" network that we virtually have nowhere to turn. The NWO system is engulfing our modern civilization. Let's be honest about this, the system we live under is corrupt. It is rotten to the core. It is simply not fair and is basically run by "Luciferian" bloodlines passed down for centuries. These people have committed crimes against humanity and everybody is awakening to this fact. These people get away with it because we let them get away with it. They control everything especially — human conscience. We let this continue since we don't know how to 'fix it' and it is the system that we have lived under for most of our lives. The reality is that we the people are not powerless. In fact, quite the opposite is true. There is really a relatively simple way to stop the NWO from continuing to oppress us. Just say STOP! Stop going along with it! The only way to make a real change in the world is through <u>NON</u>-compliance to the "system." Stop going along with the current agenda. Does this mean to quit your job and burn all your money and live under a bridge? NO! The answer to any question like this is, "No, of course not." Non-compliance is about doing the right thing. Doing what is actually just in the face of adversity and peer pressure of the masses. It is about disconnecting yourself from the system and directing yourself to be responsible for your own thoughts, your own actions and your own intentions. It is all within your own potential. Do what is right in all that you do.

'If you want to stop prejudism…you must first stop it in yourself.'

Realize your connection to others. Think humanitarianly – rather than economically. Do not base your existence on useless ideas, material trinkets or social status that absolutely serves no purpose or usefulness. To do the right thing there is nothing to decide or learn. You already know and understand this in your heart. Our intuition knows what is right or just. You're not taught this, it is innate in all humans. We must be honest with ourselves. We must look inside and consciously know what each action we are doing. If you're doing something that needs to be justified to yourself, then it is more than likely the wrong thing to be doing. In hesitation (or the process of hesitation) you are justifying a wrong action. Basically, you're "talking yourself into" an action that you may not be comfortable doing. These unjustified decisions usually happen in an instant and it is these compromised decisions that we continue to do hundreds of times daily. We don't notice that we are convincing ourselves to go against our intuition. It is automatic. Know the knowledge is in our heart and you have the innate ability to make the correct choice through your intuition without debate or compromise.

To understand how the energy works, first ask, "Where is the energy being drawn from?" We must look past imaginary restraints that have been put in front of us. The academic systems coupled with the societal limitations you have been taught stifle your full energy potential. Religion and science teachings have also limited our full understanding of who we are and what we know. All of these institutions are taught to compartmentalize knowledge. All factual knowledge is so different from one institution to another there is little positive collective consciousness. It is up to you to harness this energy to enable yourself to connect your understanding of all things that are constructed, contained and manipulated into one paradigm. Look beyond the imposed limitations. Open your mind to the multitude of possibilities. Look at the whole. Science and religion also teach us limitations by telling us "this is the way it is." But that is for you to decide after you have gathered the knowledge to make your own rational decisions.

'Don't jump to the most negative outcome...'

We should open our eyes to the connection between religion and science, if for no other reason, for the sole purpose of expanding our scope and understanding of the true knowledge. We should not be locked down into restrictive patterns of this paradigm. Religion and science can never fully make the connection to this reality solely by themselves. Therefore one can never think that we can be brought to salvation or reach utopia without better understanding the true nature of the world, and even more importantly, understanding life. Often due to the limitations in our 'belief system' it is hard to discuss these concepts with people that so steadfastly embrace science or religion. You may be able to sit down with them and talk rationally about God, salvation, goodness or even evolution, but as soon as you start talking about sacred geometry, occult teachings, numerology (or anything esoteric) most people either 'close up' or will argue with you since it is not a part of their core knowledge of teachings. They'll say "it's *God's will*" and that is the way it is. These people have essentially 'depowered' themselves by closing down any open discussion of what else is out there. So they sit back and wait for 'Armageddon' since they believe that is God's will.

Some say that pursuing knowledge and teachings of a higher understanding of ourselves is demonic in nature. This is not true. Seeking knowledge is always right and just. Scientists try to explain the mechanics of life, but in doing so they refuse to add spirituality into the equation. Quantum physics is the only science that scientists attempt to introduce when discussing or quantifying the universe into the equation of life.

Science generally only adheres to laws on a mathematical or mechanical level. Actually both approaches (science and spirituality) are inherently flawed – neither will consider the argument of the other (divide and conquer). Neither fully takes into account or embraces the variable of feelings or emotions, yet feelings and emotions are the language that is used to create and mold all reality. Feelings and emotions are the true nature of 'prayer' and it is the only language that we can ultimately communicate with the "Prime Creator" in all of us. What is the true nature of this divinity of what we call God? The creator is the intelligence that underlies all realities. The creator exists as one – a single consciousness that is in all of us. As self-awareness grows, we awaken to the relationship of who we are and how we fit into all of this. Institutionalized religion extenuates these powers of the consciousness of expansion - and suggests that God is something external from Man. That God is a benefactor that is looking down on you and judging you right now. This (is not the case and) is really an unhealthy way to view reality and live your life here on Earth.

Many "New Age" religion believers take on a different perspective and internalize this into that man can become a God. These understandings are erroneous. Man cannot become God; man is already created in the image of God. Everybody who is a part of this beautiful creation here on this Earth – in this reality – is an eternal living soul and an expression of the collective consciousness of God. When you hear that 'Man' can attain 'God-like' abilities in this lifetime, you are not remembering the most important thing in that all the "ability" is already within you.

We are taught that reality follows certain rules and we are taught to fear this reality – fear the world around us – people instill fears within us and keep us in fear from childhood. We are educated in fear. But it is indoctrination into a fictional system. Where did we get off track with our human consequences? We are the source of every evil we have seen on this planet. Man has been shifted so far from its core values that we have 'almost' completely lost our humanity. We have been trained to be totally dependent on the system that has been placed before us. We have been robbed of our true will, our self-esteem, our independence and our true calling. We have been trained to believe whatever the TV tells us…is the way it is; that life's purpose…we should only be concerned with social status, meaningless trinkets and material consumption. But this is not so. You have been 'sold' a lie, a meaningless existence. Through TV, mass media and the ingestion of brain inhibiting toxins such as fluoride, Zoloft and Paxil, we have been robbed of our power and the ability to think critically and objectively. Ultimately, we have been deprived of our wonderful innate life skills. This has created a precarious situation for humanity because right now is when it is most crucial for us to possess these life skills of knowledge and creativity because it is at this time the world is experiencing the most turmoil. Mankind is vulnerable right now. Throughout all recorded history, this may be the only time that each person has some form of dependence on this corrupt, corporate apparatus for survival.

This 'apparatus' places profit and wealth above people. It has little to do with the true nature of man or his relationship to Earth and others. Yet, we are dependent on it for food, housing, for our information and even for our entertainment. It tells us what to do, how to dress, how to act, where to go, what to eat, what we should look like, what to think and what we should think about the world and everyone around us. If you can get people to accept a certain state of affairs and servitude, you can get them to do almost anything. Techniques exist within our society which will enable the controlling hierarchy to get people to actually like their servitude. People can be made to think that they are actually free when in fact they are not. They enjoy the current 'status quo' and by any decent measure, a person with a good mind should not accept this subtle form of slavery (but they do). Puzzling isn't it? The question is: What if this 'corporate apparatus' were to fail, or shut down? What would happen then?

Over the past few thousand years we have 'warped' our own history; the story has changed so dramatically from the original that we really don't know much about our true origins. The procession of life on Earth has been misunderstood. Modern interpretations of our history have forgotten and ignored many vital pieces of information that are a part of a larger puzzle. Do our 'genetics' tell us anything about how we are perhaps 'millions' of years old. The Sumerians were an extremely advanced civilization. They are the very first culture on Earth (that we know of) and lived near modern day Iraq at the Tigris and Euphrates River. The Sumerians had writings, textbooks, clocks, calendars (zodiac), schools and laws before anyone. Mythology began with Sumerians. It all started here. They are the most influential and inventive culture and, in ways, more advanced than Babylon or any other Mesopotamian civilizations to follow. It is thought that the Annunaki (super gods or elders) came to Earth and genetically altered us (disconnected our DNA) so that we could mine for monatomic gold, but not remember who we were. What has changed so dramatically in our history that the writings of the Sumerians from 4000 years ago have been forgotten or overlooked? They explained how the "Gods" came to Earth and the disconnection of man. It seems that our history or more specifically our present-day knowledge of our history does not accurately account for some crucial, historical facts.

Important knowledge like the fact that we have never been alone in our universe should make people want to know more. The controlling elite don't want us to know the truth, fearing that they will lose their power over us. Important knowledge like of the Annunaki (The Reptilian Gods) and man's disconnection has been purposely omitted from history books and teachings. If there is another 'parallel' history of how extraterrestrials came here thousands of years ago and from these visits we got much of our mythology, religion and esoteric teachings — it is our right as citizens of the Earth to know.

Every history book will have to be 'rewritten' when the truth does finally come to us. The truth is those 'people' that came before us, were just like us - and came from great civilizations...

What happens when we finally come to the point where all of these 'entities' have unfolded the potential which is in them? According to theology and legends, we give 'birth' to another generation of creators. Another race of divine beings that become the parents of worlds, the parents of systems and the parents of creation that takes their place in the great hierarchy of eternal growth that goes on forever. Beyond the horizon, beyond the stars, beyond the galaxies and beyond the infinite there is a new beginning. We may not be able to comprehend the full extent of what lies beyond, but it is of a higher conscience and exists on the highest spiritual plateau. We do not know the 'infinite' good until we have achieved the finite good here on Earth, but it's coming, it has to come, and in "the fullness of time," we will see that we are 'one being' flowing through space and eternity, to the fulfillment of the benevolent purpose for which we were intended.

"The universe and stupidity are both infinite and endless."

– Albert Einstein

What if everything that you thought you knew about the past 100 years was actually a lie? What if an elite international banking cartel infiltrated the American Government in 1913 (or before)? What if, in 1917, this elite banking cartel funded both sides of the First World War? What if, in 1929, this elite banking cartel internationally caused the Great Depression? What if the goal all along was to build up America to a supreme economic, super power and then ship off all its industry overseas; then force so much debt on the people through consumerism, taxes and money printing to extract all the wealth and ultimately bankrupt it? What if all unconstitutional taxes on wages including the "Social Security Tax" were levied as collateral to pay the debt to the bankers? What if, in 1933, your birth certificate became legal evidence of your share of this debt? What if this banking cartel pulled the same scam in nearly every country on this planet? What if this banking cartel funded all sides of the Second World War including Hitler? What if the goal of the Second World War was to set up the State of Israel so as to have a military base in the Middle East? What if the goal of World War II was also to create the United Nations? What if the United Nations was designed as a framework for a future world government? What if all the events of 9/11 were used by the bankers to justify invading any country not under their control or not using the "petrodollar"? What if 9/11 was used as a pretext to destroy the American Constitution and set up a police state that monitors all their citizens? What if this global, police state were to be used as a way to enforce the future world government takeover of all aspects of your life? What if environmental issues such as "global warming" or "climate change" were used across the globe to implement a tax on every nation? What if world terrorists emerge from nowhere to inflict terrorism upon sovereign nations so that your personal freedom has been compromised? What if none of this was true? Then I guess you would not have to worry.

The public has been conditioned to condemn conspiracies. The very word conjures emotional overload but look at your history books. Anytime anything 'happened' throughout history, it 'conspired' to happen. It is hard to come up with an event in history that wasn't conspired. Conspiracies are very real in present day and have always been throughout our history. There are three basic elements of a conspiracy: 1) Two or more people involved. 2) Using deceit, secrecy or force. 3) To accomplish an illegal, immoral or evil objective. The first two points are a given. The third point is debatable in that the conspirators may not believe what they are doing is illegal. It may be immoral and evil, but may not be illegal. The elite have the control and ability to write laws and in any court they would never be found guilty. Is the goal of this elite group immoral? Well, in their eyes, their actions are moral and just. They firmly believe that their actions are justified (of the highest morality) and certainly placed far higher than yours or mine.

There is much controversy and debate associated with the phrase "Conspiracy Theory" today and we have been 'led' to think this way. By definition, a theory is an idea, a supposition, a hypothesis. In 'theory,' if you buy a raffle ticket you could win the lottery. As long as you don't buy the ticket it is just a theory. But when you purchase the ticket it becomes not a theory but a probability. The more tickets you purchase the stronger the probability it will be to win. A 'conspiracy theory' is just that – a theory, as long as there is no evidence, to support it. But once you have a piece of evidence even the smallest, slightest piece of evidence then that theory is no longer a theory but a probability. The more evidence one has, the more probable that the theory is truth. Possible turns to probable. In your search for the truth if you uncover any group or person that has purposely suppressed or hidden facts of the event in question, then you may not need to look any further than that same group or person is behind the event itself. A corrupt government will go to great lengths to cover up what they are really doing. Even lie to its people.

In America, false flag operations have been conspired to affect the human conscious...most notably Pearl Harbor and 9/11. The goal of the conspirators was to frighten the people enough to make them willing to go to war, but not for freedom as they were told, but instead, to further the objectives and goals of the New World Order. It was all based on a lie. When you tell one lie you will eventually have to tell five more lies to continue the first lie. After a while, telling the story becomes more difficult to keep the lie going. If you always tell the truth then you don't have to remember what you said because you will always be telling the truth—no matter what.

The first job of a conspiracy is to convince the world that conspiracies do not exist. Many assist and help this agenda without even knowing they are doing so. Media will avoid any hint that events in the news were orchestrated through a conspiracy. They always try to prove otherwise (by happenstance). One may openly talk about the MAFIA or The Watergate Conspiracy, but any suggestion that a conspiratorial group has a grip on our political, financial or governmental system including the media is met with immediate retaliation, ridicule or even character assassination. Conspirators and the defectors will go to great lengths that the existence of their plot remains hidden. The best way to combat a conspiracy is to expose it by shedding light on it.

I am not anti-government, anti-CIA or anti-Pentagon, but I am anti-lies. For the record, I want to be on the right side of truth and only stand against people and organizations that perpetuate lies and dishonesty. Many employees of these organizations don't know that they are working for dishonest and corrupt entities that are under the umbrella of what appears to be just. I am not here to criticize the entire government. There are many fine people working for the government, intelligence, military, police and fire departments. But like many of us—we have been brainwashed to believe that the agendas in place are for the betterment of humanity. Many events are orchestrated to instigate changes in society that will have us give up our freedoms. The 'shadow government' is purposely frightening the population to give up our rights for a

New World Order. Fabricated events are devised to enrage the American people and, in turn, have Congress pass legislation that would 'override' our civil liberties and further erode our civil rights—ultimately destroying our Constitution. The guidelines for the antiterrorist legislation pre 9/11 were more than adequate to interrogate any domestic or international terrorists.

So what really happened on 9/11? The immediate take—away from this sensitive subject and the fallout events stemming from 9/11 is not to blame our entire military or all government representatives. We could also point fingers and highlight the fact that many systems curiously broke down on that day that could have avoided the tragedy (e.g., NORAD, FAA and Pentagon), but certain elite global powers wanted the event to happen just the way it did. It had been planned for years and the ultimate goal was manifold, but to be able to invade other sovereign countries with coveted resources and do all this erratic manipulation in the name of fighting terror was one of the main ones. When it is said that 9/11 was planned for years, it can be traced back to as early as 1945. It was in 1945 that the first concept of the World Trade Centers was conceived. The elite wanted to build the tallest buildings in the world right in the powerhouse of America, New York City, to symbolize America's greatness worldwide. Right after the war, America was rising to new powers of economic, political and military. The twin towers, which symbolize the two Masonic pillars of Boaz and Jachin and a gateway to sacred places and mysterious realms, started construction in 1966 and opened in 1973. Following the numerology cycle of 'seven' years, it was brought down on September 11, 2001 which symbolized the 'beginning' of the slowdown of America's rule as a world leader.

There is a 'ton' of clear-cut evidence that 9/11 was an 'inside' job. Only a very small group of people in our government had prior knowledge of the event. The majority are innocent bystanders. In so discussing, one could highlight a 'landslide' of documented facts, stories and information too numerous to mention here to show you how the event was 'pulled off.' Little known facts like some of the "alleged Saudi Arabian hijackers" were going to 'strip joints' snorting cocaine and drinking booze on Jack Abramowitz's Sunny Cruise Ship the nights before 9/11 or the fact that "Five Dancing Israelis" where spotted on the morning of 9/11 celebrating the building's collapse, or even the strange but true fact that Marvin Bush (George W. Bush's brother) was overseeing the security company Securicom, who provided security at the World Trade Center, Dulles Airport and United Airlines, but there is one item that stands above the rest and what many consider to be the "smoking gun," and that is Building 7. Building 7, also known as the Salomon building, housed offices for Salomon Smith Barney, U.S. Securities and Exchange Commission, U.S. Secret Service, Internal Revenue Service and the 'ultra-fortified emergency bunker' for Rudy Giuliani that was never used on that day. It is interesting to note that Building 7 also housed investigative, financial records by the SEC of notable fraudulent corporations and banks that were being investigated which could have 'constituted manifold Enron's' that all were destroyed on that day. Building 7, located about a block-and-a-half from the World Trade Center, fell at 'free fall' speed within its own footprint at about 5:20 pm on 9/11.

Up until September 11, 2001, there had never been a steel building collapse due to fire in all of the world's history, yet on 9/11 three buildings collapsed "due to fire" as officially reported. The 'catch' is that on that day only two buildings were hit by airplanes. The foundation of Building 7 was not compromised either or it would have fallen sideways or unevenly, but it did not. The news stations reported Building 7 had fallen even before it actually collapsed (at 4:57 pm) and the pictures and video clearly show this to be true—that it was brought down by a systematic demolition with use of nano-thermite. Silverstein said in a post 9/11 interview that they decided to "pull" and they watched it collapse.

The event was orchestrated by an elite, Zionist Globalist using Israeli Intelligence (Mossad) along with United States Intelligence, Saudi Arabia Intelligence and Pakistan. Vice President Cheney was a pivotal part of the operation that day "calling off" the fighter jets that would have intercepted the planes when they went off course. 9/11 was the ultimate deception to implement a multi-layered agenda (grand deception) which ultimately results in a takeover and control of the world and all its resources by the elite.

Some helpful guidance and advice: If you're having a discussion with someone that worked at the Pentagon on September 11th, 2001 and may have lost a coworker on that day, this is probably not the right person to try to convince that a missile hit the building and not a 747. Nothing you can tell them will change their perception of that day and no debate will make either of you feel any better in the end. The topic is too sensitive, so I suggest you pick a 'peripherally related' topic that might interest them and let them connect the dots on their own. Once they take on the 'house of knowledge' and accept whatever information they investigate as fact, then they have stepped onto the path of enlightenment. All you are here for is to lay the 'seed' and let them grow the tree of knowledge themselves…if they so desire. And most importantly, let them do this at their own pace.

People have been told a lie so long that when they finally hear the truth it sounds like a lie, and they ignore it. The public has been "dumbed down," anesthetized, and void of integrity. Everything is artificial and disconnected from our true spirit and nature. It is 'learned helplessness' which seems to be the type of teachings and lessons that are being passed down to our children. Philosophy is about finding truth. Manipulative people believe only in selected truth. The current thinking in America is about overprotection of everything and everyone instead of just thinking about self-reliance. What is right or wrong? Who defines this? You actually have the right to do anything as long as you don't take anything away from someone else's individual rights. If we all did that we would not need 50,000 rules and extraneous laws and statutes on the books. We seem to not want to teach right from wrong (or fact from fiction) or the simple underlying laws of nature.

The laws of Nature supersede everything, yet many like to complicate this and confuse us into thinking we need all of these other laws. The powers that be dehumanize people in order to control them and are implementing the 'rise of the surveillance state' with these extraneous laws. The way we have been educated and raised in America is part of a very sophisticated control system. Most people think that money is somehow a measure of wealth. Money is not a measure of real wealth and hides true power. True wealth and power is knowledge and wisdom. As long as we don't see wisdom as wealth we will be misguided. By passing this wisdom onto future generations as a form of 'wealth,' it will be vital to our future survival—especially survival for our children's sake.

Some people want to hold on fiercely to the false reality of the right/left paradigm or the Republican/Democratic duality way of thinking. This is an illusion and is similar to a 'mental terrarium' in that it is made up of an artificial environment that is not real and is confined and controlled. The more people that "awaken" and provide 'mental resistance' and 'intellectual self-defense' on a non-aggressive basis, the easier it will be to break free from our mental terrarium. Through spreading conscious awareness to other people we could be free at last. It is a growing trend to wake up now and start understanding what is going on "behind the curtain." Many people may not care if they are being controlled, watched or if their personal information is not secure. If you don't care then that is your choice, but what if your bank account information was made public or your private emails exposed? You have privacy for a good reason and like most of us, you may not have anything to hide, but at some point each person has an innate need and a civil right to his or her own privacy. The contempt and hatred for America from other countries' has increased dramatically over the past 15 years. This is due mostly through our invasive involvement with other countries political and financial affairs. America has little respect for sovereign nations worldwide. Our government and military have stuck their fingers into things that really should not be any of our business. We have been forced by the Central Bankers to invade sovereign countries and have toppled regimes that had been voted in by their citizens (e.g., Ukraine). When all this manipulation comes to light, the Middle East and Europe will retaliate by dropping use of the American dollar (Petrodollar) and this will have a tremendous, negative effect upon the American people financially.

Your vote may very well be an illusion of choice. The decision has already been made—before you even check the ballot. At the Bilderberg's Conference in Chantilly, Virginia in 2011, it was overheard that some of the elite wanted to put Senator Ron Paul who was running for President (and all his supporters) on a plane piloted by a Muslim on a suicide mission. This was a horrible statement in its own right, but the real tyranny is that Obama was already preselected to win another term and it was decided on at this meeting. No matter how the votes would be cast, the winner would be Obama. The Bilderbergers, an elite group of world economic and political leaders, get together each year in a posh location and decide the agenda of the planet for the next year or so. Every four years they pick who is going to be President of the United States. Some speculated that the 2016 Presidential election would be between two tyrannical families of the Bush's and the Clinton's. Once again, it would have been a faux choice whereby the voter essentially has no real vote and only the 'illusion' of a vote. Perhaps Donald Trump could be the true 'wild card.' As president, Trump will very likely expose the corruption of Washington and bring light upon the events of 9/11. This threatens the 'establishment' and the elite ruler's stranglehold on us.

"The truth is there is no Islamic Army or terrorists group called Al Qaeda. And any informed intelligence officer knows this, but there is a propaganda campaign to make the public believe in the presence of an identified entity representing the devil only in order to drive TV watchers to accept a unified international leadership for a war against terrorism. The country behind this propaganda is the U.S..."

-Former British Foreign Secretary Robin Cook

Most all "terrorism" is manufactured and exaggerated. Osama Bin Laden was a CIA operative who possibly died of kidney failure way back in 2001 in a hospital. He has even used the alias name of Tim Osman. They will keep lying to the citizens as long as we let them. We should have a sense of integrity and sense of morality. The methodology of the corrupt elite is if you're a hammer ...then all your problems start looking like a nail. Is all this about controlling the world oil supply and protection of the 'Petro dollar?" *'We are here to spread democracy, freedom to protect human rights with a 50 caliber machine gun.'* Manufactured terrorism operates like this: 1) Create a problem 2) create opposition to the problem; (so that people 'fear' this and that they demand that something is done to get rid of the problem) and 3) offer solution to the problem. This, in-turn, limits or restricts those individuals' rights or some other predetermined goal of the controlling party (elite). This ultimately brings about a 'sort of' change that might normally not have been possible under normal conditions. Emotional stress and mental confusion occurs – judgment is impaired and suggestibility is increased under these conditions. People will allow their rights to be diminished without them knowing the full ramifications.

"Operation Northwoods" is the name of a top-secret plan in 1962 to have our own military attack America in some capacity and kill innocent people by committing acts of terrorism in U.S. cities. It would create public support to blame it on and invade Cuba. This event never occurred, but the 'plan' sounds eerily just like 9/11. It is because of the events of 9/11 that our government claims they have to 'watch everyone' to avoid new terror threats. More than 15 years later our mainstream media would have us believe the threat is still imminent and virtually no real progress has been made. Eric Snowden (who may be controlled opposition by the elite) showed the public how they are being spied on by their own government, and really nothing has changed or come from this revelation. The fact is that many people had knowledge of the surveillance spying prior to Snowden's whistleblowing. The only difference now is the government passed the 'spying baton' on to the corporations and the corporations (AT&T, Verizon, etc.) who then, in turn, hand over the information back to the government, but the public is still being spied on. Ironically, the government will say that it must "spy" on every American citizen in order to protect us (from what?...the terrorist that they invented).

Dead men tell no tales. Nor can they defend themselves or their ideas since the killers or victors report the official, historical events of what happened. Have our history books gone through the same type of revisions in that some of our real history has been 'rewritten' to match the current dialog and stories being told to us by our controllers?

Consistency has never been the maker of stupidity. If the diplomats who have mishandled our money and our relations with Russia were merely stupid, they would occasionally make a mistake in our favor once in a while. Those who methodically seek government power and control are consistent...and very smart.

"Our Constitution was made for only a moral and religious people. It is wholly inadequate to the government of any other."
                                                                      -John Adams

When you were a baby you knew who you were even though you don't remember. Some refer to this as the "Oceanic-feeling." The baby cannot determine the separation of the world and how it acts upon the world. Instead, it is just one process. But at some point, we learn very quickly in early life what is you and what is not you — what is voluntary and involuntary — and we somehow feel we can be punished for the voluntary and so we in essence unlearn what we had already known in the beginning. Through the course of life some of us are fortunate to experience and uncover who and what we really are: that each one of us is what would be called "the Son of God." "The son of" is the same as saying "The Nature of." Son of God is a divine person and is a human being who has realized their relationship with God. Jesus of Nazareth was a human being who early in life had a colossal experience called a Cosmic Conscience. You don't have to subscribe to any type of religion to have this experience. It can happen to anyone — at any time — and is just like falling in love. It is that powerful. Many people experience this "Cosmic Conscience" and share this with others around the world. When this event happens to individuals, it is because you are usually asking for knowledge or seeking a higher state of conscience or truth. You're asking questions. When this happens to you-it is an unforgettable life-changing event. Sometimes people ask for this because they want to know and sometimes it happens to people for no known reason. It is the grace of God that controls who may get this experience or not. The dramatic event brings light to who we really are and the answer to the question of mistaken identity. Are you just 'Joe' or are you a part of something bigger and greater. Is this just an act and a show? Here, what I thought was just little old me, was only completely superficial and that I am an expression of external entity. In one moment you understand why everything is the way it is. You feel a direct connection to the pulse of life and there are no boundaries anymore. It is all there and you are all of it! All that goes on is created by you, and you understand the connection to this. There is no longer the separate you and just a great happening — the following of 'Tao' (Dao) or 'Brahma.' This experience makes you see the divine in everybody else. Everyone is playing the part in this colossal, life drama that is unfolding now.

Knowing something and experiencing it, are two quite different things. Spirits long to understand this experience while in the physical world. Conceptual awareness was not enough for you so we devised a plan and the most incredible idea from a creation made. Collaboration occurred and the plan was that "we" spirits would enter the 3-D universe just created (like a playground). The reason for becoming physical is that this is the only way to know conceptually. It is in fact why the cosmos was created to begin with; the system of 'relativity' which governs it and all creation.

You think you "know" yourself, but first — to truly know yourself you must also know the opposite of yourself. In clearer English, you cannot really know yourself unless you become aware of what you're not. For example, you cannot experience the meaning of "mean" unless you know what "nice" is. Ultimate logic tells us that you can't experience yourself as what you are until you have encountered what you are not. This is juxtaposition of the Theory of Relativity and all physical life. It is by that which you are not that you yourself are defined. Ultimately knowing yourself as the creator, you cannot experience yourself as creator until or unless you create, and you cannot create yourself until you "un-create" yourself. In a sense, first, you have to *not be* in order to be!

You are a pure, creative spirit. To come to Earth and have this earthly physical experience you caused yourself to forget who you really are. Upon entering the physical universe, you relinquished your remembrance of yourself. This allows you to choose who you want to be (who you really are). Remembering who you are is a return to God. So your job here on Earth (if you choose to take it) is not to learn, but to remember. You already have all the information and knowledge within you. It is encoded in your DNA. Your job after you have awakened is to assist others to remember who they are too. That is your "soul purpose!" The Trinity or the 'Triune Truth' some describe as the Father, the Son and the Holy Ghost. On a more analytical level it is the Conscience, the Sub-conscience and the Super-conscience (mind, body and spirit). Dyads are duality concepts of this Earth such as black or white, one or the other and hot or cold, but a higher conscience sees and experiences things in triads. Time is past, present and future or what 'appears' to be three distinct moments in our perception. Past, present and future is a triad and exists all in the same space and in the same time.

It is much easier to change yourself than to convince others to change. We are all one conscience though we can create individually as well as collectively. The life and times we are experiencing are for the sole purpose of evolving. You have the ability to change the way you view the physical life here on Earth by the way you behold it. If you want to feel bad because of the impending extinction of the rare Artic spotted owl, then feel bad. It is your choice and there is no right or wrong way to feel, but unfortunately society makes us feel guilty if we don't conform to or embrace a certain way of thinking. Just remember — that which you condemn will condemn you and that which you judge — will — one day, judge you. Rather we should seek to change these things by use of our own perception and not by forcing it on others.

When I was younger, I thought that Bill Gates was the richest person in the world and Warren Buffet stood for 'good old' American wealth and enterprise. I thought how lucky we are to live in the same country as them and that we are all 'free' to seek fortunes as they have; and that we have the protection of our Constitution and Bill of Rights to follow the American Dream. I also thought how fortunate there was no small group of people that controlled us or our economy and anyone could achieve whatever they wanted as long as they worked hard. Then, as I got older and wiser, I realized that all of this was the furthest thing from the truth because multi-generational banking families exist (Rothschilds, Rockefellers, Morgans and Warburgs) and have spread their tentacles far and wide across the globe. Their wealth 'trumps' the wealth of the "Nuevo riche" Americans by at least one hundred fold. These old line families have literal ownership of more than half the world's wealth and more importantly, control over governments, companies, NGOs and anything else you can think of as far as international companies. When you come to realize this is the way the world is, you lose faith in the entire system. You lose faith in just about anything you have been told. You realize those few who achieved that level of success and their wealth is fabricated and a scam and did so circumventing the system by being 'fed' off fat government contracts. Then you also come to the realization that we really don't have the protection of our constitution.

If you seek real knowledge, then a path will be set before you. But you (and only you) must make the decision to 'play' forward and go down this path. This path is less traveled and is not for the faint of heart, but is the correct one for higher knowledge and understanding. The alternative path that has been put before many of us is full of lies and manipulation; most people have forgotten to listen to their soul. It is time to change. We need to erase all negative emotions and learn to evolve and concentrate on positive emotions. Compared to most intelligent life, humans are relatively young, rambunctious and immature, like an adolescent teenager. Use this youthfulness and passion to gain knowledge about our world. Don't let others disturb your journey. They are stealing your inner energy and hiding information to keep you primitive like they are.

We must not have hatred towards those who have oppressed us. Anger arises and this is all based on fear! Instead, we must dig deep into our hearts and try to find forgiveness. Within every being, however seemingly dark, there is light. That which you give emotion to becomes your reality! Emotion is the one item that is not quantitative.

Our nature is rampant with destruction in today's world. This is not meant to scare you, but inspire you. It is of the utmost importance that mankind wake up to this reality and to the true situation that the world is facing. The future that we are creating is all of us racing around completely enslaved and dependent upon a future that most of us really don't want to live in. What is required to fix it is for people to establish themselves as human beings and get back in touch with humanity and our true spirit of home and take control of our actions and life. Grow your own food (if you can) exchange paper money for something of real value (gold, commodities). Take responsibility for yourself (no government) and our connection to others. Inform yourself of what's truly going on and this is important since it is a situation that your government is lying to you. Washington's enemy is an enemy that they create. We are supposedly fighting an enemy that hates us for the fact that we hold elections, women can work and we are a democracy with certain freedoms. America is actually being attacked because of its foreign policy and unprecedented support for Zionist leaders of the Jewish/American lobby.

Time is a social evolution. There is no 'real time' in the astral world. Time is abstract. There are rhythms and there are motions. Constant stimulation of your consciousness can make you become more 'desensitize' to that stimulation such as a beautiful meadow that you see every day. This is not a bad experience as long as we don't take for granted the beauty it possesses. Cease one's thoughts for a moment. Silence your thoughts...for one cannot find out the 'mysteries' of the universe through talk or idle chatter. You can only do this by awareness. Awareness can only happen when you're quiet. In the silence, one can listen to your intuition and discover everything there is to know about yourself and your relationship to the environment around you.

Every conscious decision is interacting with an energy field around you. You are shaping this physical reality with your inner thoughts and emotions. This information may be discomforting to many people – because there comes a great responsibility — that your inner thoughts shape your world. How will you accept this responsibility? How will you choose to live your life now? Will you act any differently? With this realization, that whatever energies you put out into this world (matrix) for others to draw upon help shapes our reality, then understand whatever you receive back from this energy will be similar to what you have put out. Express nothing — you'll receive nothing. Express hate — you'll receive hate. Express love — you'll receive love.

A little known fact overlooked in our teachings and knowledge, is that there were actually eight American 'Presidents' before George Washington. Why have we always been told that Washington was the first? Technically, there were eight presidents of the Continental Congress that predated our New Constitution. Many use the year 1776 as the beginning of our "'Independence," yet it wasn't until 1789 that George Washington assumed the first presidency. Yes, Washington was the first under the New Constitution and he was also the first to be elected to a four year term, but it was John Hanson who was chosen unanimously by Congress to be the first to oversee the country. Seven other presidents were elected after him: Elias Boudinot (1782-83), Thomas Mifflin (1783-84), Richard Henry Lee (1784-85), John Hancock (1785-86), Nathaniel Gorhan (1786-87), Arthur St. Clair (1787-88), and Cyrus Griffin (1788-89) – all prior to Washington taking office.

You don't hear about the prior presidents because the Articles of the Confederation did not work well according to the 'international elite' since the individual states had too much power. Another interesting fact is that George Washington was a Freemason and there is a correlation between the time he gained office and the rise of the Illuminati in America.

Martin Luther King, Jr. was an American Baptist, minister and activist who literally sacrificed his life for civil rights. During his movement, his message of nonviolent, civil disobedience touched all people universally and resonated with people of all races, creeds and colors. He was assassinated on April 4th, 1968 in Memphis, Tennessee. On December 9, 1999 the King family's attorney won a civil trial that found the U.S. government agencies guilty of assassination/wrongful death. The overwhelming evidence found by the jury is as follows:

- U.S. 111th Military Intelligence Brigade was at Dr. King's location during the assassination.

- 20th Special Forces Group had an 8-man sniper team at the assassination that day.

- Memphis Police special bodyguards were advised they "weren't needed" that day.

- Dr. King's regular police protection was removed one hour before the assassination.

- Military Intelligence had photographers on the roof of nearby buildings during the event.

- Dr. King's room was changed from a secure first floor to an exposed balcony room.

- The crime scene was prematurely 'sanitized' and virtually no witnesses were interviewed.

- The bullets from Mr. James Earl Ray's (the supposed assassin) rifle did not match the one that killed King.

Dr. King was a dangerous man because he was able to access people's collective conscience and bring them together in very large numbers in peaceful protest. The amazing fact is that very few people are aware of this civil trial results because the U.S. corporate media did not cover it and just about every textbook omits this information. ...It seems justice still has not been served.

What the world elite desire for the general public is to keep us just happy enough to take all the crap that is dished out on us and to continue to work and pay taxes; while keeping us distracted and consumed with fear so that we do not have the time to pay attention and ask the question: Are we part of a fair system? Be cognizant that the elite keep us in a "state of fear" by inventing a 'Bogeyman.' The Bogeyman can be anything that creates fear in the individual, but the Bogeymen is not real...and neither should be the fear.

One has to go back centuries to understand the origins of the control of knowledge. The original group who received parts of the secret knowledge of the Annunaki as well as the "Ark of the Covenant" was the Jewish people who carried the Ark on the journey from Egypt to the Promised Land. Before the Jews (Kabbalah) had possession of the Ark, the Ark was in the hands of the Sumerians, Babylonians, and also Tibetans. The Ark had powers beyond human imagination. It could revitalize and provide a tremendous amount of energy and power. It could provide long lives (e.g., Methuselah who lived for 950 years) to those who understood its power in conjunction with monatomic gold. The Ark moved from Jerusalem to Rome to London, etc. and continued to move west. The Ark is currently in the U.S. now. The owners of the Ark provide immense care for its handling and use their own bloodline to protect and continue its journey. The Ark is moving from what many believe to be near Washington, D.C. (possibly in Virginia) and is being moved east to China. The rate at which the movement is occurring is speeding up. It took centuries for it to move through the middle east and it sped up around 1,200 AD with its rate increasing through Europe changing 'hands' at a quicker pace from Greeks to Romans, to France, Spain, England, Germany and faster yet over the past 250 years to its current day place in America.

Apparently Zionists will stop at nothing to crush all inquiries of the Jewish Holocaust by every possible means. They create elaborate documentaries and movies that tell us "the way it was" so that no one else can even entertain another opinion, show proof or provide facts. The overreach and obstruction of this is awesome. They have a 'million eyes' watching everything (websites and social media) and everybody, to ensure that the pre-scripted story does not change and is strictly enforced with laws and jail time in some countries if you question the "official" story. Every inch of the 'story' is protected and if you question any of it, you are immediately labeled as "anti-Semitic." What are they afraid of?' Is the Holocaust a "house of cards?" If it falls, do Zionism, Israel, the lucrative Jewish lobby and the entire Holocaust industry also fall? Despite the conditioning and concerted effort of the Zionists-owned, media monopoly, people everywhere are waking up to the deceptions. There is absolutely no denying that the Holocaust happened; it just may not have been exactly as it was reported. Did millions of Jews die? Yes, but so did millions of Polish and Russian citizens as well as Germans and Americans too. The hard fact and truth is that the concentration camps' primary purpose was not to just kill people. The powers that be, after breaking the spirit and stealing all the valuables from the Jews, wanted to keep many of the healthier people in the camps alive so that they could be relocated to Israel at the end of the war.

Setting up the Zionist state of Israel through the original

Balfour Declaration of 1917 was always the 'master plan' for the elite because they could then have a strategic military base in the Middle East. When I was in Hebrew school many of my teachers were Holocaust survivors and they told me stories of what really happened. Yes, there are many horrible accounts, but I find it peculiar that when I was in school the total death count was around "3 million" then it became "4 million" then "5 million" and now all you hear is "6 million" Jews were killed. It is upsetting that the number needs to keep pace with the increasingly 'embellished' version of the story that we are being told. The saying goes that the Jews will "inherit the Earth." Many people throughout history have pointed to reasons they believe this from historical documents.

An interesting fact is that the English House of Windsor is not really English. The real name of the family was Saxe-Coburg Gotha, which was of German and Jewish ancestry. In 1917, from pressure of the Great War with Germany, George V and the Royal family changed the name to Windsor which sounded more English and less German/Jewish. This phenomenon of changing from a Jewish 'sounding' surname also occurred in other countries such as Belgium, which was also experiencing anti-German sentiment of the time. So much of European elite come from Jewish and German bloodlines, but have hidden this fact through history. Famous families such as the Rothschilds have hidden their Jewish ancestry for political and possibly social reasons too.

The protocols of the Meetings of the Learned Elders of Zion is an outline (notes in document form) purporting a "Jewish" and "Masonic" plan for global, world domination (a single world government) by bringing down western civilization. First published in 1897 by Phillip Stepanov (specifically for private distribution) and later re-published by Sergei Nilus several times in other publications including Henry Ford printing 500,000 copies that was distributed throughout the U.S. in the 1920s. Henry Ford was quickly expanding his car operations and needed money and went to Kuhn Loeb & Co. for a bank loan. The bankers wanted a controlling interest in his motor car company if they lent him money, but Henry Ford did not want to 'give up' this indecent percentage so he decided to re-publish the Protocols of the Elders of Zion to expose the corrupt businessmen and their practices. He did not like being robbed by the International Zionist Bankers and associated the indebtedness as slavery. Originally translated from Russian to French and then into English, much controversy surrounds this document and organized Jewry (and other groups) claimed that it is a 'fraud.' The interest in these documents should not focus on whether they were authored from a satirical or esoteric perspective or by a particular culture or religion, but rather encourage a 'critical review' of historical events that have unfolded very closely 'in step' with what is really going on today. If not the Zionist Jews, then some 'connected' power group has integrated these Protocols into their own agenda and has systematically used the 'fake' or 'forgery' document as the outline to push us into a one world governmentally controlled society. Also, all forgeries are based on 'something real' which further proves there was a real document somewhere—at some time. To follow are the twenty-four Chapters (Protocols) of the meeting minutes and a comprehensive list of bylaw extracts from those minutes:

Protocol I   The Basic Doctrine

Protocol II   Economic Wars

Protocol III   Methods of Conquest

Protocol IV   Materialism Replaces Progress

Protocol V   Despotism and Modern Progress

Protocol VI   Take-Over Techniques

Bylaws

- Place Zionist agents and helpers everywhere.

- Take control of the media and use it in propaganda for our plans.

- Start fights between different races, classes and religions.

- Use bribery, threats and blackmail.

- Use Freemason lodges to attract potential public officials.

- Appeal to successful people's pride.

- Appoint puppet leaders who can be controlled by blackmail.

- Replace royal rule with socialist rule, then communism, then despotism.

- Abolish all rights and freedoms of individuals.

- Sacrifice people when necessary.

- Eliminate religion; replace it with science and materialism.

- Control the education system to spread deception and destroy intellect.

- Rewrite history to the benefit of the victors.

- Create entertaining distractions.

- Corrupt minds with filth and perversion.

- Encourage people to spy on one another.

- Keep the masses in poverty and perpetual labor.

- Take possession of all wealth, property and (especially) gold.

- Use gold to manipulate the markets, cause depressions, etc.

- Introduce a progressive tax on wealth.

- Replace sound investments with speculation.

- Make long-term interest-bearing loans to governments.

- Give bad advice to governments and everyone else.

The key to success lies within each of you. Look within yourself. Understand that this message, thru words, is genuine. These words and the knowledge they possess will provide personal freedom. Stop complying with the system. It is time to wake up. Everything is emerging in different frequencies of energy. It is up to you to reach out and assimilate these information frequencies into your 'arsenal' of knowledge. Understand that the stars do not create light, but rather the light creates the stars. You are the light...

MEDIA

BOOK 28

It seems the goal of the media nowadays is to detach human beings from our creative source of power, suppress true knowledge, and the banishment of religion and true patriotism. Race, class, and wealth warfare has been waged on the public and is visibly evident in how the media uses divisive subject matter to separate and divide people. The media, and more specifically the news media, exist as a propaganda tool of the elite and are designed to brainwash us and will use anything to make us feel separate from one another and from the planet we live on. The main tool to achieve this is 'fear.' And it is all being done by design. We are not aware of the 'true beginnings' of our existence so we can only understand what has been presented to us by an authoritative source of information, the media. Mainstream media will never disclose the true facts surrounding the news. It is all packaged for the purpose to control you. The media actually has little to do with keeping people informed and everything to do with control of what you think and how you think.

"The media's the most powerful entity on Earth. They have power to make the innocent guilty and to make the guilty innocent, and that's power...because they can control the minds of the masses."
-Malcolm X

The news media has everything to do with controlling the flow of information and shaping your thoughts, your understanding and your beliefs of this information that is put in front of us. It exists to directly influence the opinions of the populous. These media institutions promote 'propaganda' and present 'theory' as fact, when it is not. Those that question this information are thought of as deviants or anti-establishments. When did it become wrong or ridiculous to question public information that has been packaged and pushed onto us for our consumption?

The 'media complex' is a cleverly constructed system, but when you figure how to see through the haze of propaganda, the real truth becomes clear. Unfortunately, just about each and every one of us is dependent in some way on this corrupt, corporative apparatus for survival. It is a love/hate relationship because when the people know they are being lied to, they still continue to watch and consume the information. News reporting has become more like pre-porting in that much of the news stories are pre-packaged with meticulous oversight. It is more a function of what is not being reported (or asked) by reporters than what they are actually reporting on. So much vital information is left out of mainstream news stories that no critical analysis is being offered. It was a gentleman from the CIA several years ago that told me in a serious and amusing tone to *"turn off the television."* He said *"turn it off,"* because there was little evidence (at that time) of anything that was being shown or reported in the news as truth. *"It is all lies or half-truths and one day in the future you will see this as I have."* Puzzled at the time, I have grown confident he was right. The news reporting is not any better today and probably is getting much, much worse.

This 'media complex' apparatus also places profit and control above people — the very people it is there to inform. Modern media has little to do with the true nature of man, his growth as an individual or his community or relationship to the Earth. Yet, we are dependent on it for telling us how to live, what to believe, for our news information) and of course for our entertainment. It tells us what to do, how to dress, how to act, where to go, what to eat, what we should look like, where to live, what to think, who to fear and what we should know and think about the world nationally and internationally. The question is: What if this 'media corporate apparatus' were to fail, or shut down? What if the electricity went out or a 'cyber-attack' knocked out the Internet? What would happen? Where would we get our information? Would every business suffer? Would stores start to close down? Would the supermarkets be emptied? Would all of our reservoirs of survival be depleted within a few days? Basically, if everything 'stopped,' most people (families) would have no more than about three days of reserves to survive on. So what if this 'shut down' was already planned, on purpose, by design?

The Internet is being shut down. The 'establishment' feels that there is too much freedom on the 'web' for people to express their own opinions. The internet has been monitored and regulated almost from its inception. Each year there are less options and freedoms of websites to visit and to freely express your personal opinions. Facebook and Google are completely connected to the government, CIA military Industrial Complex. These and other popular websites provide information on every citizen back to the government. I always wondered how a very 'hip' website such as Myspace, which had over 100 million users at one point, was superseded by the very boring and unimpressive Facebook and search engines, that were excellent such as 'Alltheweb,' lost out to Google. The situation for the average person 'surfing the web' is in for cold and unfriendly waters in the future.

Facebook was 'set up' as a tool by the CIA It is a data-mining project, used to collect as much information on as many people as they can. The purpose was (and is) to find everything they could on where people are going, what people are doing, what people are eating, who they are talking to and what kind of books, movies and entertainment they like. Most importantly, it keeps track of political thoughts and views on how you feel about the government. Facebook is a brilliant plan because never before have so many people been so willing to give up so much information about themselves and do this voluntarily. It would take decades (if not longer) for a government agency to collect so much personal data on individuals, especially information that is usually private. Ironically, the name 'Facebook' in itself is very telling. Every picture that is posted of you on Facebook is processed into a facial recognition database. The entire website is a database of 'faces' in order to keep track of what you look like and be able to ID you, but this is just the beginning.

When you want to analyze a company like Facebook the best place to start is to follow the money. Facebook officially launched its current platform around 2004, and the movie 'The Social Network' documented the company from its inception to how it became a multi-billion dollar corporation during its early years. The interesting part is the movie does not tell the whole truth and has been used as a 'propaganda' tool in order to have people believe that Facebook and Mark Zuckerberg got its first real funding from Peter Thiel. It was actually James Breyer who was associated with the venture capital company called 'In-Q-tel' which is a data mining, information technology group set up by the CIA back in 1999 that 'invested' about 13 million dollars. Invested may be a misleading phrase in that many believe that the government outright bought Facebook before it went total mainstream and Zuckerberg and the other public investors are merely 'front men' to protect the illusion; albeit very well-paid frontmen. There is also a connection to D.A.R.P.A., which is The Defense Advanced Research Projects Agency, which created and uses the internet to track internet activity, credit card purchases and even more private information on people such as medical records and tax returns. Facebook, in conjunction with Google (NSA), through this government agency's oversight, has the ability to monitor every 'key' touch on your computer and track every site you visit on the internet. Just about every internet website you visit today purposely has a Facebook 'like' or 'share' button or some link to your Facebook account. Even if you don't even use Facebook, it can still track your activity on the internet. The government has access to just about every website of interest through built in 'back doors' which provides entry to people's personal information. The 'Timeline' feature on Facebook basically hands over a chronological timeline of everything you do and when you do it; people could not have made it any easier for your private information to be public.

Net Neutrality is a ploy to have each user of the internet monitored, regulated and taxed. In addition, it has nothing to do with 'fairness' for all internet providers and users will be charged a monthly fee similar to a utility bill. Just look at the big corporations who are sponsoring the Net Neutrality legislation and also follow the money to the senators and politicians who are supporting and sponsoring this overreaching law. When you compromise the integrity of the internet you are essentially shutting down a society. It has only been about 20 years or so since the introduction of the internet, but western life has become helplessly dependent on our internet connection and society has changed dramatically right along in step with it. We have become so dependent on its use and that dependence will never go away...unless it is taken away from us.

Over the past 25 years or so there has been a conscious effort by the elite to consolidate the media empire. The numbers of ownership entities that control the media outlet have shrunk to only a few companies and individuals by means of corporate merges and takeovers (very similar to what occurred in the banking industry). This ongoing consolidation has been carefully designed and methodically implemented whereby the average person has no knowledge of the consolidation. Why should it matter anyway? We basically get all of our current events and news from these media outlets and the result of this consolidation means that we are continuing to get our information from less and less of a variety of news entities. If all the news and daily information comes from only a handful of media companies and all these companies are pushing the same general agenda, then we the viewer is being conditioned (brainwashed) to think a certain way about current issues. The biggest ploy in the media industrial complex is that the left news liberal (Democratic) and right news conservative (Republican) are both part of the same elite group ownership behind the scenes (divide and conquer). Even though on the surface they may look like competing media companies with different 'principles' and 'beliefs' they are essentially disguised just like different tentacles of the same octopus.

Group Think is very much controlled by media. One of the greatest examples of group think is the way people react to the words "question authority." Is it really wrong to question things? Is it heresy or unpatriotic to question the words of our leaders? Our leaders are the first ones that should be questioned! Politics is a microcosm of 'group think' (e.g., think tanks). The fear of standing out or being different influences many inquisitive minds so they don't ask questions and are 'OK' with 'being molded' into the group think mentality. Group think places a stigma on those who "think alternatively" and has such a profound impact on society that it makes it very difficult for an individual to break free and start thinking and questioning on their own.

"If you're going to tell a lie - tell a big one."

-Joseph Goebbels

Government cover-ups all seem a bit too fantasy for the average person and events like 9/11 are more like a Hollywood script than reality when you step back and observe them with objective eyes. The 'official story' sounds made up and this is understandable — it sounds made up because it is made up and through embellishment, lies, misinformation and omissions — these stories resemble little or nothing to the truth. What better way to control much of the 'group think' population than to make these stories sound even more bizarre than they are? Mainstream media is put there in place to persuade at least 80% - 90% of the population and sets a precedent that you're stupid, ignorant or naïve to think or keep an open mind about conspiracy theories. Movies, books, television, even fairytales are all tools to condition us and make the average person feel 'insane' for supporting, believing, suggesting or even thinking alternatively to the mainstream, politically correct, media agenda.

So if you don't think for yourself, you leave others to think for you and that is possibly why there are 500 different cable stations. Yet, the messages on television are the same from all of them; entertain and control. Every aspect of your life is taxed, regulated and controlled, not for the betterment of you, but for the control and profitability of corporations. The modern, corporate controlled mass media is being used as a massive vehicle of social engineering to train, condition, and mold this current generation into thinking, which aligns with the New World Order mindset. As the world becomes more and more unstable (environmentally, economically, politically and morally), each trial we go through is a test to prepare each soul for the final revelation of the great day of reflection. The final test on this planet will be either obedience to the word of God or to the word of man. It seems nobody talks anymore – at least not about really meaningful topics – they just regurgitate what they heard on TV, in the news or on the radio or internet. When was the last time you had a real, meaningful conversation with someone? Without them being distracted by a video screen, cell phone or texting? When was the last time you had a conversation that was not gossip, about the weather or about celebrities, sports or 'pop' politics?! Conversations should be enlightening and about something important to help uplift you on a personal level. We have a civilization, yet most people cannot be civilized amongst each other...

"Don't just teach your children to read – teach them to question what they read. Teach them to question everything."

-*George Carlin*

The distraction of American media to influence us has been:

1) Deliberate
2) Planned
3) Systematic and
4) Intended to do harm

Symptoms of being trapped in the 'media' matrix:

1) Your main source of news or information is the 'mainstream' media or the newspaper.
2) You believe most (if not all) of what the 'government' and its officials tell you.
3) You accept what's been told to you 'hearsay' even without proof, hard facts or evidence.
4) You don't believe in 'conspiracy theories' and you judge others poorly if they do believe.
5) You never would believe (and stand firmly on this) that you have ever been brainwashed.
6) You occasionally catch a glimpse of the truth, but you quickly disregard it or ignore it.
7) You are 'OK' with allowing many 'injustices' to continue as long as they don't affect you.
8) You believe the big 'lie' and you have no desire to investigate or find out the real truth.

9) You feel 'powerless' and use this and other excuses for not getting involved.
10) You know your politicians lie, yet you look the other way or continue to vote for them.

The average American is heavily distracted - worried about miniscule things such as celebrities as if they were their own family members. The powers that be who own/control the media industrial complex understand how our conscious and sub-conscious mind works. They understand how our brain functions scientifically and more importantly on a psychological level. They know about sociology and social conditioning and have used the media and entertainment for decades to establish social trends. They also have 'clogged' our minds with the most extraneous, unimportant issues that don't mean anything or really matter. When the news media treats certain events as the most important issues, then in fact, they become the most important issues. This is no accident. It is to keep us (the sheeple) preoccupied and focused on certain, cultural issues that can divide and separate us as a society such as race relations or income inequality. In addition, while you're focused on social condition issues the media is distracting you away from more important issues like unjust laws that are being passed by Congress or the latest banking scandal that would affect your bank account. They rather your attention be focused or 'worried' about the latest celebrity break up, who got cut from the food competition or your sport's team trying to win the 'Superbowl' or 'World Series.' And there are so many stations on just celebrities, food and sports that it will 'mesmerize' you into a 'stupor' so much that you won't even care about the real issues that are really important. The news media should be reporting news and information objectively, but can't because they are owned and controlled for the sake of corporate profits and must keep us 'entertained' and full of fear so that we keep tuning in. The news is not supposed to make us feel good or enlighten us to information that would be beneficial in our life.

All game shows and reality TV are conditioning us to think a certain way; just about every show pits one person competing against another or one person competing against a group of people. It is this type of conditioning that demonstrates how our society works today; that it is you against the world and there is only one winner. There is no collective bargaining or working together for the good of the group or the whole. This divides us and keeps us separate. Through reality game shows we continue to see this pattern of individual survival verses the group survival in real life. This breaks down the idea of community and elevates the individual needs above the rest. It perpetuates the concept that people are 'in it' for themselves and there is no personal interest in the public's welfare. All the while the people are constantly 'scheming' to get ahead personally and the 'status quo' of a divided population seems to be the new normal. It also flaunts a life style that is impossible to live up to in real life, resulting in an incomplete, desperate individual seeking approval and acceptance from others. The 'Invisible Empire' is there to control the populous with powerful, behind the scenes forces, and manipulation tools as they distract us with the latest celebrity's scandal, newest cell phone device and favorite sporting events.

Edward Bernes, the father of modern advertising, said that you can create a demand of things even if there is really no need for it. It can be fabricated. The authorities want to stop people from talking publicly in ways that are at odds with the mainstream belief of repeating. This is why so called visionaries are seen as dangerous by the authorities because they are offering another possibility of reality that is at odds with the world view and the belief of central government systems. Most people cannot be reached or helped. They are lost without guidance and will follow the media wherever it takes them. These are the people that will most likely fall victim to unimaginable hardship, suffering and hunger during the coming collapse of our modern economy. Most of the "sheeple" do not possess the intellectual curiosity to seek this out. For those awake at this time it is important to keep your eyes and ears open and evaluate the news carefully.

Ed Bernes on advertising:

1) Creating carefully calculated associations with the subconscience fears and desires of individuals.
2) Influence opinion leaders and perceived authority figures in order to reach these who follow them.
3) Initiating the contagion of behaviors and ideas through social conformity.

Whenever you read a newspaper story or hear anything on the news, you should ask yourself two questions: 1) Who stands to profit from what happened and 2) Who stands to gain control or power from what happened? If you are not able to answer these questions from the information provided, then you are most likely not being told the entire truth. To further this point is that teachers don't teach to ask questions anymore, people don't analyze or use constructive criticism, and this passive demeanor has been passed down to our children.

Never before in history have so few taken so much from so many. It is a form of mind control in that you have been convinced to go along with the program (without even knowing). The New World Media in conjunction with the War Lords of Wall Street and the international 'Banksters' have taken our once-sovereign land from one of the largest creditor nations to the largest debtor nation on Earth. The standard of living has dropped dramatically and the wealth of the middle class is evaporating. The 'war for your mind' has been propagated by the mass media industrial complex and through the transformation of the American education system. George Orwell forewarned us of this exact scenario taking place whereby the people will be endangered of losing their human qualities and freedoms by mind conditioning — without being aware of it while it was happening. The best defense to protect you against being psychologically or intellectually manipulated or 'mind controlled' is to be aware of how it works. What the conscious mind believes the subconscious acts on. It's like a programmed computer and the computer acts on it even if the information is proven wrong. If a person believes something, even if it is not true, the memory banks of the subconscious mind does not correct the error – but rather acts on it. The human mind automatically and involuntarily rejects information that is not in 'line' with the previously accepted thoughts and beliefs; many things people believe are not questioned especially when information comes from a reliable source.

People can be led to believe something that is not true if the information is carefully presented at the appropriate time and by an accepted and respectable authority (government official or well-known media personality). The purposes of propaganda are to 'short circuit' all conscience thinking and 'operate' on the individual subconsciously. Propaganda uses the same principles of mind control, hypnotic suggestion and mutual programming (distraction and repetition). The MK Ultra mind control methods used by our central intelligence also uses similar techniques, but on a much more severe level. Distraction and/or repetition focuses the attention away from the conscience mind and into the subconscious programming by using one of our five (5) senses that produces a state of mind control that is similar to daydreaming. When you stop 'conscience thinking' and your mind goes blank, this is considered a hypnotic state of mind. Watching TV brings about an altered state of conscience similar to a hypnotic state. The TV flickers (even digital) in a wave of repeating sound and light placing us in an altered state. Patterned speech from newscasters can also put us into a hypnotic state. This subconscious 'state' is most vulnerable to mental programming. Trust in the source of the information being presented and the repetition of the message solidifies not only the desired conditioned response, but also the truth and accuracy in the subconscious programming. Subliminal perception conditioning – like in a movie theater the hidden messages in advertising that you 'see' subconsciously without even being aware of it – yet it works its way into our subconscious which in turn controls our conscious behavior. Repetition is mental programing usually achieved through radio, music, TV, and movies. It is possible to have a 'large population' of people react a certain way to new ideas or concepts by repeating, seeing or experiencing them over and over again.

In 1983, there were over 50 corporations controlling most of America's media. In 1988, there were 29 and in 1990 there were 26. Today there are perhaps 5. The consolidation of the media empire makes it easier to use propaganda over the masses. The primary control of people is pivotal to the control of the information. Many in power withhold truthful information for selfish ends. They will present false information as a division to steer you away from the ultimate truth. They can inform or misinform people through 'information schools' which would normally command trust, respect and confidence but are gate keepers of information. Most people would not believe that a published book would have false information or incorrect historical facts and so they accept it as truth. Unfortunately, much of the news and information we get has been manipulated – even printed books. If you want to know if the media is telling the truth, you must investigate the stories yourself. There is public pressure to accept what is being told to us by these so called 'accredited' media groups, but as more people are able to investigate the facts (as best they can), they will be able to wake up to see the truth for themselves.

The 'BIG' Six:

1) GE – NBC, CNBC, Universal, MSNBC, Syfy
2) Disney – AE, ESPN, Pixar, ABC, History
3) Viacom – MTV, Spike, CMT, BET, Nickelodeon, Paramount
4) CBS – CW, Showtime, CBS TV and Radio
5) News Corp – Fox, Fox News, WSJ, NY Post, Myspace
6) Time Warner – Time, WB, HB, CNN, AOL, TMC, Cinemax

Some believe that when you take a picture of yourself you are stealing a part of your soul. Imagine the thousands of selfies for some people! It is narcissistic. It seems the more famous or noteworthy you are, the more photos and pictures are taken of you. Photography has only been around since the late 1800s so, a relatively short period of time. It has only been in the past 15-20 years that digital photography has been used and even less for the cell phone/camera technology. Therefore, many more pictures have 'progressively' been taken of people each year. As we move into the later stages of the technology age it would make rational sense that the millions upon millions of pictures being taken today are affecting the shift in human conscience. The little stealing of the soul is escalating to a tipping point where enough pictures will be taken to effect and bring this paradigm to an abrupt end.

To provide final examples of how powerful the 'Media Industrial Complex' is you need to look no further than the suspicious deaths of some alternative media reporters such as Andrew Breitbart, Michael Hastings and William (Bill) Cooper. Breitbart of the news agency Breitbart.com uncovered many stories of corruption in government and government-related agencies and was the man accredited with bringing to light the ACORN scandal in 2009. At the time of his death in 2012, he was on the verge of publishing some more controversial information specifically on the Obama 'pre-second term' election when he suspiciously dropped dead at the age of 43. Michael Hasting's death was a little more dramatic. Hastings, a reporter for *Rolling Stone magazine*, was responsible for exposing the back story and 'bringing down' General Stanley McChrystal. Hastings was on the verge of another big story when he was found to have run into a tree with his car at 4:25 am in Los Angeles. The suspicious part of the accident was that the engine of his Mercedes was found more than a block from the crash site. It is thought that an explosion of some kind caused the accident since Hastings was about to go public on more damaging news about another General, David Petraeus, among other harmful information on the Obama administration. Lastly, William 'Bill' Cooper, a Naval Intelligence Veteran, author of the book <u>Behold a Pale Horse</u> and radio broadcaster, had a radio show which he talked about government conspiracies. It was on June 28th 2001 that he would make a prediction on his radio show that an event like '9/11' would happen in a couple of weeks and that Osama bin Laden would be blamed. His broadcast went on to explain the Federal Government's foreknowledge and compliance of the event months before it happened. His name, reputation and back story has been smudged, altered and changed to fit an 'unstable' crazy person, yet he was very sane and very dangerous to the establishment. Bill Cooper was killed by authorities outside of his home on November 5th 2001.

MUSIC

BOOK 29

Music is 'sound vibration' and is extremely important to our human condition here on Earth. All of creation started with a sound. Much of our historical accounts tell us that everything came from light ("let there be light"), but light originally came out of sound. Everything we see and hear originated from the physical principles of sound. It was a sound that started the universe in motion from which all matter was created. Music is sound and sound is vibration and vibration is the 'pulse' of life. Sound can move energy (even matter) from one place to another. Sound vibration can also affect the human body – it can keep you healthy and feeling good or even make you ill. Music is no different. It can be beneficial and beautiful, yet it can also have a negative impact on your health and your body. Music is an essential part of our enjoyment of life. But be cautious of what you listen to (especially angry or violent music) because it can literally influence your emotions, your feelings and your vibrational energy.

The 528 Hz vibration holds many secrets and can evolve human consciousness and even emotions and feelings of love; music is the universal language of our existence. All of nature is vibrating at 528 Hz frequency and is commonly called the love frequency of nature. You may not be able to see this with your 'naked eye,' but the light from the sun is beaming to Earth, radiating at 528 Hz by way of nine, core frequencies. These nine, core frequencies are the music scales and tones that originally were based on the six note Solfeggio scale of music. This original Solfeggio scale (396, 417, 528, 639, and 741) frequencies have been hidden from our modern music tuning. Why? It may have to do with the fact that these frequencies are harmonious to our bodies and have beautiful qualities and certain malevolent entities don't want you to listen to them. The current western world of music uses a different frequency; A – 440 Hz standard tuning. It is clearly evident, at some point, that this was changed from a more harmonious frequency that is 'in tune' naturally with our bodies to a less natural frequency. The A – 440 Hz vibrates in dissonance compared to 528 Hz. This dissonant vibratory frequency can negatively affect your physiology and make a person feel like a prisoner of a certain consciousness. The unnatural, standard tuning frequency has removed us from sacred vibrations and overtones and has declared war on the subconscious mind of western man. This unnatural frequency is 'herding' populations into greater aggression, psycho-social agitation and emotional distress predisposing people to physical illness. This destructive frequency provokes thoughts of disruption, disharmony and disunity which ultimately create disease and war.

When we laugh we make a 'ha' sound. This sound is in tune with our body resonate and not only makes us feel good, but it heals us through the love vibration. Note that the word 'Yahweh' which is the word for God contains this same 'ha' sound. Also note that many ancient music forms such as sacred Gregorian Chants which have healing powers and a calming effect on the human body have been omitted from our music libraries. The Solfeggio healing tones were used in many Gregorian chants, such as the Hymn to St. John the Baptist, along with others that church authorities say were lost centuries ago. These frequencies were delivered to impart tremendous spiritual blessings. Sound and specifically music plays an important part in our 'energy matrix field' mostly because sound vibrations have a huge impact on water. Water carries vibrational frequencies and the human body is mostly made of water (around 80%).

The Nazis stole our 'pitch!' If sound can be used for harnessing goodness, it can also be used as a weapon. The Western World acquired its standard concert tuning pitch in 1939 from the Rockefeller Foundation Institute through the British Standards Institute which was a 440 Hz frequency. This frequency was derived from military acoustic warfare research which determined the most dissonant, stressful and the most psychosocially damaging to humans. This 'demonic,' diseasing frequency originated by the Nazi propaganda minister Joseph Goebbels and was to be instituted across all modern civilizations to hamper mass populations. The timing of this was to occur a few months before Germany invaded Poland. Psychological warfare started with the Nazis and by altering the pitch of music, it had immense control over the populations.

"If you wish to understand the Universe, think of energy, frequency and vibration."

-Nikola Tesla

In 1955 the international community then fully implemented through the International Organization of Standardization, the A – 440Hz frequency for all audio, frequencies calibrations for pianos, violins and other musical instruments. A – 440 Hz means that the 'A' note above middle 'C' is tuned to 440 Hz. This actually went against the preferred A – 432 Hz, known as Verdi's 'A,' which was unanimously acclaimed as the best frequency by most all musicians. Even though the musicians knew the A-432 Hz was much more natural to the human body, the elite wanted to change the frequency. The purpose of the change was to remain hidden by the elite and for good reason because the change was for a very sinister and corrupt agenda. It was for the same reason they added fluoride to water, chemicals to air and toxins in our food and that was to cause harm to the populations of the world. The multi-pronged assault on our human condition through a slow methodical degradation of all our bodily senses and the 'altered' music would cause a disharmonic vibration in us that would place our body on edge. The Elite knew that the A – 432 Hz was the only resonant frequency that had a perfect harmonic balance. The math clearly supports the A – 432 Hz tuning too, because this demonstrates what is called 'The Plato Code.' The elite possesses hidden knowledge of this Plato Code and believe that this frequency is the only frequency that is capable of naturally reproducing what is called the 'Pythagorean Musical Spiral' which is the same frequency sequence that all life grows and follows. It uses the 'PHI' or the Fibonacci formula which is also known as the "Golden Mean or Rule." The classical composers as well as the craftsman who constructed violins such as the famous and coveted Italian Stradivarius, all were made and calibrated to the 432 Hz. The 432 Hz is special in that it touches the full, twelve scale, octave overtones of all natural music. The 440 Hz only touches eight scale octave overtones and does not 'sync' up with our inner natural body resonant vibration. All modern recorded radio, TV and film music follow that disharmonic 440 Hz frequency.

So why is music at 432 Hz so important? Specifically the A 432 Hz pitch frequency is the same frequency as water, as the solar system and our body. 432 Hz vibrate on the principles of the golden mean (PHI Ratio and Fibonacci series of numbers) which is the mathematical formula and the measurement that all living things on this planet follow and grow. Frequencies have a direct effect on every living organism. A 432 Hz is logical; pure, spiritual, scientific and mathematically consistent with the universe whereas A 440 Hz enhances materialism hostility and disconnects humans from nature and may generate an unhealthy effect or anti-social behavior in the consciousness. Fibonacci sequences appear in Indian mathematics and are in connection with ancient Sanskrit language. 432 Hz transmits beneficial healing energy and unifies the properties of light, time, space, matter, gravity, magnetism, biology, the DNA code and consciousness. 432 Hz natural tuning has profound effects on consciousness and also on the cellular levels of our bodies. By retuning musical instruments and using concert pitch at 432 Hz instead of 440 Hz, atoms and DNA start to resonate in harmony with PHI spiral in nature. 444 Hz is the harmonic equivalent to 528 Hz on the piano.

"If one should desire to know whether a kingdom is well governed, if its morals are good or bad, the quality of its music will furnish the answer."
-Confucius

Our inner ear works on the basis of "Phi" or Fibonacci spiral dampening system whereby the seashell-like structure of the cochlea helps keep us feeling balanced, centered and grounded. The 'spiral' acts as a self-regulator of inertia that stays balanced with the natural environment around us. If this balance is disrupted, then we can experience a disconnected feeling or fog-like condition. Sound and especially music comes into the ear via the cochlea and has a huge effect on the inner ear and in turn affects our mind, body and even our DNA. The general health of the human body is directly related to the things we consume such as water, food and yes the music we listen to. If the music has been adulterated, specifically the frequency of the notes, it can adversely affect our body's physical health. An unharmonic key or a frequency that vibrates against our body's 'tuning' can, in fact, affect our mood and disposition. Music can also heal. Healing is the art of restoring the balance in the body; music provides the power of putting art into the harmonic laws of healing.

The point of performing music, song and dance is not to get to the end of the 'piece' or dance the fastest...then the quickest player and fastest dancer would be regarded as the best, but rather the point is to be 'in the moment' as one plays along and enjoys the journey to the end.

There was a time if you were a talented band or singer you could make an honest living at being a musician. That is not necessarily the case anymore. At the top tier talent comes secondarily to the 'image' that needs to be portrayed first and foremost to sell 'records.' The music industry is carefully controlled just like most of the other entertainment and media industries nowadays and any of the 'big' acts are controlled by 'Mega Music Media Complex.' Many artists have 'sold their soul' to the devil and are hair jelled, airbrushed, lip-synched and voiced-boxed to make them look and sound better than they really are to help sell records. If you're super talented and will not 'play the game' then your music will not be promoted or played on the radio. The music industry was never easy or void of manipulation, but it seems the consolidation of the music industry has undergone the same corrupt turn in the road as all the other media outlets. Many of these artists are influenced by the Illuminati/occult or Kabbala teachings. The foundation behind this is Satanic and evil. Even if the artist appears fairly normal—if they have reached a certain level of success and notoriety—there is usually some kind of Luciferian deviant behavior associated with them.

The implementation of the A - 440 Hz has been a huge 'con-job' on us and the purpose was to suppress the heart chakra while stimulating the left brain 'Ego' mind. It is as if science has taken over God's role and substituted a man-made product that is not in tune with the human body. Pure 'unadulterated' music is one of the most powerful truths to humans and it has been suppressed for the reason to depower. It can affect human creativity, spirituality and consciousness and suppress the human awakening experience by replacing it with fear and disharmony. Then it's possible to more easily control individuals. This disharmony also accentuates the separation of groups from each other; blacks from whites, Jews from Christians and even Democrats from Republicans. Polarizing the populous (Polar Thinking) in order to affect division among the ranks so that we will never all come together as one. As one, we are very powerful and merely the collective thought would change the world (for the better), but the power elite would lose control. Music is a special medium that can bring large groups of people together in one consciousness. Musical vibration can elevate the heart, but if it is listened to in the wrong frequency then it will have an adverse effect. The elite want to play on our fears. This is not how we are supposed to live; under constant fear. This is not the way for us to be whole or at peace with ourselves. We are supposed to love the creator with our heart and soul and love each other as brothers and sisters. If you follow this principal, then you have begun to embrace life without fear and hopefully contribute to a much better world for all. Hopefully you will be to experience this through much song and dance accompanied by a beautiful music score of life...

ENTERTAINMENT

BOOK 30

The entertainment industry wants you to pay attention. They spend billions of dollars each year to keep you distracted from the real world. Entertainment is an escape from the all too 'consuming life' that many of us lead. But there is more. The very same entertainment industry that is there for your distraction and your money is also there for a specific more sinister purpose. This purpose is partially hidden, but it is hidden in plain sight. Much of the entertainment industry whether it be music, motion pictures or television has a certain message that is being telegraphed out to each person. It does not matter if you like a particular type of music or film, the message is constant, consistent and pervasive. The message is one of control, obedience and separation. It is a programmed message that 'dumbs us down' to the degree that we may never figure out the 'big picture.' The message is creatively packaged with beautiful art, sounds and performances that are very convincing and very enjoyable. But the outgoing message is mostly influenced by a negative (Satanic) energy that is looking to harness more negative energy and steal our goodness. Even though many movies from the past are very thought provoking, the more contemporary movies all seem to have the same underlying agenda of putting fear into us, separating us from others and just plain scaring us to death.

Going back centuries civilizations have used entertainment

as a form of distraction from everyday life. In Roman times the 'Games' were introduced as a public form of entertainment for the citizens. Back then the 'Games' were seasonal where today there are many forms of entertainment each minute of each day all year long. Sports, theater, music, television, film and even art are all modern-day forms of entertainment. Car racing is no different than the chariot races at the Circus Maximus Arena where every spectator is awaiting an exciting finish to the race or perhaps the anticipation of a fatal accident. Something about our nature as humans, embraces this type of distraction. It's literally 'entertaining.' We enjoy watching a show because it takes us away from the rigorous routine of life. We want to escape and explore something new that brings intrigue and excitement into our life. But the distraction should only proceed so far in that when the distraction is preventing us from a 'normal existence' it affects our ability to think clearly. In the end times of Rome the councils argued about what vices they needed to make legal to keep the citizens entertained. Now is a time we should take pause. We should take pause because the distraction has 'two folds' to it with one being entertaining and the other being controlling. The controlling aspect explains that these 'distractions' have been placed there for the purpose of keeping your mind from the fact that you are being over taxed, or unfair laws are being passed that will impede your liberties.

These distractions are to be so numerous in your life (Dancing with the Stars, football, and golf) that you won't have the time or even care to investigate anything that the establishment is doing. At the end of the movie, "Tommy" by The Who, all of Tommy's Holiday Camp followers copy his "deaf, dumb, and blind boy" persona by placing blinders on with attached ear plugs and mouth cork. This creates the ultimate human distraction because by cutting off all of the people's sensory abilities, a complete control over their existence can be established. But this situation may only be temporary since people don't like being 'dumbed down' and when the people have had enough they will rise up and revolt.

Over a hundred years ago, numerous Jewish immigrants from a concentrated area in Eastern Europe (mostly Russia and Ukraine) came to America as moguls to start up a brand new motion picture industry in a suburban part of Los Angeles called *"Hollywoodland"* From the beginning of the movie industry, the movie makers wanted to make a point. Yes, it was and still remains a creative medium, but when you analyze the industry on a more microscopic level, it becomes very clear that there is an agenda taking place. Most people love watching movies yet they may not see the 'motives' behind making most of the movies throughout history. Many movies were made to entertain, but many were made to influence the conscience and sub-conscience of its viewers. Movies were, and still are, used to 'rewrite' history and as propaganda to influence and establish a new (more progressive) way of thinking. Before movies and movie theaters, the only way people got their news was from printed material such as books, magazines and newspapers. After businessmen realized that the movie industry was 'taking off' they built small movie theaters everywhere in every city and every town in America. For a nickel you could spend the afternoon 'taking in' a movie or two and also get the day's news via the 'Newsreels' which were short documentary films containing news stories and topics of interest. As time progressed into the 1930's and the movie industry blossomed, so did the people's thirst for new movies, news and especially international news. The 'powers that be' understood that when you watch movies you are placed in a semi-conscience 'hypnotic trance' that can easily be influenced by certain information. Messages appeared in movies to make its viewers think a certain way or 'help' form an opinion on a subject.

As time moved into the mid-nineteen thirties the Newsreels became a medium for propaganda of war and to propagate fear into the masses of moviegoers. Through carefully scripted words and selected film clips, it was easy for the moviemakers to make a news documentary that would have you loving your country and hating Germany in one afternoon. Throughout history nothing has changed. Today you are still seeing the same exact 'recipe' on your corporate news station. Is it a coincidence that nowadays most of the television, newspapers and movie companies are owned or controlled by Zionist and Jewish families? Look no further than Louis B. Mayer, Samuel Goldwyn, William Fox, Harry Cohn, The Warner Brothers (Sam, Albert, Harry and Jack), Adolph Zukor, Carl Laemmle, Marcus Loew and other men like Lew Wasserman, Sumner Redstone and Michael Ovitz that have influenced our society through this prolific medium. Being Jewish, I used to applaud this fact that 'my people' were so successful. Yet, as I grow older with wisdom I see how this close knit club has adversely controlled the information that we are receiving through the mainstream media complex.

"You have been entertained!" It is difficult to accept that somehow our 'true reality' is really far different than what we are experiencing. Our lives have many similarities to the character, Neo, in the "Matrix" movie where he lives his life here on earth unaware of 'who' he really is. The general concept of the 'Matrix' is that the characters are living (in) an allusion— so much has been 'pulled over their eyes' to blind them from truth—the truth that they are slaves to a system that they cannot see, taste, touch or even smell. And as the story unfolds you'll see that our lives are not very far from truth or those inside the Matrix movie. Unfortunately, many will not be prepared and will have a hard time accepting all of this, like Neo, when we start to uncover the truths about our true existence here on Earth.

"It is nice to be important, but it is far more important to be nice."
-John Templeton

Some actors and musicians at some point, usually early in their career, ask for something so strongly — such as to be voted best guitar player or to win an Academy Award that they are literally willing to do anything for that level of success or notoriety. This request, this wish, this prayer invites an 'evil' presence (the devil) 'in' and your wish may be granted if you are willing to make a deal. That deal usually comes with a price or condition and that compromise may come in exchange for your soul. But when you want something so 'badly' that you are willing to 'sell' your soul to get it, shows how far off the path of nature we, as a society, have traveled. Our integrity has been marginalized, trivialized, 'ego-sized' and compromised all to embrace a superficial life of fame fortune and notoriety.

Nowadays, it seems that just about every movie produced has an alternate agenda. Most Science Fiction movies and television shows demonstrate either the 'alien agenda' with a self-destructive, violent backdrop of our planet or the relationship of artificial intelligence coming of age and its conflict with man. Contemporary movies have become more of an indoctrination to the way the elite want us to live in the next century (New World Order) as opposed to just entertainment. There always seems to be a message and that message is usually not a humanitarian one even if it is subtly disguised as one. The following are a series of lists of movies, directors, actors and singers that either have a certain life message that is important in telling us what is really going on in the world or that are used to perpetuate the New World Order mentality in movies. This by no means is a complete list of 'enlightened' or 'mind controlling' movies:

MOVIES:

Soylent Green - 1972
Notorious - 1946
2001: A Space Odyssey - 1968

North by Northwest - 1958
The Shining - 1986
Eyes Wide Shut - 1999
Fahrenheit 451 - 1972
Eiger Sanction - 1972
Network - 1976
A Clockwork Orange - 1968
Three Days of the Condor - 1972
The Conversation - 1972
'1984' - 1984
The Matrix - 1999
Terminator - 1980
Fight Club – 1999
Inception - 2012
House of Rothschild - 1932
Wag the Dog - 1995
From Hell - 1998
The Manchurian Candidate – 1962
They Live - 1986
Logan's Run - 1976
American Psycho - 2000
Cosmopolis - 1929
Being There - 1976
The Ninth Gate - 2000
Metropolis - 1929
Her - 2013
*Fantasia - 1936
The Andromeda Strain - 1973
The Firm - 2001
All the President's Men - 1970
The China Syndrome - 1976
Capricorn One - 1978
The Boys from Brazil - 1978
The Andersen Tapes -1974
The Odessa Files - 1974
The Candidate – 1972
Total Recall - 1999
Syriana - 2005

Seven Days in May - 1964

Futureworld - 1976

The Domino Principal - 1973

The Brotherhood of the Bell - 1960

Blow Out - 1980

The Parallax View – 1974

 Dr. Strangelove/Love the Bomb - 1962

The Truman Show - 2000

Blade Runner - 1978

Equilibrium - 2010

The Hunger Games - 2012

Eraser - 1996

The Skulls - 2000

The Day of the Jackal - 1976

Oblivion - 2013

Minority Report - 2000

Rosemary's Baby - 1974

The Man Who Would Be King - 1969

Stargate - 1980

*The Wizard of 'OZ' - 1939

The Fifth Element - 1999

Enemy of the State - 2000

Elysium - 2013

Planet of the Apes - 1968

Omegaman/I am Legend - 1970/2008

Running Man - 1970

The Wicker Man - 1973

Mulholland Drive - 2001

Atlas Shrugged - 2010

Marathon Man - 1976

There Will Be Blood - 2008

Now You See Me - 2000

Margin Call - 2011

The Men Who Stare at Goats - 2009

The Golden Compass - 2009
Things to Come - 1936
The Thirteenth Floor - 2009
Tommy - 1975
Contact - 1997
The Game - 1997
*A Bug's life - 2000

DIRECTORS:

Sydney Lumet   Alfred Hitchcock
Stanley Kubrick   Wackowski Brothers
James Cameron   Sydney Pollack
Roman Polanski   Christopher Nolan
Steven Spielberg   Ridley Scott

ACTORS:

Leo Dicaprio   Jodie Foster
Brad Pitt   Halle Berry
Angelina Jolie   Mark Whalberg
Christian Bale   John Travolta
Nicolas Cage   Heath Ledger
Johnny Depp   Jim Carey
Russell Crow   Keanu Reeves
Matt Damon   Will Smith
Robert Downey, Jr.   Tom Cruise
Shia LaBeouf   Nicole Kidman

MUSICIANS:

Jay Z   K$sha
Eminem   Kanye West
Madonna   Beyoncé Knowles
Rihanna   Justin Timberlake
Lady Gaga   Miley Cyrus
Britney Spears   Justin Bieber

Katy Perry

David Bowie

Taylor Swift

Lil' Wayne

Michael Jackson

Nicki Minaj

As an important side note – most all children's movies are used to indoctrinate our children into the 'New World Order' subservient system through sub-conscious and subliminal messaging.

There are numerous examples of how the entertainment industry has influenced our thoughts and actions, but none may be as fascinating or telling as the story behind Stanley Kubrick. His dynamic tale covers so many different interesting aspects of the movie industry. Kubrick only made thirteen full length movies during his life and yet each one tells a unique insightful perspective to man and his relationship to the world in the 21st century. More specifically, he left us coded information via his movies to help make us understand the incredible lies and manipulation of the hidden elite's control over the average man. Since he became acquaintances during his lifetime with the elite, he was able to understand first hand and provide this information to us. Whether it was for spite or payback, he wanted to expose the evil master agenda of these people because the elite 'used' him most notably for 2001: A Space Odyssey, but never let him join their elite club. Starting with 'Paths of Glory' in 1957, which was at its core an anti-war movie, and moving forward with 'Dr. Strangelove or: How I stopped worrying and learned to love the Bomb,' '2001: A Space Odyssey,' 'A Clockwork Orange,' 'The Shining,' 'Full Metal Jacket' and 'Eyes Wide Shut.' Each movie is rich in codes, information and secrets to the discriminating viewer.

Because of his relentless attention to detail on the movie props 'Hollywood elite' got notice of Kubrick's work on Dr. Strangelove and essentially 'partnered' with him to make a space movie. 2001, whose purpose was many-fold, was made prior to our landing supposedly on the moon. The movie set details in this film were unprecedented and the cinematography was so realistic that it looked as if it was filmed in space, which was the point. The movie execs had NASA and other government agencies work together with Kubrick on the film. Fast-forward two years and the United States went to the moon (supposedly). Much factual evidence points to 'most' of the 'film' and still 'pictures' that the world saw of the Apollo missions in space and on the moon were made in a film studio in London—created by Kubrick using his rear screen projection method—the same one he used on 2001. Kubrick, having been paid extremely well, knew the sensitivity of this information and feared for his and his family's life if he were ever to breathe a word of 'the truth' to anyone. He became a recluse settling into his rural London home. As an artist there were only a few ways that he could disseminate information without obviously gaining attention and that is through the medium of his film work itself. So he cleverly created hidden messages in the next few movies he would make. The Shining, on the surface, appears to be a very well made scary movie, yet it has been carefully analyzed as a masterpiece of hidden secrets to the real events of the Apollo 11 mission. Did we ever really go to the moon? Kubrick knew the truth. Space Odyssey 2001 was also foretelling the events of September 11, 2001 through Masonic codes and rituals. The Twin Towers are representative of the twin (towers) pillars of Boaz and Jachin along with the 'sacred' Pentagon make up the three symbols visible in every masonic lodge. New World Order planned 9/11 as a sacrifice. From the ashes will come order as prophesized by a group of elite, high level 'maji.'

Kubrick's next project were 'A Clockwork Orange' which was a futuristic analysis of society, crime and government - and 'Full Metal Jacket' which was a more modern version of his 'anti-war' message that was nothing short of on screen brilliance. In 'Full Metal Jacket,' Kubrick was making a statement not only about the

Vietnam War, but war in general and future wars. War is a very dangerous 'game' and we could end up blowing ourselves up if we are not careful (e.g., 'Dr. Strangelove'). Kubrick demonstrated through 'art' just how dangerous war is and how you can take an innocent 'kid' from 'Middle America' and turn him into a killing machine. It is noteworthy to point out that several times he was making a particular movie that other movie productions were putting out similarly themed scores, with the possible purpose of diluting the impact of his films on the unsuspecting public. For example, 'Platoon' came out right before 'Full Metal Jacket' and obviously diminished its impact. Kubrick took a long time to make his movies so it was not a stretch for another production company to 'quickly' put out a competing product before his was done. Furthermore, not too many people want to go see two war movies in one movie season.   This happened several more times with movies slated to be made such as 'Aryan Papers,' 'Napoleon' and 'A.I.' (Artificial Intelligence) that were never made during his life due to conflicts with studios or competing productions.

But it was his last movie that was his most telling. "Eyes Wide Shut" was released in 1999 and stared Tom Cruise and Nicole Kidman. The term 'Eyes Wide Shut' is an expression or catch phrase used amongst the global elite meaning—for the crimes that we commit that you will be silent and that you will keep your 'eyes wide shut' to what 'I' am doing. It was in this last movie that Kubrick tried to subtlety shed light and expose the world global 'elite' to their sinister, secret, corrupt and perverse ways. Dr. Bill Harford's portrayal was possibly Kubrick himself who was never quite accepted into the ranks of the elite since he was not of the 'proper' bloodline. It was about five days after Kubrick delivered his final version of the film to the executive studio heads that he died under suspicious causes. The film that you see today (even the unedited version) does not make 'complete' sense since there is clear evidence that the movie after Kubrick's death was severely edited. No doubt, the movie we see today is quite different than the one Kubrick originally and intentionally made for distribution. Certain critical story lines, scenes and dialogue purposely ended up on the editing room floor never to be seen.

"I don't have to tell you things are bad. Everybody knows things are bad. It's a depression. Everybody's out of work or scared of losing their job. The dollar buys a nickel's worth, banks are going bust, (and) shop-keepers keep a gun under the counter. We know the air is unfit to breathe and our food is unfit to eat, and we sit watching our TV while some local newscaster tells us that today we had fifteen homicides and sixty-three violent crimes, as if that's the way it's supposed to be. We sit in the house, and slowly the world we are living in is getting smaller, and all we say is, 'Please, at least leave us alone in our living rooms. Let me have my toaster and my TV and my steel-belted radials and I won't say anything. Just leave us alone.' Well, I'm not 'going' to leave you alone. I want you to get mad! I don't want you to protest. I don't want you to riot – I don't want you to write to your congressman because I wouldn't know what to tell you to write. I don't know about the depression and the inflation and the Russians and the crime in the street. All I know is that first you've got to get mad. You've got to say, 'I'm a HUMAN BEING, damn it! My life has VALUE!"

-Howard Beale

A motion picture studio can show the 'world' and make the public familiar with any topic or subject in a way no book, college professor or any other form of entertainment medium could do. Presenting ideas and concepts through movies in the form of entertainment is one of the most powerful methods of converting and convincing the public mind. The reason is, because often what you see in the movies is made to look so real that you never question its validity. The James Bond '007' movie series comes to mind because they not only give an interesting technological glimpse, but they also provide intriguing and telling story lines. The reason being is that these movies have been financed, produced and brought to you directly from the elite and have many 'hidden clues' that not only telegraph specific 'storylines' of what is happening in the world (at that time), but also to show you some of the advanced technology that exists in real life. Ian Fleming the author of the original '007 books, was in fact the real '007 and was an undercover British Secret Service (MI5) and agent for the elite. Many story lines are very specific like 'Gold Finger' which is about stealing the 'gold' located supposedly at Fort Knox. The movie is very convincing that there is 8,000 tons of gold there, yet in real life there may be none. In 'Diamonds are Forever' there is a particular scene that highlights a Moon landing being 'faked' in a film studio. How 'ironic' is this scene which shows the viewer that somewhere a film crew was 'mock' filming scenes on the moon.

"This used to be a hell of a country. I can understand what is going on with it. They are not scared of you...they are scared of what you represent to them. Oh no, all you represent to them is freedom. That is what it's all about, but talking about it and being it... that is two different things. I mean it is real hard to be free when you're bought and sold in the market place. Of course don't ever tell anyone that they are not free 'cause they are going to get real busy killing and maiming to prove to you that they are... Oh yea, they are going to talk to you and talk to you and talk to you about individual freedom, but when they see a free individual it's going to scare them. No, it makes them dangerous."

-Jack Nicholson in 'Easy Rider'

All doomsday and end of times prophesies are propagated to instill fear by Hollywood. They are tools used to control the thoughts and actions of people. Movies mix truths and lies to create a distorted story version of reality and fearful visions of the future. As an end-note: Druids performed magic to control large segments of the populations and used magic wands to cast powerful spells on people. Ironically, the wands were made of 'holy—wood' from the Holly—wood tree and the creators of "Hollywood" knew exactly why they called – it *Hollywood*.

EDUCATION

BOOK 31

Our public education system in America has been hijacked. It has been a very slow methodical process whereby the 'hijacking' has taken place over many years. It has deteriorated into no more than a 'check list' for the teachers to be evaluated by how well your students perform on a series of standardized tests. What is disheartening is that the average American feels that our public education system is one of the best in the world, but when you look at how we actually rank compared with other countries this is far from the truth. We rank low and it's getting worse. Alternatives to the government sponsored public schools are private schools, home schooling and the ever-growing online schooling programs. All of these are adequate options, but for the purpose of this discussion we will focus primarily on the public school system.

When both parents are working they most likely place their children into a public school system. They drop them off early in the morning and pick them up after work in the early evening leaving the child there virtually all day. Public schools are basically indoctrination camps which don't really teach children how to be creative or self-sufficient, but to listen to instructions, follow them and then regurgitate them back. The child that does this the best will get the good grades. This type of education teaches your child to be a 'worker' as a 'cog' in a big machine..."*do your job and don't ask questions.*" Schooling has been debased down to having students learn how to fill out forms. People are not educated in a 'classical' sense anymore and are being tested in levels of obedience. Today, school is about memorizing what you are told and repeating it. The bulk of how you are graded is completely based on testing and daily busy work. The most important quality in a 'worker bee' when they join the work force, is obedience. We have no real choices as long as money is our only means of survival. The system trains us and does not inspire us. Memorization and not innovation is required to fill employment positions in large governments and large corporations. That is what the current education system is basically structured for... training the next generation to be 'slaves' of a corrupt system. Learning in the current education system has become a production line. Each student slotted, evaluated and programmed into a system that does not account for individuality or creativity. And why is it important to divide children into separated ages? All of this seems to separate and divide the kids into control groups. Any outstanding child with a super intellectual mind is singled out and tracked where one day he/she will be recruited into the corporate system or special covert government programs.

Common Core is the new wave of education in the America public school system. For decades, the government had centralized control over the education system and now they have taken it so far as to use federal funds to coerce states to adopt a national academic curriculum to implement Common Core. The Common Core agenda is the systematic and intentional 'dumbing down' of our children. There is a disconnection between Washington, D.C. and our local schools. If the school system took any federal incentive money that was dished out during the 2010 recession period then they must implement this teaching curriculum to our kids. This is overreaching of our government, involving themselves into what should be a more localized, jurisdiction choice. The standard Common Core curriculum is teaches our children by fitting them all into one mold in a standardization of schooling. It seems the result of this system is stagnation of the individual's creativity and ability to think on their own only to serve the collective group. The history books have been rewritten to match much of the present day socialist agenda that our educators are pushing. Our history was not 'politically correct' then, so why should our historical accounting of it be? Why is our history being re-written for today's books and publications? The public schools need to get away from all monetary inducements that in turn push the false agenda and get back to education for the sake of universal truth. America is possibly one of the 'best' educated populations in the world with the least common sense.

Our public school systems are just as subservient to the Global Central Bankers. The Central Bankers wish to keep certain history from our students so they control the dissemination of historical information through ownership of the publishing companies of school text books. A good example of this is how the Civil War is being taught in our public schools. The true, financial dimensions of the Civil War are not well known or written about often. It is portrayed in our text books and in our popular media as an internal dispute over slavery. The Civil War had little to do with slavery and much more to do with money manipulation. It is well known with historians that several states had already abolished slavery before the Civil War even started. For some reason the 'powers that be' want you think that race relations have been bad for centuries here in America and continue to 'stir the pot' on race issues even today. The Central Bankers do not want you to focus on the 'money war' that was taking place during the Civil War, but the fact is the war was about the Confederacy seceding from the U.S. and the bankers, once again, saw an opportunity for the rich to take advantage of the situation and offer to fund President Lincoln's efforts to bring the south back into the Union at 30% interest. Lincoln knew this would indebt Americans to the bankers so he issued interest free Green Backs. Green Backs were American dollars printed by our own Government and could be borrowed without any interest or debt attached. This was a direct threat to the wealth and power of the Central Bankers so they did what they do best...shift the attention off themselves and their banks onto other current social issues going on at the time, i.e., slavery. This is a perfect representation of 'divide and conquer' that the elite have used for hundreds of years to control and manipulate the masses. The Central Bankers were not happy with Lincoln and after he was assassinated his Greenbacks were immediately repealed.

Today, these same International Bankers are also pushing for the implementation of Agenda 21 which is like new 'commandments' issued by the United Nations by which all nations will abide in the future. Through the education system, they are slowly teaching our children the false doctrines of Agenda 21 and soon to be Agenda 2030. Although at first glance, reading the doctrine, one may not see the underlying evil purpose because much of the agenda list sounds positively good. Much of what seems positive is really hidden agendas for a much more sinister purpose.

The following list outlines some Agenda 21 stances on issues:

1) Put nature above man.
2) Replace nature with world government.
3) Destroy the family and depopulate the planet.
4) Indoctrinate children in environmental-socialism.
5) Regulate, nationalize or abolish poverty.
6) Ration fossil fuels, energy and mobility.
7) Ban farming by the individual.
8) Confine humans to 'settlement zones.'

We need a new holistic approach to our education system and not just try to fix or improve the existing, broken one. Education today targets teaching our children to ultimately get a decent well-paying job after graduation (if they can find one). If our education could be more focused on learning the 'teachings of life' rather than focus on endless memorization of relatively useless information then you provide a child with a real foundation of knowledge. If we could elevate our society to a level of enlightenment and accomplishment, so that we could concentrate on creativity and innovation instead of regurgitation, that would be a huge step forward for all. What we should be striving for as a nation is fewer jobs, not more jobs. Administrations always push for more and more jobs. Why? Because that is how governments make money by taxing your wages. If you're not working, they can't tax your salary. Per our Constitution, it is illegal to place taxes on wages. This is an illegal practice by an illegal government.

"Education is a wonderful thing, provided you always remember that nothing worth knowing can ever be taught."
                                                            –Oscar Wilde

Understand - The word's definition literally means to 'stand under' such as to 'stand under' (or look under) a 'floor' of a house from 'underneath' to see how the crossbeams and flooring were built. When you 'understand' how the cross beams connect to each other and see how it was constructed then you know and 'understand' how it was made. You also understand the relationship of the floor above to the floor below. This axiom is an example of our life.

Our whole life seems to be in a constant state of preparation for what's next—but the 'rub' is you may never actually get there. We have a system of schooling that starts with grade levels that are always 'preparing' for what will happen next.

Nursery school is preparation for elementary school. Elementary school is preparation for middle school, then high school, and then if you're fascinated enough with this education system, they can get you to go on and pay for college. If you're really 'smart' (or wealthy, then onto professional or graduate school. But eventually after commencement (which ironically means beginning), society wants you to go out into the work force...'the big world.' So you have finally arrived and you go into your first 'sales' meeting and you realize the entire cycle starts over again. If you do well and meet your quota, you move up the corporate ladder with bigger titles and more money until maybe you're 45 years old and you become Vice President (or another important sounding title) that says to the world you finally have arrived. Success at last! So it dawns on you that maybe you have arrived – but also with a certain sense that you have been cheated – because life feels the same as it always did. Nothing internally has really changed. You are still you. You feel as though, to a certain degree, life is a hoax. You are conditioned to be in desperate need of a future and in reality that future never comes as you anticipated.

The education of the 'Power of thought': Nothing comes into your life without an invitation. Your thoughts and words open up doorways to different experiences. You are the creator of this reality. The greatest advantage of speaking the truth is that you don't have to remember what you said previously. Believe in what you want so much that it has no choice but to materialize. Never force anything. Give it your best effort and then let it be. If it is meant to be, it will be. Create the things you wish existed.

As I look back on my life...I realize that every time I thought I was rejected from something good, I was actually being redirected to something better.

There are two major problems with our current education system:

(1) The U.S. Department of Education costs billions of dollars and yet quality in education is decreasing. It seems our investment in education has a direct, inverse relationship; the more we spend the worse the quality.

(2) Common Core is the purposeful implementation of an education system to 'dumb down' our children, stifle independent thinking and teach them to be subservient to the state.

"Thinking is the hardest work – that is why so few of us do it."

–Henry Ford

People used to ask me what I wanted to be when I was older and I thought that was a ridiculous question. I could have answered with a humorous, rhetorical response of 'younger,' 'richer' or 'happier,' but really the better question is what do you want to be right now. All the rules in the world were made by someone no smarter than you are, so make your own rules and decisions. Schooling is the tool the controlling parties use to mold the youth and set specific agendas into motion. If newborn babies could speak, they would say some of the most wonderful and brilliant things; so what happens between birth and middle school to our children? Would our planet be a lot more 'intelligent' if we let them explore more during the early years of development?

Why do 'I' have to go to school? So that I can be molded into a state-approved homogenous drone that cannot think outside of the prescribed consensus. I will learn to repeat information instead of how to think for myself so that I don't become a threat to the status quo or the governmental state. When I graduate I will get a job, pay my taxes and vote for my politicians in order to perpetuate the corporate system of indentured servitude. It also seems most academic institutions are there for the purpose of teaching teachers. This vicious circle of 'teachers teaching teachers' will invariably work our way into a very narrow corner of intellect. No new conscience or alternate methodology of thinking is really introduced and the same ideas will be rehashed and taught over and over again. The double talk that is taught in our education system should shed some light on what is going on. Double talk can create 'Double Think.' In order to perpetuate this illusion it demands a continual alteration of the past. Historical revisions to our history books have been done and continue to be done to this day. Changes are made to conform to what is being taught in today's world that are not based on historically accurate facts.

"If you think you're more creative than the present job you're doing...then in fact you are."

-Anonymous

We work most days with the anticipation of coming home to finally relax. It is ironic that our homes' landscapes have become more of a graveyard of items not much used after purchase, not too dissimilar as a spoiled child's nursery full of abandoned toys. We hurry home from work or school and begin the real business of life to enjoy ourselves – and for the vast majority of people what seems to be the real point of life. What we are really rushing home to is an electronic reproduction of life and TV dinners. We are consumed with so much technology and technological devices that when it comes time to living our life as we want, we regress into the world that is not our own, but broadcast over the tube. This life has no taste, no smell, no love and no soul. You would think that when we finally get home from our busy work day that we would have more of a purpose of enjoyment and be able to recline into a colossal banquet of food and perhaps later in the evening a rousing night of music, dance and lovemaking. Yet, nothing of the kind happens like this. Purely a passive existence of contemplation occurs in front of a flickering, electronic screen that is telling us how to think, how to act, what to eat, how to dress and what to fear. At night during the work week you can go anywhere in suburban America and see the miles of darkened houses with one or two rooms that are barely illuminated by the flickering light of a TV. Each person isolated from one another watching someone else's life on an electronic device. This isolation of people is creating a mindless crowd of watchers. A crowd is defined as a group of people not in mutual communication with each other which certainly describes much of suburban America today.

Why do we go to school? You may find something you're interested in and you want to learn more about that topic or subject. The entire point of going to school is because you hope that 'interest' will provide a way to make enough money to sustain a career. We somehow got off track when we started giving honors to go to school. Now it becomes a competition and he who wins this competition is rewarded with the prospect of a better job that pays more money and a prestigious sounding title. Is school's sole purpose to make more money or is it about growing from point 'A' to point 'B'? For example: You learn to speak French and the reward is that you can use this language to communicate with other French speaking people, understand their culture and be able to order French food in fancy restaurants. When the point and/or reward is to just fill a university 'credit' and get a degree, then learning and mastering the French language immediately becomes secondary.

There are programs now being installed in public schools whereby teachers and school staff are to observe children's behaviors. Any students acting out of 'normal' behavior are noted. The schools are taking on a certain 'snitch culture' which is being encouraged, supported and mandated by government funding.

They are watching your children for deviant behavior defined as anything out of the parameters of the 'Common Core' agenda.

The agenda is to control behavior and implement mind controlling tactics over every student so that they fit into the mold. If someone is acting out in class or they don't fit into the 'cookie cutter' approach to education, they are put on a list. Ultimately, they want to suppress the leaders, activists, gifted artists, creative scientists (especially people who ask questions) and those that are restless with the 'lifeless' lessons of schooling. They are systematically removing our next, natural-born leaders out of society and targeting them now at a very early age. And instead of nurturing the individual, they want to "Pharmacate" children with prescription drugs to make them more compliant.

The big hindrance is that our schools and universities do not encourage us to question accepted norms. Instead there is apathy...and through apathy...they are breaking the will and spirit of the students. The schools are programming our children to not speak out — because if you do you will be called out. Additionally, nowadays students are "hypersensitive" to political correctness. It seems they feel conversations should be void of any social profiling. It is this type of conditioning that is being taught in our public schools which actually divide us as a society.

Depower the establishment by peaceful noncompliance and take your children out of the corrupt system. We need to take back our schools and re-implement a sound foundation that allows for individuality and empowers our children—not stifle their innate abilities.

TECHNOLOGY

BOOK 32

Technology is like a double edged sword. On the one side, it has provided amazing advancements and conveniences for civilization, but on the other it has taken us farther away from our natural core. As we move further into the technology and information age, the more inventions, computers, weaponry and medicines become a part of our life. Artificial Intelligence (AI) is advancing so quickly that it could be within our lifetime that the point of 'Singularity' is reached whereby computers essentially become as smart as humans. That seems to be the goal of many scientists; to create a computer (AI) that can do everything our human minds can do, but on a much faster and adaptable platform. This possesses dangers to our society and could bring about a quicker demise and downfall of humanity as we know it. So be careful what you ask for. Has technology really benefitted us? Are we that much better off today than we were yesterday? Are we any happier? Most people (in America) have grown very fond of their 'Smart Phones' and fast Internet computers, but where is all of this leading us? Are we on the brink of a 'technological utopia' or of a 'technical self-destruction?' Much depends on how technology is being used and implemented. Is it being used to help empower ourselves and make things better, or is it enslaving us to a system of subservience? Time will tell how we'll end up, but as each one of us becomes more and more dependent on the creature comforts of technology, the more difficult it will be for us to survive when the lights do go out.

The 'Bomb' has been and will continue to be used as a psychological and technological weapon against humanity and is more effective than any military force by using the constant threat of nuclear annihilation. We accepted concessions and compromises, which in turn defeat our last liberties which would be unimaginable without the 'giant mushroom' clouds deep in our subconscious. The 'Bomb' is used as propaganda and as a psychological weapon every single day on the American people.

Movies such as *"On the Beach," "Seven Days in May," "Dr. Strange Love," "Failsafe"* and *"Planet of Apes"* are all well-produced entertaining movies that have done a professional job of strengthening the sub-conscience premise of the 'grand design' of annihilation. Motion pictures of course are not the only source of this 'tech' conditioning of the public mindset. Radio, TV, books, magazines and newspapers have all played a part in influencing a free society of people even though it is the public willingly choosing to buy and consume these products. In a socialist society, people are forced to stand in line for these products as well as more important items such as food. When the line gets long enough you will need authority or police protection to oversee the process and this is the essence of a totalitarian existence. It is a society whereby someone is telling you who can have and who cannot. The police state is the beginning of the commensurate socialistic state bureaucracy and is there to keep 'order.' They know who is to get the 'RFID Chip' and who will not...and who has to wait. Those who run socialism use tough government rule over all aspects of your life.

Doesn't that sound like what is going on right now? Since many Americans have never been in a socialist state, they are not seeing the trending towards it and are not aware of the quiet changes going on. The system is already in place, which we created by allowing it, is more and more government and then even more government until they control everything. Total government is 'coming to America' and is being ushered in through technology.

Right now, for the first time in history, we are facing an enemy that has mastered the corruption of total warfare. "WWIII" is raging around us right now and although it may seem packaged as a military war, which is the least crucial aspect, it is also a political, economic, spiritual and more specifically a technological war. For the past half century American's grand designers had you busily choosing between choices [A] or [B] by keeping you distracted with unimportant choices which take your attention off the real concern of how technology is being used to control you and how technology has been held back from you. The elite group has hidden technology under the blanket of privileged information and national security—they are really 25 years (or more) advanced in technology than they tell us. When a new technology is invented, the 'powers that be' will figure out how it can be used best on the populations of the world and after that is in place they will then provide the 'boiled down' less technical version to the public later.

For example, drones are being used by our military, but the civilian version of drones has been slow to evolve mostly because it is hard to regulate, control and monitor them. The government really does not want you to have your own drone. As a side observation: We have become detached from humanity in modern warfare. Drones are used to kill people. The operators of these drones are essentially no different than players playing a video game. The person pushing the button (dropping the 'Bomb') never personally interacts with the enemy they are attacking or killing. This has detached, desensitized and dehumanized us from having to fight by 'hand to hand' combat. The act of pushing a button is a much easier killing tool than having to face your enemy in person with a gun or bayonet.

Nikola Tesla's work was way ahead of his time. His inventions were so profound that if we had embraced all his accomplishments then, today we would be living in quite a different world. A better world filled with free energy, a cleaner environment and technology that would make our life much easier and more enjoyable. Unfortunately, much of his inventions have been suppressed and/or taken to be used in a more malicious way; against humanity. Tesla's particle rays, which should have been used as a defense mechanism, have been used as an aggression weapon towards other countries. It should also be noted that Tesla may have experienced communications with extraterrestrials. This could be an explanation for so much of his advanced technological knowledge; technology that should have been used to propel mankind...not harm it.

For example, 'Smart Meters' are killing us. Smart Meters that are placed on suburban houses use a microwave technology (similar to your microwave oven) that sends microwaves from a substation to all the houses in your neighborhood. At some time, usually in the night, all the Smart Meters talk to each other and then send back information to the substation on usage. The problem is that the meters are using microwaves that are being sent through the air similar to a microwave oven. Those microwaves affect water by changing the vibration of water (i.e., heating it) and our human bodies are mostly water. These microwaves are doing irreversible damage to people that live in the houses. Smart Meters are placed on the outside of houses and apartment buildings and will have a digital number (not a dial or clock face) on the front. Ask to have your 'not so smart meter' removed from your home by your electric company and be replaced with the 'traditional' dial clock face version. It is you that pays for the electricity on your property.

You have the right to say 'no' to this unproven technology.

Your cell phone and more specifically your 'Smartphone' is a mini-computer that you carry wherever you go. Most people nowadays can't even leave their home without hauling their cell phone with them. It has become a part of our culture and the reality is that most people just could not live without them. Your cell phone has a camera, a video camera, GPS and many other tracking devices as well as keeping record of every email, text message and phone call you make. It may even be listening to you now. It is almost unconscionable to think that we are willing candidates to carry a tracking device virtually everywhere we go. The reality is that most people have nothing to hide. If they are being tracked, monitored or spied on, they may not care. The concern has more to do with the fact that this is being done covertly by use of 'backdoor technology' without the person knowing it is being done. There are laws now that allow for 'infringement' upon our privacy, yet they still deny they are collecting data on each and every one.

Question: Why does man not use his mind more? The mind is standard equipment at birth. It's free. And the things that are given to us free (that cost nothing), ironically, we put little value on.

The following is a portion of the final speech from 'The Little Dictator' movie from 1940:

"I'm sorry, but I don't want to be an emperor. That's not my business. I don't want to rule or conquer anyone. I should like to help everyone if possible; Jew, Gentile, black man, white. We all want to help one another. Human beings are like that. We want to live by each other's happiness, not by each other's misery. We don't want to hate and despise one another. In this world there is room for everyone, and the good Earth is rich and can provide for everyone. The way of life can be free and beautiful, but we have lost the way. Greed has poisoned men's souls, has barricaded the world

with hate, (and) has goose-stepped us into misery and bloodshed. We have developed speed, but we have shut ourselves in. Machinery that gives abundance has left us in want. Our knowledge has made us cynical; our cleverness, hard and unkind. We think too much and feel too little. More than machinery, we need humanity. More than cleverness, we need kindness and gentleness. Without these qualities, life will be violent and all will be lost. The airplane and the radio have brought us closer together. The very nature of these inventions cries out for the goodness in men; cries out for universal brotherhood; for the unity of us all. Even now my voice is reaching millions throughout the world, millions of despairing men, women, and little children, victims of a system that makes men torture and imprison innocent people. To those who can hear me, I say, do not despair. The misery that is now upon us is but the passing of greed, the bitterness of men who fear the way of human progress. The hate of men will pass, and dictators die, and the power they took from the people will return to the people. And so long as men die, liberty will never perish. Soldiers! Don't give yourselves to brutes, men who despise you, enslave you; who regiment your lives, tell you what to do, what to think and what to feel! Who drill you, diet you, treat you like cattle, (and) use you as cannon fodder. Don't give yourselves to these unnatural men — machine men with machine minds and machine hearts! You are not machines, you are not cattle, you are men! You have the love of humanity in your hearts! You don't hate! Only the unloved hate; the unloved and the unnatural. Soldiers! Don't fight for slavery! Fight for liberty! In the seventeenth chapter of St. Luke, it is written that the kingdom of God is within man, not one man nor a group of men, but in all men! In you! You, the people, have the power, the power to create machines, the power to create happiness! You, the people, have the power to make this life free and beautiful, to make this life a wonderful adventure. Then in the name of democracy, let us use that power. Let us all unite. Let us fight for a new world, a decent world that will give men a chance to work, that will give youth a future and old age a security. By the promise of these things, brutes have risen to power. But they lie! They do not fulfill that promise. They never will! Dictators free themselves but they enslave the people. Now let us fight to fulfill that promise. Let us fight to free the world! To do away with national barriers! To do away with greed, with hate and intolerance! Let us fight for a world of reason, a world where science and progress will lead to all men's happiness. Soldiers, in the name of democracy, let us all unite! "

- Charlie Chaplin

We visualize from 'futuristic' stories that we will be controlled in our gated cities by 'robotic' policemen in riot gear with weapons similar to the ones seen in modern video games or movies. But the weaponry they will use — you have never seen before. They will have Electromagnetic Pulse (EMP) and Vibrational Wave weaponry. They will be able to control (kill) large amounts of people with these types of guns. Super cities will be high-tech and will only be on state-controlled land. All cities will be completely 'monitored' and 'surveillanced' by sophisticated real-time camera networks and anything you do, anything you buy, or anything you say, will be tracked, recorded and documented. Your freedom will only be a perception. The most important aspect of your existence is that you serve the state and your allegiance to the state of affairs. Any problem we have shall be handled by the government. It is at this time that you will not be able to walk down the street without being watched. There is no longer the ability for free speech and even free thought will be suppressed. The Internet will be completely regulated, and everything you earn or spend will be taxed. There will be no arts, music or theater and any creativity will be suppressed. For many, it will be hell on Earth.

"The mediator between head and hands is the heart."

-Joh Fredersen

George Orwell in his book, <u>1984</u> stated, *"In a time of universal deceit telling the truth is a revolutionary act."* Many things that happened in <u>1984</u> are happening to us now. I also compare so much of what is happening today with what happens in 'The Matrix' film. Morpheus tells Neo that the life he has been living is an illusion and after Neo takes the red pill he realizes that it's true. Morpheus says, *"I didn't tell you it would be easy, I told you it would be the truth."* You can either take it at face value or you can do the research and find out yourself that we are literally living in a pre-programmed, matrix illusion. I believe that every man, woman and child on this plant is being controlled by the system without them even being aware of the control. We are manipulated to think that we can live our lives free from being conditioned or brainwashed, yet by way of the mental programming in this matrix the whole human race is unknowingly and unwittingly imprisoned. Mankind will never reach its full potential in this world as long as the 'matrix' exists. At first glance this seems absurd and you may say, *"We have free will."* We try to live our lives the way we want to, but beyond the faux surface, it does seem that we are all conditioned to think a certain way and have certain thoughts and opinions that are so similar that it seems very clear that we have been brainwashed to all think with the same limited conscience just as George Orwell foretold and warned us. That is what technology has done to us, but through the process of enlightenment people can become aware and not be so lured...so easily...for so much longer.

"Who is John Galt...?"

DEATH

BOOK 33

What happens when we die? Most people don't want to think about death and go to great lengths to avoid this topic. The main reason people don't want to think about dying is because they fear that when they die they will have no memory of this life in the afterlife. That all the memories of things you did and the people you touched and loved are lost. *Forever.* The question is, if there is an 'afterlife' experience is it any different than our 'before' life experience? If so how? Would a person even know or be cognizant of the difference they are experiencing at that time? Some people firmly believe, without conviction, that when you die, you go to a place called "heaven" or "hell" and that your actions or what you 'did' in this life here on Earth predicts where you will go when you do die. Other people are of the mindset that all you have is this life and nothing more and when you die you're going to experience 'forever nothingness' for the rest of time, similar to the 'non-memory' most of us recall before we were born. Who is right? The living doesn't know about death, obviously, since they have never experienced it. Some people have had a very rare experience where they have seen the 'other side.' Usually a person that has a 'near death' or out-of-body experience (or what I like to call a "Cosmic Event") would have this brought on from a trauma related event. This could occur either by an accident of some kind or from a near 'fatal' episode that would usher in the experience (not of this world). Either way, the event brings insight and clarity to what happens when a person dies. It can also occur in a non-life-threatening manner through reaching a higher state of consciousness.

I personally experienced this one night. I did not specifically ask to die, but leading up to the event I was asking many questions about life and death. Fortunately, in my case it was not a life-threatening event because I did not have an accident nor did I experience any real trauma. But for the better part of a year, previously to my event, I was asking the hard questions of *"whom am I?"* and *"where did I come from?"* and *"where does my soul go when I die?"* I really wanted to know and I was reciting every night to myself that, *"I want my DNA to be connected…I want my DNA to be connected,"* so I could have the knowledge of the universe and be able to know where I came from and what happened to me before I was born and what happens to me after I die.

Here is my story…

It started off as a night really no different than any other night. I had been 'under the weather' the previous week and had congestion in my lungs. I remember coughing quite vigorously for an extended period of time right as I laid down to go to sleep. At some point, soon after, I felt a little strange, a little out of sorts, perhaps I felt lighter or disconnected. But this 'lightness' or 'disconnection' was far different from any 'light-body' feeling that I had experienced previously. This was a more suspended feeling as if I was leaving my body. I realized that the coughing must have 'shaken' my body and that maybe I was still reverberating from that and yet an inner tension ensued that was quickly followed by worry and fear. I was losing control and continued to seep into a scary separation feeling of my body from my (mind) consciousness. At one point, I remember it felt as if my legs became detached from my body. As I lay there in bed, slightly propped up, my legs seemed to go straight into the bed as if I was standing yet I was lying perfectly flat. I felt strange and the feeling was growing more uncomfortable. I was paralyzed with fear, and was afraid to move. I felt dizzy and disassociated. I wanted to call out for help, but decided I did not want to concern my family at this point. Later, I would cry out for help. I felt my heart beat fast and my blood course through my body. My hands and feet became damp and cold. I imagined that this feeling was like a person overdosing on drugs and losing total control of reality. At that point, I really felt as though I was dying. I lay there and thought that for some reason I was being taken at this time perhaps because I was asking so many questions about what happens to us when we die. Be mindful of what you seek. This passing thought did not help and at that moment I had lost all control of my body. I felt completely out of body, but not in a good way. This was the scariest feeling. I sensed I was going somewhere and not coming back. At some point I remember just closing my eyes very tightly and clenching my hands holding on to the sheets and having a feeling of uncontrollable movement. An upward and forward movement as if my body was floating like on a carnival ride. This was a very uncomfortable feeling and I wanted more than anything for it to just stop. I am not sure how long I felt like this, but it seemed to go on for a very long time. I tried to push my body down into the bed as if to 'ground' myself, but the movement was too strong. I kept my eyes closed. I decided to accept my fate (whatever it was) and at that point my concentration shifted from my physical state to my mental state. I could still feel some ascension, but at this point I became more conscious of my mind and what I was thinking. This was actually a semi-good thing because it took my mind off the physical nature of the 'bad trip' I was having. At this point I was making decisions in my mind about my condition and fate. I really sensed I had gone somewhere and that it was not a 'return ticket trip' either. To have that feeling was ominous. It was easily the most frightening event to go through and still be conscious. I focused in on how my kids and family would find me the next day and what people would say about my passing. This was not easy to deal with at the time, and my sudden demise was quite upsetting, but it did take my mind off the horrible suspended feeling that I was experiencing. It was at this point that I gave up (in a sense) or I wanted to give up. It had been fifteen minutes or so, maybe longer and I thought that if I stopped breathing or if my heart burst from the racing gear it was in at least I would not have to endure any more of this feeling.

I continued to feel an uneasy 'shift' in my body and even more ascension (at this time) and came to the point of acceptance of my sudden and premature demise…

It was at this time that I finally 'popped' into what I call 'home.' Home was the most beautiful place I have ever experienced. It wasn't so much a place as a feeling, but even more than a feeling. It was here that I experienced heightened out-of-body perception. Within an instant I was at ease. Not completely, but I knew that I had traveled to a place where I was supposed to be. No question. It felt that I had moved into another dimension. Even though my eyes were closed I had full vision and all my senses were in hyper drive. For the first time in my life I finally felt connected. Connected to what I was not absolutely sure. It was a feeling of extreme ease. The difficulty here is that what I was experiencing cannot be articulated with just mere words or even drawings. There is no way to really describe the profound volume of feelings and emotions that came over me. It was as though a wave had 'washed' over me and cleansed any fear I had in that moment. I felt that I was home. Extreme inner peace and joy flooded my entire existence. The feeling of unconditional love washed over me and through me. I began to understand. I felt connected to all information and knowledge of the universe and had extreme clarity of who I was. All of the answers to my life questions were within my grasp. I felt as though I could go anywhere. I could just pick a place anywhere in the world (universe) and I could virtually be there in a second, but at this moment I just wanted to be there. I felt as though I could be male or female—king or pauper—creator or destroyer—it did not matter—I had the ability to create whatever image (glamorous or not) I wanted to be and I could wear any type of clothing I desired at that instant. I *virtually* could be 'anyway' or 'anyone' I wanted. My body was just an extension of whoever I wanted to be. The most profound feeling was that I was still at ease with all this cosmic energy swirling through me. For the first time in my entire life (that I could remember) my 'body' and 'mind' was absolutely void of pain, worry, fear and the weight of the world. I had experienced a feeling in that moment I did not have to do anything, just exist, and it was peaceful and perfect. I felt no need to sleep, eat, or do anything unless I wanted to. This moment was timeless. The concept of time was 'nonexistent.' It was as if I had all the time in the world to do whatever I wanted and when I was done with that, I could move on and 'take' as much time as I wanted with creating something else with no repercussions and no worry. What I visually saw, and felt, was light. A light not of this world. It was a bright, white light that was not the sun and certainly not artificial. It was pure energy light, the likes I had never seen before or really experienced. Along with this beautiful glow were colors around the edges. The colors I can't describe with any justice. The colors were not of this world...every possible shade and hue of color and so vivid and alive. The colors coupled with the light were surreal.

It was as if I was not just 'seeing' it, but more of 'being' it. I was now in control and the heaviness of my body and the weight of air in my lungs and the force of gravity upon my chest were gone. It was the most beautiful profound moment of my life. Fundamentally, it has changed me forever.

But the episode was not over....

I am not sure how long I was there, but it was long enough to sense and experience everything. Soon afterwards I began to feel awkward again. I felt a slight descending movement and I began to be aware of 'me' again. It was here I started to see and sense a 'blackness' that was growing around me. It was a slower moving, dark matter that was beginning to cover my lower body starting on my legs. I soon felt and sensed that this blackness would cover and engulf me. A feeling of suffocation and worry ensued and I started to again panic. Not the same as before, because I was still out-of-body and my eyes were still tightly clenched. Within an instant the blackness paralyzed me and at that instant I was in front of a barrier. I say barrier, but it was like a door or a solid structure with no hardware or frame of reference. The best way to describe it was a large metal-type black door that had a repeating design on it. Like a raised ornate pattern of pagan design or something that had special meaning yet it was something I did not understand. The door scared me. It was a feeling or a sense of concern that if I were to go beyond the door things would change. It was a feeling that if I went through I would never come back. Not back to where I just was (the most beautiful place I ever experienced) nor my previous earthy life either. This was not any door it was like 'the door.' And I sensed behind the door was nothingness, a place void of anything, void of life, nothing living just everlasting nothingness. It was the scariest feeling I had ever experienced. It was as if I was staring at the incarnation of death itself without feeling that I was dead. I felt that it was worse than any preconceived notions of death. (As I self-reflected these moments afterwards I knew that even the 'Hell' as described in any book, movie or story was not nearly as horrid as what was beyond the door). I had an urge to go through this door, but my feeling was that if I went through the doorway (door) to the other side that I would be suspended in a limbo state of nothingness. Not necessarily death, and certainly not life, but the worst-ever non-existence of being. It was absolutely void of life or anything living. It was a constant state of uneasiness, without the ability to understand, reflect or communicate with anyone, or anything. It was like being locked in a closet of darkness for the rest of eternity with not one shred of joy or creativity or entertainment. This was the final turning point of my out-of-body experience. I wanted so much to get away from this place and this moment that I forced myself to move away and separate myself from this door. I never went through, I never looked in and everything I felt was a sense of knowing what was on the other side. This was the second most memorable experience of my life with the first being just minutes before. I knew that I was not going through the door because I wanted to come back to this reality. Still somewhat paralyzed with anxiety, I was back to a place that I could feel my body — materialize — and I could feel myself trying to open my eyes.

At this point I quickly came around and acquainted myself 'back' to this reality. My cosmic event was over and I slowly was able to sit up slightly in my bed and continue to try to open my eyes. It felt as though my eyes had been glued shut since it was ever difficult to reopen them. They had been closed, and tightly closed at that, for about a half hour now (maybe longer). I was back, but clearly it was not over and still one of the strangest things was still to occur. As I finally unclenched my eyes and opened them for the first time, I looked out across my bed and onto my room. My vision was a little cloudy, but what I saw was unbelievable. The room, my bed, the walls did not look real. They

They looked flat, like a cardboard movie set. No dimension. Like a toy train model set. The colors seemed dead and lifeless, the light was artificial. It seemed like I was confined in a really small area and I remember I kept thinking, Am I back? Or is this just another continuation of the event? I knew I was back, but nothing looked the same. Or felt the same. It was not as I remembered before closing my eyes and it was just all very artificial and two— dimensional looking. I was relieved and disappointed at the same time. I had never had this feeling, but I was slightly more relieved that I was not dead and that I was back. I thought how I could see my family again and how happy to be able to look at myself in the mirror. I still felt like I had died. Or a part of me died and I had come back. I was not positively sure why, but knew for some reason that it was not my time to go. I was still stricken with fear and could only just waver in my non-lucid state of consciousness at this point. I still didn't feel right, but at least I was not at that horrible door. It took a while for me to reacquaint myself to the bedroom. Even after a few minutes it still seemed flat, lifeless and had 'dull' colors and light. It was very quiet too. It was like I was at a huge concert event with grand music and an amazing light show, and all of a sudden it just ended and I was alone again. It took a while for the room to return to normal. In fact it seemed different for the remainder of the night. It was at this point I was able to push myself from the bed and sit up and assess my situation. I was still completely on edge from this experience and it was at this time that my heightened sense of memory, visual acuity and hearing was turned off. I felt disconnected from the hyper-sensation and was back to just me. But I was shaken. I could remember everything that just happened to me, but the rest of the night is really pretty much a blur. I remember trying really hard to get some help at this point. Unable to call out I decided to try to move. My wife was sleeping with one of our children which happened often when she would fall asleep; lying next to them, while putting them to bed. I was able to finally get enough energy and balance to get out of my bed and stumble into the other bedroom. I had to wake her. I had to see if I was really back and maybe she could help with calming me down. I woke her up, and I told her to come into the other room so I could tell her something. Since this was very late into the evening it took some coaxing to get her to get up and come back to our bedroom. I tried to explain to her what I had just been through. She is pretty much a straight shooter, so this did not make any sense to her at all. I remember her telling me that I was cold. My body and especially my hands were very (very) cold and my eyes were red. She told me later that I kept saying that I was dead or I had died. I still felt really weird and thought if I took a warm shower that I would feel better. Afterwards, I changed into some comfortable night clothes to try to lie down once again. I asked her to not leave my side and during that time, which may have been at least an hour after my shower, I laid back in the bed and I 'recounted' as much as I could of what I saw on my journey. But my replaying of the night's events was not so much a play-by-play, but rather an entire dissertation on life and its meaning. I do not remember speaking so profoundly or so eloquently in my entire life. It was as if I was plugged in and received valuable cosmic teachings. I do remember rambling for quite a while, then lying gently back on my pillows. I was tired at this point, having felt like I traveled a great distance. I did finally begin to get sleepy and it was at some time later that I had the ability to close my eyes again, but this time to fall asleep.

As I reflect back on that night a few questions come to mind. Could it be 'we' have the innate power within us to bring upon an event, like a near death experience, and actually experience it without trauma? Certainly, I asked for some questions to be answered and many of them were answered. Does that make me powerful? I feel like I got what I asked for. That may very well be the power of our super-conscience mind which we can all access through connected thought and enlightenment. The other is what was really behind the door that I saw. I felt I had an idea, but with having not gone through, I can only speculate. I can only say that I still have fear of dying, but not a fear of what happens after death.

Perhaps the door represented a decision and by going through that door I would have made a change in the direction of my life. Perhaps it was symbolic of the doors of perception of one's mind. Whether behind the door was something good or not so good, I felt it was not a part of me at that time.

Near death experiences occur when most people are involved in some type of trauma to the body such as an accident or severe illness. This is why people who have survived near-death experiences have consistently reported the experience as being hyper-reality. It feels like it is a "thousand times" more real than life on Earth. It is truly cosmic and supernatural. During this time people will experience extreme mental clarity, vivid sensory imagery, a clear memory of the experience and an experience more real than their everyday life. The fascinating aspect of this is that much of the experience of heightened awareness comes at a time that the body is shutting down and even when brain functions are severely hampered. This means that the consciousness that occurs is not dependent upon a healthy brain or body functioning to sustain life, yet the person has the ability to tap into the cosmic energy of the altered state. After one has a near death experience there are many changes in the emotional state, paranormal features and other worldly features. Changes in thinking during near-death experience include a sense of time being altered and often people report that time stopped or ceased to exist during the experience. It also includes a sense of revelation or sudden understanding in which everything in the universe becomes crystal clear. Everything is clearer and faster than your normal waking state. The thinking is also logical; everything within an instant makes sense. Sometimes the person experienced a life review or a panoramic memory in which the person's entire life seems to flash before them.

The panoramic view happens more often when the person is much closer to death. Typical emotions reported during a near-death experience include an overwhelming sense of peace and well-being, a sense of cosmic unity or being one with everything a feeling of complete joy and a sense of being loved unconditionally. The paranormal features often reported in near-death experiences include a sense of leaving the body sometimes called an out-of-body experience. The experience of a person's physical vision and hearing becoming more intense and vivid than ever before; sometimes people report seeing colors and hearing sounds that do not exist in this life. A sense of extrasensory perception of knowing the things beyond the range of normal physical sense such as the ability to know what a distant land may feel and look like or visions of the future. Many feel they have entered some other unearthly world or realm of existence. Sometimes it is a border that they could not cross or a point-of-no-return...that if they had crossed they would not be able to return to life. Some say they have seen deceased spirits of people they recognize either welcoming them in or sending them back.

When you die a physical death you die, but your energy goes to another place. It will always exist, forever. The frequency that is 'me' will always be 'me.' The feeling of pure love comes through you and flows everywhere. Again, it is very hard to explain in words how intense and strong this feeling is having personally gone through this. It consumed me and still consumes me completely to this day. You no longer feel as a fragment of the universe; you 'are' the universe.

One of the most interesting aspects of the near-death experience is the profound after-effects. People reliably report a consistent pattern of changes in attitudes, beliefs and values that do not seems to fade over time. Near-death experiences report that they are more spiritual after the experience, that they have more compassion for others and a greater desire to help others with greater appreciation for life and a stronger sense of meaning or purpose, in life. The overwhelming majority of people report a stronger belief that we survive death of the body and just as many report they no longer have fear of death. Many who survive near-death experiences have lost interest in material possessions and many report less interest in personal prestige, status or competition. To many, it sounds like these people are following the 'Buddha' because they show more compassion they tend to try to help others they're less attached to material possessions and status. But these values are not uniquely Buddhist and are universal values. Almost all spiritual traditions teach compassion and the transience of worldly rewards.

Prophesies tell us the destruction that accompanies the "End of Days" has been given to us to help a forgetful humanity to remember the impermanent nature of our material existence. So that we may be inspired to seek and therefore find the greater spiritual purpose of our existence, and with the dramatic acceptance of 'End of Days' comes many facing the possibility of their own demise and loss of everything that they worked to achieve in the material world – all of which will occur for the divine purpose of shifting humanity's perspective from the physical to the spiritual. In a world where so many are living only for material achievement it will not be until that material reality is threatened with extinction and where money and luxury fail to satisfy our needs, that the majority of people will awaken to find a new purpose and meaning for life.

Everybody who appears in front of you is you, but you can only experience this 3-D reality as one person. Death is like an end of a dream. Nothing can enslave the 'real' you. There is <u>NO</u> everlasting non experience. The time between reincarnations can vary. You come back when you are ready. It will be your choice. You may ask, *"Why would anyone want to re-live many lives here on Earth"*? If you are a spiritual creation that lives forever and you wanted to experience new and exciting adventures, you would 'incarnate' into this world whenever you desire. There is nothing like the Earthly experience. The ability to see, touch, feel, hear, taste and love in the human body form are the greatest gifts that a spiritual entity can experience. I equate it to being the 'boss' of a company pretending to be an employee for a week and seeing how it feels. The only difference is that you made a deal with yourself that you would not remember that you're the boss. So it comes to be that your incarnation's success here is measured by your actions and your emotions. Did you love or did you hate? Did you give or did you take? Think about how you would grade yourself. Were you able to 'wake up' during this incarnation or did you go through the entire time not realizing who you were?

Did you 'sleep' through this life only to think that what was real were the only things that were in front of you? Were you able to break free of everything that you were taught to make your own decisions, your own ideas and your own thoughts? Did you follow the path in front of you, or did you go down the path to the side that is less traveled? Did you investigate or dig deep to find out the true meaning of your existence, or did you just accept what you were told by others that did not understand you? What is the point of life? Is this a test? Are you being tested? Are you testing yourself? Perhaps it is a test of sorts and if you 'pass' this go round then you can take the liberty of more time between incarnations. Either way, at some point you will always come back. If only we took ourselves a little less seriously, maybe our time here on Earth would be more enjoyable.

In America, we love to elevate the deceased, often too far beyond where they were when alive. The entire fanfare of expensive funerals and the gathering of all the people that supposedly knew the deceased to give their condolences seem contrived. Is the funeral for the dead, or more for the living? (Or, perhaps the funeral home business.) I am not here to 'criticize' the current grieving process, but when you see past the illusion and understand it, is the physical body that has died and not your 'real Spirit,' then we should be able to provide a more grounded and appropriate send off.

Experience your own death philosophically. Visualize the process and imagine you have died. You no longer need to hide yourself, explain yourself or protect yourself. Just be yourself. And when you're done with that exercise come back to life and start living again...

SUMMARY...?

Just outside of space, time... is a place you've always been –
Even though you can't quite remember - all of what you have seen.
All of you...of who you are – is there – not just ten percent –
The real you 'is' quantum - you vibrate with pure intent.
A frequency of light and sound...direct it here or there -
You don't exist at all - yet you are always everywhere.
The 'moment' is all there is...and can't be measured on a line -
There is no right or wrong because the 'moment' is divine.
You are the creator of the frequency of youth –
Born in swirling symphonies...of nothing but the truth.
Age cannot affect you... the moment is now -
And your mission is delightful to explore yourself but how?
In truth you are the answer to the question with no name -
The journey lasts forever and is nothing but a game.
So when you last decided to come to Earth –
To explore human beings from birth.
You knew what you were doing – your choice to come was true -
You manifested simply the frequency of...you.
But somewhere you fought the truth... you let if far away -
You forgot this was a game and your mission is to play.
But now you are remembering...truth is who you are -
That you're not your body or your thoughts about your car.

Your marriage or your spectrum of emotion -
You are a drop of water looking for the ocean.
We are scared of life. And we are scared of death.
Scared of being bold… we are scared of one another…and growing old…
We are scared if we join the ocean that we will disappear -
We are scared of what will happen if we gave in to fear.
…But just beyond the fear - is zero point - the place of birth calling me 'one'-
…and the 'zero point'…will shine brightly…through us…
… Just as brightly…as the 'sun'…

You were <u>never</u> 'originally' created to live depressed, defeated, scared, guilty, fearful, separated, poor, condemned, manipulated, ashamed, alone, sad or unworthy… you were created to be victorious. You are the most amazing creation with the most profound ability to experience a physical existence here on the most dynamic and beautiful planet in the universe, Earth. You are truly blessed to be here right now — at one of the most dynamic times in all of history — and it is all in how you interpret 'everything' – as to how you will experience it.

The Dalai Lama, when asked what surprised him most about humanity, answered:

"Man, because he sacrifices his health in order to make money. Then he sacrifices money to recuperate his health and then he is so anxious about the future that he does not enjoy the present; the result is being that he does not live in the present or the future; he lives as if he is never going to die, and then dies having never really lived."

- Dalai Lama

I didn't tell you it would be easy. I told you it would be the truth. Somehow during this life, it is your responsibility to remember who you are. It is purely your choice, if you so desire, to follow this path that lies before you. You don't have to wake up if you don't want to. You don't have to do anything. Again, it is your choice and you are in control of this reality. But those that do choose this path—by uncovering the 'mystery of life' you will elevate your conscience and in turn enable you to guide others to do the same. All the knowledge and information you need is already within you. It is encoded in every cell in your body and when you do finally 'connect' to it, the world won't seem so strange. You will be able to reach out to the higher realms and harness the energy and knowledge that is meant for you. You will understand and know the questions you need to ask yourself and others. You will remember how and why you are living in a 'pre-programmed' matrix illusion where every person is being controlled by the system. Some of us are able to balance ourselves within the system, but many of us want to break free of its confines. A lot depends on where you are spiritually with your personal growth, but at some point, and at some time, you'll want to grow beyond your physical self. The soul's natural quest is to aspire and mature in parallel to the wisdom that is already you. Understand, that we are clearly conditioned to think and conduct our lives a certain way and that the entire human race is unwittingly imprisoned. —Mankind will never reach its full potential as long as we are controlled, but all it takes…is just one person to reach out and break free. Others will follow.

"You have the rest of your life to do what you want to do."

-Anonymous

Yes... Yes, life is tough. Yes, truths have been hidden. Yes, freedoms have been suppressed. Yes, our spirit has been broken. Yes, sexuality is pervasive. Yes, war is rampant. Yes, food has been adulterated. Yes, water is poisoned. Yes, air is not fit to breath. Yes, egos are ruling us. Yes, the elite class really exists. Yes, religion is being banished. Yes, money rules the planet. Yes, governments are corrupt. Yes, nature is being harmed. Yes, we are under a surveillance state. Yes, knowledge has been forged. Yes, media pushes evil agendas. Yes, music has been 're-toned.' Yes, education brainwashes. Yes, death is scary. Yes, you have been lied to. Yes, you have been manipulated on the 'grandest' of scales... Yes, you have been...

But... life goes on...

After all of this is said and done, life still must be lived as best you can. *"We must still chop wood and carry water."* Though, with knowledge and love, the world can 'awaken' one person at a time to make it good and just for all.

I am not going to tell you that you must fight or battle our oppressors. You know what is 'at stake'...the survival of the planet and all of its inhabitants. The way to overcome adversity is through conscience awareness, through conscience endeavor and through conscience enlightenment...actions will materialize.

"Any fool can make things bigger, more complex and more violent. It takes a touch of genius—and a lot of courage—to move in the opposite direction."

-Albert Einstein

If we can conceptualize the 'matrix fields' as being removed, we understand there is no 'space' that remains, since space does not have an independent existence. Reality is mainly an illusion... albeit a very persistent one. So we can conclude that the content of 'consciousness' is the ultimate, universal reality. This beautiful knowledge could be used to elevate mankind to finally reach the place that we all want to go to and that is...'home'...

So what is the point of all of this? Is there a point? Does there have to be a point? Perhaps the point is whatever you want to make of it. Perhaps the point is there is no point and we are here for whatever you want to create and experience. Take away the teachings and thoughts that you want to embrace...and hold onto them...let them become a part of you ...and those things of lesser desire... let them go...

...after all...it is your life.

Set yourself free...

And just be...

CPSIA information can be obtained
at www.ICGtesting.com
Printed in the USA
LVOW03s0707170417
531055LV00036B/1718/P